CALIFAUNA

A LITERARY FIELD GUIDE

Edited by Terry Beers and Emily Elrod

10658581

Santa Clara University, Santa Clara, California
Heyday Books, Berkeley, California

This book is made possible in part by funding from the National Endowment for the Arts.

© 2007 by Heyday Books
Foreword © 2007 by Terry Beers
Cover art © 2007 by Edward Rooks
All images by Andrea Rich are courtesy of the artist.

All rights reserved. No portion of this work may be reproduced or transmitted in any form or by any means, electronic or mechanical, including photocopying and recording, or by any information storage or retrieval system, without permission in writing from Heyday Books.

Library of Congress Cataloging-in-Publication Data

Califauna : a literary field guide / edited by Terry Beers and Emily Elrod.
     p. cm. — (A California legacy book.)
  Includes bibliographical references and index.
  ISBN-13: 978-1-59714-049-2 (pbk. : alk. paper)
 1. California—Literary collections. 2. Plants—California. 3. Animals—California.
4. American literature—California 5. American literature—21st century. I. Beers,
Terry, 1955- II. Elrod, Emily.
  PS571.C2C275 2007
  810.8'09794--dc22

                                 2006035818

Cover Art: Edward Rooks
Cover and Interior Design: Lorraine Rath
Printing and Binding: Sheridan Books, Ann Arbor, MI

Orders, inquiries, and correspondence should be addressed to:
       Heyday Books
       P. O. Box 9145, Berkeley, CA 94709
       (510) 549-3564, Fax (510) 549-1889
       www.heydaybooks.com

Printed in the United States of America on recycled paper (50% post-consumer waste).

10 9 8 7 6 5 4 3 2 1

For Mary Louise Mackin and in memory of Orville and
Marge Beers and Edward S. Mackin—*Terry Beers*

For Lawrence and Annette Elrod and
Bobbie Bockes—*Emily Elrod*

CONTENTS

Foreword · xi
Acknowledgments · xvii

Red Abalone
Gladys Nomland, "Origin of Abalone" · 3
George Sterling, "The Abalone Song" · 4

Giant Carpenter Ant
John Muir, "Biters" · 6

Grizzly Bear
Jessie Benton Fremont, "My Grizzly Bear" · 9
Joaquin Miller, "The Grizzly as Fremont Found Him" · 12

Honey Bee
John Muir, "The Bee-Pastures" · 15

Stink Beetle
John Steinbeck, from *Cannery Row* · 33

Burro
George Wharton James, from *The Wonders of the Colorado Desert* · 35

Cabezon
Robert Hass, "On the Coast near Sausalito" · 39

Cat
Ishmael Reed, "My Thing Abt Cats" · 41
Mark Twain, from *Roughing It* · 41

California Condor
Gerald Haslam, "Condor Dreams" · 45

Cow and Ox
Gelett Burgess, "The Purple Cow," "The Purple Cow: Suite" · 52
William Heath Davis, from *Sixty Years in California* · 52
Arnold R. Rojas, from *California Vaquero* · 56

Coyote
T. C. Boyle, from *The Tortilla Curtain* · 59
William Bright, "Coyote's Journey" (from the Karuk) · 61
Alejandrina Murillo Melendres, "Coyote Baptizes the Chickens" · 66

Mule Deer
Darryl Babe Wilson, "Dose!" · 68

American Dipper
Harriet Monroe, "The Water Ouzel" · 74
John Muir, "The Water-Ouzel" · 74

Dog
Mary Austin, "The Go-Betweens" · 85
Floyd Salas, "To Sergie My Sweet Old Dog Who Died in Old Age" · 90

Dolphin
Georgiana Valoyce-Sanchez, "The Dolphin Walking Stick" · 94

Mourning Dove
Ambrose Bierce, "To the Happy Hunting Grounds" · 97

Mallard Duck
Jim Dodge, from *Fup* · 99

Elk
Joaquin Miller, from *Life Amongst the Modocs* · 105

Human Flea
Edwin Bryant, from *What I Saw in California* · 107

Red-legged Frog
Mark Twain, "The Celebrated Jumping Frog of Calaveras County" · 109

Gila Monster
George Wharton James, from *The Wonders of the Colorado Desert* · 115

Snow Goose
Barry Lopez, "A Reflection on White Geese" · 119

Pocket Gopher
John Steinbeck, from *Cannery Row* · 129

Red-tailed Hawk
Walter Van Tilburg Clark, "Hook" · 132
Hildegarde Flanner, "Hawk Is a Woman" · 145

Horse
Lincoln Steffens, from "A Boy on Horseback" · 147

Steller's Jay
William Dawson, from *The Birds of California* · 151
Louise Wagenknecht, from *White Poplar, Black Locust* · 152

Desert Horned Lizard
William Saroyan, from *My Name Is Aram* · 157

Western Fence Lizard
David Mas Masumoto, "Lizard Dance" · 160

Louse
G. Ezra Dane, from *Ghost Town* · 162

Mosquito
James M. Hutchings, from *Scenes of Wonder and Curiosity in California* · 166

Mountain Lion
Charles Bukowski, "the lady and the mountain lion" · 168
Charles F. Lummis, "The California Lion" · 170

Pocket Mouse
Steve Kowit, *"Perognathus fallax"* · 173

Mule
John Randolph Spears, from *Illustrated Sketches of Death Valley* · 176

Giant Pacific Octopus
Walter Nordhoff, from *The Journey of the Flame* · 186

Sea Otter
Charles Melville Scammon, from *The Marine Mammals of the North-Western Coast of North America* · 188

Great Horned Owl
Yokuts, "The Man and the Owl" · 195

California Quail
John Steinbeck, "The White Quail" · 197

Rabbit
Frank LaPena, "Rabbit Crazy" · 200

Common Raccoon
Kenneth Rexroth, "Raccoon" · 202

Rat
William K. McGrew, "The Rats of Sacramento" · 204

Western Rattlesnake
Charley Brown, "The Girl Who Married Rattlesnake" · 213
Bill Hotchkiss, "Rattlesnakes" · 214

King Salmon
Alexandre Dumas, from *A Gil Blas in California* · 217
Freeman House, from *Totem Salmon* · 217

Sheep
Mary Austin, "The Flock" · 228
Helen Hunt Jackson, from *Ramona* · 235

Desert Tarantula
George Wharton James, from *The Wonders of the Colorado Desert* · 238

California Western Toad
David Rains Wallace, from "Gardening with Pests" · 240

Rainbow Trout
Richard Brautigan, from *Trout Fishing in America* · 242
Austen D. Warburton, "Steelhead, the Trickster" · 244

Turkey Vulture
Robinson Jeffers, "Vulture" · 247
George Sterling, "The Black Vulture" · 247

Long-tailed Weasel
Sally Carrighar, from *One Day on Beetle Rock* · 249

Humpback Whale
Richard Henry Dana, Jr., from *Two Years Before the Mast* · 253
David Rains Wallace, "Humphrey: Goodwill Ambassador" · 254

Killer Whale
Robinson Jeffers, "Orca" · 257

Gray Wolf
Jack London, from *White Fang* · 259
Julian H. Steward, "The Theft of Pine Nuts" · 265

Acorn Woodpecker
Ursula K. Le Guin, "What Is Going On in the Oaks around the Barn" · 269

Author Sketches · 271
Timeline · 277
Selected References · 286
Permissions · 287
Index · 291
About the Editors · 293

～ FORCWORD ～

By Terry Beers

> Not that animals do not care what we feel about them. But when we divert
> the current of feeling that flows between ourself and an animal into words, we
> abstract it forever from the animal. Thus the poem is not a gift to its object,
> as the love poem is. It falls within an entirely human economy in which the
> animal has no share.
>
> —from Elizabeth Costello, by J. M.
> Coetzee

Melissa and I are driving dogs. It's a few degrees below zero and our trail—Blue
Lakes Road near Hope Valley, California—rises gently toward Border Ruffian Flat.
Overhead the early morning sky is already a blinding blue; the snow surrounding us is
a blinding white. Today, no snowmobile's roar breaks the relative stillness. We only hear
the skishing sound of our sled runners over packed powder and the easy, rhythmic
breathing of happy working dogs. Northern breeds thrive in these conditions.

We've split our eight huskies into two teams of four, each team pulling a light
basket sled at a steady trot of about six miles an hour. We will maintain this slow pace.
Two of our dogs are very young yet, puppies really, and they're still getting used to
working in a team. We won't go far with them today. Just enjoy the morning quiet,
the sight of snow-laden firs and pines, the surprise of occasional gray outcroppings of
Sierra granite standing in stark relief against the almost uniform whiteness. The dogs
are keenly aware of the landscape around them—so we are too.

The connection we always make with these beautiful animals feels almost mystical
sometimes, as if we share the same emotions, the same visceral feelings about our
shared world, the same enthusiasm that we are part of it. But I know we can't really be
that much in tune with another species. Or can we? Judging by the work of the many
California writers who have taken animals for their subjects, we can at least imagine
that possibility. Whatever the limitations scientists and philosophers may feel when
speculating about animal consciousness, writers have often claimed license to exceed
them. When they do, the results seem to me particularly relevant when we ask: How
do we define our relationship to the other species with which we share our world?
Or put another way: How well can I really know my sled dogs?

If we judge by the work of Sally Carrighar, maybe the answer is pretty damn well.

When Carrighar published her groundbreaking book *One Day on Beetle Rock* in 1944, she was at the beginning of a long and prolific career as an American nature writer. Her work was distinctive, based on careful background research and countless hours of direct observation of her subjects. As a sled dog owner I'm partial to *Wild Voice of the North*, Carrighar's 1959 chronicle of living with a Siberian husky during the time she was researching the behavior of lemmings in the Alaskan bush. But *Beetle Rock*, her first book, is most often thought to be her best one. Set in a remote section of California's Sequoia National Park, the book depicts a twenty-four-hour period as imagined from the points of view of nine different animals: a weasel, a Sierra grouse, a chickaree (Douglas's squirrel), a black bear, a lizard, a coyote, a deer mouse, a Steller's jay, and a mule deer. *Beetle Rock* was a popular and a critical success, so much so that it set a pattern for some of Carrighar's later works, like *One Day at Teton Marsh*, her 1947 study of another wild region.

To get a feel for Carrighar's insight into the minds of other species, here is a selection from her second chapter, "What Happened to the Weasel." The chapter opens at night's end, when nocturnal creatures, a female weasel and her five kits among them, are seeking their shelters for day:

> From the frail defense of an oak leaf a deer mouse stared at a passing coyote, sensing its safety by the mechanical tread of the great paws. A frog and an owl at opposite ends of the same tree closed their eyes. A black bear, trampling a new bed at the base of a cedar, broke into the burrow of a ground squirrel. With heavy eyes he saw it leap to a rock-pile; then he made a last slow turn and curled himself against the trunk.

Many of Carrighar's main subjects appear in this passage—the deer mouse, the coyote, the squirrel, and the bear—their lives interrelated within the habitat. But what most strikes a reader is the quality of the narration, nearly straight reporting except for one or two moments when some plausible sensibility is attributed to one of the animals. Carrighar's method here is to resist romanticizing or overly anthropomorphizing her subjects; instead, she infers from her observations and research plausible emotional states for these sentient creatures and lightly embeds these into the narrative, as when the deer mouse senses its safety by the "mechanical tread" of the coyote's stride. Moreover, the bear's careless destruction of the squirrel's burrow arouses no sympathy from the narrator. The act appears as unadorned incident, a fact of life on Beetle Rock, leaving it up to the reader to recognize the indifference of the larger creature to the plight of the smaller.

As the animals settle into their shelters, the weasel is disturbed by the ruckus of a deer bounding through nearby brush. She emerges with three of her young to investigate any possible danger, and serendipity brings her prey:

> A golden-mantled squirrel made the mistake of jumping over a log without stopping on top to see what was on the other side. He came down at the mouth of the weasels' den, in the very midst of the four who had awakened.

The squirrel had seen them before he touched the ground, and had twisted his body so that he was able instantly to dodge back towards the Rock. But the mother Weasel cleared the log on his heels and caught him.

The two fought back and forth across the granite. The squirrel was larger, the Weasel faster; in fury they were matched. Every breath of the squirrel was a shriek of rage and protest....

The Weasel has caught the squirrel around the haunches. All her attention is given to coiling herself around his body. She shifts her hold until it is more and more secure and her teeth can approach the base of the squirrel's skull. Finally she sinks them in a precise and fatal puncture.

Despite the swift action, the narrative again stays close to straight reporting, breaking with that technique only to hint at specific emotional qualities—for example, the rage attributed to the squirrel—or to underscore states of mind—for example, the focused attention attributed to the weasel. No words are wasted on sentiment for the death of the weasel's prey. The incident closes when "the feast is shared by all the family except the two still sleeping the den."

Despite her great care, though, there surely are moments when Carrighar can't help but humanize her subjects, though often in subtle and perhaps inevitable ways. When she characterizes the mother weasel and her kits as a "family," for example, she not only names a genetic relationship, she evokes a whole constellation of social ones that readers may unconsciously project onto these animals. But, as David Rains Wallace says, the value of Carrighar's book is not that it's entirely free of human bias. In fact, her very presence during the nine years she spent off and on observing animals at Beetle Rock certainly affected the behaviors she cataloged. Rather, the value of her work is that by inviting us to imagine non-human perspectives, it helps us to alleviate "a pervasive alienation from the natural world." Part of that alienation surely comes from too little direct experience observing other species, sometimes the consequence of urban living and busy lives squeezed for time. And part of that alienation also comes from our often unthinking and arrogant assumption of human superiority. But I wonder if sometimes another factor is at work, an ironic one: our adoption of an analytical or an ecological point of view so careful of not anthropomorphizing the natural world that it undervalues the possible sympathies that may exist between the lives of our species and those of others. I think we get a better imaginative understanding of this issue by looking at another writer, Charles M. Scammon, a nineteenth-century whaling captain and author of *Marine Mammals of the Northwestern Coast of North America*, published in 1874.

Scammon's background and point of view couldn't have been more different from Carrighar's. He commanded twenty different ships between 1848 and 1883, a testament to his skills as a mariner; he presided over the slaughter of countless gray whales in Baja California; and as a Revenue Marine officer during the civil war, he commanded, according to environmental journalist Dick Russell, "the only official U.S. guardship patrolling the West Coast against Confederate Raids." During his voyages, however, Scammon kept scrupulous notes and produced detailed maps and drawings, including sketches of the marine mammals he encountered. Doubtless his early commercial

interests were served by his careful observations of his prey. But they later served him
even better when he turned to writing, publishing articles in *Overland Monthly* beginning
in 1869. Many of these would provide material for his book.

Like Carrighar, Scammon writes from direct observation that has been sharpened
with extensive reading. But rather than effacing the role of human beings, he
routinely privileges it, which many of us today—unused to unapologetic descriptions
of commercial hunting—will find disturbing, especially so when the animal being
stalked is now listed as threatened by the United States Fish and Wildlife Service.
Here is Scammon's description of how hunters once stalked sea otters—"the most
valuable fur-bearing animals inhabiting the waters of the North-Western Coast of
North America"—while perched between the gunwales of a three-man boat called
an "Otter-canoe":

> They leave the quiet waters of the harbor and put to sea, following the general
> trend of the land, but at times making a broad deviation, to hunt about some
> islands, miles from the main land. When an Otter is seen within rifle-shot,
> instantly the hunter fires; and if only wounding the animal, it dives under water,
> but soon re-appears, to be repeatedly shot at until killed. Sometimes, three
> boats will hunt together. Then they take positions, one on each side, but in
> advance of the third, and all three in the rear of where an animal is expected to
> be seen. It is only the practiced eye of the experienced men that can detect the
> tip of the animal's nose peering above water, and frequently disguised by a leaf
> of kelp.

Scammon's narrative features no second thoughts about the hunt, no moral asides
that might raise doubts about the businesslike killing of sea otters, creatures that early
in the twentieth century would be nearly extinct thanks to the value human beings
placed on their pelts. Even so, Scammon's description expresses an almost covert
sentimentality. Note, for example, his description of an elusive otter, "the animal's
nose peering above water, and frequently disguised by a leaf of kelp." Consciously or
not, Scammon anthropomorphizes these animals, lending them a coyness that makes
them endearing: the kind of quality that makes some animals seem cute and accessible.
This is also the kind of quality that generates sympathy for endangered animals like
sea otters but that we unfortunately may find absent in animals like the California
red-legged frog, animals that some might argue deserve equal attention. The irony
is that Scammon's description of otter hunting—a human activity that very nearly
wiped out the sea otter along the West Coast—contains within it the genius of their
eventual salvation.

Scammon's personification of otters emerges more strongly in a later passage, this
one devoted to describing mothers and their pups.

> In sunny days, when looking, it sometimes shades its eyes with one fore paw,
> much in the same manner as a person does with the hand. The females rarely
> have more than a single one at a birth—never more than two—which are
> "brought forth upon the kelp," say the white hunters, that abounds at nearly all

points known as their favorite resorting-places. The mothers caress and suckle their offspring seemingly with much affection, fondling them with their fore paws—reclining, in their usual manner—and frequently uttering a plaintive sound, which may have given rise to the saying that "Sea Otters sing to quiet their young ones," and gives some credence to the suggestion that human-like actions of the animal originated the story about mermaids.

Notice that Scammon grounds his observations firmly within a human frame, using our values and behaviors as an explanatory analogy for the habits of a wild animal. It is ironic that such a seemingly different point of view than that of Sally Carrighar—who consistently seeks to avoid overt human comparisons—yields a similar result, a figurative kinship between human and non-human creatures. In Scammon's writing this kinship finally transcends the familiar dichotomy of predator and prey and to some degree undercuts his unsentimental reporting on the techniques of otter hunting. The result is a description that is ambiguous, compelling, disturbing, and haunting. Scammon does not offer us a simple portrait of animal species so much as he sketches an outline that invites us to imagine our complex relationship to them.

In an essay on fiction and the animal mind, Dan Wylie has pointed out that recent research has questioned conventional distinctions between human and animal. "Rationality, language, self-awareness, consciousness of death, problem-solving, altruism, play: all these and other traits have been singled out as marking the distinctively 'human.' All have to some extent been eroded," he writes. Perhaps that's ultimately what all of the writers featured in this collection do for us—erode the barriers between human beings and other species and ultimately make us confront how we think about ourselves.

For myself, I'll continue to enjoy the outdoors with our sled dogs, ever hopeful that whenever we share a bright morning run, whatever enthusiasms I feel might be their enthusiasms, too.

References

Coetzee, J. M. *Elizabeth Costello*. New York: Penguin, 2003.

Russell, Dick. *Eye of the Whale: Epic Passages from Baja to Siberia*. Washington, D.C.: Island Press/Shearwater Books, 2004.

Wallace, David Rains. Foreword to *One Day on Beetle Rock*, by Sally Carrighar. Berkeley: Heyday Books, 2002.

Wylie, Dan. "The Anthropomorphic Ethic: Fiction and the Animal Mind in Virginia Woolf's *Flush* and Barbara Gowdy's *The White Bone*." *Interdisciplinary Studies in Literature and the Environment* 9, no. 2 (2002): 115–131.

⊱ ACKNOWLEDGMENTS ⊰

Califauna: A Literary Field Guide is the first California Legacy volume to benefit from the talents of students enrolled in the California Legacy Practicum, a course offered within the English Department at Santa Clara University wherein undergraduates hone research, writing, and editing skills aimed at producing work for a public audience. Over the last year and a half, ten students have made substantial contributions to the production of this book and it is with deep gratitude that we acknowledge them here. Our thanks to Adrianne Anderson, Meghan Bass, Sarah Bonnel, Laurie Cvengros, Kerrie Foy-Babbage, Marissa Gonzalez, Phi Le, Rebecca Rissman, and Matthew Weyand. Special recognition is also due to Mike Lysaght, a California Legacy intern, who not only provided research and editorial assistance but also helped to supervise practicum sessions.

Meghan Bass, another California Legacy intern, undertook the daunting task of managing the collection of material and organizing a review process for the work we were collecting. Meghan's dedication and imagination served the book especially well.

We are also grateful to Professor Janice Edgerly-Rooks of SCU's biology department. Janice reviewed the "field guide"–style head notes that we prepared for each selection and offered many useful suggestions and corrections. Any errors that remain are ours. Christie Genochio, another California Legacy intern, did invaluable work researching the graphics and crafting the timeline, which took a surprising— and illuminating—shape. Susan Snyder at the Bancroft Library at the University of California, Berkeley, was also wonderfully helpful when it came to tracking down the images included in this anthology.

From Heyday Books we wish to thank Malcolm Margolin, Gayle Wattawa, and William Justice for their support and invaluable guidance. We were very lucky to draw upon the talent of Lorraine Rath, who designed the book. And finally we owe a substantial debt to Lisa K. Manwill, whose editorial eye has made the book much better.

We have made every effort to identify the animals in the following selections according to common and scientific names. Since common names are often inclusive of several species and scientific names change as scientists consider new genetic evidence, there are some differences in the names that appear in our field guide headnotes and the selections they accompany.

Terry Beers
Emily Elrod

~ RED ABALONE ~

Haliotis rufescens

Family Haliotidae

Height: to 3"; Length: 6–12"; Width: to 9 ¼"

Habitat:

Intertidal rocks and crevices exposed to heavy surf with depths from 20–100'

Range:

Common along the coastline of California

Comments:

The red abalone—an oval, slightly flat, brick-red mollusk—is the largest species of abalone in the world. The inner surface of the shell is iridescent pink, green, and blue. The shell also has three to four holes in a row to eject water from its gill chamber and to expel waste products.

The red abalone's diet consists mainly of algae, kelp, and plankton, which it eats by placing its foot over the food source and consuming it with teeth and an extruding tongue. The red abalone is a sedentary creature, remaining near one place for most of its life. Its muscular foot serves as a giant suction cup, making it difficult for predators to pry it away from its rock. The red abalone can live up to twenty years.

The red abalone is prized as a delicacy, and its meat brings high prices. After humans, sea otters are the red abalone's main predator, but others include rock crabs and octopuses.

Gladys Nomland
"Origin of Abalone"

A girl came from the south—came and stood a long way off from a man. He wanted to get her because she was covered with Indian money. He said to his grandmother, "How am I going to get that woman?" His grandmother said, "Sing a song to her and she will come to you." So the grandmother gave him a song and he sang it to the woman. His grandmother told him that he must be out hunting when the girl came.

One day the grandmother heard shells on a dress and saw the girl coming. She shone all over with the abalone shell, she looked just like a rainbow. Then the man came home dressed in finery, dressed just like a hummingbird. He saw the girl was old and ugly, so he turned his back on her. She went away to the north, and his grandmother told the boy he did very wrong. The girl went a short distance and came to a creek where she changed back to a beautiful young woman. He saw her and followed her again. She went on and on. She stopped at Klamath river and he followed and caught up with her there on the left side of the river.

He wanted her to go back with him but she said no. He said he would cut her up so that she would never be pretty again. She would not go back, so he cut her. He left then, and she went to Trinidad and washed the blood and her body came back beautiful again. That man saw her again and he wanted to get her. She came toward him and told him that she would not go back with him but that she would always leave abalone shell for him to see so that he should not come after her again. Then she cried and sang a song.

That love song is the oldest song the Bear River people have. After she came back to her family, her sister said, "What happened to you?" She said, "I've been all cut up. I'll never follow another man." The tiny abalone shells are the oldest girl's body. When she arrived home south, the man was already there. She would not marry him, but he stayed there with her and that is why abalone money stays at Trinidad and that is the reason women do not follow men but have the men follow the women. Abalone is found only where that girl stopped to swim when she traveled, and it is always rough because she was all cut up by that man.

George Sterling (and others)
from "The Abalone Song"

Oh! some folks boast of quail on toast,
Because they think it's tony;
But I'm content to owe my rent,
And live on abalone.

Oh! Mission Point's a friendly joint,
Where every crab's a crony,
And true and kind you'll ever find
The clinging abalone.

He wanders free beside the sea,
Where e'er the coast is stony;
He flaps his wings and madly sings—
The plaintive abalone.

By Carmel Bay, the people say,
We feed the lazzaroni
On Boston beans and fresh sardines
And toothsome abalone.

Some live on hope, and some on dope,
And some on alimony;
But my tom-cat, he lives on fat
And tender abalone.

Oh! some drink rain, & some champagne,
Or brandy by the pony;
But I will try a little rye,
With a dash of abalone.

Oh! some like jam, and some like ham,
And some like macaroni;
But bring me in a pail of gin
And a tub of abalone.

Some stick to biz, some flirt with Liz,
Down on the sands at Coney;
But we, by Hell! stay in Carmel,
And nail the abalone.

We sit around and gaily pound,
And hold no acrimony,
Because our object is a gob
Of toothsome abalone.

Our servant girl is sure a pearl—
Her name is Meg Mahoney,
You ought to see the way that she
Serves up the abalone.

He hides in caves beneath the waves—
His ancient patrimony,
And so, 'tis shown that faith alone
Reveals the abalone.

The more we take, the more they make
In deep-sea matrimony;
Race-suicide cannot betide
The fertile abalone.

GIANT CARPENTER ANT

Camponotus laevigatus

Family Formicidae

Length: ¼"–⅜"

Habitat:

    Dead wood of tree trunks, timber, houses

Range:

    Common throughout the Sierra Nevada

Comments:

    The giant carpenter ant is shiny black to reddish brown. Like other ants, the giant carpenter ant has well-developed eyes and elbowed antennae that consist of one long first segment and eleven shorter segments.

    As is true for all ants, the social structure of the giant carpenter ant consists of a worker class of sterile females and a fertile reproductive caste of winged males and females. After mating, the males die and the females return to begin a new colony. When disturbed by humans, they protect themselves by biting.

    They live in tunnels of dead wood and set up trails between a main colony and satellite colonies. Their diet consists of other insects or sweets, such as juice from ripe fruit.

John Muir
"Biters"

Mastodons and elephants used to live here [on the Merced North Fork] no great geological time ago, as shown by their bones, often discovered by miners in washing gold gravel. And bears of at least two species are here now, besides the California lion or panther, and wildcats, wolves, foxes, snakes, scorpions, wasps, tarantulas; but one is almost tempted at times to regard a small savage black ant as the master existance of this vast mountain world. These fearless, restless, wandering imps, though only about a quarter of an inch long, are fonder of fighting and biting than any beast I know. They attack every living thing around their homes, often without cause as far as I can see. Their bodies are mostly jaws curved like ice-hooks, and to get work for these weapons seems to be their chief aim and pleasure. Most of their colonies are established in living oaks somewhat decayed or hollowed, in which they conveniently build their cells. These are chosen, probably, because of their strength as opposed to the attacks of animals and storms. They work both by day and by night, creep into dark caves, climb the highest trees, wander and hunt through cool ravines as well as on hot, unshaded ridges, and extend their highways and byways over everything but water and sky. From the foothills to a mile over the level of the sea nothing can stir without their knowledge; and alarms are spread in an incredibly short time, without any howl or cry that we can hear. I can't understand their ferocious courage; there seems to be no common sense to it. Sometimes, no doubt, they fight in defense of their homes, but they fight anywhere and always, wherever they can find anything to bite. As soon as a vulnerable spot is discovered on man or beast, they stand on their heads and sink their jaws, and though torn limb from limb, they will yet hold on and die biting deeper. When I contemplate this fierce creature so widely distributed and so strongly intrenched, I see that much remains to be done ere the world is brought under the rule of universal peace.... When you happen to sit down near a colony, some wandering hunter is sure to find you and come cautiously forward to discover the nature of the intruder and what ought to be done. If you are not too near the town and keep perfectly still he may run across your feet a few times, over your legs and hands and face, up your trousers, as if taking your measure and getting comprehensive views, then go in peace without raising an alarm. If, however, a tempting spot is offered, or some suspicious move excites him, a bite follows, and such a bite! I fancy that a bear or wolf bite is not to be compared with it. A quick electric shock of pain flashes along the outraged nerves, a shriek, a grab for the animal, and a bewildered stare follow this bite of bites as one comes back to consciousness from sudden eclipse. Fortunately, if careful, one need not be bitten oftener than once or twice in a lifetime. This wonderful electric species is about three fourths of an inch long. Bears are fond of them, and tear and gnaw their home-logs to pieces, and roughly devour the eggs, larvae, parent ants, and the rotten and sound wood of the cells, all in one spicy acid hash. The Digger Indians also are fond of the larvae, and even of the perfect ants, so I have been told by old mountaineers. They bite off and reject the head, and eat the tickly acid body with keen relish. Thus are the poor biters bitten, like every other biter, big or little, in the world's great family.

∾ GRIZZLY BEAR ∾

Ursus arctos horribilis

Family Ursidae

Height: 4'3"; Length: 5'11"–7'; Weight: 324–1,499 lb

Habitat:

Open country, usually mountainous, but also in grasslands or along coasts and rivers

Range:

Extirpated species

Comments:

The grizzly bear has a concave facial profile, long claws, and yellowish brown to dark brown fur with white-tipped hairs. It has a hump above the shoulders, which conceals a large muscle mass. It moves with a slow, clumsy walk but can break into a gallop.

Omnivorous, the grizzly bear eats mostly small mammals, carrion, fish, insects, grasses, berries, and fungi. It often hides its kill in shallowly dug depressions, covered with branches, earth, or natural debris, and returns later to finish off all the meat. It will also dig up roots, bulbs, and tubers, or tear up logs to get ants and termites. Ragged, overturned rocks and torn-up berry patches are signs of a grizzly feeding area.

Although not considered a true hibernator because it can be quickly awakened, the grizzly bear puts on a layer of fat in the winter. Some populations do not hibernate at all because they spend winters at lower elevations. Others den up in protected spots, such as caves or crevices, and will return to good dens year after year.

A nocturnal animal, the grizzly bear normally avoids humans. Its legendary ferocity can sometimes be observed along rivers, where aggressive grizzlies erupt in vicious fights over the best salmon feeding stations.

Jessie Benton Fremont
"My Grizzly Bear"

Bear Valley was the name of the busy mining town nearest us on our mining place in the Lower Sierra. It troubled our sense of fitness to call a town a valley, but it was fixed by custom and fitness; for this had been a happy hunting-ground of the grizzlies. Acorns of the long variety, tasting like chestnuts, abounded here as well as the usual smaller varieties, while the rich oily nut of the piñon-pine made their delight. These acorns and piñones were the chief bread-supplies of the Indians also who did not give them up easily, and consequently bear-skeletons and Indian skulls remained to tell the tale to the miners, who came in to the rich "diggings" there. American rifles, then the pounding of quartz mills and strange shrieks of steam engines drove them away, and only the name remained.

To my objection of using "valley" and "town" as one and the same, I was told best let it alone or worse would follow, for there was a strong party intending to change the name of the place to "Simpkinsville," and how would I like that? The postmaster was the Simpkins—a tall, "showy" young man with an ambitious wife much older than himself; he was a London footman and she Irish, active, energetic, with a good head, and with ambition for her Simpkins. That neither of them could read or write was a trivial detail that did not seem to disturb the public. Men would swing down from horse or wagon-box, go in and select from the loose pile of letters their own and those of their neighbors, and have their drink at the bar over which Simpkins presided (they kept a tavern and the post-office was only a little detail).

But with the instinct of a man who "had seen the world" toward people of somewhat the same experience, the postmaster treated us with the largest courtesy, for everything with a capital "F" on it was laid aside for us.★ Isaac, our part-Indian hunter, who generally rode in for the mail, did not read either, and often had to make return-trips to give back what was not ours. It was in the time of Mr. Buchanan's administration, and had Simpkins sent in a petition signed as it would have been by the habitues of his bar, of course so faithful a political servant would have been granted this small favor, of change of name. You may be sure I lay low in my valley to avert this cruel address on my letters.

I had never before gone up to this property, and now it was chiefly as a summer open-air and camping-out tour to be over in three months, when we were to return to Paris where all arrangements had been made for a three-years stay.

Although the bear had long disappeared from this favorite old haunt I felt nervous about horseback excursions. Mountains are grim things at best, but all those deep clefts and thickets in ravines and horrid stony hill-slopes barred me from any but the beaten stage and wagon-roads, with our cool, brave Isaac to drive me. However, there was one view Mr. Fremont wanted me to see which we could get only on horseback, with a short climb at the peak of the mountain. From the summit we could see eighty

★ *This "F" was the brand on all the tools and belongings of the works—in these countries whatever else was defied, the brand had to be respected. —J. B. F.*

miles off the line of the San Joaquin River, defined by its broad belt of trees, running north and south parallel to our mountains; connecting the two were many mountain rivers crossing the broad plain and glittering like steel ribbons in the afternoon sun— the Merced, the Stanislaus, the Tuolumne and others; a turn of the head showed the peaks of the Yosemite thirty miles off, and lines of blue mountains back to the everlasting snow of Carson's Peak—a stretch of a hundred and fifty miles.

It was a rough ride up, and rougher climbing after the horses could go no further and had to be left tied to trees with one man to watch them—only one other was with us; our party was only myself and my daughter with her father and the two men.

We were growing more and more enthusiastic as glimpses of this rare view came to us. Mr. Fremont told us the distances, which only singularly pure mountain air could have let the eye pierce. "And the ear, too," I said. "We must be three miles from the village and yet how near sounds the barking of that dog!"

Dead silence fell on our animated people. They listened, as the rough, low bark— broader and rougher even than that of a bull-dog—rose again, sounding really close to us.

I never question any acts of some few people but was surprised, and not too pleased, to find myself hurried back down the steep, stony peak with only, "It is too late to finish the climb—we must hurry—do not speak—keep all your breath for walking." And hurry we did. I was fairly lifted along. Mr. Burke had disappeared and was now with Lee bringing the horses to meet us—the horses refractory.

Without a word I was lifted into the saddle—Mr. Fremont gathered up my reins himself and kept close to my side—and we fairly scurried down the mountains, I shamelessly holding to the saddle as the steep grade made me dizzy. This dizziness so preoccupied me with the fear of fainting that I felt nothing else. We gained the stage-road by the shortest cut, and then a loping gallop soon brought us home, where I was carefully lifted down and all the consideration and care which they dared not give me on the hurried ride was now lavished on me. I had been seriously ill not long before and could not understand why I was so roughly hauled along.

There was reason enough.

It was no dog, but a grizzly bear that made that warning bark, and we were very close to it.

My ignorance spared me the shock of this knowledge, but the practised mountain men knew it was not only a bear, but a she-bear with cubs. They knew she would not be likely to leave her cubs at that hour when they were settling for the night unless we came nearer or irritated her by talking and noises. Horses are terribly afraid of this powerful and dangerous animal, and one danger was that our horses would break away and run for safety leaving us to the chances of getting off on foot. There I was the weak link in the chain. My daughter was fleet of foot and so steady of nerve that she was told the truth at once, and did her part bravely in keeping me unaware of any unusual condition. Fortunately our riding horses were, each, pets and friends, and only required to be safe with their masters; Burke had got back instantly to help Lee, and once mounted we were moved by one intelligence, one will.

Very quickly our bright drawing-room filled with eager men gun in hand. Armed men rode down the glen intent on that bear—first coming to get all information of the exact locality, then to ride and raise the countryside for a general turnout against it. For every one had kept from "the Madam" the fact that a she-bear had been prowling about for some time seeking what she could devour; and that she had devoured some and mangled more of "Quigley's hogs"—Quigley having very fine and profitable hogs at a small ranch three miles from us.

Lights frighten off wild beasts. I had no shame in illuminating the house that night. Men laughed kindly over it, but they all felt glad that I had come off so safely, and next day I was early informed that the cubs were all killed. The bear went as usual to Quigley's for her raw pork supper, the digestion of a bear making this a pleasure without drawback, but the stir about the place was evident to the keen senses of the grizzly and the men watched that night in vain. Her tracks were plain all around about, and the poor thing was tracked to her return to her cubs. She had moved them—made sure they were all dead, and her instinct sent her off into close hiding.

The watch was kept up, but she was wary and kept away.

At length one dark night the Quigley people heard sounds they were sure came from the bear though the hogs in the big pen were quiet. They were stifled sounds blown away by a high wind. There was but one man in the house, and he said his wife would not let him go after them; it was so desperately dark the odds would be all against him.

The woman said she was not sure it was a bear. She half thought it was men fighting, an equally great danger in that isolated way of living. So they shut their ears and their hearts although human groans and stifled blown-away cries made them sure it was no animal.

The sounds passed on. In the morning they went to the wagon-road which ran near their enclosure and found a trail of blood. Followed up, it led to a little creek close by with steep clay banks. Dead, his face downward in the water, lay a young man in a pool of blood—shockingly mangled across the lower part of the body. His sufferings must have been great, but his will and courage had proved greater.

He had not been torn by a bear as was first thought, but by a ball from his own pistol. This was found, a perfectly new pistol, in his trousers pocket; the scorched clothing showing it had gone off while in the pocket. The trail was followed back, leading to a brook where he must have stopped to drink when the pistol, carrying a heavy ball, went off. Yet such was his courage and determination that he crawled that long way in a state plainly told by the place where he had rolled in agony—the last was where he made his vain appeal for help at the Quigley house. Perhaps he fell face downward into the shallow streams and was mercifully drowned.

His good clothing, a geologist's hammer, and some specimens of quartz wrapped in bits of a German newspaper told of an educated, worthy sort of man. But there was nothing to identify him, and the poor fellow was never inquired after. One of the many who came from afar with high hopes, and whose life was summed up in that most pathetic of words, "Missing."

The grizzly had disappeared and was, I am told, the last ever known in that valley, which still has as postmark for the town "Bear Valley"; it is to be presumed the succeeding post-masters have been men who knew the whole of the alphabet as well as the letter "F."

Joaquin Miller
"The Grizzly as Fremont Found Him"

General Fremont found this powerful brute to be a gregarious and confiding creature, fond of his family and not given to disturbing those who did not disturb him. In his report to the government—1847—he tells of finding a large family of grizzly bears gathering acorns very much as the native Indians gathered them, and this not far from a small Mexican town. He says that riding at the head of his troops he saw, on reaching the brow of a little grassy hill set with oaks, a great commotion in the boughs of one of the largest trees, and, halting to cautiously reconnoiter, he noticed that there were grouped about the base of the tree and under its wide boughs, several huge grizzlies, employed in gathering and eating the acorns which the baby grizzlies threw down from the thick branches overhead. More than this, he reports that the baby bears, on seeing him, became frightened, and attempted to descend to the ground and run away, but the older bears, which had not yet discovered the explorers, beat the young ones and drove them back up the tree, and compelled them to go on with their work, as if they had been children.

In the early '50s, I myself saw the grizzlies feeding together in numbers under the trees, far up the Sacramento Valley, as tranquilly as a flock of sheep. A serene, dignified and very decent old beast was the full-grown grizzly as Fremont and others found him here at home. This king of the continent, who is quietly abdicating his throne, has never been understood. The grizzly was not only every inch a king, but he had, in his undisputed dominion, a pretty fair sense of justice. He was never a roaring lion. He was never a man-eater. He is indebted for his character for ferocity almost entirely to tradition, but, in some degree, to the female bear when seeking to protect her young. Of course, the grizzlies are good fighters, when forced to it; but as for lying in wait for anyone, like the lion, or creeping, cat-like, as the tiger does, into camp to carry off someone for supper, such a thing was never heard of in connection with the grizzly.

The grizzly went out as the American rifle came in. I do not think he retreated. He was a lover of home and family, and so fell where he was born. For he is still found here and there, all up and down the land, as the Indian is still found, but he is no longer the majestic and serene king of the world. His whole life has been disturbed, broken up; and his temper ruined. He is a cattle thief now, and even a sheep thief. In old age, he keeps close to his canyon by day, deep in the impenetrable chaparral, and at night shuffles down hill to some hog-pen, perfectly careless of dogs or shots, and, tearing out a whole side of the pen, feeds his fill on the inmates.

One of the interior counties kept a standing reward for the capture of an old grizzly of this character for several years. But he defied everything and he escaped everything but old age. Some hunters finally crept in to where the old king lay, nearly blind and dying of old age, and dispatched him with a volley from several Winchester rifles. It was found that he was almost toothless, his paws had been terribly mutilated by numerous steel traps, and it is said that his kingly old carcass had received nearly lead enough to sink a small ship. There were no means of ascertaining his exact weight, but it was claimed that skin, bone and bullets, as he was found, he would have weighed well nigh a ton.

～ HONEY BEE ～

Apis mellifera

Family Apidae

Length: ⅛"–1"

Habitat:

  Mainly manmade hives in well-vegetated and flower-rich areas

Range:

  Common throughout California

Comments:

  The honey bee's body is a brightly colored pattern of gold and black. Honey bees live in hives, where they are divided into three types: queen, drone, and worker. The queen's primary function is to lay eggs. Drones—the queen's sons—do not work in the hive but fly off to mate with new and future queens of other colonies. Workers fashion the honeycomb, tend to the young, ventilate the hive with their wings, and obtain nectar and pollen from flowers. They defend the hive by stinging invaders, soon after which they die of abdominal rupture.

  Pollen is the main source of protein and vitamins for the hive, and nectar provides the carbohydrate supply. A mixture of honey and pollen, called "bee bread," is used for food.

  Honey bees allow plants to reproduce by carrying pollen from flower to flower, each of which attracts bees through its particular fragrance and color. When they find areas abundant in flowers, honey bees communicate with each other through a dance that indicates the location of the flowers in relation to the hive.

  The honey bee was originally from Southeast Asia but has been introduced throughout the world.

John Muir
"The Bee-Pastures"

When California was wild, it was one sweet bee-garden throughout its entire length, north and south, and all the way across from the snowy Sierra to the ocean.

Wherever a bee might fly within the bounds of this virgin wilderness—through the redwood forests, along the banks of the rivers, along the bluffs and headlands fronting the sea, over valley and plain, park and grove, and deep, leafy glen, or far up the piny slopes of the mountains—throughout every belt and section of climate up to the timber line, bee-flowers bloomed in lavish abundance. Here they grew more or less apart in special sheets and patches of no great size, there in broad, flowing folds hundreds of miles in length—zones of polleny forests, zones of flowery chaparral, stream-tangles of rubus and wild rose, sheets of golden compositae, beds of violets, beds of mint, beds of bryanthus and clover, and so on, certain species blooming somewhere all the year round.

But of late years plows and sheep have made sad havoc in these glorious pastures, destroying tens of thousands of the flowery acres like a fire, and banishing many species of the best honey-plants to rocky cliffs and fence-corners, while, on the other hand, cultivation thus far has given no adequate compensation, at least in kind; only acres of alfalfa for miles of the richest wild pasture, ornamental roses and honeysuckles around cottage doors for cascades of wild roses in the dells, and small, square orchards and orange-groves for broad mountain-belts of chaparral.

The Great Central Plain of California, during the months of March, April, and May, was one smooth, continuous bed of honey-bloom, so marvelously rich that, in walking from one end of it to the other, a distance of more than 400 miles, your foot would press about a hundred flowers at every step. Mints, gilias, nemophilas, castilleias, and innumerable compositae were so crowded together that, had ninety-nine per cent. of them been taken away, the plain would still have seemed to any but Californians extravagantly flowery. The radiant, honeyful corollas, touching and overlapping, and rising above one another, glowed in the living light like a sunset sky—one sheet of purple and gold, with the bright Sacramento pouring through the midst of it from the north, the San Joaquin from the south, and their many tributaries sweeping in at right angles from the mountains, dividing the plain into sections fringed with trees.

Along the rivers there is a strip of bottom-land, countersunk beneath the general level, and wider toward the foot-hills, where magnificent oaks, from three to eight feet in diameter, cast grateful masses of shade over the open, prairie-like levels. And close along the water's edge there was a fine jungle of tropical luxuriance, composed of wild-rose and bramble bushes and a great variety of climbing vines, wreathing and interlacing the branches and trunks of willows and alders, and swinging across from summit to summit in heavy festoons. Here the wild bees reveled in fresh bloom long after the flowers of the drier plain had withered and gone to seed. And in midsummer, when the "blackberries" were ripe, the Indians came from the mountains to feast—men, women, and babies in long, noisy trains, often joined by the farmers of the neighborhood, who gathered this wild fruit with commendable appreciation of its superior flavor, while their home orchards were full of ripe peaches, apricots, nectarines, and figs, and their vineyards were laden with grapes. But, though these luxuriant, shaggy river-beds were thus distinct from the smooth, treeless plain, they made no heavy dividing lines in general views. The whole appeared as one continuous sheet of bloom bounded only by the mountains.

When I first saw this central garden, the most extensive and regular of all the bee-pastures of the State, it seemed all one sheet of plant gold, hazy and vanishing in the distance, distinct as a new map along the foot-hills at my feet.

Descending the eastern slopes of the Coast Range through beds of gilias and lupines, and around many a breezy hillock and bush-crowned headland, I at length waded out into the midst of it. All the ground was covered, not with grass and green leaves, but with radiant corollas, about ankle-deep next the foot-hills, knee-deep or more five or six miles out. Here were bahia, madia, madaria, burrielia, chrysopsis, corethrogyne, grindelia, etc., growing in close social congregations of various shades of yellow, blending finely with the purples of clarkia, orthocarpus, and oenothera, whose delicate petals were drinking the vital sunbeams without giving back any sparkling glow.

Because so long a period of extreme drought succeeds the rainy season, most of the vegetation is composed of annuals, which spring up simultaneously, and bloom together at about the same height above the ground, the general surface being but slightly ruffled by the taller phacelias, pentstemons, and groups of *Salvia carduacea,* the king of the mints.

Sauntering in any direction, hundreds of these happy sun-plants brushed against my feet at every step, and closed over them as if I were wading in liquid gold. The air was sweet with fragrance, the larks sang their blessed songs, rising on the wing as I advanced, then sinking out of sight in the polleny sod, while myriads of wild bees stirred the lower air with their monotonous hum—monotonous, yet forever fresh and sweet as every-day sunshine. Hares and spermophiles showed themselves in considerable numbers in shallow places, and small bands of antelopes were almost constantly in sight, gazing curiously from some slight elevation, and then bounding swiftly away with unrivaled grace of motion. Yet I could discover no crushed flowers to mark their track, nor, indeed, any destructive action of any wild foot or tooth whatever.

The great yellow days circled by uncounted, while I drifted toward the north, observing the countless forms of life thronging about me, lying down almost anywhere on the approach of night. And what glorious botanical beds I had! Oftentimes on awaking I would find several new species leaning over me and looking me full in the face, so that my studies would begin before rising.

About the first of May I turned eastward, crossing the San Joaquin River between the mouths of the Tuolumne and Merced, and by the time I had reached the Sierra foot-hills most of the vegetation had gone to seed and become as dry as hay.

All the seasons of the great plain are warm or temperate, and bee flowers are never wholly wanting; but the grand springtime—the annual resurrection—is governed by the rains, which usually set in about the middle of November or the beginning of December. Then the seeds, that for six months have lain on the ground dry and fresh as if they had been gathered into barns, at once unfold their treasured life. The general brown and purple of the ground, and the dead vegetation of the preceding year, give place to the green of mosses and liverworts and myriads of young leaves. Then one species after another comes into flower, gradually overspreading the green with yellow and purple, which lasts until May.

The "rainy season" is by no means a gloomy soggy period of constant cloudiness and rain. Perhaps nowhere else in North America, perhaps in the world, are the months of December, January, February, and March so full of bland, plant-building sunshine. Referring to my notes of the winter and spring of 1868-69, every day of which I spent out of doors, on that section of the plain lying between the Tuolumne and Merced rivers, I find that the first rain of the season fell on December 18th. January had only six rainy days—that is, days on which rain fell; February three, March five, April three, and May three, completing the so-called rainy season, which was about an average one. The ordinary rain-storm of this region is seldom very cold or violent. The winds, which in settled weather come from the northwest, veer round into the opposite direction, the sky fills gradually and evenly with one general cloud, from which the rain falls steadily, often for days in succession, at a temperature of about 45° or 50°.

More than seventy-five per cent of all the rain of this season came from the northwest, down the coast over southeastern Alaska, British Columbia, Washington, and Oregon, though the local winds of these circular storms blow from the southeast. One magnificent local storm from the northwest fell on March 21. A massive, round-browed cloud came swelling and thundering over the flowery plain in most imposing majesty, its bossy front burning white and purple in the full blaze of the sun, while warm rain poured from its ample fountains like a cataract, beating down flowers and bees, and flooding the dry watercourses as suddenly as those of Nevada are flooded by the so-called "cloud-bursts." But in less than half an hour not a trace of the heavy, mountain-like cloud structure was left in the sky, and the bees were on the wing, as if nothing more gratefully refreshing could have been sent them.

By the end of January four species of plants were in flower, and five or six mosses had already adjusted their hoods and were in the prime of life; but the flowers were not sufficiently numerous as yet to affect greatly the general green of the young leaves. Violets made their appearance in the first week of February, and toward the end of this month the warmer portions of the plain were already golden with myriads of the flowers of rayed compositae.

This was the full springtime. The sunshine grew warmer and richer, new plants bloomed every day; the air became more tuneful with humming wings, and sweeter with the fragrance of the opening flowers. Ants and ground squirrels were getting ready for their summer work, rubbing their benumbed limbs, and sunning themselves on the husk-piles before their doors, and spiders were busy mending their old webs, or weaving new ones.

In March, the vegetation was more than doubled in depth and color; claytonia, calandrinia, a large white gilia, and two nemophilas were in bloom, together with a host of yellow compositae, tall enough now to bend in the wind and show wavering ripples of shade.

In April, plant-life, as a whole, reached its greatest height, and the plain, over all its varied surface, was mantled with a close, furred plush of purple and golden corollas. By the end of this month, most of the species had ripened their seeds, but undecayed, still seemed to be in bloom from the numerous corolla-like involucres and whorls of chaffy scales of the compositae. In May, the bees found in flower only a few deep-set liliaceous plants and eriogonums.

June, July, August, and September is the season of rest and sleep,—a winter of dry heat,—followed in October by a second outburst of bloom at the very driest time of the year. Then, after the shrunken mass of leaves and stalks of the dead vegetation crinkle and turn to dust beneath the foot, as if it had been baked in an oven, *Hemizonia virgata*, a slender, unobtrusive little plant, from six inches to three feet high, suddenly makes its appearance in patches miles in extent, like a resurrection of the bloom of April. I have counted upward of 3,000 flowers, five eighths of an inch in diameter, on a single plant. Both its leaves and stems are so slender as to be nearly invisible, at a distance of a few yards, amid so showy a multitude of flowers. The ray and disk flowers are both yellow, the stamens purple, and the texture of the rays is rich and velvety, like the petals of garden pansies. The prevailing wind turns all the heads round to the southeast, so that in facing northwestward we have the flowers looking us in the face. In my estimation, this little plant, the last born of the brilliant host of compositae that glorify the plain, is the most interesting of all. It remains in flower until November, uniting with two or three species of wiry eriogonums, which continue the floral chain around December to the spring flowers of January. Thus, although the main bloom and honey season is only about three months long, the floral circle, however thin around some of the hot, rainless months, is never completely broken.

How long the various species of wild bees have lived in this honey-garden, nobody knows; probably ever since the main body of the present flora gained possession of the land, toward the close of the glacial period. The first brown honey-bees brought to California are said to have arrived in San Francisco in March, 1853. A bee-keeper by the name of Shelton purchased a lot, consisting of twelve swarms, from some one at Aspinwall, who had brought them from New York. When landed at San Francisco, all the hives contained live bees, but they finally dwindled to one hive, which was taken to San Jose. The little immigrants flourished and multiplied in the bountiful pastures of the Santa Clara Valley, sending off three swarms the first season. The owner was killed shortly afterward, and in settling up his estate, two of the swarms were sold at auction for $105 and $110 respectively. Other importations were made, from time to time, by way of the Isthmus, and, though great pains were taken to insure success, about one half usually died on the way. Four swarms were brought safely across the plains in 1859, the hives being placed in the rear end of a wagon, which was stopped in the afternoon to allow the bees to fly and feed in the floweriest places that were within reach until dark, when the hives were closed.

In 1855, two years after the time of the first arrivals from New York, a single swarm was brought over from San Jose, and let fly in the Great Central Plain. Bee-culture, however, has never gained much attention here, notwithstanding the extraordinary abundance of honey-bloom, and the high price of honey during the early years. A few hives are found here and there among settlers who chanced to have learned something about the business before coming to the State. But sheep, cattle, grain, and fruit raising are the chief industries, as they require less skill and care, while the profits thus far have been greater. In 1856 honey sold here at from one and a half to two dollars per pound. Twelve years later the price had fallen to twelve and a half cents. In 1868 I sat down to dinner with a band of ravenous sheep-shearers at a ranch on the San Joaquin, where fifteen or twenty hives were kept, and our host advised us not to spare the large pan of honey he had placed on the table, as it was the cheapest article he had to offer. In all my walks, however, I have never come upon a regular bee-ranch in the Central Valley like those so common and so skillfully managed in the southern counties of the State. The few pounds of honey and wax produced are consumed at home, and are scarcely taken into account among the coarser products of the farm. The swarms that escape from their careless owners have a weary, perplexing time of it in seeking suitable homes. Most of them make their way to the foot-hills of the mountains, or to the trees that line the banks of the rivers, where some hollow log or trunk may be found. A friend of mine, while out hunting on the San Joaquin, came upon an old coon trap, hidden among some tall grass, near the edge of the river, upon which he sat down to rest. Shortly afterward his attention was attracted to a crowd of angry bees that were flying excitedly about his head, when he discovered that he was sitting upon their hive, which was found to contain more than 200 pounds of honey. Out in the broad, swampy delta of the Sacramento and San Joaquin rivers, the little wanderers have been known to build their combs in a bunch of rushes, or stiff, wiry grass, only slightly protected from the weather, and in danger every spring of being carried away by floods. They have the advantage, however, of a vast extent of fresh pasture, accessible only to themselves.

The present condition of the Grand Central Garden is very different from that we have sketched. About twenty years ago, when the gold placers had been pretty thoroughly exhausted, the attention of fortune-seekers—not home-seekers—was, in great part, turned away from the mines to the fertile plains, and many began experiments in a kind of restless, wild agriculture. A load of lumber would be hauled to some spot on the free wilderness, where water could be easily found, and a rude box-cabin built. Then a gang-plow was procured, and a dozen mustang ponies, worth ten or fifteen dollars apiece, and with these hundreds of acres were stirred as easily as if the land had been under cultivation for years, tough, perennial roots being almost wholly absent. Thus a ranch was established, and from these bare wooden huts, as centers of desolation, the wild flora vanished in ever-widening circles. But the arch destroyers are the shepherds, with their flocks of hoofed locusts, sweeping over the ground like a fire, and trampling down every rod that escapes the plow as completely as if the whole plain were a cottage garden-plot without a fence. But notwithstanding these destroyers, a thousand swarms of bees may be pastured here for every one now gathering honey. The greater portion is still covered every season with a repressed growth of bee-flowers, for most of the species are annuals, and many of them are not relished by sheep or cattle, while the rapidity of their growth enables them to develop and mature their seeds before any foot has time to crush them. The ground is, therefore, kept sweet, and the race is perpetuated, though only as a suggestive shadow of the magnificence of its wildness.

The time will undoubtedly come when the entire area of this noble valley will be tilled like a garden, when the fertilizing waters of the mountains, now flowing to the sea, will be distributed to every acre, giving rise to prosperous towns, wealth, arts, etc. Then, I suppose, there will be few left, even among botanists, to deplore the vanished primeval flora. In the mean time, the pure waste going on—the wanton destruction of the innocents—is a sad sight to see, and the sun may well be pitied in being compelled to look on.

The bee-pastures of the Coast Ranges last longer and are more varied than those of the great plain, on account of differences of soil and climate, moisture, and shade, etc. Some of the mountains are upward of 4,000 feet in height, and small streams, springs, oozy bogs, etc., occur in great abundance and variety in the wooded regions, while open parks, flooded with sunshine, and hill girt valleys lying at different elevations, each with its own peculiar climate and exposure, possess the required conditions for the development of species and families of plants widely varied.

Next the plain there is, first, a series of smooth hills, planted with a rich and showy vegetation that differs but little from that of the plain itself—as if the edge of the plain had been lifted and bent into flowing folds, with all its flowers in place, only toned down a little as to their luxuriance, and a few new species introduced, such as the hill lupines, mints, and gilias. The colors show finely when thus held to view on the slopes; patches of red, purple, blue, yellow, and white, blending around the edges, the whole appearing at a little distance like a map colored in sections.

Above this lies the park and chaparral region, with oaks, mostly evergreen, planted wide apart, and blooming shrubs from three to ten feet high; manzanita and ceanothus of several species, mixed with rhamnus, cercis, pickeringia, cherry, amelanchier, and adenostoma, in shaggy, interlocking thickets, and many species of hosackia, clover, monardella, castilleia, etc., in the openings.

The main ranges send out spurs somewhat parallel to their axes, inclosing level valleys, many of them quite extensive, and containing a great profusion of sun-loving bee-flowers in their wild state; but these are, in great part, already lost to the bees by cultivation.

Nearer the coast are the giant forests of the redwoods, extending from near the Oregon line to Santa Cruz. Beneath the cool, deep shade of these majestic trees the ground is occupied by ferns, chiefly woodwardia and aspidiums, with only a few flowering plants—oxalis, trientalis, erythronium, fritillaria, smilax, and other shade-lovers.

But all along the redwood belt there are sunny openings on hill-slopes looking to the south, where the giant trees stand back, and give the ground to the small sunflowers and the bees. Around the lofty redwood walls of these little bee-acres there is usually a fringe of Chestnut Oak, Laurel, and Madroño, the last of which is a surpassingly beautiful tree, and a great favorite with the bees. The trunks of the largest specimens are seven or eight feet thick, and about fifty feet high; the bark red and chocolate colored, the leaves plain, large, and glossy, like those of *Magnolia grandiflora,* while the flowers are yellowish-white, and urn-shaped, in well-proportioned panicles, from five to ten inches long. When in full bloom, a single tree seems to be visited at times by a whole hive of bees at once, and the deep hum of such a multitude makes the listener guess that more than the ordinary work of honey-winning must be going on.

How perfectly enchanting and care-obliterating are these withdrawn gardens of the woods—long vistas opening to the sea—sunshine sifting and pouring upon the flowery ground in a tremulous, shifting mosaic, as the light-ways in the leafy wall open and close with the swaying breeze—shining leaves and flowers, birds and bees, mingling together in springtime harmony, and soothing fragrance exhaling from a thousand thousand fountains! In these balmy, dissolving days, when the deep heart-beats of Nature are felt thrilling rocks and trees and everything alike, common business and friends are happily forgotten, and even the natural honey-work of bees, and the care of birds for their young, and mothers for their children, seem slightly out of place.

To the northward, in Humboldt and the adjacent counties, whole hillsides are covered with rhododendron, making a glorious melody of bee-bloom in the spring. And the Western azalea, hardly less flowery, grows in massy thickets three to eight feet high around the edges of groves and woods as far south as San Luis Obispo, usually accompanied by manzanita; while the valleys, with their varying moisture and shade, yield a rich variety of the smaller honey-flowers, such as mentha, lycopus, micromeria, audibertia, trichostema, and other mints; with vaccinium, wild strawberry, geranium, calais, and goldenrod; and in the cool glens along the stream banks, where the shade of trees is not too deep, spiraea, dog-wood, heteromeles, and calycanthus, and many species of rubus form interlacing tangles, some portion of which continues in bloom for months.

Though the coast region was the first to be invaded and settled by white men, it has suffered less from a bee point of view than either of the other main divisions, chiefly, no doubt, because of the unevenness of the surface, and because it is owned and protected instead of lying exposed to the flocks of the wandering "sheepmen." These remarks apply more particularly to the north half of the coast. Farther south there is less moisture, less forest shade, and the honey flora is less varied.

The Sierra region is the largest of the three main divisions of the bee-lands of the State, and the most regularly varied in its subdivisions, owing to their gradual rise from the level of the Central Plain to the alpine summits. The foot-hill region is about as dry and sunful, from the end of May until the setting in of the winter rains, as the plain. There are no shady forests, no damp glens at all like those lying at the same elevations in the Coast Mountains. The social compositae of the plain, with a few added species, form the bulk of the herbaceous portion of the vegetation up to a height of 1,500 feet or more, shaded lightly here and there with oaks and Sabine Pines, and interrupted by patches of ceanothus and buckeye. Above this, and just below the forest region, there is a dark, heath-like belt of chaparral, composed almost exclusively of *Adenostoma fasciculata*, a bush belonging to the rose family, from five to eight feet high, with small, round leaves in fascicles, and bearing a multitude of small white flowers in panicles on the ends of the upper branches. Where it occurs at all, it usually covers all the ground with a close, impenetrable growth, scarcely broken for miles.

Up through the forest region, to a height of about 9,000 feet above sea-level, there are ragged patches of manzanita, and five or six species of ceanothus, called deer-brush or California lilac. These are the most important of all the honey-bearing bushes of the Sierra. *Chamoebatia foliolosa*, a little shrub about a foot high, with flowers like the strawberry, makes handsome carpets beneath the pines, and seems to be a favorite with the bees; while pines themselves furnish unlimited quantities of pollen and honey dew. The product of a single tree, ripening its pollen at the right time of year, would be sufficient for the wants of a whole hive. Along the streams there is a rich growth of lilies, larkspurs, pedicularis, castilleias, and clover. The alpine region contains the flowery glacier meadows, and countless small gardens in all sorts of places full of potentilla of several species, spraguea, ivesia, epilobium, and goldenrod, with beds of bryanthus and the charming cassiope covered with sweet bells. Even the tops of the mountains are blessed with flowers,—dwarf phlox, polemonium, ribes, hulsea, etc. I have seen wild bees and butterflies feeding at a height of 13,000 feet above the sea. Many, however, that go up these dangerous heights never come down again. Some, undoubtedly, perish in storms, and I have found thousands lying dead or benumbed on the surface of the glaciers, to which they had perhaps been attracted by the white glare, taking them for beds of bloom.

From swarms that escaped their owners in the lowlands, the honey-bee is now generally distributed throughout the whole length of the Sierra, up to an elevation of 8,000 feet above sea-level. At this height they flourish without care, though the snow every winter is deep. Even higher than this several bee-trees have been cut which contained over 200 pounds of honey.

The destructive action of sheep has not been so general on the mountain pastures as on those of the great plain, but in many places it has been more complete, owing to the more friable character of the soil, and its sloping position. The slant digging and down-raking action of hoofs on the steeper slopes of moraines has uprooted and buried many of the tender plants from year to year, without allowing them time to mature their seeds. The shrubs, too, are badly bitten, especially the various species of ceanothus. Fortunately, neither sheep nor cattle care to feed on the manzanita, spiraea, or adenostoma; and these fine honey-bushes are too stiff and tall, or grow in places too rough and inaccessible, to be trodden under foot. Also the cañon walls and gorges, which form so considerable a part of the area of the range, while inaccessible to domestic sheep, are well fringed with honey-shrubs, and contain thousands of lovely bee-gardens, lying hid in narrow side-cañons and recesses fenced with avalanche taluses, and on the top of flat, projecting headlands, where only bees would think to look for them.

But, on the other hand, a great portion of the woody plants that escape the feet and teeth of the sheep are destroyed by the shepherds by means of running fires, which are set everywhere during the dry autumn for the purpose of burning off the old fallen trunks and underbrush, with a view to improving the pastures, and making more open ways for the flocks. These destructive sheep-fires sweep through nearly the entire forest belt of the range, from one extremity to the other, consuming not only the underbrush, but the young trees and seedlings on which the permanence of the forests depends; thus setting in motion a long train of evils which will certainly reach far beyond bees and bee-keepers.

The plow has not yet invaded the forest region to any appreciable extent, neither has it accomplished much in the foot-hills. Thousands of bee-ranches might be established along the margin of the plain, and up to a height of 4,000 feet, wherever water could be obtained. The climate at this elevation admits of the making of permanent homes, and by moving the hives to higher pastures as the lower pass out of bloom, the annual yield of honey would be nearly doubled. The foot-hill pastures, as we have seen, fail about the end of May, those of the chaparral belt and lower forests are in full bloom in June, those of the upper and alpine region in July, August, and September. In Scotland, after the best of the Lowland bloom is past, the bees are carried in carts to the Highlands, and set free on the heather hills. In France, too, and in Poland, they are carried from pasture to pasture among orchards and fields in the same way, and along the rivers in barges to collect the honey of the delightful vegetation of the banks. In Egypt they are taken far up the Nile, and floated slowly home again, gathering the honey-harvest of the various fields on the way, timing their movements in accord with the seasons. Were similar methods pursued in California the productive season would last nearly all the year.

The average elevation of the north half of the Sierra is, as we have seen, considerably less than that of the south half, and small streams, with the bank and meadow gardens dependent upon them, are less abundant. Around the head waters of the Yuba, Feather, and Pitt rivers, the extensive table-lands of lava are sparsely planted with pines, through which the sunshine reaches the ground with little interruption. Here flourishes a scattered, tufted growth of golden applopappus, linosyris, bahia, wyetheia, arnica, artemisia, and similar plants; with manzanita, cherry, plum, and thorn in ragged patches on the cooler hill slopes. At the extremities of the Great Central Plain, the Sierra and Coast Ranges curve around and lock together in a labyrinth of mountains and valleys, throughout which their floras are mingled, making at the north, with its temperate climate and copious rainfall, a perfect paradise for bees, though, strange to say, scarcely a single regular bee ranch has yet been established in it.

Of all the upper flower fields of the Sierra, Shasta is the most honeyful, and may yet surpass in fame the celebrated honey hills of Hybla and hearthy Hymettus. Regarding this noble mountain from a bee point of view, encircled by its many climates, and sweeping aloft from the torrid plain into the frosty azure, we find the first 5,000 feet from the summit generally snow-clad, and therefore about as honeyless as the sea. The base of this arctic region is girdled by a belt of crumbling lava measuring about 1,000 feet in vertical breadth, and is mostly free from snow in summer. Beautiful lichens enliven the faces of the cliffs with their bright colors, and in some of the warmer nooks there are a few tufts of alpine daisies, wall-flowers and pentstemons; but, notwithstanding these bloom freely in the late summer, the zone as a whole is almost as honeyless as the icy summit, and its lower edge may be taken as the honey-line. Immediately below this comes the forest zone, covered with a rich growth of conifers, chiefly Silver Firs, rich in pollen and honey-dew, and diversified with countless garden openings, many of them less than a hundred yards across. Next, in orderly succession, comes the great bee zone. Its area far surpasses that of the icy summit and both the other zones combined, for it goes sweeping majestically around the entire mountain, with a breath of six or seven miles and a circumference of nearly a hundred miles.

Shasta, as we have already seen, is a fire-mountain created by a succession of eruptions of ashes and molten lava, which, flowing over the lips of its several craters, grew outward and upward like the trunk of a knotty exogenous tree. Then followed a strange contrast. The glacial winter came on, loading the cooling mountain with ice, which flowed slowly outward in every direction, radiating from the summit in the form of one vast conical glacier—a down-crawling mantle of ice upon a fountain of smoldering fire, crushing and grinding for centuries its brown, flinty lavas with incessant activity, and thus degrading and remodeling the entire mountain. When, at length, the glacial period began to draw near its close, the ice-mantle was gradually melted off around the bottom, and, in receding and breaking into its present fragmentary condition, irregular rings and heaps of moraine matter were stored upon its flanks. The glacial erosion of most of the Shasta lavas produces detritus, composed of rough, sub-angular boulders of moderate size and of porous gravel and sand, which yields freely to the transporting power of running water. Magnificent floods from the ample fountains of ice and snow working with sublime energy upon this prepared glacial detritus, sorted it out and carried down immense quantities from the higher slopes, and reformed it in smooth, delta-like beds around the base; and it is these flood-beds joined together that now form the main honey-zone of the old volcano.

Thus, by forces seemingly antagonistic and destructive, has Mother Nature accomplished her beneficent designs—now a flood of fire, now a flood of ice, now a flood of water; and at length an outburst of organic life, a milky way of snowy petals and wings, girdling the rugged mountain like a cloud, as if the vivifying sunbeams beating against its sides had broken into a foam of plant-bloom and bees, as sea-waves break and bloom on a rock shore.

In this flowery wilderness the bees rove and revel, rejoicing in the bounty of the sun, clambering eagerly through bramble and hucklebloom, ringing the myriad bells of the manzanita, now humming aloft among polleny willows and firs, now down on the ashy ground among gilias and buttercups, and anon plunging deep into snowy banks of cherry and buckthorn. They consider the lilies and roll into them, and, like lilies, they toil not, for they are impelled by sun-power, as water-wheels by water-power; and when the one has plenty of high-pressure water, the other plenty of sunshine, they hum and quiver alike. Sauntering in the Shasta bee-lands in the sun-days of summer, one may readily infer the time of day from the comparative energy of bee-movements alone—drowsy and moderate in the cool of the morning, increasing in energy with the ascending sun, and, at high noon, thrilling and quivering in wild ecstasy, then gradually declining again to the stillness of night. In my excursions among the glaciers I occasionally meet bees that are hungry, like mountaineers who venture too far and remain too long above the bread line; then they droop and wither like autumn leaves. The Shasta bees are perhaps better fed than any others in the Sierra. Their field-work is one perpetual feast; but, however exhilarating the sunshine or bountiful the supply of flowers, they are always dainty feeders. Humming-moths and humming-birds seldom set foot upon a flower, but poise on the wing in front of it, and reach forward as if they were sucking through straws. But bees, though as dainty as they, hug their favorite flowers with profound cordiality, and push their blunt, polleny faces against them, like babies on their mother's bosom. And fondly, too, with eternal love, does Mother Nature clasp her small bee-babies, and suckle them, multitudes at once, on her warm Shasta breast.

Besides the common honey-bee there are many other species here—fine mossy, burly fellows, who were nourished on the mountains thousands of sunny seasons before the advent of the domestic species. Among these are the bumblebees, mason-bees, carpenter-bees, and leaf-cutters. Butterflies, too, and moths of every size and pattern; some broad-winged like bats, flapping slowly, and sailing in easy curves; others like small, flying violets, shaking about loosely in short, crooked flights close to the flowers, feasting luxuriously night and day. Great numbers of deer also delight to dwell in the brushy portions of the bee-pastures.

Bears, too, roam the sweet wilderness, their blunt, shaggy forms harmonizing well with the trees and tangled bushes, and with the bees, also, notwithstanding the disparity in size. They are fond of all good things, and enjoy them to the utmost, with but little troublesome discrimination—flowers and leaves as well as berries, and the bees themselves as well as their honey. Though the California bears have as yet had but little experience with honey-bees, they often succeed in reaching their bountiful stores, and it seems doubtful whether bees themselves enjoy honey with so great a relish. By means of their powerful teeth and claws they can gnaw and tear open almost any hive conveniently accessible. Most honey-bees, however, in search of a home are wise enough to make choice of a hollow in a living tree, a considerable distance above the ground, when such places are to be had; then they are pretty secure, for though the smaller black and brown bears climb well, they are unable to break into strong hives while compelled to exert themselves to keep from falling, and at the same time to endure the stings of the fighting bees without having their paws free to rub them off. But woe to the black bumblebees discovered in their mossy nests in the ground! With a few strokes of their huge paws the bears uncover the entire establishment, and, before time is given for a general buzz, bees old and young, larvae, honey, stings, nest, and all are taken in one ravishing mouthful.

Not the least influential of the agents concerned in the superior sweetness of the Shasta flora are its storms—storms I mean that are strictly local, bred and born on the mountain. The magical rapidity with which they are grown on the mountain-top, and bestow their charity in rain and snow, never fails to astonish the inexperienced lowlander. Often in calm, glowing days, while the bees are still on the wing, a storm-cloud may be seen far above in the pure ether, swelling its pearl bosses, and growing silently, like a plant. Presently a clear, ringing discharge of thunder is heard, followed by a rush of wind that comes sounding over the bending woods like the roar of the ocean, mingling rain-drops, snow-flowers, honey-flowers, and bees in wild storm harmony.

Still more impressive are the warm, reviving days of spring in the mountain pastures. The blood of the plants throbbing beneath the life-giving sunshine seems to be heard and felt. Plant growth goes on before our eyes, and every tree in the woods, and every bush and flower is seen as a hive of restless industry. The deeps of the sky are mottled with singing wings of every tone and color; clouds of brilliant chrysididae dancing and swirling in exquisite rhythm, golden barred vespidae, dragon flies, butterflies, grating cicadas, and jolly, rattling grasshoppers, fairly enameling the light.

On bright, crisp mornings a striking optical effect may frequently be observed from the shadows of the higher mountains while the sunbeams are pouring past overhead. Then every insect, no matter what may be its own proper color, burns white in the light. Gauzy-winged hymenoptera, moths, jet-black beetles, all are transfigured alike in pure, spiritual white, like snowflakes.

In Southern California, where bee-culture has had so much skilful attention of late years, the pasturage is not more abundant, or more advantageously varied as to the number of its honey-plants and their distribution over mountain and plain, than that of many other portions of the State where the industrial currents flow in other channels. The famous White Sage *(Audibertia),* belonging to the mint family, flourishes here in all its glory, blooming in May, and yielding great quantities of clear, pale honey, which is greatly prized in every market it has yet reached. This species grows chiefly in the valleys and low hills. The Black Sage on the mountains is part of a dense, thorny chaparral, which is composed chiefly of adenostoma, ceanothus, manzanita, and cherry—not differing greatly from that of the southern portion of the Sierra, but more dense and continuous, and taller, and remaining longer in bloom. Stream-side gardens, so charming a feature of both the Sierra and Coast Mountains, are less numerous in Southern California, but they are exceedingly rich in honey-flowers, wherever found,—melilotus, columbine, collinsia, verbena, zauschneria, wild rose, honeysuckle, philadelphus, and lilies rising from the warm, moist dells in a very storm of exuberance. Wild buckwheat of many species is developed in abundance over the dry, sandy valleys and lower slopes of the mountains, toward the end of summer, and is, at this time, the main dependence of the bees, reinforced here and there by orange groves, alfalfa fields, and small home gardens.

The main honey months, in ordinary seasons, are April, May, June, July, and August; while the other months are usually flowery enough to yield sufficient for the bees.

According to Mr. J. T. Gordon, President of the Los Angeles County Bee-keepers' Association, the first bees introduced into the county were a single hive, which cost $150 in San Francisco, and arrived in September, 1854.★ In April, of the following year, this hive sent out two swarms, which were sold for $100 each. From this small beginning the bees gradually multiplied to about 3,000 swarms in the year 1873. In 1876 it was estimated that there were between 15,000 and 20,000 hives in the county, producing an annual yield of about 100 pounds to the hive—in some exceptional cases, a much greater yield.

In San Diego County, at the beginning of the season of 1878, there were about 24,000 hives, and the shipments from the one port of San Diego for the same year, from July 17 to November 10, were 1,071 barrels, 15,544 cases, and nearly 90 tons. The largest bee ranches have about a thousand hives, and are carefully and skilfully managed, every scientific appliance of merit being brought into use. There are few bee-keepers, however, who own half as many as this, or who give their undivided attention to the business. Orange culture, at present, is heavily overshadowing every other business.

A good many of the so-called bee-ranches of Los Angeles and San Diego counties are still of the rudest pioneer kind imaginable. A man unsuccessful in everything else hears the interesting story of the profits and comforts of bee-keeping, and concludes to try it; he buys a few colonies, or gets them from some overstocked ranch on shares, takes them back to the foot of some cañon, where the pasturage is fresh, squats on the land, with, or without, the permission of the owner, sets up his hives, makes a box cabin for himself, scarcely bigger than a bee-hive, and awaits his fortune.

Bees suffer sadly from famine during the dry years which occasionally occur in the southern and middle portions of the State. If the rainfall amounts only to three or four inches, instead of from twelve to twenty, as in ordinary seasons, then sheep and cattle die in thousands, and so do these small, winged cattle, unless they are carefully fed, or removed to other pastures. The year 1877 will long be remembered as exceptionally rainless and distressing. Scarcely a flower bloomed on the dry valleys away from the stream-sides, and not a single grain-field depending upon rain was reaped. The seed only sprouted, came up a little way, and withered. Horses, cattle, and sheep grew thinner day by day, nibbling at bushes and weeds, along the shallowing edges of streams, many of which were dried up altogether, for the first time since the settlement of the country.

In the course of a trip I made during the summer of that year through Monterey, San Luis Obispo, Santa Barbara, Ventura, and Los Angeles counties, the deplorable effects of the drought were everywhere visible—leafless fields, dead and dying cattle, dead bees, and half-dead people with dusty, doleful faces. Even the birds and squirrels were in distress, though their suffering was less painfully apparent than that of the poor cattle. These were falling one by one in slow, sure starvation along the banks of the hot, sluggish streams, while thousands of buzzards correspondingly fat were sailing

★ *Fifteen hives of Italian bees were introduced into Los Angeles County in 1855, and in 1876 they had increased to 500. The marked superiority claimed for them over the common species is now attracting considerable attention.*

above them, or standing gorged on the ground beneath the trees, waiting with easy faith for fresh carcasses. The quails, prudently considering the hard times, abandoned all thought of pairing. They were too poor to marry, and so continued in flocks all through the year without attempting to rear young. The ground-squirrels, though an exceptionally industrious and enterprising race, as every farmer knows, were hard pushed for a living; not a fresh leaf or seed was to be found save in the trees, whose bossy masses of dark green foliage presented a striking contrast to the ashen baldness of the ground beneath them. The squirrels, leaving their accustomed feeding-grounds, betook themselves to the leafy oaks to gnaw out the acorn stores of the provident woodpeckers, but the latter kept up a vigilant watch upon their movements. I noticed four woodpeckers in league against one squirrel, driving the poor fellow out of an oak that they claimed. He dodged round the knotty trunk from side to side, as nimbly as he could in his famished condition, only to find a sharp bill everywhere. But the fate of the bees that year seemed the saddest of all. In different portions of Los Angeles and San Diego counties, from one half to three fourths of them died of sheer starvation. Not less than 18,000 colonies perished in these two counties alone, while in the adjacent counties the death-rate was hardly less.

Even the colonies nearest to the mountains suffered this year, for the smaller vegetation on the foot-hills was affected by the drought almost as severely as that of the valleys and plains, and even the hardy, deep-rooted chaparral, the surest dependence of the bees, bloomed sparingly, while much of it was beyond reach. Every swarm could have been saved, however, by promptly supplying them with food when their own stores began to fail, and before they became enfeebled and discouraged; or by cutting roads back into the mountains, and taking them into the heart of the flowery chaparral. The Santa Lucia, San Rafael, San Gabriel, San Jacinto, and San Bernardino ranges are almost untouched as yet save by the wild bees. Some idea of their resources, and of the advantages and disadvantages they offer to bee-keepers, may be formed from an excursion that I made into the San Gabriel Range about the beginning of August of "the dry year." This range, containing most of the characteristic features of the other ranges just mentioned, overlooks the Los Angeles vineyards and orange groves from the north, and is more rigidly inaccessible in the ordinary meaning of the word than any other that I ever attempted to penetrate. The slopes are exceptionally steep and insecure to the foot, and they are covered with thorny bushes from five to ten feet high. With the exception of little spots not visible in general views, the entire surface is covered with them, massed in close hedge growth, sweeping gracefully down into every gorge and hollow, and swelling over every ridge and summit in shaggy, ungovernable exuberance, offering more honey to the acre for half the year than the most crowded clover-field. But when beheld from the open San Gabriel Valley, beaten with dry sunshine, all that was seen of the range seemed to wear a forbidding aspect. From base to summit all seemed gray, barren, silent, its glorious chaparral appearing like dry moss creeping over its dull, wrinkled ridges and hollows.

Setting out from Pasadena, I reached the foot of the range about sundown; and being weary and heated with my walk across the shadeless valley, concluded to camp for the night. After resting a few moments, I began to look about among the flood-boulders of Eaton Creek for a camp-ground, when I came upon a strange, dark-looking man who had been chopping cord-wood. He seemed surprised at seeing me, so I sat down with him on the live-oak log he had been cutting, and made haste to give a reason for my appearance in his solitude, explaining that I was anxious to find out something about the mountains, and meant to make my way up Eaton Creek next morning. Then he kindly invited me to camp with him, and led me to his little cabin, situated at the foot of the mountains, where a small spring oozes out of a bank overgrown with wild-rose bushes. After supper, when the daylight was gone, he explained that he was out of candles; so we sat in the dark, while he gave me a sketch of his life in a mixture of Spanish and English. He was born in Mexico, his father Irish, his mother Spanish. He had been a miner, rancher, prospector, hunter, etc., rambling always, and wearing his life away in mere waste; but now he was going to settle down. His past life, he said, was of "no account," but the future was promising. He was going to "make money and marry a Spanish woman." People mine here for water as for gold. He had been running a tunnel into a spur of the mountain back of his cabin. "My prospect is good," he said, "and if I chance to strike a good, strong flow, I'll soon be worth $5,000 or $10,000. For that flat out there," referring to a small, irregular patch of bouldery detritus, two or three acres in size, that had been deposited by Eaton Creek during some flood season,—"that flat is large enough for a nice orange grove, and the bank behind the cabin will do for a vineyard, and after watering my own trees and vines I will have some water left to sell to my neighbors below me, down the valley. And then," he continued, "I can keep bees, and make money that way, too, for the mountains above here are just full of honey in the summer-time, and one of my neighbors down here says that he will let me have a whole lot of hives, on shares, to start with. You see I've a good thing; I'm all right now." All this prospective affluence in the sunken, boulder-choked flood-bed of a mountain stream! Leaving the bees out of the count, most fortune-seekers would as soon think of settling on the summit of Mount Shasta. Next morning, wishing my hopeful entertainer good luck, I set out on my shaggy excursion.

About half an hour's walk above the cabin, I came to "The Fall," famous throughout the valley settlements as the finest yet discovered in the San Gabriel Mountains. It is a charming little thing, with a low, sweet voice, singing like a bird, as it pours from a notch in a short ledge, some thirty-five or forty feet into a round mirror-pool. The face of the cliff back of it, and on both sides, is smoothly covered and embossed with mosses, against which the white water shines out in showy relief, like a silver instrument in a velvet case. Hither come the San Gabriel lads and lassies, to gather ferns and dabble away their hot holidays in the cool water, glad to escape from their commonplace palm-gardens and orange-groves. The delicate maidenhair grows on fissured rocks within reach of the spray, while broad-leaved maples and sycamores cast soft, mellow shade over a rich profusion of bee-flowers, growing among boulders in front of the pool—the fall, the flowers, the bees, the ferny rocks, and leafy shade forming a charming little poem of wildness, the last of a series extending down the flowery slopes of Mount San Antonio through the rugged, foam-beaten bosses of the main Eaton Cañon.

From the base of the fall I followed the ridge that forms the western rim of the Eaton basin to the summit of one of the principal peaks, which is about 5,000 feet above sea-level. Then, turning eastward, I crossed the middle of the basin, forcing a way over its many subordinate ridges and across its eastern rim, having to contend almost everywhere with the floweriest and most impenetrable growth of honey-bushes I had ever encountered since first my mountaineering began. Most of the Shasta chaparral is leafy nearly to the ground; here the main stems are naked for three or four feet, and interspiked with dead twigs, forming a stiff *chevaux de frise* through which even the bears make their way with difficulty. I was compelled to creep for miles on all fours, and in following the bear trails often found tufts of hair on the bushes where they had forced themselves through.

For 100 feet or so above the fall the ascent was made possible only by tough cushions of club-moss that clung to the rock. Above this the ridge weathers away to a thin knife-blade for a few hundred yards, and thence to the summit of the range it carries a bristly mane of chaparral. Here and there small openings occur on rocky places, commanding fine views across the cultivated valley to the ocean. These I found by the tracks were favorite outlooks and resting places for the wild animals—bears, wolves, foxes, wildcats, etc.—which abound here, and would have to be taken into account in the establishment of bee-ranches. In the deepest thickets I found wood-rat villages—groups of huts four to six feet high, built of sticks and leaves in rough, tapering piles, like musk-rat cabins. I noticed a good many bees, too, most of them wild. The tame honey-bees seemed languid and wing-weary, as if they had come all the way up from the flowerless valley.

After reaching the summit I had time to make only a hasty survey of the basin, now glowing in the sunset gold, before hastening down into one of the tributary cañons in search of water. Emerging from a particularly tedious breadth of chaparral, I found myself free and erect in a beautiful park-like grove of Mountain Live Oak, where the ground was planted with aspidiums and brier-roses, while the glossy foliage made a close canopy overhead, leaving the gray dividing trunks bare to show the beauty of their interlacing arches. The bottom of the cañon was dry where I first reached it, but a bunch of scarlet mimulus indicated water at no great distance, and I soon discovered about a bucketful in a hollow of the rock. This, however, was full of dead bees, wasps, beetles, and leaves, well steeped and simmered, and would, therefore, require boiling and filtering through fresh charcoal before it could be made available. Tracing the dry channel about a mile farther down to its junction with a larger tributary cañon, I at length discovered a lot of boulder pools, clear as crystal, brimming full, and linked together by glistening streamlets just strong enough to sing audibly. Flowers in full bloom adorned their margins, lilies ten feet high, larkspur, columbines, and luxuriant ferns, leaning and overarching in lavish abundance, while a noble old Live Oak spread its rugged arms over all. Here I camped, making my bed on smooth cobblestones.

Next day, in the channel of a tributary that heads on Mount San Antonio, I passed about fifteen or twenty gardens like the one in which I slept—lilies in every one of them, in the full pomp of bloom. My third camp was made near the middle of the general basin, at the head of a long system of cascades from ten to 200 feet high, one following the other in close succession down a rocky, inaccessible cañon, making a total descent of nearly 1,700 feet. Above the cascades the main stream passes through a series of open, sunny levels, the largest of which are about an acre in size, where the wild bees and their companions were feasting on a showy growth of zauschneria, painted cups, and monardella; and gray squirrels were busy harvesting the burs of the Douglas Spruce, the only conifer I met in the basin.

The eastern slopes of the basin are in every way similar to those we have described, and the same may be said of other portions of the range. From the highest summit, far as the eye could reach, the landscape was one vast bee-pasture, a rolling wilderness of honey-bloom, scarcely broken by bits of forest or the rocky outcrops of hilltops and ridges.

Behind the San Bernardino Range lies the wild "sage-brush country," bounded on the east by the Colorado River, and extending in a general northerly direction to Nevada and along the eastern base of the Sierra beyond Mono Lake.

The greater portion of this immense region, including Owen's Valley, Death Valley, and the Sink of the Mohave, the area of which is nearly one fifth that of the entire State, is usually regarded as a desert, not because of any lack in the soil, but for want of rain, and rivers available for irrigation. Very little of it, however, is desert in the eyes of a bee.

Looking now over all the available pastures of California, it appears that the business of bee-keeping is still in its infancy. Even in the more enterprising of the southern counties, where so vigorous a beginning has been made, less than a tenth of their honey resources have as yet been developed; while in the Great Plain, the Coast Ranges, the Sierra Nevada, and the northern region about Mount Shasta, the business can hardly be said to exist at all. What the limits of its developments in the future may be, with the advantages of cheaper transportation and the invention of better methods in general, it is not easy to guess. Nor, on the other hand, are we able to measure the influence on bee interests likely to follow the destruction of the forests, now rapidly falling before fire and the ax. As to the sheep evil, that can hardly become greater than it is at the present day. In short, notwithstanding the wide-spread deterioration and destruction of every kind already effected, California, with her incomparable climate and flora, is still, as far as I know, the best of all the bee-lands of the world.

STINK BEETLE

Eleodes dentipes

Family Tenebrionidae

Length: ½"–1 ½"

Habitat:

Desert and arid regions

Range:

Common throughout California

Comments:

Beetles are the largest order of insects, with more than 166 families and 370,000 species. They are known for their hard outer shells, or their elytra, which are tough forewings that cover their bodies and protect their abdomens and hind wings.

The stink beetle, a member of the darkling beetle family, has an oval shape and is black. It is known for the position it takes when disturbed: it does a kind of headstand and sometimes emits a foul smelling liquid from glands at the tip of its abdomen. It eats decaying vegetable or animal matter.

John Steinbeck
from *Cannery Row*

On the black earth on which the ice plants bloomed, hundreds of black stink bugs crawled. And many of them stuck their tails up in the air. "Look at all them stink bugs," Hazel remarked, grateful to the bugs for being there.

"They're interesting," said Doc.

"Well, what they got their asses up in the air for?"

Doc rolled up his wool socks and put them in the rubber boots and from his pocket he brought out dry socks and a pair of thin moccasins. "I don't know why," he said. "I looked them up recently—they're very common animals and one of the commonest things they do is put their tails up in the air. And in all the books there isn't one mention of the fact that they put their tails up in the air or why."

Hazel turned one of the stink bugs over with the toe of his wet tennis shoe and the shining black beetle strove madly with floundering legs to get upright again. "Well, why do *you* think they do it?"

"I think they're praying," said Doc.

"What!" Hazel was shocked.

"The remarkable thing," said Doc, "isn't that they put their tails up in the air—the really incredibly remarkable thing is that we find it remarkable. We can only use ourselves as yardsticks. If we did something as inexplicable and strange we'd probably be praying—so maybe they're praying."

"Let's get the hell out of here," said Hazel.

∽∾ BURRO ∽∾

Equus asinus

Family Equidae

Height: 36–48"; Weight: 400–500 lb

Habitat:

 Ranches, farms, semi-rural and rural stables, and arid areas to 11,000"

Range:

 Common throughout California; feral in arid regions from Inyo to Imperial Counties

Comments:

 The probable ancestor of the domestic donkey is a subspecies of the Nubian wild ass. The donkey was developed as a beast of burden in North Africa, where it helped make possible long-distance trade routes through Egyptian deserts. Valued for their hardiness and intelligence, donkeys were eventually brought to Europe, and from there a supply ship brought donkeys to the New World in 1495.

 Although they resemble horses, donkeys are easily distinguished by their long ears, their stiff manes, and their tails, which are covered with short hair and end in tassels. Donkeys appear in a variety of colors—black, white, gray, and brown—but the most familiar color is gray-dun. Donkeys make a distinctive sound, the familiar bray "aw ee, aw ee."

 Wild populations exist in some areas of southern California. These wild burros (*burro* is the Spanish word for donkey) feed on native grasses and compete with bighorn sheep for grazing land and for water.

 The donkey has been the symbol of the Democratic Party since the time of Andrew Jackson, who had been labeled a "jackass" for his populist views.

George Wharton James
from *The Wonders of the Colorado Desert*

On the desert fourteen-fifteenths of the travel away from wagon roads would be impossible without the burro. It is the standby of the prospector and the desert enthusiast.

Centuries before the camel was brought to our American shores the burro had proven his worth, had demonstrated his strength, endurance, and reliability. Sweet-tempered and patient, too much of a philosopher to ever hurry or worry, he becomes a mental and spiritual guide, voiceless but practical, unobtrusive but insistent, to every intelligent man who is long in his company on the desert. I think much of the burro and his intelligence. I gladly claim kinship with him, though that means that I write myself down an ass. The burro knows many things better than most white men, even the intelligent ones—desert-intelligent I mean—such as I am *a little*. Twice burros have saved my life by finding water when my intelligence could not discover it, and often their trail-craft has proven safer to follow than mine.

True, they can be as mean as humankind at times. They will provokingly get off the trail, hide in the dark, and let you leave them behind for miles, even when they have a pack on their backs. True, they sometimes have the provoking habit of going down on their knees, purposely, I verily believe, when they are on the worst possible places on the mountain trails, and they know you will pitch heels over heads—their heads—to your eminent danger and discomfort.

True, they will wander off sometimes and leave you in the lurch if you do not bind them to you with cords of—stomachic—affection. A pint or, better still, a quart of grain three times a day makes a "threefold cord" that binds as much as love.

Yet in spite of all these things the burro is man's invaluable companion and servant on the desert.

On our trips we had three burros, Babe, Kate, and Jennie. Babe was happy in the recent acquisition of a baby, and as soon as I saw her I dubbed her Marchioness, exactly for the same reason that Dick Swiveller called the little kitchen maiden by the same name.

The Marchioness was a sweet looking, cute little creature and I was at once undone by her charms. She had a tiny, dainty, clean white muzzle, with white patches of perfect evenness and balance under her eyes. Her color was of brown, shading off into mouse, and on the course of her spine, as straight as if it had been put there by a ruler, was a line of black, reaching from between her ears to the very tip of her tail.

But she was a deceitful piece of baggage. I shall never forget how she wandered away one night from her pseudo owner, following in the sweet moonlight some Indians or Mexicans who thought to lure her away and keep her. My friend, riding on the back of her patient and devoted mother, followed her for long weary miles over the salt-bush strewn, effloresced soils of the region northwest of the Salton Sea to Fig

Tree John's. She refused to be called back home even by the voice of her own mother, and the poor rider simply had to keep chasing her, as an enthusiast chases a butterfly, or an irate sleeper a flea, and like the butterfly or the flea, whenever he dismounted to catch and tie her, the irresponsible, irrepressible, bewitching, aggravating little creature, with a flap of her long ears, a flit of her tail, and a snicker, as if in derision, would kick up her heels and run off, and the chase had to be begun again.

The way we happened to find this out was that we had been visiting at the Indian village of Martinez. We started for Mecca late in the evening. We were indifferent and careless about roads, and the desert air and the witchery of moonlight made it impossible for us calmly to decide where we were and which road we ought to take. So blindly and wildly we drove across the desert, back and forth, up and down, as the sweet will prompted of the one who held the reins, and thus in our inconsequent shuttling back and forth—for we should have got nowhere until morning on the plan we were following, and didn't much care whether we did or not—we ran into our friend just as he had succeeded in catching the Marchioness and was dragging her behind him, a captive against her will.

But she never resented any kind of treatment, and though thus dragged home, the next day she was as naïvely affectionate, familiar, and confidential as before.

When we started off for the Brooklyn Mine I took the box of the wagon and Van rode Kate and was to drive along Babe and Jennie who were packed.

He confidently expected the Marchioness would follow. She did, but it was her own sweet will, rather than her mother, that she followed. Unconscious of his difficulties, we in the wagon ahead slowly plodded on, until in desperation he decided to leave her behind. Fortunately she was cared for in our nine days' absence, and having perforce become weaned in this time she found herself henceforth, to her mother, merely as any other burro, and the sweet relationship of mother and daughter ceased to exist.

The burro has been made the object of many a poet's lofty strains. Here is a quatrain I found in the heart of the Colorado Desert posted on a prospector's cupboard door. I congratulate the unknown poet.

> "I am a burro, the loftiest peaks all unafraid I scale,
> Picking my way, sure-footed, along the dizziest trail;
> I lead in pioneering work which, but for me, must stop;
> I am a burro, patient, dumb, but always at the top."

While the merciful man is as merciful to his beast on the desert as in any other place, it must not he forgotten that an animal on the desert means far more to a man than in any other place. The mule or burro he has taken with him is his sole and absolute dependence. Without it his life is in danger, much travel is almost an impossibility, for man unaided cannot carry the food supply he needs, and while the desert does, in its own peculiar way, afford browse and picking for the animal, it offers but little except to the very well informed, and not much to him, in the way of food. Hence it is imperative that a desert traveler do two things: he must take as good care of his animals as he possibly can, yet he must under no circumstances run any risk of letting them get away from him. These two imperative conditions often seem to come in direct conflict, yet they must never be lost sight of or forgotten. Let me enlarge somewhat to make the grave importance of the matter clear. Many of the desert tragedies that have been recorded, and hundreds that have not, have come about through carelessness about tying up the mules or burros; allowing them to wander unhobbled in search of food; or leaving them untied (only hobbled) at night in order that they may "pick up all they can." It is in strict accordance with the first imperative condition I have laid down that animals be given every possible chance to get all the food they need, but in doing that it is more imperative still that nothing be done to jeopardize human life. An untied mule or burro, unhobbled, may be frightened away from the prospector's camp, or be maddened by a horsefly or gnats until he has traveled twenty miles. If water is scarce a hobbled animal will often travel twenty miles at night in order to reach it. I have been a personal sufferer several times from this very cause. Once on the Painted Desert our animals, all hobbled, deserted us and went back many miles where we found them digging for water. On another occasion when on the way to Lee's Ferry, I spent a lonely day in camp, my driver having started off to fetch in his horses before breakfast, and following them for sixteen miles before they were caught. Had he not been an exceptionally desert-hardened man, that thirty-two miles—sixteen on foot and sixteen on a saddleless horse—would have so exhausted him as to tender his return to where I was camped somewhat problematical. What then could I have done had he failed to return? On a road where water could be found only by the well informed, hidden away in secret tanks up tiny canyons, or under unmarked arroyo banks, no ordinary traveler can conceive the horrors of the situation.

To walk in the intense heat without water is almost an impossibility. To carry provisions is to add to the difficulty, and yet to go without them equally impracticable. Then, too, it is disturbing, to say the least, to the peace of mind of the strongest-hearted to find himself in a strange place, uncertain as to the road, often where there is no road at all,—nothing but landmarks over a trackless desert,—short of water, and *alone*. No wonder that many men break down under it, grow confused, become delirious and finally perish in their aimless wanderings.

Hence the emphasis of my caution: never run any risk in tying your animals. See that your tie-ropes are of the strongest and most reliable. See that you tie only to the strongest of trees or around the base of bushes that are secure. Be ever alert in this regard, as one act of carelessness may cause the loss of your life, as well as those of others who are dependent upon you. In my "Indians of the Painted Desert Region" I have explained how an animal may be picketed to a hole in the ground with perfect safety, so that there is no excuse for not tying up securely even though there seems to be nothing to tie to. If animals are thus tied up at night it is necessary that a day-rest be taken, their packs removed, and an opportunity given to them to eat whenever a place that seems to afford feed is reached. In the daytime they can be watched, and while vigilance must not be lessened it is then more readily and easily exercised.

⤜ CABEZON ⤏

Scorpaenichthys marmoratus

Family Cottidae

Length: 18"–3'3"; Weight: 15–25 lb

Habitat:

    Rocky areas in intertidal zones and under kelp beds; to depths of 250'

Range:

    Common off the coast of California

Comments:

    The cabezon is mottled brown, red, or green, with a white or green underbelly. The fish gets its name from the Spanish word *cabezon,* which means big-headed or stubborn, and the head is certainly its most notable feature. The fish is elongate and has a somewhat blunt snout. There is a large cirrus—a finger-like protuberance—on the midline of the snout and over each eye. It has a skin flap on its snout, and its eyes are placed high on its head. It has a stiff pelvic fin, five soft supporting rays, and fanlike pectoral fins. The cabezon's body is unscaled.

    The cabezon's diet consists mostly of crustaceans, mollusks, and small fish. Its coloring allows for camouflage as it sits still, watching for prey it can swiftly attack. Younger cabezon are eaten by, among other predators, rockfishes and larger members of their own species.

    The cabezon spawns in the winter. Its eggs are greenish to purplish and the male guards them until they hatch. Although the eggs are poisonous to humans, the cabezon is still often caught for its flesh.

Robert Hass
"On the Coast near Sausalito"

1
I won't say much for the sea
except that it was, almost,
the color of sour milk.
The sun in that clear
unmenacing sky was low,
angled off the grey fissure of the cliffs,
hills dark green with manzanita.

Low tide: slimed rocks
mottled brown and thick with kelp
like the huge backs of ancient tortoises
merged with the grey stone
of the breakwater, sliding off
to antediluvian depths.
The old story: here filthy life begins.

2
Fish-
ing, as Melville said,
"to purge the spleen,"
to put to task my clumsy hands
my hands that bruise by
not touching
pluck the legs from a prawn,
peel the shell off,
and curl the body twice about a hook.

3
The cabezone is not highly regarded
by fishermen, except Italians
who have the grace

to fry the pale, almost bluish flesh
in olive oil with a sprig
of fresh rosemary.

The cabezone, an ugly atavistic fish,
as old as the coastal shelf
it feeds upon
has fins of duck's-web thickness,
resembles a prehistoric toad,
and is delicately sweet.

Catching one, the fierce quiver of surprise
and the line's tension
are a recognition.

4
But it's strange to kill
for the sudden feel of life.
The danger is
to moralize
that strangeness.
Holding the spiny monster in my hands
his bulging purple eyes
were eyes and the sun was
almost tangent to the planet
on our uneasy coast.
Creature and creature,
we stared down centuries.

≫ CAT ≪

Felis catus

Family Felidae

Length: to 30"; Tail: to 15"; Weight: Males 9–14 lb; Females 6–10 lb

Habitat:

Wherever humans are established; open fields for hunting

Range:

Common throughout California

Comments:

The domestic cat, or house cat, was domesticated from *Felis silvestris,* a wild cat found in Africa and Eurasia. Domestic cats have been human companions for at least four thousand years, and today there are as many as seventy different breeds recognized by cat registries.

Breeds vary in coloring and fur length. Many domestic breeds, like the Russian blue and Maine coon, naturally occur in certain geographic regions; others, like the Himalayan, are a result of selective breeding. Newer breeds, like the hairless Sphynx, began as genetic mutations and were then cultivated into separate breeds. Most cats are not purebreds, however, and are identified as being either "domestic longhair" or "domestic shorthair" based on their fur length.

Cats are skilled predators and help control populations of vermin, especially on farmland. They have excellent senses and compact bodies, making them superb hunters. Their hunting skills are similar to those of leopards and tigers: they pounce, deliver a neck bite with their canine teeth, or asphyxiate their prey by crushing their windpipes.

Other traits include: conserving energy by sleeping from thirteen to fourteen hours a day, a general dislike of getting wet, and incredible balance and flexibility that allows them to almost always land on their feet after a fall. They communicate by a series of vocalizations—"meows," purrs, hisses, and growls—and body language.

Ishmael Reed
"My Thing Abt Cats"

In berkeley whenever
black cats saw dancer &
me they crossed over to
the other side. alan &
carol's cat jumped over
my feet. someone else's
cat pressed its paw against
my leg, in seattle it's
green eyes all the way.
"they cry all the time when
ever you go out, but when
you return they stop," dancer
said of the 3 cats in the back
yard on st mark's place. there
is a woman downstairs who makes
their sounds when she feeds them.
we don't get along.

Mark Twain
from *Roughing It*

One of my comrades there—another of those victims of eighteen years of unrequited toil and blighted hopes—was one of the gentlest spirits that ever bore its patient cross in a weary exile: grave and simple Dick Baker, pocket miner of Dead-House Gulch. He was forty-six, gray as a rat, earnest, thoughtful, slenderly educated, slouchily dressed and clay-soiled, but his heart was finer metal than any gold his shovel ever brought to light—than any, indeed, that ever was mined or minted.

Whenever he was out of luck and a little downhearted, he would fall to mourning over the loss of a wonderful cat he used to own (for where women and children are not, men of kindly impulses take up with pets, for they must love something). And he always spoke of the strange sagacity of that cat with the air of a man who believed in his secret heart that there was something human about it—maybe even supernatural.

I heard him talking about this animal once. He said:

"Gentlemen, I used to have a cat here, by the name of Tom Quartz, which you'd a took an interest in, I reckon—most anybody would. I had him here eight year—and he was the remarkablest cat *I* ever see. He was a large gray one of the Tom specie, an' he had more hard, natchral sense than any man in the camp—'n' a *power* of dignity— he wouldn't let the Gov'ner of Californy be familiar with him. He never ketched a rat in his life—'peared to be above it. He never cared for nothing but mining. He knowed more about mining, that cat did, than any man *I* ever, ever see. You couldn't tell *him* noth'n' 'out placer diggin's—'n' as for pocket mining, why he was just born for it. He would dig out after me an' Jim when we went over the hills prospec'n', and he would trot along behind us for as much as five mile, if we went so fur. An' he had the best judgment about mining ground—why you never see anything like it. When we went to work, he'd scatter a glance around, 'n' if he didn't think much of the indications, he would give a look as much as to say, 'Well, I'll have to get you to excuse *me,*' 'n' without another word he'd hyste his nose into the air 'n' shove for home. But if the ground suited him, he would lay low 'n' keep dark till the first pan was washed, 'n' then he would sidle up 'n' take a took, an' if there was about six or seven grains of gold *he* was satisfied—he didn't want no better prospect 'n' that—'n' then he would lay down on our coat and snore like a steamboat till we'd struck the pocket, an' then get up 'n' superintend. He was nearly lightnin' on superintending.

"Well, by an' by, up comes this yer quartz excitement. Everybody was into it— everybody was pick'n' 'n' blast'n' instead of shovelin' dirt on the hillside—everybody was put'n' down a shaft instead of scrapin' the surface. Noth'n' would do Jim, but *we* must tackle the ledges, too, 'n' so we did. We commenced put'n' down a shaft, 'n' Tom Quartz he begin to wonder what in the dickens it was all about. *He* hadn't ever seen any mining like that before, 'n' was all upset, as you may say—he couldn't come to a right understanding of it no way—it was too many for *him.* He was down on it, too, you bet you—he was down on it powerful—'n' always appeared to consider it the cussedest foolishness out. But that cat, you know, was *always* agin newfangled arrangements—somehow he never could abide 'em. *You* know how it is with old habits. But by an' by Tom Quartz begin to git sort of reconciled a little, though he never *could* altogether understand that eternal sinkin' of a shaft an' never pannin' out anything. At last he got to comin' down in the shaft, hisself, to try to cipher it out. An' when he'd git the blues, 'n' feel kind o' scruffy, 'n' aggravated 'n' disgusted—knowin' as he did that the bills was runnin' up all the time an' we warn't makin' a cent—he would curl up on a gunny sack in the corner an' go to sleep. Well, one day when the shaft was down about eight foot, the rock got so hard that we had to put in a blast—the first blast'n' we'd ever done since Tom Quartz was born. An' then we lit the fuse 'n' clumb out 'n' got off 'bout fifty yards—'n' forgot 'n' left Tom Quartz sound asleep on the gunny sack. In 'bout a minute we seen a puff of smoke bust up out of the hole, 'n' then everything let go with an awful crash, 'n' about four million ton of rocks 'n' dirt 'n' smoke 'n' splinters shot up 'bout a mile an' a half into the air, an' by George, right in the dead center of it was old Tom Quartz a goin' end over end, an' a snortin' an' a sneez'n', an' a clawin' an' a reachin' for things like all possessed. But it warn't no use, you know, it warn't no use. An' that was the last we see of *him* for about two minutes 'n' a half, an' then all of a sudden it begin to rain rocks and rubbage, an' directly he come down ker-whop about ten foot off where we stood. Well, I reckon he was p'raps the orneriest-lookin' beast you ever see. One ear was sot back on his neck, 'n' his tail was stove up, 'n' his eyewinkers was swinged off, 'n' he was all blacked up with powder an' smoke, an' all sloppy with mud 'n' slush f'm one end to the other. Well sir, it warn't no use to try to apologize—we couldn't say a word. He took a sort of a disgusted look at hisself, 'n' then he looked at us—an' it was just exactly the same as if he had said—'Gents, maybe *you* think it's smart to take advantage of a cat that ain't had no experience of quartz minin', but *I* think *different*'—an' then he turned on his heel 'n' marched off home without ever saying another word.

"That was jest his style. An' maybe you won't believe it, but after that you never see a cat so prejudiced agin quartz mining as what he was. An' by an' by when he *did* get to goin' down in the shaft agin, you'd a been astonished at his sagacity. The minute we'd tetch off a blast 'n' the fuse'd begin to sizzle, he'd give a look as much as to say: 'Well, I'll have to git you to excuse *me*,' an' it was surpris'n' the way he'd shin out of that hole 'n' go f'r a tree. Sagacity? It ain't no name for it. 'Twas *inspiration!*"

I said, "Well, Mr. Baker, his prejudice against quartz mining was remarkable, considering how he came by it. Couldn't you ever cure him of it?"

"*Cure him!* No! When Tom Quartz was sot once, he was *always* sot—and you might a blowed him up as much as three million times 'n' you'd never a broken him of his cussed prejudice agin quartz mining."

The affection and the pride that lit up Baker's face when he delivered this tribute to the firmness of his humble friend of other days will always be a vivid memory with me.

∼∞∽ CALIFORNIA CONDOR ∼∞∽

Gymnogyps californianus

Family Cathartidae

Length: 46–55"; Wingspan: 8 ½–9 ½'; Weight: 22 lb

Habitat:

Arid foothills and mountains; prefers isolated, rocky cliffs for nesting but may also roost in tall trees

Range:

Central and southern California

Comments:

The California condor is the largest flying bird in North America, with reported wingspans of up to thirteen feet, although documented measurements—still impressive—fall into the nine-foot range. Its wings and body are black, with white wing-linings visible in flight. The head is "naked" and pale orange in color.

Condors soar on rising air currents, which carry them high aloft as they search for large carrion—wild game like deer or domestic stock like cattle and sheep—over a range that may cover hundreds of miles in a day. Most of their time, however, is spent grooming and sunning near their roosts.

California condors are extremely rare. At one time, they were routinely hunted, until populations declined precipitously, due to, among other reasons, their ingestion of carcasses of poisoned rodents and coyotes, as well as a steady loss of habitat. At one time the population was probably fewer than twenty-five birds, although conservation efforts and captive breeding programs have expanded numbers somewhat in recent years and several birds have been released into the wild in California and Arizona.

Gerald Haslam
"Condor Dreams"

Standing with his nearly empty coffee cup in one hand, Dan gazed into tule fog dense as oatmeal. It obscured the boundary between sky and earth, between breath and wind, and he was momentarily uncertain where or what he was. He could see nothing. He could not be seen. This must be what nothingness is, he thought, what extinction is…like what's happened to the condors. Then he chuckled at himself: Don't lose it, pal. Don't lose it. Stress will do that to you.

He rubbed his chest where it was again tightening. This field is real and those critters are gone, as defunct as family farmers soon will be. As I'll be, Dan thought. His chuckle turned grim.

Nearly fifty years before, on a morning as sunny and clear as this one was foggy and obscure, he had stood next to his father in this same field and seen for the first time a wonder soaring high above—a vast black shape like death itself. Frightened, he moved closer to his father. Then he noticed the bird's bare head and its vast wings. Those dark sails were cored with white, their farthest feathers spread like fingers grasping sky. It appeared to belong to another, sterner time.

"Look, Daniel," his father said, "that's a California condor. See, its wings, they never move. It rides the wind."

"It rides the wind? How, Papa?"

"Ahhh…it is just a wind rider, I guess."

"Can I be one?"

"Only in your dreams, Daniel."

"Where did he come from, Papa?" Dan asked.

His father pointed southeast, where the Tehachapi Mountains loomed, where mysterious canyons slashed into them. "There," he explained. "They live where men can't. Years ago, when I come here from the old country, those condors they'd fly out here over the valley every spring to eat winter kills. Sometimes fifty or sixty of 'em. Sometimes maybe a hundred. You could hear their beaks clicking. Now, only four or five ever come."

"Why, Papa?"

"Why?" His father had migrated here from the Azores and worked for other people until he could buy a patch of worn-out range, which he'd then turned into this farm. "I don't know," he finally replied. "Things they changed, eh? Maybe some ranchers they shoot 'em 'cause they think those condors take calves…or for the fun of it. Maybe there's not so much for 'em to eat no more. All I ever seen 'em eat is winter kills. I don't know…" His voice trailed off, and he seemed genuinely puzzled. A few years later, the boy's father had been a winter kill, drowned by a freak flood pouring from one of those mountain canyons.

Just a few days before his father's death, the two of them had stood on the edge of this very field and spied a dot high against the mountains. They leaned on their shovels and watched it grow larger, closer, since by then appearances of condors over the valley had become rare indeed. A young heifer had died and, as was his habit, his father had left the carcass next to the reservoir, and a cluster of buzzards busied themselves cleaning it up.

Neither man said anything and they stood waiting: Perhaps the great condor might strip this heifer's bones. As though tantalizing them, it approached slowly, so slowly, its white-splotched wings tipping, never pumping, as it sailed far above, then began to swing lower, its great shadow sliding over these acres. Finally, the antique flier swooped down from the wind, and the smaller, squabbling birds quickly bounced away and scrambled into the sky. As the condor began to feed, father and son turned and smiled at one another; they were gazing at a California older than memory.

Dan stood now on the land his family had reclaimed, and he could not see the sky because of the fog that had risen, as it so often did following rains, obscuring nearly everything. If the condors were out there anymore, they were as hidden as other people's dreams. If they were there. Crazy thoughts.

He walked up one long row, grapevines staked on both sides of him, their bare branches trained on wires. Normally the campesinos would be pruning them now, but not this year. Not any year, perhaps. Dan had grown up working these fields that his father and uncle had originally cleared and plowed, that his brothers and sisters and he had irrigated and cultivated and reaped. Now a bank would take it all, the land and the memories. It was grinding to accept. One part of him wanted to weep, another wanted vengeance. He wandered the field now because he could not bring himself to tell Mary everything he had heard the day before at the bank. It was the first significant thing he had ever withheld from her, and that too compounded his tension. Thank God the kids were grown.

He stopped, far from house or road, surrounded by the gray-velvet haze, and listened closely. He had heard a voice. Then he realized it was his own, arguing with himself. That's what this was doing to him, driving him nuts. It would take nearly $300,000 to convert his fields to profitable crops now that table grapes with seeds no longer sold well, but five consecutive losing years had so eroded his credit that he could not raise that kind of backing. His note was due and the once friendly banker demanded payment.

Dan tilted his face skyward and stared into the colorless miasma surrounding him, wanting to scream like a dying animal. Were there condors left up there? Would they come clean his bones? He trudged back toward the house to give his wife the bad news.

The next morning, they sat at the dinette table sipping coffee and gazing out the window at fog as soft as kittens' fur. "Another cold one," he sighed, meaningless talk to fill the silence.

"Why don't you start the pruning?" his wife asked. "It's not like you to give up."

"What's the point?" His voice edged toward anger, for he'd sensed reproach even before she spoke. She didn't understand. This land was his body, and now it would be torn from him. Her way was to stay busy; when her mother'd died, Mary had cooked for three days. But you can't stay busy when your land, your flesh, is being devoured like so much carrion. She didn't understand that.

No, Dan simply wanted revenge. But on whom? The banker who had urged him to expand and had staked him for so many years? The public that ate only Thompson seedless grapes and Perlettes? The county agriculture agent who hadn't warned him about changing tastes? Who?

There was the sharp sound of a car door slamming, then a light knock at the kitchen door. It was 6:45 A.M., and the two glanced at each other across the table before Dan stood and strode to the door.

"Buenos días, Señor Silva," said the old man who stood there, battered five-gallon hat in hand. "Estoy aquí para trabajar." His chin was not quite half shaven, and his faded jeans were only partly buttoned.

"Come on in, Don Felipe," Dan smiled. "You want coffee?"

"Sí, por favor."

"Como? Americano o Mexicano?" It was an old joke between them.

"Solo Mexicano, por favor." The grin was nearly toothless.

Despite the gentle humor, here was one more problem. Felipe Ramirez had been working on this land as long as Dan could remember. His father had originally employed the old man years before. Despite his name and fluent Spanish, he was more than half Yokuts—local Indian. In his prime he had been a vaquero in those faraway condor mountains. Dan had always liked him, with his strange but amusing yarns, his unabashed belief in the supernatural—which he said *was* natural.

The old man now lived with a niece in Bakersfield, and Dan annually hired him to help prune grapevines, then kept him on over the summer as a general helper. He was a link to the past, to Dan's own father. Don Felipe remained a strong worker, but his peculiar tales—amusing during good times—would be a burden now.

At the table, Don Felipe bowed to Mary, who smiled and greeted him. He seated himself and accepted a steaming mug of coffee into which he spooned a great mound of sugar. Their conversation was, as always, conducted in two languages, a comfortable weaving of Spanish and English. "Where are the others?" asked the old man.

Dan was suddenly embarrassed. "We haven't begun pruning yet."

"It is too wet?"

There was a long silence, for the old man would not ask why. It was not his way to probe. "It will be a fine growing year," he finally observed, "all this rain. In my dream, the great green gods were touching you."

"It could be a good year," Dan responded.

"Tell him," said Mary. Her husband briefly glared at her. This was difficult enough without being rushed. She had never understood how men speak to one another...or don't speak to one another about some things.

Again there was silence. The old man did not appear anxious. "Would you like some tobacco?" he asked, extending his pouch of Bull Durham.

"No thanks."

Don Felipe knew Mary did not smoke, so no tobacco was offered her. Instead, he rolled a drooping cigarette, carefully twisting both ends. "Do you no longer wish to employ me, Daniel?" He pronounced the name "Don-yale."

"We are losing our ranch, Don Felipe. A bank will take it. But I want you to work with me because there are still some things to be done."

"I am your servant."

"Just take it easy today. Tomorrow I'll have a list of jobs."

"As you wish, Daniel."

Two hours later, a brisk wind broke from the mountains and cleared the fog. Dan emerged from the barn when he heard its swift whine, and walked into cold sunlight, then noted on what they called the old section a lone figure among the vines. What the hell? He strode to the place where Don Felipe pruned grapes.

"Why are you doing this?" he asked, almost demanded, for this land would soon no longer be his, and to work it was suddenly a personal offense. He had not even told Mary that it was rumored the bank would subdivide ranchettes here, a prospect too painful for words.

"It must be done."

"Don't you understand, I won't own this land much longer. I won't harvest grapes this year."

"Daniel," the old man said in a tone Dan had heard before, "no one owns the land. The earth must be nurtured, never owned. Your father knew that and you, deep within, you know that too. It is like a woman, to be loved but never owned. It is not an empty thing but full of life. And these vines are our children."

"Tell the bank that," Dan spat.

"They will build no houses here."

"Houses? Who won't?"

"The bank will build no houses here."

"Of course not. Who said they would?" How had the old man guessed that?

A smile lit the leathery face and the eyes rolled skyward. "Your father started here with only eighty acres, true?"

"Yes."

"How many do you plant now?"

"About thirteen hundred. Why?"

"I am pruning the old eighty acres. You must save them. No houses here, Daniel."

This conversation was crazy. He didn't need it; he had problems enough. "I'm saving all of it or none of it," he snapped. His chest began tightening as he fought rage. Why didn't the old man sense the trouble he was causing? Dan was tempted to call Don Felipe's niece and have her come back for him.

Wind was picking up, blowing north from the distant mountains, and dust was beginning to pepper them. The old man removed a thong from one pocket, wrapped it over his sombrero, and tied it under his chin. "It is the dust of the condors," he said, squinting toward the peaks and canyons to the south. "They will protect this land."

"The condors are dead."

The old man's eyes seemed to crackle for a second, then he smiled. "No, not all of them."

"I'll need some condors, or buzzards maybe, when the bank is through with me."

"The condors, my son, are not mere carrion birds. They bring life from death. They renew, that is why their dust is a good sign. It will be a good year."

"For the bank," Dan said, and he turned toward the house.

That night he could not relax. In the cusp between sleep and wakefulness near dawn, he saw the earth rupture and a gray flatus ooze out, then a great inky bird seemed to swim from it while he struggled to find light...find light. He awoke, his breast tight, and immediately stared out the window: Heavy fog pressed against the glass, the world rendered low-contrast and colorless. He couldn't even see the land he was about to lose, and the compression in his chest and jaw were edging toward pain.

He rose quietly, but Mary stirred. "Getting up?" she asked drowsily.

"Yeah." He headed for the bathroom, where he gulped two antacid tablets, then pulled on his jeans and boots, shrugged on a shirt, and finally washed up. In the kitchen, he started coffee, one hand holding his aching breast, then put on his hat and walked out the back door to smell the morning fog.

As he stood in that near-darkness, he heard—or thought he heard—an irregular clicking. Condors? Condors' beaks? For a moment he was puzzled, rubbing his chest, then realized what it had to be: Someone was pruning grapes.

On the old field, he confronted Don Felipe. "Why are you doing this? I'm going to lose the ranch, don't you understand?"

The leathery face smiled, and the old man, still bent with pruning shears in one hand, replied, "When I was a young man, I worked with an old Indian named Castro on the Tejon Ranch in those mountains. He was what you call it? a...a wizard, maybe, or a...a medicine man. He could do many strange things. He could turn a snake by looking at it. One time I saw him touch a wolf that had killed some sheep and the wolf understood; it never came back. No horse ever bucked him.

"That guy, one time he told me that this life we think is real isn't real at all. He said we live only in the dreams of condors. He said that us Indians were condors' good dreams, and you pale people were their nightmares." The old man smiled, then he continued, "He said we can live only if those birds dream of us."

Dan didn't need this nonsense. "Condors are extinct," he pointed out. He was sure he'd read that in the newspaper.

The old man only grinned. "Then how are we talking? We are still here, Daniel, so the condors cannot be gone. You are still here." The old man paused, then added, "I think that guy he was a condor."

Too much, this was just too damned much. He would have to call Don Felipe's niece as soon as he returned to the house. He just didn't need this mumbo jumbo on top of the distress he was already suffering. "Why do you think that?" the younger man snapped.

"Because one day he flew away up a canyon into the heart of the mountains, and we never saw him again. He said that if the condors disappeared, so would their dreams. That's what that old Indian told me."

"*Right*," said the despondent farmer, turning away. Why couldn't this old man understand? Why couldn't he deal with reality? Dan was becoming agitated enough to fire Don Felipe on the spot.

Before he could speak, though, the pain surged from his chest into his arm and jaw. "Listen…," he began, but did not finish, for breath left him. "Listen…," he croaked just before he swayed to the damp soil.

"Daniel!" Don Felipe cried. He knelt, and his hard old hands, like talons, touched the fallen man's face. Dan was straining to speak when he sensed the fog beginning to swirl and vaguely saw the old man's body begin to deepen and darken and oscillate. A shadowy shape suddenly surged and a liquid wing swelled beneath Dan, lofting him from his pain.

A startled moment later, he hovered above a great gray organism that sent misty tendrils into nearby canyons and arroyos, that moved within itself and stretched as far north into the great valley as his vision could reach. It was…all…so…beautiful, and his anxiety drained as he skimmed wind far above the fog, far beyond it, as he rode his own returning breath, and below the mist began clearing. His fields focused as the earth-cloud thinned. The land too was breathing, he suddenly realized, its colors as iridescent as sunlight on the wings of condors. It was all so alluring that he stretched a hand to touch…touch…it.

"Dan," Mary's voice startled him, "are you all right?" She cradled his head in her hands and her own face was tight with fear.

It was like waking from his deepest dream but, after a second of confusion, he managed a smile. "I'm okay." An edge of breathlessness remained, that and pain's shadow, so he hesitated before, with her help, climbing to his feet. Past his wife's shoulder he saw the old man, whose dark eyes merged momentarily with his. "I just let tension get to me," he explained. Rising, he brushed wet earth from his jeans. "I'll drive into town and see the doc just in case."

The easy tone of his voice seemed to reassure his wife. "Let's go have our coffee," she urged.

"Sure," he replied, putting an arm around her waist, his relief at being able to touch her as tangible as breath itself, then turning toward the old man. "Don Felipe, are you coming in?"

"I must finish the field."

"Okay," Dan replied, "I'll bring something out, and I'll give you a hand when I get back from the doctor's." This place, even eighty acres of it, was worth saving. There had to be a way.

"I will be grateful," the old man nodded.

After Dan and Mary turned, they could hear Don Felipe's shears clicking like a condor's beak. Arm in arm, they walked toward home. The fog had dissipated enough so that their house shone sharp and white across the field of dormant vines. Behind it, bordering the hazy valley, those mountains, the Tehachapis, bulked like the land's surging muscles: creased and burnished and darkened with bursts of oaks and pines, flexing into silent summits and deep canyons where valley winds were born, into the hidden heart of the range where Dan now knew a secret condor still dreamed.

∼ COW AND OX ∼

Bos taurus

Family Bovidae

Height: 49–52"; Weight: 1,150 lb

Habitat:

   Ranches, farms, and dairies as well as open rangeland with sufficient grazing

Range:

   Common throughout California

Comments:

   Domestic cattle and oxen (oxen are cattle trained as draft animals) are large, short-haired, hoofed animals with unbranched, hollow horns, and they appear in a variety of colors and shades. The species may have been first domesticated over eight thousand years ago, and there are now 275 cattle breeds worldwide. Some more recent varieties have been specially bred to respond to harsh, dry conditions in the western United States. Forty distinct breeds of cattle are currently produced in California, although most from the state are breed crosses.

   Cattle gather in herds and feed on grasses, stems, and other plant material, which they thoroughly chew before passing it to a four-chambered stomach where the food is partially digested, then regurgitated (this material is called "cud"), chewed again, then swallowed once more for further digestion.

   Cattle are raised for meat and dairy products. Carcasses provide leather and may also be rendered into glue, soaps, and other products. Mechanization has largely replaced the use of oxen as draft animals, but they were a common choice of immigrants for pulling wagons across the prairies to California.

Gelett Burgess
"The Purple Cow"

Reflections on a Mythic Beast
Who's Quite Remarkable, at Least.

I never saw a Purple Cow,
I never hope to See One;
But I can Tell you, Anyhow,
I'd rather See than Be One!

"The Purple Cow: Suite"

Ah, yes, I wrote the "Purple Cow"—
I'm Sorry, now, I wrote it;
But I can tell you Anyhow
I'll Kill you if you Quote it!

William Heath Davis
from *Sixty Years in California*

Although the cattle belonging to the various ranchos were wild, yet they were under training to some extent, and were kept in subjection by constant rodeos. At stated times, say, two or three times a week at first, the cattle on a particular ranch were driven in by the vaqueros, from all parts thereof, to a spot known as the rodeo ground, and kept there for a few hours, when they were allowed to disperse. Shortly they were collected again, once a week perhaps, and then less seldom, until after considerable training, being always driven to the same place, they came to know it. Then, whenever the herd was wanted, all that was necessary for the vaqueros to do was, say twenty-five or thirty of them, to ride out into the hills and valleys and call the cattle, shouting and screaming to them, when the animals would immediately run to the accustomed spot; presently the whole vast herd belonging to the ranch finding their way there.

At times, cattle strayed from one ranch to another and got into the wrong herd. Whenever a rodeo was to be held, the neighbors of the ranchero were given notice and attended at the time and place designated.

If any of these cattle were found in the band, they were picked out, separated, and driven back to the rancho where they belonged. As the cattle were all branded, and each rancho had ear-marks, this was not difficult.

Sometimes when cattle were being herded in a rodeo, an obstinate or unruly animal, cow, steer or bull—commonly a bull—watching an opportunity, suddenly darted from the herd and ran away at full speed. The vaquero, being always on the alert and knowing his duty well, immediately dashed out after the animal. Being on a fleet horse he presently came up with the runaway, and by a dexterous movement, leaning over his horse, seized the creature by the tail, when, urging the steed to an extra effort, the horse dashed forward, giving a sudden jerk, and the tail being let go by the vaquero at the right moment, the animal was rolled over and over on the ground. When it regained its legs it was completely subdued, tamely submitted to be driven back to the herd and was not inclined to repeat the experiment.

The capture was called *colliar*. It was highly enjoyed by the vaquero, and was a feat requiring no little skill, strength, nerve and horsemanship on his part. The ranchero himself when out riding with his friends, for their amusement and his own, would sometimes separate an animal from the herd, run him off to one side, gallop alongside, catch him by the tail and skillfully turn him over and over, creating a good deal of merriment. At times the sagacious animal, knowing what was coming, would draw his tail down under his body. This manœuvre did not prevent its being seized, nevertheless.

The rodeo ground was of circular shape; the vaqueros always left the cattle together in that form. When a rodeo took place, six or eight *cabestros*, or tame cattle, were brought together in a stand, or *parada*, about one hundred yards or more from the rodeo, in charge of a vaquero. When the cattle were to be selected from the rodeo, the vaqueros rode quietly in among them, in pairs, and two of them, seeing one they wanted to remove, gently approached the animal, one on each side, and, without making any disturbance, edged him along to one side of the rodeo ground opposite to where the *parada* stood. When they got just to the edge, they gave him a sudden start, by shouting "*hora*" (now), and off he went at full speed, followed by them. Seeing the *parada* a little distance off, the wild steer or cow generally made for that, or, if he or she turned to one side, was guided by the vaqueros, and, on reaching it, stopped with the tame cattle, or was compelled to if not so inclined. The cattle when taken first in this way to the *parada*, finding themselves with a strange set and few in number, were uneasy; but the vaqueros continuing to bring in others, the numbers increasing rapidly, the new comers would feel more at home, and generally remained quiet. If one bolted from the *parada*, a vaquero pursued him and performed the *colliar* movement, and he returned tamely and made no more trouble. As many as were required were brought to the *parada* by the vaqueros, until fifty or seventy-five were thus collected at times, as in the killing season, or a less number if selected to be returned to their owners, or for sale. Several pairs of vaqueros, or *apartadores*, were often engaged at the same time in the rodeo ground, taking out cattle to be removed and conducting them to different *paradas*.

When the owners of adjoining ranchos came to the rodeo ground to select their cattle, they brought their own *cabestros*, and their own vaqueros, who went in and picked out the cattle belonging to their special ranchos, and took them to their own *paradas*. Two or three hundred cattle belonging to a neighboring ranch would be taken from a rodeo at a time.

The work of separating the cattle, while a necessity, was really more of an amusement than a labor, and I have frequently participated in it for the sport. On such occasions many persons from the different ranchos came, as at a cattle fair in the country in our day, to exchange greetings and talk over affairs. Sometimes they would amuse themselves by joining in the work with the vaqueros, in pairs, a point being not to disturb or frighten the whole mass of cattle on the rodeo ground.

The *cabestros* had holes in their horns, with a small spike inserted, by which an unruly beast could be attached to one or two other cattle, so to be taken from one place to another, when necessary.

When the horses became disabled, or too poor for use, they were generally given away to the poorer people of the country, or to Indians who could make them useful.

The California horses were originally from Arabian stock, imported from Spain by the Padres at the time of the first establishment of the Missions. They had multiplied here extensively. At first it was very fine stock, but it became degenerated by breeding in, generation after generation, for over a hundred years. No attention was given by the rancheros to the production of good stock, either cattle or horses.

All *orejanos* (calves without ear-mark or brand) not following the cow were considered as belonging to the rancho on which they were found.

The marking season always commenced about the first of February in the southern counties, before the hot weather came on, and ended about the middle of May, when both horses and cattle were branded, ear-marked and castrated. Rodeos were held at marking and slaughtering times, and at other periods often enough to keep the animals subdued, and accustomed to the premises of the owner.

At the killing season, cattle were driven from the rodeo ground to a particular spot on the rancho, near a brook and forest. It was usual to slaughter from fifty to one hundred at a time, generally steers three years old and upward; the cows being kept for breeding purposes. The fattest would be selected for slaughter, and about two days would be occupied in killing fifty cattle, trying out the tallow, stretching the hides and curing the small portion of meat that was preserved. The occasion was called the *matanza*.

The mode of killing cattle was thus: About fifty were driven into a corral near the *matanza* ground; a vaquero then went in on horseback and lassoed a creature by the horns, the end of the reata being already fastened to the pommel of the saddle, with as much thrown out as was necessary, only a portion being used in a small space like the corral, the remainder being held in the hand in a coil, to be let out or drawn in, as circumstances should require. The animal was brought out of the corral, and, another vaquero coming up, the animal when it reached the spot where it was wanted was lassoed by one or both hind legs, and at that moment the horse, by a sudden movement, jerked the animal to one side or the other, and it was thrown instantly to the ground. The man who had him by the head then backed his horse, or the horse, understanding the business perfectly, backed himself, until the whole reata was straightened out; and the horse of the vaquero who had the creature by the hind legs did the same, the latter vaquero meanwhile fastening his reata more securely to the saddle, and the two lines were drawn taut. The man at the tail end, then dismounting, tied the fore legs of the animal together with an extra piece of rope, and the hind legs also, drawing all the feet together in a bunch and tying them. During this operation the man and horse at the head stood firm, and the horse without the rider did the same, watching every movement, his ears moving back and forth; if there was any slacking of the reata from the motions of the animal, he backed a little further, without any direction from the vaquero, so intelligent and well-trained was the faithful beast. After the steer was thus tied, and powerless to rise, the reatas were taken from him entirely, and the man on foot stuck a knife in his neck. When he was dead, the two took off the skin in a short time, not over half an hour, so expert were they at the business. At other times, not during the killing season, if a beef was required for family use, two vaqueros were detailed by the ranchero to go out and bring in a fat creature. They selected the best they could find from the cattle in the field, lassoed him and brought him in to the side or rear of the house, about 100 feet distant and convenient to the kitchen, where the steer was lassoed by the hind legs, thrown over and killed, as above. The skin was laid back on the ground as it was taken off, and the creature was cut up on the skin. At this time nearly the whole of the meat was used, not merely the choice parts, as at the *matanza*. In cutting up the animal they first took off in a layer the *fresada* (literally, blanket), that is, the thick portion covering the ribs, which, though tough, was very sweet and palatable; and as the Californians, both men and women, old and young, were blessed with remarkably sound teeth, the toughness was no impediment to its being eaten. I never knew an instance of a person of either sex or any age among the Californians suffering from toothache or decay of teeth, but all preserved their teeth in good condition to extreme old age; at the same time, they did not take any special care of them. I can account for the excellent preservation of the teeth only upon the ground of an extremely simple mode of living and their temperate habits.

This mode of slaughter of cattle—lying flat upon the ground—preserved a great deal more of the blood in the meat than the method in use by Americans. The meat was therefore sweeter and more nutritious than if the blood had been drained as much as possible, as is the custom with us; though the slaughtering in this way seemed somewhat repugnant to a stranger, at first. I have heard Americans express this feeling, and have experienced it myself, but we soon became accustomed to it, and were convinced that the mode of the Californians was superior to ours. Capt. Richardson said to me that he could account for the fine appearance, the health and longevity of the Californians only from the fact that their chief article of food was beef; and the beef being dressed in the way I have described was more nutritious and sustaining than ours.

Arnold R. Rojas
from *California Vaquero*

Their skill in roping and tying wild cattle in brush and mountain would have availed the vaqueros nothing in getting them to the home corral, had they not had that faithful servant of man from time immemorial, the ox, to aid them. The man who trained and managed the *cabestros* was one of the most important members of the ranch crew in the old days. His title was *caporal de cabestros*. He taught each ox to know its name, to know and keep its position in the band when traveling, to follow its leader, the *capitán*, as the lead steer was called, and when reaching a destination to stand with the rest of the band until some wild steer was roped and tied. Then, when its name was called, it was taught to approach and kneel to be yoked to the hogtied *bronco* he was to lead home.

Training oxen as leaders is an old skilled art in the peninsula, a profession as old as bull fighting in Spain. It is with *cabestros* (leaders) that fierce bulls are handled and moved. To rope and throw a bull intended for the arena will ruin the animal as a fighter. Each *cabestro* had a hole bored through one horn. On some ranches each vaquero carried a drill of fine steel, the handle of which was the hollow tip of a bull's horn. This handle was filled with tallow to grease the drill when boring a hole in the horn of a wild steer when it was caught. Two steel pins went with each *cabestro*, one pin went into the hole in the ox's horn, the other into that of the wild steer, then they were yoked up and were turned loose, the leader invariably bringing the wild one home to the corral, though it sometimes took several days for the pair to arrive.

Many old vaqueros believe the ox to be a reasoning animal. A *cabestro* will lead any animal whatever the breed, out of the brush, and take care of himself, while the burro will fail when lashed to a wild mule. Not being afraid of it he will not pull it home for someone to relieve him of it. The ox never leaves the road or trail when turned loose with a wild one. The instant the captive heads for the brush, the *cabestro* will stop, and only when it starts in the right direction will the *cabestro* go on again.

Lead oxen had a hole bored in either the right or left horn, never in both. Sometimes after years of wear the hold wore through and another was bored, always in the same horn. An ox will work only on the side he is trained on. They are either near or off side. Whenever available, one was *mancornado* (lashed) to each side of a bull and that gentleman was marched home in record time.

A bull is the most troublesome to lead because he will gore the ox if not lashed horn to horn. The *mancuernas* (thongs) were tied to the ox's horns then around the base of the bull's, and down to a forefoot which prevented him from hooking his *cabestro*.

Cattle were still plentiful when the great fire of 1888 swept through the mountains. Great numbers of the wild-eyed *cimarones* escaped the flames by moving down upon the plains and canyons, where riders seeing them were surprised at the vast amount of cattle those mountains could hold.

Each vaquero was given a number of *ligas* (thongs) a *brasada y media* (roughly nine feet) in length. A *brasada* from *brazos* (arms) is a measure, the length from left to right hand when the arms are spread horizontally, about the height of the person measured. These *ligas* were used to tie the wild cattle when they were caught and left to wait for the oxen to lead them home. The record on the Tejon for roping and tying wild cattle in the mountains was eight head roped and hogtied in one day.

~ COYOTE ~

Canis latrans

Family Canidae

Height: 23–26"; Length: 3'5"–4'4"; Weight: 20–40 lb

Habitat:

Prefers open country but can be found near and within urban areas, rural farmland, and forests; mountain populations may move to lower elevations in autumn

Range:

Common throughout California

Comments:

The coyote is typically gray, buff, and/or brown in color, and resembles a mid-sized, lanky dog. It has prominent, pricked ears and a bushy tail with a black tip. Legs are long, with a dark line on the lower forelegs.

The coyote may bark in defense of its young or its food but it is more often known by its nocturnal barks, yips, and howls. Once begun by an individual coyote, howling may evoke a chorus of responses from others.

The coyote can run up to forty miles per hour for short distances and can maintain speeds of up to thirty miles per hour. The coyote is also a good swimmer and will enter water after prey. Although the coyote does not keep a permanent home, a female will establish a den for raising young.

The coyote is a resourceful carnivore that dines on a variety of small mammals, including rabbits, mice, gophers, and squirrels. It will also eat carrion, insects, frogs, and various fruits. Coyotes prefer to hunt by themselves but will occasionally team with others to chase and tire prey. They may also follow foraging badgers in order to pounce on rodents who escape them. Coyotes occasionally take lambs, calves, poultry, cats, and small dogs, making them a nuisance to farmers and ranchers, who often hunt, trap, and poison them. Nonetheless, the versatile and opportunistic coyote is currently sustaining its population numbers and even extending its range.

T. C. Boyle
from *The Tortilla Curtain*

As I sit here today at the close of summer, at the hour when the very earth crackles for the breath of moisture denied it through all these long months of preordained drought, I gaze round my study at the artifacts I've collected during my diurnal wanderings—the tail feathers of the Cooper's hawk, the trilobite preserved in stone since the time the ground beneath my feet was the bed of an ancient sea, the owl pellets, skeletons of mouse and kangaroo rat, the sloughed skin of the gopher snake—and my eye comes to rest finally on the specimen jar of coyote scat. There it is, on the shelf over my desk, wedged between the Mexican red-kneed tarantula and the pallid bat pickled in formalin, an innocuous jar of desiccated ropes of hair the casual observer might take for shed fur rather than the leavings of our cleverest and most resourceful large predator, the creature the Indians apotheosized as the Trickster. And why today do my eyes linger here and not on some more spectacular manifestation of nature's plethora of wonders? Suffice it to say that lately the coyote has been much on my mind.

Here is an animal ideally suited to its environment, able to go without water for stretches at a time, deriving the lion's share of its moisture from its prey, and yet equally happy to take advantage of urban swimming pools and sprinkler systems. One coyote, who makes his living on the fringes of my community high in the hills above Topanga Creek and the San Fernando Valley, has learned to simply chew his way through the plastic irrigation pipes whenever he wants a drink. Once a week, sometimes even more frequently, the hapless maintenance man will be confronted by a geyser of water spewing out of the xerophytic ground cover the community has planted as a firebreak. When he comes to me bewildered with three gnawed lengths of PVC pipe, I loan him a pair of Bausch & Lomb 9x35 field glasses and instruct him to keep watch at dusk along the rear perimeter of the development. Sure enough, within the week he's caught the culprit in the act, and at my suggestion, he paints the entire length of the irrigation system with a noxious paste made of ground serrano chilies. And it works. At least until the unforgiving blast of the sun defuses the chilies' potency. And then, no doubt to the very day, the coyote will be back.

Of course, a simpler solution (the one most homeowners resort to when one of these "brush wolves" invades the sanctum sanctorum of their fenced-in yard) is to call in the Los Angeles County Animal Control Department, which traps and euthanizes about one hundred coyotes a year. This solution, to one who wishes fervently to live in harmony with the natural world, has always been anathema (after all, the coyote roamed these hills long before *Homo sapiens* made his first shaggy appearance on this continent), and yet, increasingly, this author has begun to feel that some sort of control must be applied if we continue to insist on encroaching on the coyote's territory with our relentless urban and suburban development. If we invade his territory, then why indeed should we be surprised when he invades ours?

For *Canis latrans* is, above all, adaptable. The creature that gives birth to four or fewer pups and attains a mature weight of twenty-five pounds or less in the sere pinched environment in which it evolved has spread its range as far as Alaska in the north and Costa Rica in the south, and throughout all the states of the continental U.S. Nineteen subspecies are now recognized, and many of them, largely because of the abundant food sources we've inadvertently made available to them (dogs, cats, the neat plastic bowls of kibble set just outside the kitchen door, the legions of rats and mice our wasteful habits support), have grown considerably larger and more formidable than the original model, the average size of their litters growing in proportion. And the march of adaptability goes on. Werner Schnitter, the renowned UCLA biologist, has shown in his radio-collaring studies that the coyotes of the Los Angeles basin demonstrate a marked decline in activity during periods coinciding with the morning and evening rush hour. This is nothing less than astonishing: you would think the coyotes were studying us.

The problem, of course, lies at our own doorstep. In our blindness, our species-specific arrogance, we create a niche, and animals like the raccoon, the opossum, the starling and a host of other indigenous and introduced species will rush in to fill it. The urban coyote is larger than his wild cousin, he is more aggressive and less afraid of the humans who coddle and encourage him, who are so blissfully unaware of the workings of nature that they actually donate their kitchen scraps to his well-being. The disastrous results can be seen in the high mortality among small pets in the foothills and even the as yet rare but increasingly inevitable attacks on humans.

I had the infinitely sad task last year of interviewing the parents of Jennifer Tillman, the six-month-old infant taken from her crib on the patio of the Tillmans' home in the hills of Monte Nido, directly over the ridge from my own place of residence. The coyote involved, a healthy four-year-old female with a litter of pups, had been a regular daytime visitor to the area, lured by misguided residents who routinely left tidbits for her on the edge of their lawns.

But forgive me: I don't mean to lecture. After all, my pilgrimage is for the attainment of wonder, of involving myself in the infinite, and not for the purpose of limiting or attempting to control the uncontrollable, the unknowable and the hidden. Who can say what revolutionary purpose the coyote has in mind? Or the horned lizard, for that matter, or any creature? Or why we should presume or even desire to preserve the status quo? And yet something must be done, clearly, if we are to have any hope of coexisting harmoniously with this supple suburban raider. Trapping is utterly useless—even if traps were to be set in every backyard in the county—as countless studies have shown. The population will simply breed up to fill in the gap, the bitches having litters of seven, eight or even more pups, as they do in times of abundance—and with our interference, those times must seem limitless to the coyote.

Sadly, the backlash is brewing. And it is not just the ranchers' and hunters' lobbies and the like pushing for legislation to remove protections on this animal, but the average homeowner who has lost a pet, humane and informed people, like the readers of this periodical, devoted to conservation and preservation. Once classified as a "varmint," the coyote had a price on his head, governmental bounties paid out in cash for each skin or set of ears, and in response he retreated to the fastnesses of the hills and deserts. But we now occupy those fastnesses, with our ready water sources (even a birdbath is a boon to a coyote), our miniature pets and open trash cans, our feeble link to the wild world around us. We cannot eradicate the coyote, nor can we fence him out, not even with eight feet of chain link, as this sad but wiser pilgrim can attest. Respect him as the wild predator he is, keep your children and pets inside, leave no food source, however negligible, where he can access it.

Little Jennifer's neck was broken as neatly as a rabbit's: that is the coyote's way. But do not attempt to impose human standards on the world of nature, the world that has generated a parasite or predator for every species in existence, including our own. The coyote is not to blame—he is only trying to survive, to make a living, to take advantage of the opportunities available to him. I sit here in the comfort of my air-conditioned office staring at a jar of scat and thinking of all the benefit this animal does us, of the hordes of rats and mice and ground squirrels he culls and the thrill of the wild he gives us all, and yet I can't help thinking too of the missing pets, the trail of suspicion, the next baby left unattended on the patio.

The coyotes keep coming, breeding up to fill in the gaps, moving in where the living is easy. They are cunning, versatile, hungry and unstoppable.

William Bright, translator (from Karuk) "Coyote's Journey"

A man lived there,
 he had many strings of shell-money
  Coyote saw him there,
   he saw him measuring shell-money,
    that person there.
And then Coyote said,
 "Where do you find it,
  that money?"
And then that person said,
 "At Klamath Falls."
And then Coyote
 he went home.
And then he thought,
 I'll make some string!
"I have to go to Klamath Falls!

"I'll go get that money,
      I like it so much."
And he made a lot of it,
      that string.
So he tied it in a bundle,
      that string.
And then he thought,
      "Now I'll start out!"…

Coyote went on upstream,
      there had been a big brushfire.
And he looked around,
      there were lots of roasted grasshoppers.
"I won't eat them."
Finally he went a little ways.
And he thought,
      "I'll just gather a few of them,
            those roasted grasshoppers."
There he was going to gather them.
And then he thought,
      "I wonder why it is,
            I'm not getting full."
And he thought,
      "I think they're coming out my rear,
            while I'm eating them."
And he thought,
      "I'll plug up my ass!"
So he gathered pitch,
      and he plugged up his ass with it.
And he thought, "There,
      now I'll get full.
I've plugged up my ass."
So he ate them—
      but there had been a BIG brushfire.
And he was sticking his butt all around there.
And he thought,
      "I think I'm getting there,
            to Klamath Falls"—
                  he heard it,
                        the thundering,
                              he heard it like that,
                                    it sort of said HUHUHUHUHU.
And he thought,
      "I'm getting there,

to Klamath Falls"—
    all he could hear was the HUHUHUHUHU.
It was really his ass,
   there it was burning.
It was really the pitch,
   what he had plugged it with,
    there it was burning.
What could he do?
He slid all around there,
   on the ground, in the sand.
And he was just saying "ATUHTUHTUHTUHTUH!"
So finally his ass stopped burning.
And he thought,
   "Now I'll never eat them again,
    those roasted grasshoppers.
That's enough, I won't eat them."...

And then he looked downriver.
There were young women downriver leaching flour,
   on the shore.
And then he said,
   "I'll turn into some pretty driftwood!"
And then he turned into some pretty driftwood.
And then he floated down from upstream,
   he watched them close by,
    while they were leaching flour.
And he said,
   "I'll float to the shore,
    I'll float to the shore!
I'll keep floating in circles just downslope from them."
And then one girl looked downslope to the river.
And she said, "Look, my dear!
   Oh, look how pretty,
    downslope,
     that driftwood!"
"All right!"
So they ran downslope,
   they went to look at it,
    where it was floating in circles.
And one said, "Come on, my dear,
   Where's a little stick?
We'll hook it out with that."
And so they hooked it out.

And oh! they took a liking to it.
Oh, how pretty it was,
    the driftwood,
        they took a liking to it!
And then one threw it to another,
    they played with it,
        that driftwood,
            the pretty little stick.
And then one girl said, "Ugh,"
    she said, "Ugh! Maybe it's Coyote,
        they said he drowned in the river, upstream."
And then they threw it back in the river,
    that driftwood.
And they took it up,
    their acorn mush,
        what they were leaching.
Sure enough, in a while, they both were pregnant.
There Coyote floated downstream,
    then he floated ashore downriver from them.
And then he traveled on,
    Coyote did,
        he turned back into a person,
            he turned back into himself....

Coyote wandered around there,
    there was a sweat-house standing.
And he looked inside,
    he saw nobody at all.
And Coyote crawled in.
And when he got inside,
    when he looked around,
        all the chairs were made of pure grease,
            their headrests too were of grease,
                and their stepladder too was of grease.
And Coyote was hungry.
And he thought,
    "I'll just taste them,
        those headrests."
And when he took a taste,
    they were very delicious.
Finally he ate them all up,
    he ate up their stepladder too.
Then suddenly he sort of heard something.
And he thought,
    "I'd better hide."

And he lay down there behind the woodpile.
And when the men came back in the sweathouse in the evening,
    as each man crawled in,
        he fell down. [Because the stepladder was eaten.]
And they said,
    "I'm thinking,
        Coyote's wandering around here.
"That's who did it,
    he ate them all up,
        our headrests."
He just lay there,
    he heard them,
        when they were talking about him.
And then they said,
    "Let's spend the night away from home,
        at Long Pond."
And then he thought,
    Coyote thought,
        "They're talking about my country."
And he jumped out—
    "Nephew, my nephews,
        "I'll go along!"…

So Coyote went with them.
And finally he kept his eyes closed for a long ways.
Suddenly they paddled ashore.
And they said,
    "We've arrived."
And then he jumped up,
    Coyote did.
And then he said,
    "My country!"
And he kicked dirt out into the river.
And he kicked it out from Camp Creek,
    he kicked it out from Kattiphirak,
        he kicked it out from Ullathorne Creek,
           Coyote was so happy,
                when he returned,
                    back to his country.
That's why he kicked it out.

Kupannakanakana!
Young brodiaea plant,
    you must come up quickly,
        hurry to me!

Spring salmon,
    shine upriver quickly,
        hurry to me!
My back has become like a mountain ridge,
    so thin,
        so hungry.

Alejandrina Murillo Melendres
"Coyote Baptizes the Chickens"

An old woman had a
hen and a rooster.
The hen had seven chicks.
Coyote came; he wanted to
carry them all off and
eat them, but he couldn't.

He saw the hen at the door;
he said, "Give me a chick.
I'll take and baptize it," said Coyote.
"All right, take it."
He took the chick and ate it.

The next day he came
and took still another one.
"Comadre, I'm taking another
  one to baptize;
the first one is sad, all by himself."
He carried if off and ate it—
the baptizing was a fake!

The next day he came
and took still another one.
He carried them all off;
he ate up every chick.

Then he came: "Comadre,
come see your children, all baptized,
very big and beautiful;
they want to see you."

"Go ahead," said the rooster.
Coyote carried off the hen;
he carried her off and ate her.

After eating he came back.
"Compadre, now Comadre cries for
  you to come…"
"All right," the rooster said, and went—
Coyote carried him off.
Coyote carried him off and ate him.

When he finished eating,
the old farmer's wife came.
"What happened to my chickens?
"They're lost, gone—what happened?"
"Who robbed me?"

She went to look: Aah, a big cave;
under a stone were a lot of feathers.
All the chicks were eaten,
the hen and all, the rooster and all,
  all were eaten.
The old woman went there and saw it;
she got furious: What could she do?
They were all gone.

MULE DEER

Odocoileus hemionus

Family Cervidae

Height: 3'–3'5"; Length: 3'10"–7'6"; Weight: Males 110–475 lb; Females 70–160 lb

Habitat:

    Forest edges, meadows, mountains, and foothills

Range:

    Common throughout California, except in open, heavily farmed regions and some desert areas

Comments:

    The mule deer is medium-sized and stocky, with long, sturdy legs. In the summer, its top half is brown, and in the winter, it is gray; its lower body is tan year-round. It has white patches on its throat, rump, and the insides of its ears and legs, and its tail is white with a black tip. The name for the animal comes from its large ears, which move independently and constantly like a mule's. The males have branched antlers.

    A grazer and a browser, the mule deer mostly feeds in the wild on herbaceous plants and the leaves and twigs of shrubs and trees such as cedar, aspen, and sage; it will occasionally eat apples. The mule deer is active in morning and evening and moves with a stiff-legged, bounding gait with all four feet hitting the ground together. It is also a good swimmer.

    California's most significant large game animal, mule deer form small herds of both males and females. They migrate to avoid heavy snow. Bucks tend to be solitary, while does stay with their offspring. Does must spread out because they tend to fight with other does.

Darryl Babe Wilson
"Dose!"

Instantaneous hunger gripped the family every day at the same time, sundown. Our hunger was fed by the excitement of living at the Old Home Place, and the thrill of our new freedom. There was no food and it seemed that it was up to Daddy and me to solve that problem, too. Now that the whole family was together again, and there would be no wasting of meat, it was time for Daddy and me to get a deer. Like wolves, we had to eat meat.

Preparing to hunt in the old way, Daddy and I built a small fire down behind the barn that evening. The flames painted Daddy's dark face with deeper shadows, alternating with dancing bright orange. And orange glinted off of his straight black hair.

As a part of our hunting ceremony, we "smoked" ourselves, sparks reaching up into the night when Daddy placed "medicine" in the flames, a mixture of leaves and bark from a variety of trees and shrubs. His brown eyes flashed orange as he looked deep into the fire. Then, after putting the fire out, we went into the barn to sleep under the hay. This was so the *dose* (deer) could not smell the human odor very well. Outside, the black sky was almost white with millions of stars. Inside the barn, sweet dust floated in the old air. *Suk'ahow* (owl) in the rafters returned a call from *suk'ahow* upon the hill.

Now that we were somewhat "cleansed," Daddy said to sleep and to dream about the *dose* we would get tomorrow. "Dream and 'see' them tonight just as they will appear tomorrow. To dream and not see the *dose* is a sign that we should not go hunting. We could go hunting, but we never would come close."

I was almost seven and thought that I was a great warrior. Maybe like Straight Arrow. He taught everybody how to hunt and survive by leaving instructions on a big card in the cereal box. I could read every word, so I learned a lot from Straight Arrow. And I bet I could do everything he said.

But still there were some things that worried me. I knew the contents of the old barn. There were pigeons and hawks, owls and crickets. There were spiders and ants. There were lizards and how'ta (rattlesnakes). Some things still frightened me. At those times I was not a warrior after all.

Daddy seemed to go to sleep quickly. Under the hay, I did not rest because I could feel a *how'ta* sliding silently toward me, drawing nearer and nearer. I knew he was there, staring at me. Even though I could not hear or see him, I could "feel" his presence, like a ghost. He was planning to strike me, to poison me to death, then swallow my blood. I was a warrior. I could not wake Daddy talking about a little thing like a *how'ta*, even if it was twenty feet long, and hungry!

I did not sleep for a long time. *Suddenly dose appeared, breathing and studying its world with huge eyes that seemed to be made of black glass. It was alert, and puffs of steam came from its nostrils. It was a beautiful doe with huge ears, but it seemed like it did not make any difference if we killed her or not. It was a feathery dream.* Dose *just kept walking away, deeper into the forest and over the hills, then vanished.*

It was still dark when Daddy woke me up. As quietly as we could, we made our way out of the old barn and into the early darkness. At first light we moved toward Lake Britton. Silver shimmered upon the horizon, yet darkness wrapped all around us, thick. We stopped and gathered skunk berries and leaves, rolled them between our hands, crushing the odor out of them, then rubbed the mixture all over our Levi's, hands, shirts, and hair. Daddy always wore Levi's. I did, too. He liked to wear his gray sweatshirt, but I didn't have one, so I wore my long-sleeved, black-checkered shirt with a tear near the pocket.

"Daddy, we smell like *ha'yanna* (skunk)!"

"Shh. In the quiet, everything can hear the human voice."

Obeying the rules of the hunter, silently, without breaking a branch or turning a leaf, we melted into the thick darkness, sneaking west through trees and buck brush. Daddy made no noise. But I often stepped on a dead branch that cracked in the silence of early morning. We stopped, waiting for nature to resume its composure. Then, after tiptoeing for what seemed to be a hundred miles, we heard the wind moving in the forest near Lake Britton. Daddy knew the trail that the deer used as they came early to water from the high country, following the backbone ridge and dropping down the chalk bank. Then the trail skirted the lake.

If I breathed too hard, steam came from my mouth, wisping up into the darkness. Better stop breathing. Creeping now, like two shadows, a big one and a little one, we eased into our position between the sleeping lake and the deer trail. "Get comfortable, son. We may have a long wait."

Silent and motionless, we waited. Long we waited. It seemed like years instead of hours. Still we waited. I was uncomfortable and wanted to change position just a little, but was afraid I would make a noise and everything would hear me, and the deer would run away.

Then! Daddy tensed slightly. "*Dose,*" he whispered softly. The urgency in Daddy's voice was a command, signifying several very important things. It meant for me to be quiet, like stone. It meant that the *dose* we dreamed of and were waiting for had arrived. It meant that I must use all of my hunting and warrior power to remain silent, now that we were within reach of our game. It meant that now the family would eat, and if I made a noise, if I breathed, if I in any manner spooked the *dose* and they took flight, I would be responsible for our family having no food.

His rifle was aimed at the target. Daddy was set.

In the dim light I stared hard, eyes riveted on the place where Daddy's rifle was aimed. Then my heart leaped! I went dizzy and thought I was going to faint. There, magically, almost at the end of Daddy's gun, appeared the *dose* that I had dreamed about last night! It stood motionless, its ears alert. Its eyes peered into tomorrow. Two small mists wisped from its shiny, black nose. It remained frozen as if a statue, its alert, shiny black eyes reflecting the whole morning world.

My spirit screamed, "Shoot! Daddy, shoot!"

Then, as magically as it appeared, *dose* disappeared. It simply vanished, like the mist from its nostrils, like the *dose* in my dream.

I was confused. We came here to kill a *dose*, and Daddy let it get away without a single shot! I wanted to scream, but remained mute and motionless. I had to. That is the way of the hunter, they always said. Daddy's rifle was still aimed at the target.

Then! The *dose* appeared again! No, this was another one. I thought I had blinked, and the first deer was still standing there. But this one held its head differently. "Shoot! Shoot!" cried my tormented spirit, again and again. In this manner many *dose* passed through the target, none breaking a branch.

Finally, for two reasons, I gave up on Daddy ever shooting. First, I had cramps everywhere. Second, I knew the *dose* would all pass by, and Daddy would not shoot. All the deer would be gone before he decided to kill one. My worried spirit and my aching body both decided that I should adjust my position, just a little. However, my will and the laws of hunting would not allow the slightest movement.

BOOM!

A thundering explosion shattered the quiet of morning. A red splotch came out of my consciousness and turned black, trimmed with silver. Faintly, I heard the rifle report echoing across the lake. The sweet, fresh air was filled with the pungent odor of smoke from the burnt gunpowder.

That BOOM! knocked me back into the thick brush, almost unconscious. I had been numb from waiting, numb from seeing the *dose* of my dreams; now I was numb from the report of the rifle. In the darkness of the brush, I lay there as if I were the one shot and not the *dose*. I tried to move my finger. It worked! Then my arm. Then my legs. Slowly I gathered myself together, and with a loud ringing in my ears, got up and looked around in the early light.

By the time I had recovered my senses and my balance and found Daddy and the *dose*, he already had the animal's stomach open with the hunting knife. Like skinny, dancing ghosts, steam wisped up into the early chill. A salty smell permeated the air. Daddy had blood on his hands, and dark blood clots lumped nearby. And pink blood foamed from its lungs.

Shivering from fright and excitement, and from sitting in one position forever, I stumbled around to the *dose*'s head. I saw the painful blue silver glitter of death in its eyes. I felt very sorry for the *dose*. Only a few moments ago it was alive and traveling with its family. Now it was food for our family and for the earth. To kill seemed like committing a crime, a bad one. Especially killing something so pretty. My stomach shook silently. I knew Straight Arrow would not cry, so I didn't either. But I wanted to. Still, again.

I thought about the deer's spirit. Eyes that only a few moments ago had seen the whole world shining now maybe saw shadows of memories. Upriver, *ma'ka'ta* (coyote) forlornly yapped to a departing night.

As is the custom of our mountain people, Daddy took out the purple liver from among the mounds of entrails and cut off a small piece for me and one for himself. He called upon *Kwaw* (the Wonder Power that created the universe) to forgive the injury to the family of the deer, and the injury to the silence of morning. Daddy licked the blood from the liver, then, in ceremony, ate it, for now his family could eat.

I looked at my piece of liver. It seemed to be looking back at me. With some hesitation I tasted the blood. I questioned my warrior spirit, and wondered how Straight Arrow would react. Then I remembered that my grandfather might be nearby, studying me as I grew a little more this morning. Yes, Grandfather was watching me from somewhere secret in the shadows. I could feel his presence. So, in the manner of my people, I put the squishy piece of blood-warm liver in my mouth. A sharp taste (which I have always remembered) attacked my tongue with a vengeance. Saliva flooded my mouth as if I had just bitten a hundred lemons. The soft flesh slipped and slid and did not want to go down my throat. I wrestled with it, and my spirit wrestled with it. Then, finally, it squiggled down. It almost got stuck, then kind of swam toward my stomach. I needed water, quick!

I ran to the lake, flopped down on my belly, and took a big swallow. Then, after waiting a few minutes to make sure the liver stayed down, I returned to Daddy and the *dose*. He had picked the carcass up and wrapped it around his neck so he could hold both front feet in his right hand and both back feet in his left. The head flopped down and the dry tongue hung out.

On the way home we stopped to rest, Daddy leaning against the fork of a tree to support the weight of the deer. He saw my tears.

"Son?"

"'Cause of...*dose*..."

Daddy gave me a pat on the head.

"There are many things you must learn. As hunters, we must kill so our family will live. All of nature knows this, and the hunter must obey all the laws of nature. One of those laws, the most important, is to talk with *Kwaw* and set things straight with the Great Powers of the world.

"In a herd that is in a following pattern, one after the other, the first *dose* is always the leader, strong, young. Do not kill this one. It is in nature that the old ones follow last. This is because the last one is the one ready to be taken; its life has been lived.

"*Maya'ki, piriki, wer'ak'mita* (Wolf, Grizzly Bear, Panther) know of this law, and they obey it. They wait beside the trail just as we did this morning. When the last *dose* passes, they spring to kill, just as we did.

"Don't worry, son. It is a great law that you have obeyed. *L'hepta* (let's go), the family is waiting."

Daddy rocked the deer back to the balance of his body and turned toward home. I was one step behind him, carrying the rifle and the knife that still had blood on it. I felt very important. After all, I had just obeyed a great law, although I didn't quite know which one. Yet something about the *dose* was not settled in my heart. Maybe it was supposed to have another baby? I could not tell.

After walking for a while, Daddy had to rest again. He saw in my eyes the emotions that had broken through to the surface of my being.

"Remember, it is because of nature that the barren doe, the one that can no longer have babies, follows behind the herd. She is a decoy. When we, or the mountain lion, take the last *dose* that moves along the trail, we are taking only one from the world. If we take the first ones, the ones that are still having babies, we do not know how many *dose* we have killed, and we upset the way of life all around us."

"...But, Daddy, *jamat* (a fawn)."

"No, Son, no more fawns. Because this deer is old and it was last. It was not as frisky as a younger doe and its neck is longer. The ears were not as alert and are large and floppy. And since *dose* moved slowly, I knew it was barren. It could not have babies."

Daddy could see all of that in the almost dark? Somehow I understood. And somehow I knew that I had just taken a big step toward becoming *It'jati'wa* (a genuine man). *It'jati'wa* with a great, new, strutting pride.

Arriving home, we created some excitement. Mom and all the kids ran out to see. Even the dogs jumped up and down. They were dreaming about bones, I bet. And I think *ha'yanna* (skunk) and *ma'ka'ta* (coyote) got the guts down near Lake Britton—and the ants got some, too.

✂ AMERICAN DIPPER ✂

Cinclus mexicanus

Family Cinclidae

Length: 7–8 ½"

Habitat:

> Mountain streams; always nests near water, sometimes behind waterfalls

Range:

> Throughout the central and northern Sierra Nevada to 12,000', and some local areas of Coast Ranges; may descend to lower elevations in winter

Comments:

> The American dipper—also called the water ouzel—is a small gray bird with a stubby tail, white eye rings, and a dark bill. Juveniles are typically paler, with mottled underparts and lighter-colored bills.
>
> These birds always live near rushing water and often perch on rocks in or near streams, typically bobbing up and down, perhaps in order to avoid surface glare and see better beneath the water. They usually maintain an exclusive territory, which serves as their feeding area. The American dipper is the only American songbird that dives below the surface of the water, where it searches for food, typically aquatic insects and larvae, but sometimes even small fish and aquatic plants. They forage underwater for up to sixty seconds before bobbing to the surface. American dippers also fly through waterfalls.
>
> The song of the American dipper is bright and varied; its call resembles a loud "zeet."

Harriet Monroe
"The Water Ouzel"

Little brown surf-bather of the mountains!
Spirit of foam, lover of cataracts, shaking your wings in falling waters!
Have you no fear of the roar and rush when Nevada plunges—
Nevada, the shapely dancer, feeling her way with slim white fingers?
How dare you dash at Yosemite the mighty—
Tall, white limbed Yosemite, leaping down, down over the cliff?
Is it not enough to lean on the blue air of mountains?
Is it not enough to rest with your mate at timberline, in bushes that hug the rocks?
Must you fly through mad waters where the heaped-up granite breaks them?
Must you batter your wings in the torrent?
Must you plunge for life and death through the foam?

John Muir
"The Water-Ouzel"

The waterfalls of the Sierra are frequented by only one bird,—the Ouzel or Water Thrush (*Cinclus Mexicanus*, Sw.). He is a singularly joyous and lovable little fellow, about the size of a robin, clad in a plain waterproof suit of bluish gray, with a tinge of chocolate on the head and shoulders. In form he is about as smoothly plump and compact as a pebble that has been whirled in a pot-hole, the flowing contour of his body being interrupted only by his strong feet and bill, the crisp wing-tips, and the upslanted wren-like tail.

Among all the countless waterfalls I have met in the course of ten years' exploration in the Sierra, whether among the icy peaks, or warm foot-hills, or in the profound yosemitic cañons of the middle region, not one was found without its Ouzel. No cañon is too cold for this little bird, none too lonely, provided it be rich in falling water. Find a fall, or cascade, or rushing rapid, anywhere upon a clear stream, and there you will surely find its complementary Ouzel, flitting about in the spray, diving in foaming eddies, whirling like a leaf among beaten foam-bells; ever vigorous and enthusiastic, yet self-contained, and neither seeking nor shunning your company.

If disturbed while dipping about in the margin shallows, he either sets off with a rapid whir to some other feeding-ground up or down the stream, or alights on some half-submerged rock or snag out in the current, and immediately begins to nod and curtsy like a wren, turning his head from side to side with many other odd dainty movements that never fail to fix the attention of the observer.

He is the mountain streams' own darling, the humming-bird of blooming waters, loving rocky ripple-slopes and sheets of foam as a bee loves flowers, as a lark loves sunshine and meadows. Among all the mountain birds, none has cheered me so much in my lonely wanderings,—none so unfailingly. For both in winter and summer he sings, sweetly, cheerily, independent alike of sunshine and of love, requiring no other inspiration than the stream on which he dwells. While water sings, so must he, in heat or cold, calm or storm, ever attuning his voice in sure accord; low in the drought of summer and the drought of winter, but never silent.

During the golden days of Indian summer, after most of the snow has been melted, and the mountain streams have become feeble,—a succession of silent pools, linked together by shallow, transparent currents and strips of silvery lacework,—then the song of the Ouzel is at its lowest ebb. But as soon as the winter clouds have bloomed, and the mountain treasuries are once more replenished with snow, the voices of the streams and ouzels increase in strength and richness until the flood season of early summer. Then the torrents chant their noblest anthems, and then is the flood-time of our songster's melody. As for weather, dark days and sun days are the same to him. The voices of most songbirds, however joyous, suffer a long winter eclipse; but the Ouzel sings on through all the seasons and every kind of storm. Indeed no storm can be more violent than those of the waterfalls in the midst of which he delights to dwell. However dark and boisterous the weather, snowing, blowing, or cloudy, all the same he sings, and with never a note of sadness. No need of spring sunshine to thaw *his* song, for it never freezes. Never shall you hear anything wintry from *his* warm breast; no pinched cheeping, no wavering notes between sorrow and joy; his mellow, fluty voice is ever tuned to downright gladness, as free from dejection as cock-crowing.

It is pitiful to see wee frost-pinched sparrows on cold mornings in the mountain groves shaking the snow from their feathers, and hopping about as if anxious to be cheery, then hastening back to their hidings out of the wind, puffing out their breast-feathers over their toes, and subsiding among the leaves, cold and breakfastless, while the snow continues to fall, and there is no sign of clearing. But the Ouzel never calls forth a single touch of pity; not because he is strong to endure, but rather because he seems to live a charmed life beyond the reach of every influence that makes endurance necessary.

One wild winter morning, when Yosemite Valley was swept its length from west to east by a cordial snow-storm, I sallied forth to see what I might learn and enjoy. A sort of gray, gloaming-like darkness filled the valley, the huge walls were out of sight, all ordinary sounds were smothered, and even the loudest booming of the falls was at times buried beneath the roar of the heavy-laden blast. The loose snow was already over five feet deep on the meadows, making extended walks impossible without the aid of snow-shoes. I found no great difficulty, however, in making my way to a certain ripple on the river where one of my ouzels lived. He was at home, busily gleaning his breakfast among the pebbles of a shallow portion of the margin, apparently unaware of anything extraordinary in the weather. Presently he flew out to a stone against which the icy current was beating, and turning his back to the wind, sang as delightfully as a lark in springtime.

After spending an hour or two with my favorite, I made my way across the valley, boring and wallowing through the drifts, to learn as definitely as possible how the other birds were spending their time. The Yosemite birds are easily found during the winter because all of them excepting the Ouzel are restricted to the sunny north side of the valley, the south side being constantly eclipsed by the great frosty shadow of the wall. And because the Indian Cañon groves, from their peculiar exposure, are the warmest, the birds congregate there, more especially in severe weather.

I found most of the robins cowering on the lee side of the larger branches where the snow could not fall upon them, while two or three of the more enterprising were making desperate efforts to reach the mistletoe berries by clinging nervously to the under side of the snow-crowned masses, back downward, like woodpeckers. Every now and then they would dislodge some of the loose fringes of the snow-crown, which would come sifting down on them and send them screaming back to camp, where they would subside among their companions with a shiver, muttering in low, querulous chatter like hungry children.

Some of the sparrows were busy at the feet of the larger trees gleaning seeds and benumbed insects, joined now and then by a robin weary of his unsuccessful attempts upon the snow-covered berries. The brave woodpeckers were clinging to the snowless sides of the larger boles and overarching branches of the camp trees, making short flights from side to side of the grove, pecking now and then at the acorns they had stored in the bark, and chattering aimlessly as if unable to keep still, yet evidently putting in the time in a very dull way, like storm-bound travelers at a country tavern. The hardy nut-hatches were threading the open furrows of the trunks in their usual industrious manner, and uttering their quaint notes, evidently less distressed than their neighbors. The Steller jays were of course making more noisy stir than all the other birds combined; ever coming and going with loud bluster, screaming as if each had a lump of melting sludge in his throat, and taking good care to improve the favorable opportunity afforded by the storm to steal from the acorn stores of the woodpeckers. I also noticed one solitary gray eagle braving the storm on the top of a tall pine-stump just outside the main grove. He was standing bolt upright with his back to the wind, a tuft of snow piled on his square shoulders, a monument of passive endurance. Thus every snow-bound bird seemed more or less uncomfortable if not in positive distress. The storm was reflected in every gesture, and not one cheerful note, not to say song, came from a single bill; their cowering, joyless endurance offering a striking contrast to the spontaneous, irrepressible gladness of the Ouzel, who could no more help exhaling sweet song than a rose sweet fragrance. He *must* sing though the heavens fall. I remember noticing the distress of a pair of robins during the violent earthquake of the year 1872, when the pines of the Valley, with strange movements, flapped and waved their branches, and beetling rock-brows came thundering down to the meadows in tremendous avalanches. It did not occur to me in the midst of the excitement of other observations to look for the ouzels, but I doubt not they were singing straight on through it all, regarding the terrible rock-thunder as fearlessly as they do the booming of the waterfalls.

What may be regarded as the separate songs of the Ouzel are exceedingly difficult of description, because they are so variable and at the same time so confluent. Though I have been acquainted with my favorite ten years, and during most of this time have heard him sing nearly every day, I still detect notes and strains that seem new to me. Nearly all of his music is sweet and tender, lapsing from his round breast like water over the smooth lip of a pool, then breaking farther on into a sparkling foam of melodious notes, which glow with subdued enthusiasm, yet without expressing much of the strong, gushing ecstasy of the bobolink or skylark.

The more striking strains are perfect arabesques of melody, composed of a few full, round, mellow notes, embroidered with delicate trills which fade and melt in long slender cadences. In a general way his music is that of the streams refined and spiritualized. The deep booming notes of the falls are in it, the trills of rapids, the gurgling of margin eddies, the low whispering of level reaches, and the sweet tinkle of separate drops oozing from the ends of mosses and falling into tranquil pools.

The Ouzel never sings in chorus with other birds, nor with his kind, but only with the streams. And like flowers that bloom beneath the surface of the ground, some of our favorite's best song-blossoms never rise above the surface of the heavier music of the water. I have often observed him singing in the midst of beaten spray, his music completely buried beneath the water's roar; yet I knew he was surely singing by his gestures and the movements of his bill.

His food, as far as I have noticed, consists of all kinds of water insects, which in summer are chiefly procured along shallow margins. Here he wades about ducking his head under water and deftly turning over pebbles and fallen leaves with his bill, seldom choosing to go into deep water where he has to use his wings in diving.

He seems to be especially fond of the larva of mosquitos, found in abundance attached to the bottom of smooth rock channels where the current is shallow. When feeding in such places he wades up-stream, and often while his head is under water the swift current is deflected upward along the glossy curves of his neck and shoulders, in the form of a clear, crystalline shell, which fairly incloses him like a bell-glass, the shell being broken and reformed as he lifts and dips his head; while ever and anon he sidles out to where the too powerful current carries him off his feet; then he dexterously rises on the wing and goes gleaning again in shallower places.

But during the winter, when the stream-banks are embossed in snow, and the streams themselves are chilled nearly to the freezing-point, so that the snow falling into them in stormy weather is not wholly dissolved, but forms a thin, blue sludge, thus rendering the current opaque—then he seeks the deeper portions of the main rivers, where he may dive to clear water beneath the sludge. Or he repairs to some open lake or mill-pond, at the bottom of which he feeds in safety.

When thus compelled to betake himself to a lake, he does not plunge into it at once like a duck, but always alights in the first place upon some rock or fallen pine along the shore. Then flying out thirty or forty yards, more or less, according to the character of the bottom, he alights with a dainty glint on the surface, swims about, looks down, finally makes up his mind, and disappears with a sharp stroke of his wings. After feeding for two or three minutes he suddenly reappears, showers the water from his wings with one vigorous shake, and rises abruptly into the air as if pushed up from beneath, comes back to his perch, sings a few minutes, and goes out to dive again; thus coming and going, singing and diving at the same place for hours.

The Ouzel is usually found singly; rarely in pairs, excepting during the breeding season, and *very* rarely in threes or fours. I once observed three thus spending a winter morning in company, upon a small glacier lake, on the Upper Merced, about 7,500 feet above the level of the sea. A storm had occurred during the night, but the morning sun shone unclouded, and the shadowy lake, gleaming darkly in its setting of fresh snow, lay smooth and motionless as a mirror. My camp chanced to be within a few feet of the water's edge, opposite a fallen pine, some of the branches of which leaned out over the lake. Here my three dearly welcome visitors took up their station, and at once began to embroider the frosty air with their delicious melody, doubly delightful to me that particular morning, as I had been somewhat apprehensive of danger in breaking my way down through the snow-choked cañons to the lowlands.

The portion of the lake bottom selected for a feeding-ground lies at a depth of fifteen or twenty feet below the surface, and is covered with a short growth of algae and other aquatic plants,—facts I had previously determined while sailing over it on a raft. After alighting on the glassy surface, they occasionally indulged in a little play, chasing one another round about in small circles; then all three would suddenly dive together, and then come ashore and sing.

The Ouzel seldom swims more than a few yards on the surface, for, not being web-footed, he makes rather slow progress, but by means of his strong, crisp wings he swims, or rather flies, with celerity under the surface, often to considerable distances. But it is in withstanding the force of heavy rapids that his strength of wing in this respect is most strikingly manifested. The following may be regarded as a fair illustration of his power of sub-aquatic flight. One stormy morning in winter when the Merced River was blue and green with unmelted snow, I observed one of my ouzels perched on a snag out in the midst of a swift-rushing rapid, singing cheerily, as if everything was just to his mind; and while I stood on the bank admiring him, he suddenly plunged into the sludgy current, leaving his song abruptly broken off. After feeding a minute or two at the bottom, and when one would suppose that he must inevitably be swept far down-stream, he emerged just where he went down, alighted on the same snag, showered the water-beads from his feathers, and continued his unfinished song, seemingly in tranquil ease as if it had suffered no interruption.

The Ouzel alone of all birds dares to enter a white torrent. And though strictly terrestrial in structure, no other is so inseparably related to water, not even the duck, or the bold ocean albatross, or the stormy-petrel. For ducks go ashore as soon as they finish feeding in undisturbed places, and very often make long flights overland from lake to lake or field to field. The same is true of most other aquatic birds. But the Ouzel, born on the brink of a stream, or on a snag or boulder in the midst of it, seldom leaves it for a single moment. For, notwithstanding he is often on the wing, he never flies overland, but whirs with rapid, quail-like beat above the stream, tracing all its windings. Even when the stream is quite small, say from five to ten feet wide, he seldom shortens his flight by crossing a bend, however abrupt it may be; and even when disturbed by meeting some one on the bank, he prefers to fly over one's head, to dodging out over the ground. When, therefore, his flight along a crooked stream is viewed endwise, it appears most strikingly wavered—a description on the air of every curve with lightning-like rapidity.

The vertical curves and angles of the most precipitous torrents he traces with the same rigid fidelity, swooping down the inclines of cascades, dropping sheer over dizzy falls amid the spray, and ascending with the same fearlessness and ease, seldom seeking to lessen the steepness of the acclivity by beginning to ascend before reaching the base of the fall. No matter though it may be several hundred feet in height he holds straight on, as if about to dash headlong into the throng of booming rockets, then darts abruptly upward, and, after alighting at the top of the precipice to rest a moment, proceeds to feed and sing. His flight is solid and impetuous, without any intermission of wing-beats,—one homogeneous buzz like that of a laden bee on its way home. And while thus buzzing freely from fall to fall, he is frequently heard giving utterance to a long outdrawn train of unmodulated notes, in no way connected with his song, but corresponding closely with his flight in sustained vigor.

Were the flights of all the ouzels in the Sierra traced on a chart, they would indicate the direction of the flow of the entire system of ancient glaciers, from about the period of the breaking up of the ice-sheet until near the close of the glacial winter; because the streams which the ouzels so rigidly follow are, with the unimportant exceptions of a few side tributaries, all flowing in channels eroded for them out of the solid flank of the range by the vanished glaciers,—the streams tracing the ancient glaciers, the ouzels tracing the streams. Nor do we find so complete compliance to glacial conditions in the life of any other mountain bird, or animal of any kind. Bears frequently accept the pathways laid down by glaciers as the easiest to travel; but they often leave them and cross over from cañon to cañon. So also, most of the birds trace the moraines to some extent, because the forests are growing on them. But they wander far, crossing the cañons from grove to grove, and draw exceedingly angular and complicated courses.

The Ouzel's nest is one of the most extraordinary pieces of bird architecture I ever saw, odd and novel in design, perfectly fresh and beautiful, and in every way worthy of the genius of the little builder. It is about a foot in diameter, round and bossy in outline, with a neatly arched opening near the bottom, somewhat like an old-fashioned brick oven, or Hottentot's hut. It is built almost exclusively of green and yellow mosses, chiefly the beautiful fronded hypnum that covers the rocks and old drift-logs in the vicinity of waterfalls. These are deftly interwoven, and felted together into a charming little hut; and so situated that many of the outer mosses continue to flourish as if they had not been plucked. A few fine, silky-stemmed grasses are occasionally found interwoven with the mosses, but, with the exception of a thin layer lining the floor, their presence seems accidental, as they are of a species found growing with the mosses and are probably plucked with them. The site chosen for this curious mansion is usually some little rock-shelf within reach of the lighter particles of the spray of a waterfall, so that its walls are kept green and growing, at least during the time of high water.

No harsh lines are presented by any portion of the nest as seen in place, but when removed from its shelf, the back and bottom, and sometimes a portion of the top, is found quite sharply angular, because it is made to conform to the surface of the rock upon which and against which it is built, the little architect always taking advantage of slight crevices and protuberances that may chance to offer, to render his structure stable by means of a kind of gripping and dovetailing.

In choosing a building-spot, concealment does not seem to be taken into consideration; yet notwithstanding the nest is large and guilelessly exposed to view, it is far from being easily detected, chiefly because it swells forward like any other bulging moss-cushion growing naturally in such situations. This is more especially the case where the nest is kept fresh by being well sprinkled. Sometimes these romantic little huts have their beauty enhanced by rock-ferns and grasses that spring up around the mossy walls, or in front of the door-sill, dripping with crystal beads.

Furthermore, at certain hours of the day, when the sunshine is poured down at the required angle, the whole mass of the spray enveloping the fairy establishment is brilliantly irised; and it is through so glorious a rainbow atmosphere as this that some of our blessed ouzels obtain their first peep at the world.

Ouzels seem so completely part and parcel of the streams they inhabit, they scarce suggest any other origin than the streams themselves; and one might almost be pardoned in fancying they come direct from the living waters, like flowers from the ground. At least, from whatever cause, it never occurred to me to look for their nests until more than a year after I had made the acquaintance of the birds themselves, although I found one the very day on which I began the search. In making my way from Yosemite to the glaciers at the heads of the Merced and Tuolumne rivers, I camped in a particularly wild and romantic portion of the Nevada cañon where in previous excursions I had never failed to enjoy the company of my favorites, who were attracted here, no doubt, by the safe nesting-places in the shelving rocks, and by the abundance of food and falling water. The river, for miles above and below, consists of a succession of small falls from ten to sixty feet in height, connected by flat, plume-like cascades that go flashing from fall to fall, free and almost channelless, over waving folds of glacier-polished granite.

On the south side of one of the falls, that portion of the precipice which is bathed by the spray presents a series of little shelves and tablets caused by the development of planes of cleavage in the granite, and by the consequent fall of masses through the action of the water. "Now here," said I, "of all places, is the most charming spot for an Ouzel's nest." Then carefully scanning the fretted face of the precipice through the spray, I at length noticed a yellowish moss-cushion, growing on the edge of a level tablet within five or six feet of the outer folds of the fall. But apart from the fact of its being situated where one acquainted with the lives of ouzels would fancy an Ouzel's nest ought to be, there was nothing in its appearance, visible at first sight, to distinguish it from other bosses of rock-moss similarly situated with reference to perennial spray; and it was not until I had scrutinized it again and again, and had removed my shoes and stockings and crept along the face of the rock within eight or ten feet of it, that I could decide certainly whether it was a nest or a natural growth.

In these moss huts three or four eggs are laid, white like foam-bubbles; and well may the little birds hatched from them sing water songs, for they hear them all their lives, and even before they are born.

I have often observed the young just out of the nest making their odd gestures, and seeming in every way as much at home as their experienced parents, like young bees on their first excursions to the flower fields. No amount of familiarity with people and their ways seems to change them in the least. To all appearance their behavior is just the same on seeing a man for the first time, as when they have seen him frequently.

On the lower reaches of the rivers where mills are built, they sing on through the din of the machinery, and all the noisy confusion of dogs, cattle, and work-men. On one occasion, while a wood-chopper was at work on the river-bank, I observed one cheerily singing within reach of the flying chips. Nor does any kind of unwonted disturbance put him in bad humor, or frighten him out of calm self-possession. In passing through a narrow gorge, I once drove one ahead of me from rapid to rapid, disturbing him four times in quick succession where he could not very well fly past me on account of the narrowness of the channel. Most birds under similar circumstances fancy themselves pursued, and become suspiciously uneasy; but, instead of growing nervous about it, he made his usual dippings, and sang one of his most tranquil strains. When observed within a few yards their eyes are seen to express remarkable gentleness and intelligence; but they seldom allow so near a view unless one wears clothing of about the same color as the rocks and trees, and knows how to sit still. On one occasion, while rambling along the shore of a mountain lake, where the birds, at least those born that season, had never seen a man, I sat down to rest on a large stone close to the water's edge, upon which it seemed the ouzels and sandpipers were in the habit of alighting when they came to feed on that part of the shore, and some of the other birds also, when they came down to wash or drink. In a few minutes, along came a whirring Ouzel and alighted on the stone beside me, within reach of my hand. Then suddenly observing me, he stooped nervously as if about to fly on the instant, but as I remained as motionless as the stone, he gained confidence, and looked me steadily in the face for about a minute, then flew quietly to the outlet and began to sing. Next came a sandpiper and gazed at me with much the same guileless expression of eye as the Ouzel. Lastly, down with a swoop came a Steller's jay out of a fir-tree, probably with the intention of moistening his noisy throat. But instead of sitting confidingly as my other visitors had done, he rushed off at once, nearly tumbling heels over head into the lake in his suspicious confusion, and with loud screams roused the neighborhood.

Love for song-birds, with their sweet human voices, appears to be more common and unfailing than love for flowers. Every one loves flowers to some extent, at least in life's fresh morning, attracted by them as instinctively as humming-birds and bees. Even the young Digger Indians have sufficient love for the brightest of those found growing on the mountains to gather them and braid them as decorations for the hair. And I was glad to discover, through the few Indians that could be induced to talk on the subject, that they have names for the wild rose and the lily, and other conspicuous flowers, whether available as food or otherwise. Most men, however, whether savage or civilized, become apathetic toward all plants that have no other apparent use than the use of beauty. But fortunately one's first instinctive love of song-birds is never wholly obliterated, no matter what the influences upon our lives may be. I have often been delighted to see a pure, spiritual glow come into the countenances of hard businessmen and old miners, when a song-bird chanced to alight near them. Nevertheless, the little mouthful of meat that swells out the breasts of some song-birds is too often the cause of their death. Larks and robins in particular are brought to market in hundreds. But fortunately the Ouzel has no enemy so eager to eat his little body as to follow him into the mountain solitudes. I never knew him to be chased even by hawks.

An acquaintance of mine, a sort of foot-hill mountaineer, had a pet cat, a great, dozy, over-grown creature, about as broad-shouldered as a lynx. During the winter, while the snow lay deep, the mountaineer sat in his lonely cabin among the pines smoking his pipe and wearing the dull time away. Tom was his sole companion, sharing his bed, and sitting beside him on a stool with much the same drowsy expression of eye as his master. The good-natured bachelor was content with his hard fare of soda-bread and bacon, but Tom, the only creature in the world acknowledging dependence on him, must needs be provided with fresh meat. Accordingly he bestirred himself to contrive squirrel-traps, and waded the snowy woods with his gun, making sad havoc among the few winter birds, sparing neither robin, sparrow, nor tiny nut-hatch, and the pleasure of seeing Tom eat and grow fat was his great reward.

One cold afternoon, while hunting along the river-bank, he noticed a plain-feathered little bird skipping about in the shallows, and immediately raised his gun. But just then the confiding songster began to sing, and after listening to his summery melody the charmed hunter turned away, saying, "Bless your little heart, I can't shoot you, not even for Tom."

Even so far north as icy Alaska, I have found my glad singer. When I was exploring the glaciers between Mount Fairweather and the Stikeen River, one cold day in November, after trying in vain to force a way through the innumerable icebergs of Sum Dum Bay to the great glaciers at the head of it, I was weary and baffled and sat resting in my canoe convinced at last that I would have to leave this part of my work for another year. Then I began to plan my escape to open water before the young ice which was beginning to form should shut me in. While I thus lingered drifting with the bergs, in the midst of these gloomy forebodings and all the terrible glacial desolation and grandeur, I suddenly heard the well-known whir of an Ouzel's wings, and, looking up, saw my little comforter coming straight across the ice from the shore. In a second or two he was with me, flying three times round my head with a happy salute, as if saying, "Cheer up, old friend; you see I'm here, and all's well." Then he flew back to the shore, alighted on the topmost jag of a stranded iceberg, and began to nod and bow as though he were on one of his favorite boulders in the midst of a sunny Sierra cascade.

The species is distributed all along the mountain-ranges of the Pacific coast from Alaska to Mexico, and east to the Rocky Mountains. Nevertheless, it is as yet comparatively little known. Audubon and Wilson did not meet it. Swainson was, I believe, the first naturalist to describe a specimen from Mexico. Specimens were shortly afterward procured by Drummond near the sources of the Athabasca River, between the fifty-fourth and fifty-sixth parallels; and it has been collected by nearly all of the numerous exploring expeditions undertaken of late through our Western States and Territories; for it never fails to engage the attention of naturalists in a very particular manner.

Such, then, is our little cinclus, beloved of every one who is so fortunate as to know him. Tracing on strong wing every curve of the most precipitous torrents from one extremity of the Sierra to the other; not fearing to follow them through their darkest gorges and coldest snow-tunnels; acquainted with every waterfall, echoing their divine music; and throughout the whole of their beautiful lives interpreting all that we in our unbelief call terrible in the utterances of torrents and storms, as only varied expressions of God's eternal love.

~ DOG ~

Canis familiaris

Family Canidae

Height: to 3'; Weight: to 190 lb

Habitat:

Wherever human beings are established, and occasionally found wild in a wide variety of habitats

Range:

Common throughout California

Comments:

Domestic dogs are ultimately descended from gray wolves, perhaps from wolves that were originally attracted to edible discards from aboriginal human villages. Over centuries the descendants of these canines have been selectively bred for desirable characteristics, and there are now more than three hundred different breeds of dogs, all of which are recognized as a single species.

Domestic dogs share many of the same traits as their wolf ancestors. They are highly social, are possessed of powerful hunting instincts, and they may be highly territorial. But unlike wolves, dogs have benefited from a tolerance for human beings—if not an outright predilection for tameness—that has created a foundation for the complex relationship between dogs and humans.

Dogs have been bred to be valuable work animals, beloved companions, and even admired ornaments. One consequence of dog breeding has been that these animals present an astonishing variety of physical characteristics: long and short fur; light, dark, or piebald coats; stocky and slim bodies; and wide and narrow heads, among other variants. Unfortunately, some breeds have developed tendencies to inherit a variety of ailments, tendencies that may be reinforced by narrow breeding programs.

Mary Austin
"The Go-Betweens"

What one wishes to know is just what the dog means to the flock. It might be something of what the dark means to man, the mould of fear, the racial memory of the shape in which Terror first beset them. It is as easy to see what the flock means to the dog as to understand what it meant before man went about this business of perverting the Original Intention. If it is a trick man has played upon the dog to constitute him the guardian of his natural prey, he has also been played upon, for even as men proved their God on the persons of the brethren and exterminated tribes to show how great He was, latterly they afflict themselves to offer up the heathen scathless and comforted.

Now that in the room of the Primal Impulse, the herder is the god of the sheep dog, the flock is become an oblation. The ministrant waits with pricked ears and an expectant eye the motion of his deity; he invites orders by eagerness; he worries the sheep by the zealousness of care; that not one may escape he threads every wandering scent and trails it back to the flock. In short, when in the best temper for his work he frequently becomes useless from excess of use. But in the half a hundred centuries that have gone to perverting his native instincts, the sheep have hardly come so far. They no longer flee the herd dog, but neither do they run to him. When he rounds them they turn; when he speaks they tremble; when he snaps they leave off feeding; but when they hear his cousin-german, the coyote, padding about them in the dark, they trust only to fleeing. For this is the apotheosis of the dog, that he fights his own kind for the flock, but the flock does not know it.

It is notable that the best sheep dogs are most like wolves in habit, the erect triangular ears, the long thin muzzle, the sag of the bushy tail, the thick mane-like hackles; as if it were on the particular aptness for knowing the ways of flocking beasts developed by successful wolves that the effective collie is moulded. No particular breed of dogs is favored by the herders hereabout, though Scotch strains predominate. Among the Frenchmen a small short-tailed, black-and-white type is seen oftenest, a pinto with white about the eyes. One may pay as much as five dollars or five hundred for a six months' pup, but mostly the herders breed their own stock and exchange among themselves. Ordinarily the dog goes with the flock, is the property of the owner, for sheep learn to know their own guardian and suffer an accession of timidity if a stranger is set over them.

The herder who brings up a dog by hand loves it surpassingly. There was one of my acquaintance had so great an attachment for a bitch called Jehane that he worked long for a hard master and yearly tendered him the full of his wage if only he might have Jehane and depart with her to a better employment. He was not single in his belief that Jehane regarded him with a like affection, for the faith a herder grows to have in the dog's understanding is only exceeded by the miracle of communication.

To see three or four shepherds met in a district of good pastures, leaning on their staves, each with a dog at his knees quick and attentive to the talk, is to go a long way toward conviction.

Many years ago, but not so long that he can recall it without sorrow, Giraud lost a dog on Kern River. There had come one of the sudden storms of that district, white blasts of hail and a nipping wind; it was important to get the sheep speedily to lower ground. The dog was ailing and fell behind somewhere in the white swarm of the snow. When it lay soft and quiet over all that region and the flock was bedded far below it in the cañon, Giraud returned to the upper river, seeking and calling; twenty days he quested bootless about the meadows and among the cold camps. More he could not have done for a brother, for Pierre Giraud was not then the owner of good acres and well-fleeced Merinos that he is now, and twenty days of a shepherd's time is more than the price of a dog. "And still," Pierre finishes his story simply, "whenever I go by that country of Kern River I think of my dog."

Curiously, the obligation of his work—who shall say it is not that higher form of habit out of which the sense of duty shapes itself?—is always stronger in the dog than the love of the herder. Lacking a direct command, in any severance of their interests, the collie stays by the sheep. In that same country of young roaring rivers a shepherd died suddenly in his camp and was not found for two days. The flock was gone on from the meadow where he lay, straying toward high places as shepherdless sheep will, and the dogs with them. They had returned to lick the dead face of the herder, no doubt they had mourned above him in their fashion in the dusk of pines, but though they could win no authority from him they stayed by the flock. So they did when the two herdsmen of Barret's were frozen on their feet while still faithfully rounding the sheep; they dropped stilly in their places and were overblown by the snow. The dogs had scraped the drifts from their bodies, and the sheep had trampled mindlessly on the straightened forms, but at the end of the third day when succor found them, the dogs had come a flock-journey from that place and had turned the sheep toward home. This is as long as can be proved that the sense of responsibility to the flock stays with the dog when he feels himself abandoned by his over-lord.

A dog might remain indefinitely with the sheep because he has the habit of association, but the service of herding is rendered only at the bidding of the gods. The superintendent of Tejon told me of a dog that could be trusted to take a bunch of muttons that had been cut out for use at the ranch house, and from any point on the range, drive them a whole day's journey at his order, and bring them safely to the home corral. Señor Lopez, I think, related of another that it was sent out to hunt estrays, and not returning, was hunted for and found warding a ewe and twin lambs, licking his wounds and sniffing, not without the appearance of satisfaction, at a newly killed coyote. The dog must have found the ewe in travail, for the lambs were but a few hours old, and been made aware of it by what absolute and elemental means who shall say, and stood guarding the event through the night.

At Los Alisos there was a bitch of such excellent temper that she was thought of more value for raising pups than herding; she was, therefore, when her litter came, taken from the flock and given quarters at the ranch house. But in the morning Flora went out to the sheep. She sought them in the pastures where they had been, and kept the accustomed round, returning wearied to her young at noon; she followed after them at evening and covered with panting sides the distance they had put between them and her litter. At the end of the second day when she came to her bed, half dead with running, she was tied, but gnawed the rope, and in twenty-four hours was out on the cold trail of the flock. One of the vaqueros found her twenty miles from home, working faint and frenzied over its vanishing scent. It was only after this fruitless sally that she was reconciled to her new estate.

Now consider that we have very many high and brave phrases for such performances when they pertain to two-footed beings who grow hair on their heads only, and are disallowed the use of them for the four-foots that have hair all over them. Duty, chivalry, sacrifice, these are words sacred to the man things. But how shall one loving definiteness consign to the loose limbo of instinct all the qualities engendered in the intelligence of the dog by the mind of man? For it is incontrovertible that a good sheep dog is made.

The propensity to herd is fixed in the breed. Some unaccountably in any litter will have missed the possibility of being good at it, and a collie that is not good for a herd dog is good for nothing. The only thing to do with the born incompetent is to shoot it or give it to the children; in the bringing up of a family almost any dog is better than no dog at all. What good breeding means in a young collie is not that he is fit to herd sheep, but that he is fit to be trained to it. Aptitude he may be born with, but can in no wise dispense with the hand of the herder over him. What we need is a new vocabulary for the larger estate which a dog takes on when he is tamed by a man.

Training here is not carried to so fine a pitch as abroad, most owners not desiring too dependable a dog. The herder is the more likely to leave the flock too much to his care, and whatever a sheep dog may learn, it is never to discriminate in the matter of pasture. An excellent collie makes an indolent herder.

Every man who follows after sheep will tell you how he thinks he trains his pups, and of all the means variously expounded there are two that are constant. It is important that the dog acquire early the habit of association, and to this purpose herders will often carry a pup in the cayaca and suckle it to a goat. Most important is it that he shall learn to return of his own motion to the master for deserved chastisement. To accomplish this the dog is tied with sufficient ropeway and punished until he discovers that the ease of his distress is to come straightly to the hand that afflicts him. He is to be tied long to allow him room for volition and tied securely that he may not once get clean away from the trainer's hand. Once a dog, through fear or the sense of anger incurred, escapes his master for a space of hours, there is not much to be done by way of retrievement. It is as if the impalpable bridge between his mind and the mind of man, being broken by the act, is never to be built again. For this in fine is what constitutes a good herd dog, to be wholly open to the suggestion of the man-mind, and carry its will to the flock. His is the service of the Go-Between. Not that he knows or cares what becomes of the flock, but merely what the herder intends toward it.

I have said the shepherd will tell you how he thinks he trains his collies, for watching them I grow certain that more goes forward than the herder is rightly aware. Working communication between them is largely by signs, since the dog manœuvres at the distance of a flock-length, taking orders from the herder's arm. Every movement of the flock can be so effected, but if the herder would have barking, he must say to him, Speak, and he speaks. The teaching methods seem not to be contrived by any rule, as if every man fumbling at the dog's understanding had hit upon a device which seemed to accomplish his end, and might or might not serve the next adventure. You would not suppose in any other case that by waving arms, buffets, pettings, and retrievings, and by no other means, so much could be communicable in violation to racial instincts, with no root in experience and only a possible one in the generational memory; nor do I for one suppose it. Moreover it sticks in my mind that I have never seen one herd dog instruct another even by the implication of behaving in such a manner as to invite imitation.

Bobcats I have seen teaching their kittens to seek prey, young eagles coached at flying, coyote cubs remanded to the trail with a snarl when wishful to leave it; but never the sheep dog teaching her young to round and guard. In this all the shepherds of the Long Trail bear me out. Assuredly the least intelligent dog learns something by imitation; to be convinced of it one has only to note the assumed postures, the look as of a very deaf person who wishes to have you believe that he has heard, the self-gratulation when some tentative motion proves acceptable, the tolerable assumption when it fails that the sally has been undertaken merely by way of entertainment. But with it all no intention of being imitated.

Since all these things are so, how then can a shepherd say to the Go-Between what the dog cannot say to another dog? It is not altogether that they lack speech, for, as I say, the work of herding goes on by signs, and I have come to an excellent understanding with some collies that know only Basque and a patois that is not the French of the books. Fellowship is helped by conversation, though it is not indispensable, and if the herder has an arm to wave has not the dog a tail to wag? If he reads the face of his master, and who that has been loved by a dog but believes him amenable to a smile or a frown, may he not so learn the countenance of his blood brother? Notwithstanding, the desire of the shepherd which the dog bears to the sheep remains with respect to other dogs, like the personal revelation of a deity, locked, incommunicable. He arises to the man virtues so long as the man's command, or the echo of it, lies in his consciousness. But we, when we have arrived at the pitch of conserving what was once our study to destroy, conceive that we have done it of ourselves.

———〜———

What a herd dog has first to learn is to know every one of two to three hundred sheep, and to know them both by sight and smell. This he does thoroughly. When Watterson was running sheep on the plains he had a young collie not yet put to the herd but kept about the pumping plant. As the sheep came in by hundreds to the troughs, the dog grew so to know them that when they had picked up an estray from another band he discovered it from afar off, and darting as a hornet, nipping and yelping, parted it out from the band. At that time no mere man would have pretended without the aid of the brand to recognize any of the thousands that bore it.

How long recollection stays by the dog is not certain, but at least a twelvemonth, as was proved to Filon Gerard after he had lost a third of his band when the Santa Ana came roaring up by Lone Pine with a cloud of saffron-colored dust on its wings. After shearing of next year, passing close to another band, Filon's dogs set themselves unbidden to routing out of it, and rounding with their own, nearly twenty head which the herder, being an honest man, freely admitted he had picked up on the mesa following after Filon the spring before.

Quick to know the willful and unbidable members of a flock, the wise collie is not sparing of bites, and following after a stubborn estray will often throw it, and stand guard until help arrives, or the sheep shows a better mind. But the herder who has a dog trained at the difficult work of herding range sheep through the chutes and runways into boats and cars for transportation is the fortunate fellow.

There was Pete's dog, Bourdaloue, that, at the Stockton landing, with no assistance, put eight hundred wild sheep from the highlands on the boat in eight minutes, by running along the backs of the flock until he had picked out the stubborn or stupid leaders that caused the sheep to jam in the runway, and by sharp bites set them forward, himself treading the backs of the racing flock, like the premier equestrienne of the circus, which all the men of the shipping cheered to see.

In shaping his work to the land he moves in, an old wolf-habit of the sheep dog comes into play. From knowing how to leap up in mid-run to keep sight of small quarry, the collie has learned to mount on stumps and boulders to observe the flock. So he does in the sage and chamisal, and of greater necessity years ago in the coast ranges where the mustard engulfed the flock until their whereabouts could be known only by the swaying of its bloom. Julien, the good shepherd of Lone Pine, had a little dog, much loved, that would come and bark to be taken up on his master's shoulder that he might better judge how his work lay. The propensity of sheep to fall over one another into a pit whenever occasion offers is as well noted by the dog as the owner; so that there was once a collie of Hittell's of such flock-wisdom that at a point in a certain drive where an accident had occurred by the sheep being gulched, he never failed afterward to go forward and guard the bank until the flock had gone by.

Footsoreness is the worst evil of the Long Trail; cactus thorn, foxtail, and sharp, hot granite sands induce so great distress that to remedy it the shepherd makes moccasins of deerskin for his dogs. Once having experience of these comforts the collie returns to the herder's knee and lifts up his paws as a gentle invitation to have them on when the trail begins to wear. On his long drive Sanger had slung a rawhide under the wagon to carry brushwood for the fire, but the dogs soon discovered in it a material easement of their fatigues, and would lie in it while the team went forward, each collie rousting out his confrère and insisting on his turn.

When one falls in with a sheep camp it is always well to inquire concerning the dogs; the herder who will not talk of anything else will talk of these. You bend back the springy sage to sit upon, the shepherd sits on a brown boulder with his staff between his knees, the dogs at his feet, ears pointed with attention. He unfolds his cigarette papers and fumbles for the sack.

"Eh, my tobacco? I have left it at the camp; go, Pinto, and fetch it."

Away races the collie, pleased as a patted schoolboy, and comes back with the tobacco between his jaws.

"I must tell you a story of that misbegotten devil of a he goat, Noé," says the shepherd, rolling a cigarette; "you, go and fetch Noé that Madame-who-writes-the-book may see."

In a jiffy the dog has nipped Noé by the ankles and cut him out of the band, but you will have to ask again before you get your story, for it is not Noé the shepherd has in mind. In reality he is bursting with pride of his dog, and thinks only to exhibit him.

It is the expansiveness of affection that elevates the customary performance to an achievement. As for the other man's dog, why should it not do well? unless his master being a dull fellow has spent his pains to no end. But in the Pinto there with the listening ears and muzzle delicately pointed and inquiring, with the eye confident and restrained as expressing the suspension of communication rather than its incompleteness, you perceive at once a tangible and exceptionable distinction.

Floyd Salas
"To Sergie My Sweet Old Dog Who Died in Old Age"

This is the reality now Sergie
this mound of earth
under the camellia bush
with a bouquet of orange poppies
alive at its foot
the shade that sprinkles it
even in the sunshine
There will always be sprinkles on this gravesite
summer or winter
raining or shining
I sprinkle it now with my tears

One of the poppies is dying though
the brown bud of a withered face
smiles out
through the bent strands
of its petals

peeking up through the bent brim
of an old straw hat
though his blooms all gone
like you did
these last two years

I suck in air to ease the cramp in my gut
Miki my Japanese puppy
nibbles some grass on your grave
A bird trill thrills me
from the big bush over your head
The sun warms me
the long branches of a thin plum tree
burst into beads of green buds
and rows of buttons of white flowers
Poppies
spin like a fleet of flying suns
over the green clover
in the speckled shade
of a knobby pear tree

This is the reality
Sergie

You down in the deep damp hole
the rain seeping into your ears
trickling through the fears
a slow movement
of flesh and bone
back to silt
back to the mud of my backyard
back to these earth clods
spongy with a whole night's rain
This is my pain

This is the reality
Sergie
dogchain
hanging from the doorknob
red cross of its rabies tab
and green heart
of its license

a breeze on me
shadow of leaves
flickering on my page
no you around
on top the ground

No Sergie
to sniff noses with
no sweet
and earthy canine smell

The reality is
there is
no trace of you
here
aside from this small mound of dirt
in the yard
and the warm coral
of my brain
the pain
in my chest

This is the reality
Sergie

~ DOLPHIN ~

Tursiops truncates

Family Delphinidae

Length: 6 ¼'–13'; Weight: to 1,100 lb

Habitat:

  Shallow inshore waters, lower areas of rivers, ocean

Range:

  Common off the coast of California, especially southern California and the
  Channel Islands

Comments:

  The bottlenose dolphin, named after its short and broad beak, has a basic color
  combination of bluish gray above, paler gray on the sides, whitish gray on the throat and
  belly, and almost-black flippers. It has a bump on its forehead and a swept-back, pointed
  dorsal fin. It is the largest beaked dolphin and is found worldwide.

  The bottlenose dolphin travels in small groups—usually no more than twenty—and is
  noted for its curiosity and friendliness. Its diet varies depending on what food is available.
  Sometimes these dolphins cooperate to catch and eat large schools of fish, and other times
  they chase individual fish. They also feed behind fishing boats.

  Bottlenose dolphins are very intelligent and are the "performing" species at marine life
  centers. They will also often interact with humans in the wild and will ride ships' bow
  waves.

Georgiana Valoyce-Sanchez
"The Dolphin Walking Stick"

He says
sure you look for your Spirit
symbol   your totem
only it's more a waiting
watching
for its coming

You listen
You listen for the way it
feels.   deep inside

Sometimes something comes
that feels   almost
right
the way that swordfish
kept cropping up with
its long nose

but no
and so   you wait
knowing it is getting
closer   knowing
it is coming

And when that dolphin
jumped out of the water
its silver blue sides all shiny
and glistening with rainbows
against the white cloud sky
and the ocean so big
and deep
it went on
forever
I knew it had come

My father rests his hand upon
the dolphin's back
the dolphin's gaze serene
above the rainbow band
wrapped around the walking stick

He leans upon his brother friend
and walks across the room

          As he walks
strings of seashells clack softly
like when ocean waves tumble
rocks and shells and
the gentle clacking song
follows each wave

as it pulls back into
the sea

The sea

So long ago
The Channel Islands filled
with Chumash people like
colonies of sea lions
along the shore so many
people
it was time for some to
make the move
across the ocean to
the mainland

Kakunupmawa the sun
the Great Mystery
according to men's ideas
said
       don't worry
I will make you a bridge
the rainbow
will be your bridge only
don't look down
or you will fall
Have Faith

So then the chosen ones began
the long walk across
the rainbow
they kept their eye straight
toward where the mainland was
and all around them
was the ocean sparkling
like a million scattered crystals
so blue-green and singing
lovely and cool

some looked down
and fell
into the deep
to become
the dolphins
they too
the People

My father turns to look at me

Someone told me that story
long before I ever heard it
It's those old ones
he says pointing up to the ceiling
as if it were sky

They sent the dolphin to me

I always loved the sea

95

MOURNING DOVE

Zenaida macroura

Family Columbidae

Length: 11–13"

Habitat:

> Woodlands, farms, and meadows, and suburban and urban areas; prefers to nest in trees but may build ground nests

Range:

> Common throughout California; leaves high mountains and deserts during winter

Comments:

> The mourning dove's back, wings, and tail are dull brown, and it has black spots on its upper wings and a single black spot beneath or below its eyes. The mourning dove's small head and underparts are pale buff or light pink, its legs are short and red, and its long tail has distinctive black and white edges. The mourning dove's wings produce a whistling sound when it takes flight.

> The mourning dove may be the most common wild dove in California. It feeds on a wide variety of seeds but may also ingest small insects.

> Its call is an unforgettable, melancholy-sounding "ooh Whoo woo woo."

Ambrose Bierce
"To the Happy Hunting Grounds"

Wide windy reaches of high stubble field;
A long gray road, bordered with dusty pines;
A wagon moving in a "cloud by day";
Two city sportsmen with a dove between,
Breast-high upon a fence and fast asleep—
A solitary dove, the only dove
In twenty counties, and it sick, or else
It were not there. Two guns that fire as one,
With thunder simultaneous and loud;
Two shattered human wrecks of blood and bone!
And later, in the gloaming, comes a man—
The worthy local coroner is he,
Renowned all thereabout, and popular
With many a remain. All tenderly
Compiling in a game-bag the remains,
He glides into the gloom and fades from sight.
The dove, cured of its ailment by the shock,
Has flown, meantime, on pinions strong and fleet,
To die of age in some far foreign land.

MALLARD DUCK

Anas platyrhynchos

Family Anatidae

Length: 1 ½–2 ¼'; Wingspan: 2 ½–3 ¼'

Habitat:

Ponds, rivers, marshes, mudflats, other open-water areas, including those located in urban settings

Range:

Throughout California west and south of the Sierra Nevada to 10,000'

Comments:

The male mallard, or drake, may be the most easily recognized duck in California. He has a gray body with a bright green head and neck, a purplish chest, a white ring separating his chest and neck, and a yellow bill. The female is buff heavily mottled with brown, with an orange bill marked with black.

Mallards are dabblers, that is, they can take flight directly from the water without running on its surface. They consume algae, snails, and worms, and even scavenge bits of floating food left behind by humans. Although mallards are migratory, they often stay through winter to form resident populations where food and shelter are available. The mallard is one of the most common ducks in California and is also the ancestor of most domestic ducks.

The male may give a "reeb" call when fighting; the female sounds the recognizable "quack."

Jim Dodge
from *Fup*

It was apparent in her first few weeks of recovery that Fup was an unusual duck. She refused to eat or shit in the house. She would wobble to the door, peeping frantically, and pound on it with her bill like a deformed woodpecker until one of them let her out.

Her appetite was omnivorous and immense. Pancakes, cheese, cracked corn, deer meat, onion peels, whatever: it got devoured. And as she ate, she grew. In four months she weighed nearly twenty pounds. Granddaddy Jake, partial to excess in any form, was so impressed he invited neighbors over to watch.

"Goddamn," Willis Hornsby muttered as Fup gobbled a pound of link sausage and started on a coffee can of cracked barley.

"Nothing the matter with her eater, is there?" Granddaddy gleamed. "Goes after it like a feathered vacuum cleaner."

Willis shook his head: "I never saw nothing like it."

"Makes me think we should've named her Electrolux," Jake opined. "Or hell, even better, Dolly P."

"Dolly P.?" Willis asked. "Sounds like a fishing boat."

"Naw, Dolly Pringle. Big redhead I run around with up in Coos Bay. A woman of amazing talents. She could suck a golfball through twenty-five yards of garden hose. Seen her siphon gas uphill. Why, you might not believe it, but I won a $1,000 bet with Big Dave Stevens one night when we took ol' Dolly out in the parking lot and she sucked the chrome completely off a trailer hitch in fourteen minutes and thirty-two seconds."

Granddaddy sighed with a forlorn fondness. "Just thinking about that gal makes my ol' pecker twitch."

"Better hope that duck don't see it," Willis mumbled, watching as Fup speared the last few flecks of barley.

It was a judicious warning, for Fup proved as fierce as she was hungry. Early on, when she could still be weighed in ounces, she had ventured out to join Granddaddy for an afternoon of sipping on the porch. Buster, a usually comatose Bluetick hound, bayed her up under the tattered green couch where she'd scurried for refuge. When the dog had finally yielded to Granddaddy pounding on its head and had sprawled back out on the porch to whimper itself back to sleep, Fup, with a single kamikaze PEEEEEP! charged from hiding and clamped her bill like a pair of eternal vise-grip pliers on Buster's sagging scrotum, hanging on fiercely as the hound spun around in howling circles, snapping at the half-pound duckling swinging on his sack. Granddaddy laughed so hard he had to crawl out in the front yard and beat his head on the ground to stop.

Besides her appetite and temper, Fup was distinguished by her walk and her talk.

Her walk was foolishly graceful, a hunched, toppling waddle that barely managed to sustain itself, a wobble continuously and precariously balanced by her outstretched neck, head swaying like a charmed cobra: a movement somewhere between a clumsy sneak and a hypnotic search. She was ungainly, yet effortlessly so; she proceeded at a steady lurch. Mass fueled momentum, but her bright orange webbed feet were not designed for such velocity, and though her progress was sure, it always seemed doubtful, and always bore that melancholy discord between biology and terrain. She showed absolutely no inclination to fly.

Her talk was more straight-forward, if by talk we mean a somatic or sonic response to one's environment. Her vocabulary was small, but rich. One quack indicated agreement. Two meant rapport. Three signified heartfelt approval. Four or more—uttered in a sharp, excited series: QUACK-WHAK-WHAK-WHAK-WHAK-WHAK—was total and joyous accord. If she opened her bill without making a sound, a gesture somewhere between a bored yawn and an attempt to retch, it signified sharp disagreement; if it was accompanied by a low hissing sound with her head lowered and wings slightly spread, it indicated profound disagreement and imminent attack. If she tucked her head under her wing, you, the proposition, and the rest of the dreary world were dismissed.

From the first few weeks she was with them, Fup displayed a strict passion for balance and order in the daily life of the household. She slept on a large foam cushion in the hallway, equidistant between Tiny's room and Granddaddy Jake's. She woke Tiny precisely an hour before sunrise by hopping up and down on his chest. She ate her pail of pre-breakfast corn while Tiny cooked the sausage, eggs, and sourdough pancakes for breakfast, which they split half and half, Fup eating outside on the porch, Tiny joining her on clement mornings. After breakfast, just at daybreak, they would set out for the day's work on the fences. Fup would watch Tiny work, adding a quacked comment here or there. Sometimes she helped, checking the plumb of a post with a cocked eye, plucking at a strand of wire to test its tautness, or occasionally holding the end of a tape, but just as often she would poke around, spear an errant insect, or rest. When Tiny dug postholes, she tucked her head under her wing.

Exactly between sunrise and mid-day they would take a half-hour break for the sandwiches and iced tea Tiny had prepared the night before. After the break, they resumed work till mid-day, then returned to the house for lunch. Tiny started the meal while Fup woke Granddaddy Jake by nibbling at his toes. After lunch Tiny returned to his fence work while Granddaddy and Fup repaired to the porch to sip a little Death Whisper, be still, and generally consider the drift of things. Fup drank from a shallow saucer; Jake straight from the jar. It pleased Granddaddy deeply that both Tiny and Fup enjoyed his whiskey. Tiny, he knew, used it to help his insomnia and to ease his dreams. He was convinced in Fup's case that the emergency dropper of Ol' Death Whisper had saved her life, and was sure she continued to use it in celebration of its life-giving powers. She drank about three tablespoons a day, and seldom more than five unless it was cold or foggy. Her only apparent reaction to the whiskey was to pound her bill on Granddaddy's shins when she wanted more.

About an hour before dusk Granddaddy Jake would rise and stretch and go in the house to start dinner while Fup waddled down to her pond and floated gracefully through the sun's setting, sometimes silently, sometimes quacking softly to herself. They had built her a pond in the first month of her recovery. It was on the same scale as Tiny's sandbox. According to Pee Wee Scranton, who'd done the excavation, the pond was more properly a small lake, or at least large enough to water most of the livestock between Santa Cruz and Petaluma.

For awhile, after dinner Tiny and Granddaddy Jake had tried to teach Fup to play checkers, but after a few months they gave up. It wasn't that she didn't comprehend the nature of the game—even, perhaps, its nuances—she just did not like it when they tried to remove one of her checkers from the board. She *did* like it when she jumped one of theirs and got to pick it up with her bill and drop it on the floor, but when one of hers was jumped she would jump too—up and down on the board with her webbed feet wildly stomping, scattering the pieces so that it was necessary to declare the game a draw and start over. Collectively, they eventually gave up.

The only exceptions to daily routine were part of a larger accord. The two primary deviations were the Friday Night Drive-In Movies and the Sunday Morning Pig Hunt.

They all enjoyed going out to the movies. The closest theater (to give it a dignity description could not bear) was the Rancho Deluxe Drive-In near Graton, some forty miles and two hours away. Fup rode in the cab, on top of the seat between them, Tiny driving, Granddaddy Jake riding shotgun.

The first time they'd taken Fup, the plump redhead in the ticket stall had squinted into the cab of the pick-up, smacked her Juicy Fruit, and asked, "What's that?"

"A duck—a female mallard," Tiny said. "And my Granddaddy."

"That's the biggest damn duck I've ever seen."

"Yes ma'am…and we wouldn't mind paying extra for her even though the sign out there says $2 a carload."

Fup lowered her head and made a hissing/retching sound.

"No, there's no extra charge—she's part of the load. Go on in. I'll talk to the manager, and if there's any problem with codes or like that, he'll come talk to you."

Grandaddy leaned across the seat. "If there's any problem, there's two problems. You savvy?"

She sighed and smacked her gum. "I kinda figured that."

The manager, a short, dour man in a Robert Hall suit, sporting a pencil moustache that just nudged being mousy, saw Tiny looming in the driver's seat and made the mistake of choosing Grandaddy's side of the truck instead.

When Granddaddy cranked down the window, the manager peered in, confirmed Fup's presence with a glance, and demanded, "What's this duck doing in my establishment?"

"She wants to watch the movie," Tiny said amiably, cutting off his Granddaddy who was already starting to froth.

"We don't want anything unusual," the manager said firmly, if without immediate reference.

Granddaddy erupted, "Well that really narrows the shit out of *your* life, don't it? This happens to be a Kung Fu Attack Duck, specially bred by the Tong Society. We'd leave her home, but she's killing all the coyotes."

"That's not really true, sir," Tiny said quickly. "We found her in a posthole and raised her up. She's kinda family."

"Listen," the manager said, raising his hands in either exasperation or surrender, "we are willing to be reasonable about this but…"

"I'm not," Granddaddy snarled, grinding the two teeth that met. "If you don't go away and leave us alone to enjoy our evening at this shithole excuse of a drive-in, we will come back tomorrow night with the bed of this truck full of wild pigs and a couple of troughs full of fermented corn mash, and if that doesn't sway your intelligence we'll come back the next night and my son Tiny will tear off your arms and pound on your head with them until you get the idea."

"I'd only do that if I was really mad," Tiny assured him.

Fup tucked her head under her wing.

"I won't be threatened," the manager shrilled.

"No, you'll be hurting," Granddaddy promised. Then he added, still sharply but somewhat softer, "A duck. A duck. What possible fucking difference could it make to your stunted heart or the world at large?"

"Alright, alright," the manager relented, backing away. "But keep it in the car. And if there's anything unusual, you're out. And no refund."

There was no trouble with admission after that.

Tiny and Granddaddy Jake were both partial to Westerns, especially those featuring gunslingers against a good-hearted Marshall. Granddaddy, who was usually pretty well into his second jar of the day, pulled hard for the outlaws and other forces of disorder, often leaning out the window to holler advice at the screen—"No, no, you dumb shits. Don't meet him on the streets…bushwhack the sumbitch from behind a watering trough!" He was also highly critical of the gunslinger's choice of weapons, ranting to Tiny and Fup, "Goddamn why do they want to use them pistols all the time? Can't hit jackshit with 'em past ten yards. Situation like that requires a sawed-off .10 gauge and nine or twelve sticks of dynamite. Idiots! No wonder they never win!"

Tiny quietly rooted for the Marshall.

Fup was generally indifferent to Westerns, except for seemingly arbitrary scenes when she would quack excitedly. It took Tiny and Granddaddy Jake about five months to figure out what all the scenes had in common were horses, and after discussing it they decided to buy her a colt for company when Bill Leland's mare foaled the coming spring. Tiny started roughing out drawings for a ten-foot-high split-rail corral when they got home that night.

Fup's favorite movies were romances, whether light and witty or murderously tragic. She watched intently from her roost on the back of the seat, occasionally tilting her head to quack in sympathy at the problems assailing love. She would not tolerate Granddaddy's derisive and consistently obscene comments, and after she'd almost torn off his ear a few times he settled for quiet mumbling. Tiny watched without comment.

Granddaddy Jake liked horror movies almost as much as Westerns. He thought they were hilarious. Tiny and Fup didn't like them at all. Tiny shut his eyes at critical points. Fup paced the back of the seat, occasionally hissing at the monster or quacking frantically to warn an unsuspecting victim, who was usually quite innocently exploring a radioactive cave or wandering around pressing buttons in a laboratory on a lightning-streaked night.

Considering the range of their tastes, it was fortunate that the Rancho Deluxe always had a double feature. Between movies Tiny would walk across the humped asphalt to the concession stand and buy them some snacks. The order was usually the same: two pieces of beef jerky for Granddaddy to work on, eight bags of salted peanuts and two large root beers for himself, and for Fup the $2.99 Family Tub of buttered popcorn and a large orange drink. They munched away as the second movie began.

ELK

Cervus elaphus

Family Cervidae

Length: 6'8"–9'9"; Height: 4'6"–5'; Weight: Males 600–1,089 lb; Females 450–650 lb

Habitat:

In summer, high, open plains and grasslands; in winter, lower slopes, often densely wooded

Range:

Northern California and isolated populations elsewhere in California

Comments:

The elk, or "red deer," is reddish brown in the summer with a dark line along its neck and back; in the winter, the elk turns dull brown. Males have antlers with multiple points. The elk is a highly adaptable animal and has been introduced to most continents, and there are twenty-eight known subspecies. The elk gets its name from the misapplication of the British word "elk," which actually means "moose." This word was used by early settlers for the "wapiti," the Shawnee word for the animal.

The elk is gregarious and travels mainly in cow/calf herds that can number up to four hundred. Female elks, or hinds, form one herd while males form a separate band, except during the fall. During this time, the males rut, or battle; they whistle and bellow, thrash their antlers, walk parallel to each other, and often lock antlers in a joust. They are not often hurt, but sometimes there are serious injuries, some of them fatal.

Elk are mostly grazers and are most active at dusk and at night. They make a variety of sounds, ranging from the squeal of a young elk to the snort or grunt of an adult. The elk has been widely farmed for its meat, hide, antler velvet, and upper teeth (which were popular as watch-fob charms in the nineteenth century). As more and more settlements and farms took over elk habitat, the animal's population dwindled. Today, however, the elk population appears to be stable.

Joaquin Miller
from *Life Amongst the Modocs*

The snow began to fall, and Paquita did not return.

Elk came down from the mountain towards spring, and we could shoot them from the cabin door. At this season of the year, as well as late in the fall, they are found in herds of hundreds together.

It seems odd to say that they should go up further into the mountains as winter approaches, instead of down into the foot-hills and plains below, as do the deer, but it is true. There are warm springs—in fact, all mountain springs are warmer in the winter than in the summer—up the mountain, where vine-maple, a kind of water-cress, and wild swamp berries grow in the warm marshes or on the edges, and here the elk subsist. When the maple and grasses of one marsh are consumed, they break through the snow in single file, led in turns by the bulls, to another.

Hundreds in this way make but one great track, much as if a great log had been drawn to and fro through the snow. The cows come up last, to protect the calves in the line of march from the wolves.

It is a mistake to suppose that elk use their splendid horns in battle. These are only used to receive the enemy upon. A sort of cluster of bayonets in rest. All offensive action is with the feet. An elk's horns are so placed on his head that when his nose is lifted so as to enable him to move about or see his enemy, they are thrown far back on his shoulders, where they are quite useless. He strikes out with his feet, and then throws his head on the ground to receive his enemy. You have much to fear from the feet of an elk at battle, but nothing from his matchless antlers.

✤ HUMAN FLEA ✤

Pulex irritans

Family Pulicidae

Size: 1/16"

Habitat:

 Adults live in dense hair and clothing; larvae can be found under rugs and in lint

Range:

 Common throughout California

Comments:

 The human flea is a small, pale to dark brown, wingless insect that is an external parasite. It has a flattened abdomen covered with spines and bristles. Its small size allows it to slip easily among the hairs of its host. The human flea also has enlarged coxae, or the first segments of its legs, that allow it to jump twelve inches or more. Unfortunately for their hosts, human fleas have tough exoskeletons, making them hard to kill.

 The adult human flea uses mouthparts with three needlelike organs to suck blood from its host. It feeds on the blood of humans, pigs, cats, dogs, and rodents, among others. Human flea larvae eat organic matter.

 The human flea can act as a carrier of diseases, including the bubonic plague.

Edwin Bryant
from *What I Saw in California*

SEPT. 19.—Several Californians came into the mission during the night or early this morning; among them the husband of our hostess, who was very kind and cordial in his greetings.

While our man Jack was saddling and packing the mules, they gathered around us to the number of a dozen or more, and were desirous of trading their horses for articles of clothing; articles which many of them appeared to stand greatly in need of, but which we had not to part from. Their pertinacity exceeded the bounds of civility, as I thought; but I was not in a good humor, for the fleas, bugs, and other vermin, which infested our miserable lodgings, had caused me a sleepless night, by goring my body until the blood oozed from the skin in countless places. These ruinous missions are prolific generators and the nurseries of vermin of all kinds, as the hapless traveller who tarries in them a few hours will learn to his sorrow. When these bloodthirsty assailants once make a lodgment in the clothing or bedding of the unfortunate victim of their attacks, such are their courage and perseverance that they never capitulate. "Blood or death" is their motto;—the war against them, to be successful, must be a war of extermination.

～ RED-LEGGED FROG ～

Rana aurora draytonii

Family Ranidae

Length: 2–5 ⅜"

Habitat:

Moist woods, forest clearings, and well-vegetated areas near ponds, reservoirs, marshes, or streams

Range:

Throughout California

Comments:

The California red-legged frog has brown to reddish smooth, thin skin, with dark flecks and blotches with light centers. It has a dark mask bordered by a pale upper jaw stripe and a ridge that goes from behind each eye to the base of each hind leg. Its underside is yellow, except for the hind legs and the lower belly, which are red. It also has well-developed folds on its back and sides. Its toes are not fully webbed.

The California red-legged frog eats insects such as beetles, caterpillars, and silverfish. It also sometimes preys on salamanders and other small frogs.

A primarily solitary amphibian, the red-legged frog is almost always in water, but it also lives in well-shaded border areas along water and occasionally ventures out to where it can be spotted on roads. It is diurnal. Its voice is a series of two- or three-second throaty noises.

The California red-legged frog has been protected by the Endangered Species Act since 1996.

Mark Twain
"The Celebrated Jumping Frog of Calaveras County"

Mr. A. Ward—Dear Sir: Well, I called on good-natured, garrulous old Simon Wheeler, and I inquired after your friend Leonidas W. Greeley, as you requested me to do, and I hereunto append the result. If you can get any information out of it you are cordially welcome to it. I have a lurking suspicion that your Leonidas W. Greeley is a myth—that you never knew such a personage, and that you only conjectured that if I asked old Wheeler about him it would remind him of his infamous *Jim* Greeley, and he would go to work and bore me nearly to death with some infernal reminiscence of him as long and tedious as it should be useless to me. If that was your design, Mr. Ward, it will gratify you to know that it succeeded.

I found Simon Wheeler dozing comfortably by the barroom stove of the old dilapidated tavern in the ancient mining camp at Angel's, and I noticed that he was fat and bald-headed, and had an expression of winning gentleness and simplicity upon his tranquil countenance. He roused up and gave me good-day. I told him a friend of mine had commissioned me to make some inquiries about a cherished companion of his boyhood named Leonidas W. Greeley—Rev. Leonidas W. Greeley—a young minister of the Gospel, who he had heard was at one time a resident of Angel's Camp. I added that if Mr. Wheeler could tell me anything about this Rev. Leonidas W. Greeley, I would feel under many obligations to him.

Simon Wheeler backed me into a corner and blockaded me there with his chair—and then sat me down and reeled off the monotonous narrative which follows this paragraph. He never smiled, he never frowned, he never changed his voice from the gentle-flowing key to which he tuned the initial sentence, he never betrayed the slightest suspicion of enthusiasm—but all through the interminable narrative there ran a vein of impressive earnestness and sincerity, which showed me plainly that so far from his imagining that there was anything ridiculous or funny about his story, he regarded it as a really important matter, and admired its two heroes as men of transcendent genius in *finesse*. To me, the spectacle of a man drifting serenely along through such a queer yarn without ever smiling was exquisitely absurd. As I said before, I asked him to tell me what he knew of Rev. Leonidas W. Greeley, and he replied as follows. I let him go on in his own way, and never interrupted him once:

There was a feller here once by the name of *Jim* Greeley, in the winter of '49—or maybe it was the spring of '50—I don't recollect exactly, some how, though what makes me think it was one or the other is because I remember the big flume wasn't finished when he first come to the camp; but anyway, he was the curiosest man about always betting on anything that turned up you ever see, if he could get anybody to bet on the other side, and if he couldn't he'd change sides—any way that suited the other man would suit *him*—any way just so's he got a bet, *he* was satisfied. But still, he was lucky—uncommon lucky; he most always come out winner. He was always ready and laying for a chance; there couldn't be no solitry thing mentioned but that feller'd offer to bet on it—and take any side you please, as I was just telling you: if there was a horse race, you'd find him flush or you'd find him busted at the end of it; if there was a dog-fight, he'd bet on it; if there was a cat-fight, he'd bet on it; if there was a chicken-fight, he'd bet on it; why if there was two birds sitting on a fence, he would bet you which one would fly first—or if there was a camp-meeting he would be there regular to bet on Parson Walker, which he judged to be the best exhorter about here, and so he was, too, and a good man; if he even see a straddle-bug start to go any wheres, he would bet you how long it would take him to get wherever he was going to, and if you took him up he would foller that straddle-bug to Mexico but what he would find out where he was bound for and how long he was on the road. Lots of the boys here has seen that Greeley and can tell you about him. Why, it never made no difference to *him*—he would bet on *anything*—the dangdest feller. Parson Walker's wife laid very sick, once, for a good while, and it seemed as if they warn't going to save her; but one morning he come in and Greeley asked how she was, and he said she was considerable better—thank the Lord for his inf'nit mercy—and coming on so smart that with the blessing of Providence she'd get well yet—and Greeley, before he thought, says: "Well, I'll resk two-and-a-half that she don't, anyway."

Thish-yer Greeley had a mare—the boys called her the fifteen-minute nag, but that was only in fun, you know, because, of course, she was faster than that—and he used to win money on that horse, for all she was so slow and always had the asthma, or the distemper, or the consumption, or something of that kind. They used to give her two or three hundred yards' start, and then pass her under way; but always at the fag-end of the race she'd get excited and desperate like, and come cavorting and spraddling up, and scattering her legs around limber, sometimes in the air, and sometimes out to one side amongst the fences, and kicking up m-o-r-e dust, and raising m-o-r-e racket with her coughing and sneezing and blowing her nose—and always fetch up at the stand just about a neck ahead, as near as you could cipher it down.

And he had a little small bull pup, that to look at him you'd think he warn't worth a cent, but to set around and look onery, and lay for a chance to steal something. But as soon as money was up on him he was a different dog—his underjaw'd begin to stick out like the for'castle of a steamboat, and his teeth would uncover, and shine savage like the furnaces. And a dog might tackle him, and bully-rag him, and bite him, and throw him over his shoulder two or three times, and Andrew Jackson—which was the name of the pup—Andrew Jackson would never let on but what he was satisfied, and hadn't expected nothing else—and the bets being doubled and doubled on the other side all the time, till the money was all up—and then all of a sudden he would grab that other dog just by the joint of his hind leg and freeze to it—not chaw, you understand, but only just grip and hang on till they throwed up the sponge, if it was a year. Greeley always came out winner on that pup till he harnessed a dog once that didn't have no hind legs, because they'd been sawed off in a circular saw, and when the thing had gone along far enough, and the money was all up, and he come to make a snatch for his pet holt, he saw in a minute how he'd been imposed on, and how the other dog had him in the door, so to speak, and he 'peared surprised, and then he looked sorter discouraged like, and didn't try no more to win the fight, and so he got shucked out bad. He give Greeley a look as much as to say his heart was broke, and it was *his* fault, for putting up a dog that hadn't no hind legs for him to take holt of, which was his main dependence in a fight, and then he limped off a piece, and laid down and died. It was a good pup, was that Andrew Jackson, and would have made a name for hisself if he'd lived, for the stuff was in him, and he had genius—I know it, because he hadn't had no opportunities to speak of, and it don't stand to reason that a dog could make such a fight as he could under them circumstances, if he hadn't no talent. It always makes me feel sorry when I think of that last fight of his'n, and the way it turned out.

Well, thish-yer Greeley had rat-tarriers and chicken cocks, and tomcats, and all them kind of things, till you couldn't rest, and you couldn't fetch nothing for him to bet on but he'd match you. He ketched a frog one day and took him home and said he cal'lated to educate him; and so he never done nothing for three months but set in his back yard and learn that frog to jump. And you bet he *did* learn him, too. He'd give him a little punch behind, and the next minute you'd see that frog whirling in the air like a doughnut—see him turn one summerset, or maybe a couple, if he got a good start, and come down flat-footed and all right, like a cat. He got him up so in the matter of catching flies, and kept him in practice so constant, that he'd nail a fly every time as far as he could see him. Greeley said all a frog wanted was education, and he could do most anything—and I believe him. Why, I've seen him set Dan'l Webster down here on this floor—Dan'l Webster was the name of the frog—and sing out, "Flies! Dan'l, flies," and quicker'n you could wink, he'd spring straight up, and snake a fly off'n the counter there, and flop down on the floor again as solid as a gob of mud, and fall to scratching the side of his head with his hind foot as indifferent as if he hadn't no idea he'd done any more'n any frog might do. You never see a frog so modest and straightfor'ard as he was, for all he was so gifted. And when it come to fair-and-square jumping on a dead level, he could get over more ground at one straddle than any animal of his breed you ever see. Jumping on a dead level was his strong suit, you understand, and when it come to that, Greeley would ante up money on him as long as he had a red. Greeley was monstrous proud of his frog, and well he might be, for fellers that had travelled and been everywheres, all said he laid over any frog that ever *they* see.

Well, Greeley kept the beast in a little lattice box, and he used to fetch him down town sometimes and lay for a bet. One day a feller—a stranger in the camp, he was— come across him with his box, and says:

"What might it be that you've got in the box?"

And Greeley says, sorter indifferent like, "It might be a parrot, or it might be a canary, maybe, but it ain't—it's only just a frog."

And the feller took it, and looked at it careful, and turned it round this way and that, and says, "H'm—so 'tis. Well, what's *he* good for?"

"Well," Greeley says, easy and careless, "he's good enough for *one* thing I should judge—he can out-jump ary frog in Calaveras county."

The feller took the box again, and took another long, particular look, and give it back to Greeley and says, very deliberate, "Well—I don't see no points about that frog that's any better'n any other frog."

"Maybe you don't," Greeley says. "Maybe you understand frogs, and maybe you don't understand 'em; maybe you've had experience, and maybe you ain't only a amature, as it were. Anyways, I've got *my* opinion, and I'll resk forty dollars that he can outjump ary frog in Calaveras county."

And the feller studied a minute, and then says, kinder sad, like, "Well—I'm only a stranger here, and I ain't got no frog—but if I had a frog I'd bet you."

And then Greeley says, "That's all right—that's all right—if you'll hold my box a minute I'll go and get you a frog"; and so the feller took the box, and put up his forty dollars along with Greeley's, and set down to wait.

So he set there a good while thinking and thinking to hisself, and then he got the frog out and prized his mouth open and took a teaspoon and filled him full of quail-shot—filled him pretty near up to his chin—and set him on the floor. Greeley he went to the swamp and slopped around in the mud for a long time, and finally he ketched a frog and fetched him in and give him to this feller and says:

"Now if you're ready, set him alongside of Dan'l, with his forepaws just even with Dan'l's, and I'll give the word." Then he says, "one—two—three—jump!" and him and the feller touched up the frogs from behind, and the new frog hopped off, but Dan'l give a heave, and hysted up his shoulders—so—like a Frenchman, but it wa'nt no use—he couldn't budge; he was planted as solid as an anvil, and he couldn't no more stir than if he was anchored out. Greeley was a good deal surprised, and he was disgusted, too, but he didn't have no idea what the matter was, of course.

The feller took the money and started away, and when he was going out at the door he sorter jerked his thumb over his shoulder—this way—at Dan'l, and says again, very deliberate: "Well—I don't see no points about that frog that's any better'n any other frog."

Greeley he stood scratching his head and looking down at Dan'l a long time, and at last he says, "I do wonder what in the nation that frog throw'd off for—I wonder if there ain't something the matter with him—he 'pears to look mighty baggy, somehow," and he ketched Dan'l by the nap of the neck, and lifted him up and says, "Why blame my cats if he don't weigh five pound," and turned him upside down, and he belched out about a double-handful of shot. And then he see how it was, and he was the maddest man—he set the frog down and took out after that feller, but he never ketched him. And—

(Here Simon Wheeler heard his name called from the front yard, and got up to see what was wanted.) And turning to me as he moved away, he said: "Just set where you are, stranger, and rest easy—I ain't going to be gone a second."

But by your leave, I did not think that a continuation of the history of the enterprising vagabond Jim Greeley would be likely to afford me much information concerning the Rev. Leonidas W. Greeley, and so I started away.

At the door I met the sociable Wheeler returning, and he buttonholed me and recommenced:

"Well, thish-yer Greeley had a yaller one-eyed cow that didn't have no tail only just a short stump like a bannanner, and—"

"O, curse Greeley and his afflicted cow!" I muttered, good-naturedly, and bidding the old gentleman good-day, I departed.

Yours, truly,
Mark Twain

GILA MONSTER

Heloderma suspectum

Family Helodermatidae

Length: 18–24"; Weight: 3–5 lb

Habitat:

Arid and semiarid regions with sandy soils and some moisture; lives under rocks and in holes

Range:

Throughout southern California

Comments:

The gila monster is a large, heavy-bodied reptile with a thick, blunt tail. It has a black face and its scales are patterned with broken blotches and bars of black and either yellow, orange, or pink. The scales, which are non-overlapping and beadlike, are osteoderms, or a kind of bony armor.

The gila monster uses its thick tongue to find prey by tasting and smelling the ground. Its powerful bite subdues victims, and venom produced in glands near the lower jaw may flow into the bite wounds of its larger victims. Since it primarily eats small birds, eggs, and rodents, however, the gila monster typically uses its venom only for defense. Humans bit by gila monsters will suffer pain but usually not die. When food is abundant, the gila monster's tail becomes fat, but during times of scarcity, it can lose up to 20 percent of this stored fat.

George Wharton James
from *The Wonders of the Colorado Desert*

The Gila monster (*Heloderma suspectum*, Cope) is seldom seen on the Colorado Desert, though in twenty years I have seen three or four. This is a large, heavily built lizard, from a foot to two feet in length, with short limbs and tail, and entirely distinct from any other lizard of the region, both in its size and stockiness of build. It and the rattlesnake are the only two dangerous or poisonous reptiles of the desert.

Many desert people will tell you that the heloderma has no poison glands and that, therefore, his bite is not dangerous. This error doubtless arises from the fact that there are well-authenticated cases of his bite that have caused nothing more than a slight inconvenience. But it is a most dangerous error. The venom of the heloderma is as poisonous as that of the rattlesnake, as several people who have been bitten have found out to their cost. For many years I have been investigating this subject and I will make quite clear why some people are bitten by the heloderma without injury and others suffer severely.

The venom glands are situated under the chin—thus being on the lower jaw, instead of the upper, as in the case of the rattlesnake. "They are modified from glands which correspond to the sublingual glands of mammals. There are four ducts leading out of each gland. These ducts perforate the lower jaw and open in front of the grooved teeth. A careful study of the dentition of the heloderma shows that there are several intermediate forms between the unmodified teeth of the reptile and the fully developed poison fangs. The poison glands are compound tubular glands, closely resembling the other salivary glands in structure. The peculiarity of their secretion is to be explained by their physiological activity rather than by their structure." So writes my friend, Dr. C. A. Whiting of the Pacific College of Osteopathy, who has given some time to the study of the teeth and glands of the heloderma. Though their poison teeth are grooved, there is no direct connection between the poison glands and the teeth, as in the case of the duct of the rattlesnake. The poison flows out onto the floor of the mouth, between the lips and the gums, that is, into the interior of the bottom jaw. Being below the teeth and not directly communicated to them, the poison sometimes fails to find its way into a wound. The saliva of the upper jaw is perfectly harmless, as is also the same saliva in the lower jaw. But it must not be forgotten that there is also a deadly venom in the lower jaw, which gets mixed with the saliva.

As a rule the Gila monster is lazy and sluggish, and one might play with him for hours and keep him as a pet for years and never see any sign of anger. But let him be angered and then he is dangerous. And the real danger comes when, as he bites, *he turns over*. With a vicious lunge he seizes the object and at the same moment turns over with lightning-like rapidity. He can hold on with the tenacity of a bulldog or he can bite so quickly that he "snips" a piece of flesh out easier than one would pinch off a piece of a cracker. I have seen this action a hundred times, and this is what one must beware of. When the reptile thus bites, holds on, and *turns over* the danger of the case is as great as the most dangerous bite of a rattlesnake, for in this position, if the poison glands are active, the saliva and poison commingle and flow freely into the teeth and thus into the wound. As will be seen in my comments upon the chuckwalla, this "turning over" is a habit of the latter reptile. Yet the chuckwalla has no poison glands. There seems, however, to be a relationship in this peculiar habit, which, as far as I know, is confined to these two reptilian inhabitants of the desert. How strange and singular the provisions of Nature for the protection of her various children!

With the chuckwalla the rapid turning over seems to be to give added purchase in biting its enemies or prey. The questions that arise are: Is the turning over of the heloderma for the purpose of rendering effective the working of its poison apparatus? If so, what is the reason of the turning over of the chuckwalla? Is it a survival of a useless and unnecessary habit in the chuckwalla, seeing that it has no poison to distribute, or is the development of the poison glands in the heloderma a later evolution, while the chuckwalla has evolved in a different line?

The treatment for the bite of the heloderma is the same as that for the bite of the rattlesnake.

In a wild state the heloderma lives largely on birds' eggs, young rabbits, and though apparently so clumsy and slow is an expert bush climber. I have seen him perched high on a mesquite and have been considerably startled at his presence. His five-toed "hands and feet" are well adapted to climbing, which he does both easily and gracefully. Certain specimens that have been in captivity are thus referred to by Professor R. L. Ditmars, their curator at the Bronx Zoölogical Park: "The Gila monster may be placed under the head of omnivorous lizards, as in captivity it feeds almost exclusively upon eggs—the food which most certainly cannot form a large proportion of its nourishment in a wild state. Our captive specimens never have been induced to take other food than eggs, either boiled or raw, the latter sometimes mixed with chopped meat. Unless mixed with eggs they will not eat meat. With stolid indifference they refuse morsels that are dear to the ordinary reptile of their size, such as very young rodents, large grubs, and meal worms. Ants and their eggs are said to furnish a large proportion of this reptile's food, but all the specimens under the writer's observation have refused them. They have lived with us for four years, and have thrived upon their simple and unvarying diet."

In referring to the changes noticed in the actions of captive animals when placed outside and under the influence of the outer air, sunshine and natural surroundings, Professor Ditmars thus writes of the heloderma: "The most interesting demonstration of this mental change has been in connection with specimens of the venomous Gila monster. In their cages these lizards are the personification of good nature, permitting themselves to be handled in the most unceremonious manner, without the least show of bad temper. Removed to a sand pile heated to a high temperature under a bright sun, and left for a few minutes, they become different creatures. They will snap viciously from side to side, and resent the least intimation of interference with sharp hisses as they lie open mouthed, awaiting an opportunity to close with bulldog tenacity upon an offending object. On several occasions when endeavoring to extract poison from these lizards, the writer has been unable to provoke them to bite, but after giving them a sun-bath for a few moments had considerable difficulty in disengaging their jaws from the glass vessel in which the fluid was collected, although the temperature of the outside air and sunlight which had aroused such hostility differed but slightly from the warm air of their indoor cages."

The heloderma is a strictly oviparous lizard. A captive specimen, measuring nineteen and a half inches, deposited four eggs, each two and three-quarters inches long, and one and a half inches in diameter. The eggs were covered with a leathery integument, but, though fertile, the conditions for development were adverse, as, in spite of every known precaution, they shriveled up and their contents solidified.

～ SNOW GOOSE ～

Chen caerulescens

Family Anatidae

Length: 19–28"; Wingspan 53–61"; Weight: 5 ½–7 ¼ lb

Habitat:

    Chiefly marshy areas and mudflats

Range:

    Fall through winter, northern California, San Francisco Bay, and inland valleys like the Great Central Valley and Salton Sea area

Comments:

    The snow goose is almost entirely white, with black primary feathers. Its legs are pink, as is its beak, which also displays distinctive black markings that create the effect of "lips." Rare in California is a "blue" or "dark" phase, once considered a separate species.

    Snow geese often fly in irregular formations of wavy lines, seldom in the familiar V shape. Large flocks may number as many as eighty thousand birds. Snow geese migrate yearly from northern Canada to the Gulf of Mexico and back, wintering in various temperate regions. They consume leaves, grass, sedges, and, when in suitable agricultural areas, wasted grain.

    Their call is a loud, raucous "honk."

Barry Lopez
"A Reflection on White Geese"

I slow the car, downshifting from fourth to third, with the melancholic notes of Bach's sixth cello suite in my ears—a recording of Casals from 1936—and turn east, away from a volcanic ridge of black basalt. On this cool California evening, the land in the marshy valley beyond is submerged in gray light, while the far hills are yet touched by a sunset glow. To the south, out the window, Venus glistens, a white diamond at the horizon's dark lapis edge. A few feet to my left is lake water—skittish mallards and coots bolt from the cover of bulrushes and pound the air furiously to put distance between us. I am chagrined, and slow down. I have been driving like this for hours—slowed by snow in the mountains behind me, listening to the cello suites—driving hard to get here before sunset.

I shut the tape off. In the waning light I can clearly see marsh hawks swooping over oat and barley fields to the south. Last hunts of the day. The eastern sky is beginning to blush, a rose afterglow. I roll the window down. The car fills with the sounds of birds—the nasalized complaints of several hundred mallards, pintails, and canvasbacks, the slap-water whirr of their halfhearted takeoffs. But underneath this sound something else is expanding, distant French horns and kettledrums.

Up ahead, on the narrow dirt causeway, I spot Frans's car. He is here for the same reason I am. I pull up quietly and he emerges from his front seat, which he has made into a kind of photographic blind. We hug and exchange quiet words of greeting, and then turn to look at the white birds. Behind us the dark waters of Tule Lake, rippled by a faint wind, stretch off north, broken only by occasional islands of hardstem bulrush. Before us, working methodically through a field of two-row barley, the uninterrupted inquiry of their high-pitched voices lifting the night, are twenty-five thousand snow geese come down from the Siberian and Canadian Arctic. Grazing, but alert and wary in this last light.

Frans motions wordlessly to his left; I scan that far eastern edge of Tule Lake with field glasses. One hundred thousand lesser snow geese and Ross's geese float quietly on riffles, a white crease between the dark water and the darkening hills.

⌇

The staging of white geese at Tule Lake in northern California in November is one of the most imposing—and dependable—wildlife spectacles in the world. At first one thinks of it only as a phenomenon of numbers—it's been possible in recent years to see as many as three hundred thousand geese here at one time. What a visitor finds as startling, however, is the great synchronicity of their movements: long skeins of white unfurl brilliantly against blue skies and dark cumulonimbus thunderheads, birds riding the towering wash of winds. They rise from the water or fall from the sky with balletic grace, with a booming noise like rattled sheets of corrugated tin, with a furious and unmitigated energy. It is the *life* of them that takes such hold of you.

I have spent enough time with large predators to know the human predilection to overlook authority and mystery in the lives of small, gregarious animals like the goose, but its qualities are finally as subtle, its way of making a living as admirable and attractive, as the grizzly bear's.

Geese are traditional, one could even say conservative, animals. They tend to stick to the same nesting grounds and wintering areas, to the same migration routes, year after year. Males and females have identical plumage. They usually mate for life, and both sexes care for the young. In all these ways, as well as in being more at ease on land, geese differ from ducks. They differ from swans in having proportionately longer legs and shorter necks. In size they fall somewhere between the two. A mature male lesser snow goose *(Chen caerulescens),* for example, might weigh six pounds, measure thirty inches from bill to tail, and have a wingspan of three feet. A mature female would be slightly smaller and lighter by perhaps half a pound.

Taxonomists divide the geese of the Northern Hemisphere into two groups, "gray" and "black," according to the color of their bills, feet, and legs. Among black geese like Canada geese and brandt they're dark. Snow geese, with rose-pink feet and legs and pink bills, are grouped with the gray geese, among whom these appendages are often brightly colored. Snow geese also commonly have rust-speckled faces, from feeding in iron-rich soils.

Before it was changed in 1971, the snow goose's scientific name, *Chen hyperborea,* reflected its high-arctic breeding heritage. The greater snow goose *(C. c. atlantica)*—a larger but far less numerous race of snow goose—breeds in northwestern Greenland and on adjacent Ellesmere, Devon, and Axel Heiburg islands. The lesser snow goose breeds slightly farther south, on Baffin and Southampton islands, the east coast of Hudson Bay, and on Banks Island to the west and Wrangel Island in Siberia. (Many people are attracted to the snow goose precisely because of its association with these little-known regions.)

There are two color phases, finally, of the lesser snow goose, blue and white. The combined population of about 1.5 million, the largest of any goose in the world, is divided into an eastern, mostly blue-phase population that winters in Texas and Louisiana, and a western, white-phase population that winters in California. (It is the latter birds that pass through Tule Lake.)

The great numbers of these highly gregarious birds can be misleading. First, we were not certain until quite recently where snow geese were nesting, or how large their breeding colonies were. The scope of the problem is suggested by the experience of a Canadian biologist, Angus Gavin. In 1941 he stumbled on what he thought was a small breeding colony of lesser snow geese, on the delta of the McConnell River on the east coast of Hudson Bay—14,000 birds. In 1961 there were still only about 35,000 birds there. But a 1968 survey showed 100,000 birds, and in 1973 there were 520,000. Second, populations of arctic-breeding species like the snow goose are subject to extreme annual fluctuations, a boom-and-bust cycle tied to the unpredictable weather patterns typical of arctic ecosystems. After a series of prolonged winters, for example, when persistent spring snow cover kept birds from nesting, the Wrangel Island population of snow geese fell from 400,000 birds in 1965 to fewer than 50,000 in 1975. (By the summer of 1981 it was back up to 170,000.)

The numbers in which we see them on their wintering grounds are large enough to be comforting—it is hard at first to imagine what would threaten such flocks. Snow geese, however, face a variety of problems. The most serious is a striking loss of winter habitat. In 1900 western snow geese had more than 6,200 square miles of winter habitat available to them on California's Sacramento and San Joaquin rivers. Today, 90 percent of this has been absorbed by agricultural, industrial, and urban expansion. This means 90 percent of the land in central California that snow geese once depended on for food and shelter is gone. Hunters in California kill about 20 percent of the population each year and leave another 4 to 5 percent crippled to die of starvation and injuries. (An additional 2 to 3 percent dies each year of lead poisoning, from ingesting spent shot.) An unknown number are also killed by high-tension wires. In the future, geese will likely face a significant threat on their arctic breeding grounds from oil and gas exploration.

The birds also suffer from the same kinds of diseases, traumatic accidents, and natural disasters that threaten all organisms. Females, for example, fiercely devoted to the potential in their egg clutches, may choose to die of exposure on their nests rather than abandon them in an unseasonable storm.

In the light of all this, it is ironic that the one place on earth a person might see these geese in numbers large enough to cover half the sky is, itself, a potential threat to their existence.

— ∘ —

The land now called Tule Lake National Wildlife Refuge lies in a volcanic basin, part of which was once an extensive 2,700-square-mile marshland. In 1905 the federal government began draining the area to create irrigated croplands. Marshland habitat and bird populations shrank. By 1981 only fifty-six square miles of wetland, two percent of the original area, was left for waterfowl. In spite of this reduction, the area, incredibly, remains an ideal spot for migratory waterfowl. On nearly any given day in the fall a visitor to the Klamath Basin might see more than a million birds—mallards, gadwalls, pintails, lesser scaups, goldeneyes, cinnamon teals, northern shovelers, redheads, canvasbacks, ruddy ducks; plus western and cackling Canada geese, white-fronted geese, Ross's geese, lesser snow geese, and whistling swans. (More than 250 species of birds have been seen on or near the refuge, and more than 170 nest here.)

The safety of these populations is in the hands of a resident federal manager and his staff, who must effectively balance the birds' livelihood with the demands of local farmers, who use Tule Lake's water to irrigate adjacent fields of malt barley and winter potatoes, and waterfowl hunters, some of whom come from hundreds of miles away. And there is another problem. Although the Klamath Basin is the greatest concentration point for migratory waterfowl in North America, caring well for birds here is no guarantee they will fare well elsewhere along the flyway. And a geographic concentration like this merely increases the chance of catastrophe if epidemic disease should strike.

———

The first time I visited Tule Lake I arrived early on a fall afternoon. When I asked where the snow geese were congregated I was directed to an area called the English Channel, several miles out on the refuge road. I sat there for three hours, studying the birds' landings and takeoffs, how they behaved toward each other on the water, how they shot the skies overhead. I tried to unravel and to parse the dazzling synchronicity of their movements. I am always struck anew in these moments, in observing such detail, by the way in which an animal slowly reveals itself.

Before the sun went down, I drove off to see more of the snow goose's landscape, what other animals there might be on the refuge, how the land changed at a distance from the water. I found the serpentine great blue heron, vivacious and melodious flocks of red-winged blackbirds, and that small, fierce hunter, the kestrel. Muskrats bolted across the road. At the southern end of the refuge, where cattails and bulrushes give way to rabbit brush and sage on a volcanic plain, I came upon mule deer, three does and four fawns standing still and tense in a meandering fog.

I found a room that evening in the small town of Tulelake. There'd not been, that I could recall, a moment of silence all day from these most loquacious of geese. I wondered if they were mum in the middle of the night, how quiet they were at dawn. I set the alarm for 3 a.m.

The streets of Tulelake are desolate at that hour. In that odd stillness—the stillness of moonlit horses standing asleep in fields—I drove out into the countryside, toward the refuge. It was a ride long enough to hear the first two movements of Beethoven's Fifth Symphony. I drove in a light rain, past white farmhouses framed by ornamental birches and weeping willows. In the 1860s this land was taken by force from the Modoc Indians; in the 1940s the government built a Japanese internment camp here. At this hour, however, nearly every landscape has a pervasive innocence. I passed the refuge headquarters—low shiplapped buildings, white against a dark ridge of basalt, facing a road lined with Russian olives. I drove past stout, slowly dying willows of undetermined age, trees that mark the old shore line of Tule Lake, where it was before the reclamation project began.

The music is low, barely audible, but the enthusiasm in some of the strong passages reminds me of geese. I turn the tape off and drive a narrow, cratered road out into the refuge, feeling the car slipping sideways in the mud. Past rafts of sleeping ducks. The first geese I see surge past just overhead like white butterflies, brushing the penumbral dimness above the car's headlights. I open the window and feel the sudden assault of their voices, the dunning power of their wings hammering the air, a rush of cold wind and rain through the window. In a moment I am outside, standing in the roar. I find a comfortable, protected place in the bulrushes and wait in my parka until dawn, listening.

Their collective voice, like the cries of athletic young men at a distance, is unabated. In the darkness it is nearly all there is of them, but for an occasional and eerie passage overhead. I try to listen closely: a barking of high-voiced dogs, like terriers, the squealing of shoats. By an accident of harmonics the din rises and falls like the cheering of a crowd in a vast stadium. Whoops and shouts; startled voices of outrage, of shock.

These are not the only voices. Cackling geese pass over in the dark, their cries more tentative. Coyotes yip. Nearby some creature screeches, perhaps a mouse in the talons of a great horned owl, whose skipping hoots I have heard earlier.

A gibbous moon shines occasionally through a wind-driven overcast. Toward dawn the geese's voices fall off suddenly for a few moments. The silence seems primordial. The black sky in the east now shows blood red through scalloped shelves of cloud. It broadens into an orange flare that fades to rose and finally to the grays of dawn. The voices begin again.

I drive back into Tulelake and eat breakfast amid a throng of hunters crowding the tables of a small cafe, steaming the windows with their raucous conversation.

Bob Fields, the refuge manager, has agreed to take me on a tour in the afternoon. I decide to spend the morning at the refuge headquarters, reading scientific reports and speaking with biologist Ed O'Neill about the early history of Tule Lake.

O'Neill talks first about the sine qua non, a suitable expanse of water. In the American West the ownership of surface water confers the kind of political and economic power that comes elsewhere with oil wells and banks. Water is a commodity; it is expensive to maintain and its owners seek to invest the limited supply profitably. A hunting club that keeps private marshland for geese and ducks, for example, will do so only as long as they feel their hunting success warrants it. If the season is shortened or the bag limit reduced by the state—the most common ways to conserve dwindling waterfowl populations—they might find hunting no longer satisfying and sell the marsh to farmers, who will turn it into cropland. Real estate speculators and other landowners with substantial surface-water rights rarely give the birds that depend on their lands a second thought when they're preparing to sell. As O'Neill puts it, "You can't outweigh a stack of silver dollars with a duck."

The plight of western waterfowl is made clearer by an anomaly. In the eastern United States, a natural abundance of water and the closure of many tracts of private land to hunting provide birds with a strong measure of protection. In the West, bird populations are much larger, but water is scarcer and refuge lands, because they are largely public, remain open to hunting.

By carefully adjusting the length of the hunting season and the bag limits each year, and by planting food for the birds, refuge managers try to maintain large bird populations, in part to keep private hunting clubs along the flyway enthusiastic about continuing to provide additional habitat for the birds. Without the help of private individuals, including conservation groups that own wetlands, the federal and state refuge systems simply cannot provide for the birds....

Some birds, the snow geese among them, have adapted to shortages of food and land. Deprived of the rootstocks of bulrushes and marsh grasses, snow geese in the West have switched to gleaning agricultural wastes and cropping winter wheat, a practice that has spread to the Midwest, where snow geese now feed increasingly on rice and corn. A second adjustment snow geese have made is to linger on their fall migrations and to winter over farther north. That way fewer birds end up for a shorter period of time on traditional wintering grounds, where food is scarcer each year.

As we spoke, O'Neill kept glancing out the window. He told me about having seen as many as three hundred thousand white geese there in years past. With the loss of habitat and birds spreading out now to winter along the flyway, such aggregations, he says, may never be seen again. He points out, too, looking dismayed and vaguely bitter, that these huge flocks have not been conserved for the viewer who does not hunt, for the tourist who comes to Tule Lake to see something he has only dreamed of.

We preserve them, principally, to hunt them.

⌒⌒⌒

In broad daylight I was able to confirm something I'd read about the constant, loud din of their voices: relatively few birds are actually vocalizing at any one time, perhaps only one in thirty. Biologists speculate that snow geese recognize each other's voices and that family units of three or four maintain contact in these vast aggregations by calling out to one another. What sounds like mindless chaos to the human ear, then, may actually be a complex pattern of solicitous cries, discretely distinguished by snow geese.

Another sound that is easier to decipher in daylight is the rising squall that signals they are leaving the water. It's like the sustained hammering of a waterfall or a wind booming in the full crowns of large trees.

One wonders, watching the geese fly off in flocks of a hundred or a thousand, if they would be quite so arresting without their stunning whiteness. When they fly with the sun behind them, the opaque white of their bodies, the white of water-polished seashells, is set off against grayer whites in their tail feathers and in their translucent, black-tipped wings. Up close these are the dense, impeccable whites of an arctic fox. Against the grays and blues of a storm-laden sky, the whiteness has a surreal glow, a brilliance without shadow.

I remember watching a large flock rise one morning from a plowed field about a mile distant. I had been watching clouds, the soft, buoyant, wind-blown edges of immaculate cumulus. The birds rose against much darker clouds to the east. There was something vaguely ominous in this apparition, as if the earth had opened and poured them forth, like a wind, a blizzard, which unfurled across the horizon above the dark soil, becoming wider and higher in the sky than my field of vision could encompass, great swirling currents of birds in a rattling of wings, one fluid recurved sweep of ten thousand passing through the open spaces in another, counterflying flock, while beyond them lattice after lattice passed like sliding walls, until in the whole sky you lost your depth of field and felt as though you were looking up from the floor of the ocean through shoals of fish.

〜

At rest on the water the geese drank and slept and bathed and preened. They reminded me in their ablutions of the field notes of a Hudson Bay trader, George Barnston. He wrote of watching flocks of snow geese gathering on James Bay in 1862, in preparation for their annual two-thousand-mile, nonstop thirty-two-hour flight to the Louisiana coast. They finally left off feeding, he wrote, to smooth and dress their feathers with oil, like athletes, biding their time for a north wind. When it came they were gone, hundreds of thousands of them, leaving a coast once "widely resonant with their petulant and incessant calls" suddenly as "silent as the grave—a deserted, barren, and frozen shore."

Barnston was struck by the way snow geese do things together. No other waterfowl are as gregarious, certainly no other large bird flies as skillfully in such tight aggregations. This quality—the individual act beautifully integrated within the larger movement of the flock—is provocative. One afternoon I studied individual birds for hours as they landed and took off. I never once saw a bird on the water move over to accommodate a bird that was landing nor a bird ever disturbed by another taking off, no matter how tightly they were bunched. In no flight overhead did I see two birds so much as brush wing tips. Certainly they must; but for the most part they are flawlessly adroit. A flock settles gently on the water like whiffling leaves; birds explode vertically with compact and furious wing beats and then stretch out full length, airborne, rank on rank, as if the whole flock had been cleanly wedged from the surface of the water. Several thousand bank smoothly against head wind, as precisely as though they were feathers in the wing of a single bird.

It was while I sat immersed in these details that Bob Fields walked up. After a long skyward stare he said, "I've been here for seven years. I never get tired of watching them."

We left in his small truck to drive the narrow causeways of Tule Lake and the five adjacent federal refuges. Fields joined the U.S. Fish and Wildlife Service in 1958, at the age of twenty-two. His background is in range biology and plant ecology as well as waterfowl management. Before he came to Tule Lake in 1974, to manage the Klamath Basin refuges, he worked on the National Bison Range in Montana and on the Charles Sheldon Antelope Range in Nevada.

In 1973 a group of visitors who would profoundly affect Fields arrived at Tule Lake. They were Eskimos, from the Yukon-Kuskokwim delta of Alaska. They had come to see how the geese populations, which they depend on for food, were being managed. In the few days they were together, Fields came to understand that the Eskimos were appalled by the waste they saw at Tule Lake, by the number of birds hunters left crippled and unretrieved, and were surprised that hunters took only the breast meat and threw the rest of the bird away. On the other hand, the aggregations of geese they saw were so extensive they believed someone was fooling them—surely, they thought, so many birds could never be found in one place.

The experience with the Eskimos—Fields traveled north to see the Yukon-Kuskokwim country, and the Eskimos returned to Tule Lake in 1977—focused his career as had no other event. In discussions with the Eskimos he found himself talking with a kind of hunter he rarely encountered anymore—humble men with a respect for the birds and a sense of responsibility toward them. That the Eskimos were dumbstruck at the number of birds led him to more sobering thoughts: if he failed here as a refuge manager, his failure would run the length of the continent.

In the years following, Fields gained a reputation as a man who cared passionately for the health and welfare of waterfowl populations. He tailored, with the help of assistant refuge manager Homer McCollum, a model hunting program at Tule Lake, but he is candid in expressing his distaste for a type of hunter he still meets too frequently—belligerent, careless people for whom hunting is simply violent recreation; people who trench and rut the refuge's roads in oversize four-wheel-drive vehicles, who are ignorant of hunting laws or who delight in breaking them as part of a "game" they play with refuge personnel.

At one point in our afternoon drive, Fields and I were watching a flock of geese feeding in a field of oats and barley on the eastern edge of the refuge. We watched in silence for a long time. I said something, about the way birds can calm you, how the graceful way they define the sky can draw irritation right [out] of you. He looked over at me and smiled and nodded. A while later, still watching the birds, he said, "I have known all along there was more to it than managing the birds so they could be killed by some macho hunter." It was the Eskimos who gave him a sense of how a hunter should behave, and their awe that rekindled his own desire to see the birds preserved.

As we drove back across the refuge, Fields spoke about the changes that had occurred in the Klamath Basin since the federal reclamation project began in 1905. Most of the native grasses—blue bench wheat grass, Great Basin wild rye—are gone. A visitor notices foreign plants in their place, like cheatgrass. And introduced species like the ringnecked pheasant and the muskrat, which bores holes in the refuge dikes and disrupts the pattern of drainage. And the intrusion of high-tension power lines, which endanger the birds and which Fields has no budget to bury. And the presence of huge pumps that circulate water from Tule Lake to farmers in the valley, back and forth, back and forth, before pumping it west to Lower Klamath Refuge.

It is over these evolving, occasionally uneasy relationships between recent immigrant and the original inhabitant that Fields keeps watch. I say good-bye to him at his office, to the world of bird poacher, lead poisoning, and politically powerful hunting and agricultural lobbies he deals with every day. When I shake his hand I find myself wanting to thank him for the depth with which he cares for the birds, and for the intelligence that allows him to disparage not hunting itself but the lethal acts of irresponsibility and thoughtless people.

———

I still have a few hours before I meet Frans for dinner. I decide to drive out to the east of the refuge, to a low escarpment which bears the carvings of Indians who lived in this valley before white men arrived. I pass open fields where horses and beef cattle graze and cowbirds flock after seeds. Red-tailed hawks are perched on telephone poles, watching for field rodents. A light rain has turned to snow.

The brooding face of the escarpment has a prehistoric quality. It is secured behind a chain link fence topped with barbed wire, but the evidence of vandals who have broken past it to knock off souvenir petroglyphs is everywhere. The castings of barn owls, nesting in stone pockets above, are spread over the ground. I open some of them to see what the owls have been eating. Meadow voles. Deer mice.

The valley before me has darkened. I know somewhere out there, too far away to see now, long scarves of snow geese are riding and banking against these rising winds, and that they are aware of the snow. In a few weeks Tule Lake will be frozen and they will be gone. I turn back to the wall of petroglyphs. The carvings relate, apparently, to the movement of animals through this land hundreds of years ago. The people who made them made their clothing and shelters, even their cooking containers, from the lake's tule reeds. When the first white man arrived—Peter Ogden, in 1826—he found them wearing blankets of duck and goose feathers. In the years since, the complex interrelationships of the Modoc with this land, largely unrecorded to begin with, have disappeared. The land itself has been turned to agriculture, with a portion set aside for certain species of birds that have passed through this valley for no one knows how many centuries. The hunters have become farmers, the farmers landowners. Their sons have gone to the cities and become businessmen, and the sons of these men have returned with guns, to take advantage of the old urge, to hunt. But more than a few come back with a poor knowledge of the birds, the land, the reason for killing. It is by now a familiar story, for which birds pay with their lives.

The old argument, that geese must be killed for their own good, to manage the size of their populations, founders on two points. Snow goose populations rise and fall precipitously because of their arctic breeding pattern. No group of hunters can "fine-tune" such a basic element of their ecology. Second, the artificial control of their numbers only augments efforts to continue draining wetlands.

We must search in our way of life, I think, for substantially more here than economic expansion and continued good hunting. We need to look for a set of relationships similar to the ones Fields admired among the Eskimos. We grasp what is beautiful in a flight of snow geese rising against an overcast sky as easily as we grasp the beauty in a cello suite; and intuit, I believe, that if we allow these things to be destroyed or degraded for economic or frivolous reasons we will become deeply and strangely impoverished.

———————

I had seen little of my friend Frans in three days. At dinner he said he wanted to tell me of the Oostvaardersplassen in Holland. It has become a major stopover for waterfowl in northern Europe, a marsh that didn't even exist ten years ago. Birds hardly anyone has seen in Holland since the time of Napoleon are there now. Peregrine falcons, snowy egrets, and European sea eagles have returned.

I drive away from the escarpment holding tenaciously to this image of reparation.

~ POCKET GOPHER ~

Thomomys bottae

Family Geomyidae

Length: 4 ½–12"; Weight: 3 ⅗–7 ⅖ oz

Habitat:

Lightly packed soil in valleys, deserts, and agricultural areas

Range:

Common throughout California

Comments:

The Botta's pocket gopher has soft, smooth, short fur that varies in color but usually matches the color of the soil it lives in, generally ranging from dull brown to black. The gopher's entire body is covered by this fur, except for its front and rear paws and the tip of its tail. It has small ears and eyes, a robust body, and short, stocky legs. Its front feet have long claws, and it also has fur-lined cheek pouches.

A burrowing animal, the Botta's pocket gopher feeds on roots, tubers, and ground plants. When it eats ground plants, it usually starts at the roots and then pulls the stem into its burrow instead of eating from the surface. It does not drink water but receives moisture from its food.

Botta's pocket gophers are solitary animals that live one to a burrow, which resembles a fan-shaped mound above ground and is very elaborate underground, with specialized areas for nests and latrines, among other uses. They are hostile to members of their own species who trespass into their burrows.

"Californian Vulture" by John James Audubon, 1838, The
Bancroft Library, University of California, Berkeley. Courtesy
of The Bancroft Library.

"Hunting the Grizzly Bear" by William H. Meyers, 1842, The Bancroft Library, University of California, Berkeley. Courtesy of The Bancroft Library.

"Ennemi de la tarantule (Californie)" by Louis Jules Rupalley, circa 1850s, The Bancroft Library, University of California, Berkeley. Courtesy of The Bancroft Library.

"*Phaethon aetherus,* red-billed bird" by Andrew Jackson Grayson, c. 1853–1869, The Bancroft Library, University of California, Berkeley. Courtesy of The Bancroft Library.

Basket by Guadalupe Arenas (Cahuilla, c. 1880–1959), c. 1910, gift of
James Smeaton Chase to the Palm Springs Art Museum. Courtesy of the
Palm Springs Art Museum.

"Morning Song" by Mark Twain, c. 1880, Mark
Twain Papers, University of California, Berkeley.
Courtesy of the Mark Twain Foundation.

"The Curse of California" by George Frederick Keller, 1882, The Bancroft Library, University of California, Berkeley. Courtesy of The Bancroft Library.

"Logging in Mendocino, 1870" by Emmy Lou Packard, 1969. Courtesy of PackardPrints.com.

"Vaqueros Lassoing a Steer" by Augusto Ferran, c. 1849, The Bancroft Library,
University of California, Berkeley. Courtesy of The Bancroft Library.

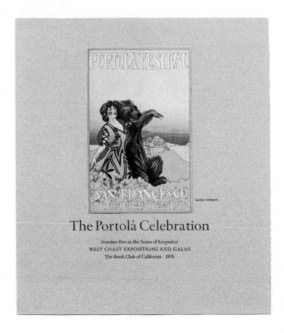

Portolá Celebration postcard by
Pacific Novelty, 1909. The Bancroft
Library, University of California,
Berkeley. Courtesy of The Bancroft
Library.

"When Can We Go Home?" by Henry Sugimoto, 1943, gift of Madeleine Sugimoto and Naomi Tagawa to the Japanese American National Museum (92.97.3). Courtesy of the Japanese American National Museum.

"Fish Dancer" by Frank Day, c. 1973–1975, collection of M. Leigh and Sandra W. Marymor. Courtesy of M. Leigh and Sandra W. Marymor.

"Monterey Deer" by Elizabeth Strong, c. 1978, Crocker Art Museum, E. B. Crocker
Collection (1872.522). Courtesy of the Crocker Art Museum.

"Deer Dance Spirit" by Frank LaPena, 1983, collection of A. P. Fenderson. Courtesy of the artist.

"Rose and the Res Sisters" by Harry Fonseca, 1981. Courtesy of the artist.

"The Rescue" by Judith Lowry, 1999. Courtesy of the artist.

ANDREA RICH'S CALIFORNIA ANIMALS

"Virginia Rail," 1999.

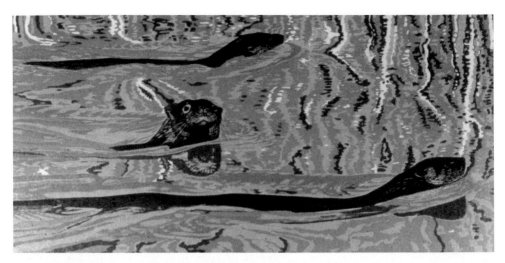

"River Otters," 1998.

"Desert Tortoise," 1999.

"Redwing Blackbirds," 2000.

"Red Fox wih Turtle Eggs," 2003.

"Full Moon," 1995.

John Steinbeck
from *Cannery Row*

A well-grown gopher took up residence in a thicket of mallow weeds in the vacant lot on Cannery Row. It was a perfect place. The deep green luscious mallows towered up crisp and rich and as they matured their little cheeses hung down provocatively. The earth was perfect for a gopher, hole too, black and soft and yet with a little clay in it so that it didn't crumble and the tunnels didn't cave in. The gopher was fat and sleek and he had always plenty of food in his cheek pouches. His little ears were clean and well set and his eyes were as black as old-fashioned pin heads and just about the same size. His digging hands were strong and the fur on his back was glossy brown and the fawn-colored fur on his chest was incredibly soft and rich. He had long curving yellow teeth and a little short tail. Altogether he was a beautiful gopher and in the prime of his life.

He came to the place over land and found it good and he began his burrow on a little eminence where he could look out among the mallow weeds and see the trucks go by on Cannery Row. He could watch the feet of Mack and the boys as they crossed the lot to the Palace Flophouse. As he dug down into the coal-black earth he found it even more perfect, for there were great rocks under the soil. When he made his great chamber for the storing of food it was under a rock so that it could never cave in no matter how hard it rained. It was a place where he could settle down and raise any number of families and the burrow could increase in all directions.

It was beautiful in the early morning when he first poked his head out of the burrow. The mallows filtered green light down on him and the first rays of the rising sun shone into his hole and warmed it so that he lay there content and very comfortable.

When he had dug his great chamber and his four emergency exits and his waterproof deluge room, the gopher began to store food. He cut down only the perfect mallow stems and trimmed them to the exact length he needed and he took them down the hole and stacked them neatly in his great chamber, and arranged them so they wouldn't ferment or get sour. He had found the perfect place to live. There were no gardens about so no one would think of setting a trap for him. Cats there were, many of them, but they were so bloated with fish heads and guts from the canneries that they had long ago given up hunting. The soil was sandy enough so that water never stood about or filled a hole for long. The gopher worked and worked until he had his great chamber crammed with food. Then he made little side chambers for the babies who would inhabit them. In a few years there might be thousands of his progeny spreading out from this original hearthstone.

But as time went on the gopher began to be a little impatient, for no female appeared. He sat in the entrance of his hole in the morning and made penetrating squeaks that are inaudible to the human ear but can be heard deep in the earth by other gophers. And still no female appeared. Finally in a sweat of impatience he went up across the track until he found another gopher hole. He squeaked provocatively in the entrance. He heard a rustling and smelled female and then out of the hole came an old battle-torn bull gopher who mauled and bit him so badly that he crept home and lay in his great chamber for three days recovering and he lost two toes from one front paw from that fight.

Again he waited and squeaked beside his beautiful burrow in the beautiful place but no female ever came and after a while he had to move away. He had to move two blocks up the hill to a dahlia garden where they put out traps every night.

RED-TAILED HAWK

Buteo jamaicensis

Family Accipitridae

Length: 1 ⅔–2'; Wingspan: 4–4 ½'

Habitat:

> Woods, plains, scrub deserts, grasslands; open areas with elevated perches; nests in trees surrounded by open land or at the edge of forests

Range:

> Throughout California

Comments:

> The red-tailed hawk is the most common hawk in California. Although its plumage is variable, its head and back are typically dark brown and its underparts are light rufous and white. Its tail is a pale orange when observed from below.

> Often seen perched on fence posts or telephone poles, or soaring aloft, red-tailed hawks are extremely territorial and stake out home ranges as large as 1.5 square miles. They are patient hunters and may perch for hours watching for prey, which they can detect at great distances. Red-tailed hawks feed on a wide variety of species, including rodents, reptiles, and small birds. Mating pairs may remain together for years in the same territory, the female guarding the nest and the male defending territory boundaries.

> Their call is a distinctive, piercing scream, "kee-eee-arr."

Walter Van Tilburg Clark
"Hook"

I

Hook, the hawks' child, was hatched in a dry spring among the oaks beside the seasonal river, and was struck from the nest early. In the drouth his single-willed parents had to extend their hunting ground by more than twice, for the ground creatures upon which they fed died and dried by the hundreds. The range became too great for them to wish to return and feed Hook, and when they had lost interest in each other they drove Hook down into the sand and brush and went back to solitary courses over the bleaching hills.

Unable to fly yet, Hook crept over the ground, challenging all large movements with recoiled head, erected rudimentary wings, and the small rasp of his clattering beak. It was during this time of abysmal ignorance and continual fear that his eyes took the first quality of hawk, that of being wide, alert, and challenging. He dwelt, because of his helplessness, among the rattling brush which grew between the oaks and the river. Even in his thickets, and near the water, the white sun was the dominant presence. Except in the dawn, when the land wind stirred, or in the late afternoon, when the sea wind became strong enough to penetrate the half-mile inland to this turn in the river, the sun was the major force, and everything was dry and motionless under it. The brush, small plants and trees alike, husbanded the little moisture at their hearts; the moving creatures waited for dark, when sometimes the sea fog came over and made a fine, soundless rain which relieved them.

The two spacious sounds of his life environed Hook at this time. One was the great rustle of the slopes of yellowed wild wheat, with over it the chattering rustle of the leaves of the California oaks, already as harsh and individually tremulous as in autumn. The other was the distant whisper of the foaming edge of the Pacific, punctuated by the hollow shoring of the waves. But these Hook did not yet hear, for he was attuned by fear and hunger to the small, spasmodic rustlings of live things. Dry, shrunken, and nearly starved, and with his plumage delayed, he snatched at beetles, dragging in the sand to catch them. When swifter and stronger birds and animals did not reach them first, which was seldom, he ate the small silver fish left in the mud by the failing river. He watched, with nearly chattering beak, the quick, thin lizards pause, very alert, and raise and lower themselves, but could not catch them because he had to raise his wings to move rapidly, which startled them.

Only one sight and sound not of his world of microscopic necessity was forced upon Hook. That was the flight of the big gulls from the beaches, which sometimes, in quealing play, came spinning back over the foothills and the river bed. For some inherited reason the big, ship-bodied birds did not frighten Hook, but angered him. Small and chewed-looking, with his wide, already yellowing eyes glaring up at them, he would stand in an open place on the sand in the sun and spread his shaping wings and clatter like shaken dice. Hook was furious about the swift, easy passage of gulls.

His first opportunity to leave off living like a ground owl came accidentally. He was standing in the late afternoon in the red light under the thicket, his eyes half-filmed with drowse and the stupefaction of starvation, when suddenly something beside him moved, and he struck, and killed a field mouse driven out of the wheat by thirst. It was a poor mouse, shriveled and lice-ridden, but in striking Hook had tasted blood, which raised nest memories and restored his nature. With started neck plumage and shining eyes he tore and fed. When the mouse was devoured Hook had entered hoarse adolescence. He began to seek with a conscious appetite, and to move more readily out of shelter. Impelled by the blood appetite, so glorious after his long preservation upon the flaky and bitter stuff of bugs, he ventured even into the wheat in the open sun beyond the oaks, and discovered the small trails and holes among the roots. With his belly often partially filled with flesh he grew rapidly in strength and will. His eyes were taking on their final change, their yellow growing deeper and more opaque, their stare more constant, their challenge less desperate. Once during this transformation he surprised a ground squirrel, and although he was ripped and wing-bitten and could not hold his prey, he was not dismayed by the conflict, but exalted. Even while the wing was still drooping and the pinions not grown back, he was excited by other ground squirrels and pursued them futilely, and was angered by their dusty escape. He realized that his world was a great arena for killing, and felt the magnificence of it.

The two major events of Hook's young life occurred in the same day. A little after dawn he made the customary essay and succeeded in flight. A little before sunset he made his first sustained flight of over two hundred yards, and at its termination struck and slew a great buck squirrel, whose thrashing and terrified gnawing and squealing gave him a wild delight. When he had gorged on the strong meat, Hook stood upright, and in his eyes was the stare of the hawk, never flagging in intensity but never swelling beyond containment. After that the stare had only to grow more deeply challenging and more sternly controlled as his range and deadliness increased. There was no change in kind. Hook had mastered the first of the three hungers which are fused into the single flaming will of a hawk, and he had experienced the second.

The third and consummating hunger did not awaken in Hook until the following spring, when the exultation of space had grown slow and steady in him, so that he swept freely with the wind over the miles of the coastal foothills, circling and ever in sight of the sea, and used without struggle the warm currents lifting from the slopes, and no longer desired to scream at the range of his vision, but intently sailed above his shadow swiftly climbing to meet him on the hillsides, sinking away and rippling across the brush-grown canyons.

That spring the rains were long, and Hook sat for hours, hunched and angry under their pelting, glaring into the fogs of the river valley, and killed only small, drenched things flooded up from their tunnels. But when the rains had dissipated, and there were sun and sea wind again, the game ran plentiful, the hills were thick and shining green, and the new river flooded about the boulders where battered turtles climbed up to shrink and sleep. Hook then was scorched by the third hunger. Ranging farther, often forgetting to kill and eat, he sailed for days with growing rage, and woke at night clattering on his dead tree limb, and struck and struck and struck at the porous wood of the trunk, tearing it away. After days, in the draft of a coastal canyon miles below his own hills, he came upon the acrid taint he did not know but had expected, and, sailing down it, felt his neck plumes rise and his wings quiver so that he swerved unsteadily. He saw the unmated female perched upon the tall and jagged stump of a tree that had been shorn by storm, and, as if upon game, he stooped. But she was older than he, and wary of the gripe of his importunity, and banked off screaming, and he screamed also at the intolerable delay.

At the head of the canyon the screaming pursuit was crossed by another male with a great wingspread and the light golden in the fringe of his plumage. But his more skillful opening played him false against the ferocity of the twice-balked Hook. His rising manœuvre for position was cut short by Hook's wild upward stoop, and at the blow he raked wildly and tumbled off to the side. Dropping, Hook struck him again, struggled to clutch, but only raked and could not hold, and, diving, struck once more in passage, and then beat up, yelling triumph, and saw the crippled antagonist sideslip away, half-tumble once as the ripped wing failed to balance, then steady and glide obliquely into the cover of brush on the canyon side. Beating hard and stationary in the wind above the bush that covered his competitor, Hook waited an instant, but, when the bush was still, screamed again, and let himself go off with the current, reseeking, infuriated by the burn of his own wounds, the thin choke-thread of the acrid taint.

On a hilltop projection of stone two miles inland, he struck her down, gripping her rustling body with his talons, beating her wings down with his wings, belting her head when she whimpered or thrashed, and at last clutching her neck with his hook, and, when her coy struggles had given way to stillness, succeeded.

In the early summer Hook drove the three young ones from their nest, and went back to lone circling above his own range. He was complete.

II

Throughout that summer and the cool, growthless weather of the winter when the gales blew in the river canyon and the ocean piled upon the shore, Hook was master of the sky and the hills of his range. His flight became a lovely and certain thing, so that he played with the treacherous currents of the air with a delicate ease surpassing that of the gulls. He could sail for hours searching the blanched grasses below him with telescopic eyes, gaining height against the wind, descending in mile-long, gently declining swoops when he curved and rode back, and never beating either wing. At the swift passage of his shadow within their vision gophers, ground squirrels, and rabbits froze, or plunged gibbering into their tunnels beneath matted turf. Now, when he struck, he killed easily in one hard-knuckled blow. Occasionally, in sport, he soared up over the river and drove the heavy and weaponless gulls downstream again, until they would no longer venture inland.

There was nothing which Hook feared now, and his spirit was wholly belligerent, swift, and sharp, like his gaze. Only the mixed smells and incomprehensible activities of the people at the Japanese farmer's home, inland of the coastwise highway and south of the bridge across Hook's river, troubled him. The smells were strong, unsatisfactory, and never clear, and the people, though they behaved foolishly, constantly running in and out of their built-up holes, were large, and appeared capable, with fearless eyes looking up at him, so that he instinctively swerved aside from them. He cruised over their yard, their gardens, and their bean fields, but he would not alight close to their buildings.

But this one area of doubt did not interfere with his life. He ignored it, save to look upon it curiously as he crossed, his afternoon shadow sliding in an instant over the chicken and crate-cluttered yard, up the side of the unpainted barn, and then out again smoothly, just faintly, liquidly rippling over the furrows and then the stubble of the grazing slopes. When the season was dry, and the dead earth blew on the fields, he extended his range to satisfy his great hunger, and again narrowed it when the fields were once more alive with the minute movements he could not only see but anticipate.

Four times in that year he was challenged by other hawks blowing up from behind the coastal hills to scud down his slopes, but two of these he slew in mid-air, and saw hurtle down to thump on the ground and lie still while he circled; and a third, whose wing he tore, he followed closely to earth and beat to death in the grass, making the crimson jet out from its breast and neck into the pale wheat. The fourth was a strong flier and experienced fighter, and theirs was a long, running battle, with brief, rising flurries of striking and screaming, from which down and plumage soared off.

Here, for the first time, Hook felt doubts, and at moments wanted to drop away from the scoring, burning talons and the twisted hammer strokes of the strong beak, drop away shrieking and take cover and be still. In the end, when Hook, having outmanoeuvred his enemy and come above him, wholly in control and going with the wind, tilted and plunged for the death rap, the other, in desperation, threw over on his back and struck up. Talons locked, beaks raking, they dived earthward. The earth grew and spread under them amazingly, and they were not fifty feet above it when Hook, feeling himself turning towards the underside, tore free and beat up again on heavy, wrenched wings. The other, stroking swiftly, and so close to down that he lost wing plumes to a bush, righted himself and planed up, but flew on lumberingly between the hills and did not return. Hook screamed the triumph, and made a brief pretense of pursuit, but was glad to return, slow and victorious, to his dead tree.

In all of these encounters Hook was injured, but experienced only the fighter's pride and exultation from the sting of wounds received in successful combat. And in each of them he learned new skill. Each time the wounds healed quickly, and left him a more dangerous bird.

In the next spring, when the rains and the night chants of the little frogs were past, the third hunger returned upon Hook with a new violence. In this quest he came into the taint of a young hen. Others too were drawn by the unnerving perfume, but only one of them, the same with which Hook had fought his great battle, was a fit competitor. This hunter drove off two, while two others, game but neophytes, were glad enough that Hook's impatience would not permit him to follow and kill. Then the battle between the two champions fled inland and was a tactical marvel, but Hook lodged the neck-breaking blow, and struck again as they dropped past the treetops. The blood had already begun to pool on the gray, fallen foliage as Hook flapped up between branches, too spent to cry victory. Yet his hunger would not let him rest until, late in the second day, he drove the female to ground among the laurels of a strange river canyon.

When the two fledglings of this second brood had been driven from the nest, and Hook had returned to his own range, he was not only complete but supreme. He slept without concealment on his bare limb, and did not open his eyes when, in the night, the heavy-billed cranes coughed in the shallows below him.

III

The turning point of Hook's career came that autumn, when the brush in the canyons rustled dryly, and the hills, mowed close by the cattle, smoked under the wind as if burning. One midafternoon, when the black clouds were torn on the rim of the sea and the surf flowered white and high on the rocks, raining in over the low cliffs, Hook rode the wind diagonally across the river mouth. His great eyes, focused for small things stirring in the dust and leaves, overlooked so large and slow a movement as that of the Japanese farmer rising from the brush and lifting the two black eyes of his shotgun. Too late Hook saw, and, startled, swerved, but wrongly. The surf muffled the reports, and nearly without sound Hook felt the minute whips of the first shot, and the astounding, breath-breaking blow of the second.

Beating his good wing, tasting the blood that quickly swelled into his beak, he tumbled off with the wind and struck into the thickets on the far side of the river mouth. The branches tore him. Wild with rage, he thrust up, clattered beak, challenging, but, when he had twice fallen over, knew that the trailing wing would not carry, and then heard the boots of the hunter among the stones in the river bed, and, seeing him loom at the edge of the bushes, crept back amid the thickest brush, and was still. When he saw the boots stand before him, he reared back, lifting his good wing and cocking his head for the serpent-like blow, his beak open but soundless, his great eyes hard and very shining. The boots passed on. The Japanese farmer, who believed that he had lost chickens, and who had cunningly observed Hook's flight for many afternoons until he could plot it, did not greatly want a dead hawk.

When Hook could hear nothing but the surf and the wind in the thicket, he let the sickness and shock overcome him. The fine film of the inner lid dropped over his big eyes. His heart beat frantically, so that it made the plumage of his shot-aching breast throb. His own blood throttled his breathing. But these things were nothing compared to the lightning of pain in his left shoulder where the shot had bunched, shattering the airy bones so the pinions trailed on the ground and could not be lifted. Yet when a sparrow lit in the bush over him, Hook's eyes flew open again, hard and challenging, his good wing was lifted and his beak strained open. The startled sparrow darted piping out over the river.

Throughout that night, while the long clouds blew across the stars and the wind shook the bushes about him, and throughout the next day, while the clouds still blew and massed until there was no gleam of sunlight on the sand bar, Hook remained stationary, enduring his sickness. In the second evening the rains began. First there was a long, running patter of drops upon the beach and over the dry trees and bushes. At dusk there came a heavier squall, which did not die entirely, but slacked off to a continual, spaced splashing of big drops, and then returned with the front of the storm. In long, misty curtains, gust by gust, the rain swept over the sea, beating down its heaving, and coursed up the beach. The little jets of dust ceased to rise about the drops in the fields, and the mud began to gleam. Among the boulders of the river bed darkling pools grew slowly.

Still Hook stood behind his tree from the wind, only gentle drops reaching him, falling from the upper branches and then again from the brush. His eyes remained closed, and he could still taste his own blood in his mouth, though it had ceased to come up freshly. Out beyond him, he heard the storm changing. As rain conquered the sea the heave of the surf became a hushed sound, often lost in the crying of the wind. Then gradually, as the night turned towards morning, the wind also was broken by the rain. The crying became fainter, the rain settled towards steadiness, and the cave and creep of the waves could be heard again, quiet and regular upon the beach.

At dawn there was no wind, and no sun, but everywhere the roaring of the vertical, relentless rain. Hook then crept among the rapid drippings of the bushes, dragging his torn sail, seeking better shelter. He stopped often, and stood with the shutters of film drawn over his eyes. At midmorning he found a little cave under a ledge at the base of the sea cliff. Here, lost without branches and leaves about him, he settled to await improvement.

When, at midday of the third day, the rain stopped altogether and the sky opened before a small, fresh wind, letting light through to glitter upon a tremulous sea, Hook was so weak that his good wing also trailed to prop him upright, and his open eyes were lustreless. But his wounds were hardened and he felt the return of hunger. Beyond his shelter he heard the gulls flying in great numbers and crying their joy at the cleared air.

He could even hear, from the fringe of the river, the ecstatic and unstinted bubblings and chirpings of the small birds. The grassland, he felt, would be full of the stirring anew of the close-bound life, the undrowned insects clicking as they dried out, the snakes slithering down, heads half erect, into the grasses where the mice, gophers, and ground squirrels ran and stopped and chewed and licked themselves smoother and drier.

With the aid of this hunger, and on the crutches of his wings, Hook came down to stand in the sun beside his cave, whence he could watch the beach. Before him, in ellipses on tilting planes, the gulls flew. The surf was rearing again and beginning to shelve and hiss on the sand. Through the white foam-writing it left, the long billed pipers twinkled in bevies, escaping each wave, then racing down after it to plunge their fine drills into the minute double holes where the sand crabs bubbled. In the third row of breakers two seals lifted sleek, streaming heads and barked, and over them, trailing his spider legs, a great crane flew south. Among the stones at the foot of the cliff, small red and green crabs made a little, continuous rattling and knocking. The cliff swallows glittered and twanged on aerial forays.

The afternoon began auspiciously for Hook also. One of the two gulls which came squabbling above him dropped a freshly caught fish to the sand. Quickly Hook was upon it; gripping it, he raised his good wing and cocked his head with open beak at the many gulls which had circled and come down at once towards the fall of the fish. The gulls sheered off, cursing raucously. Left alone on the sand, Hook devoured the fish, and, after resting in the sun, withdrew again to his shelter.

IV

In the succeeding days, between rains, he foraged on the beach. He learned to kill and crack the small, green crabs. Along the edge of the river mouth, he found the drowned bodies of mice and squirrels and even sparrows. Twice he managed to drive feeding gulls from their catch, charging upon them with buffeting wing and clattering beak.

He grew stronger slowly, but the shot sail continued to drag. Often, at the choking thought of soaring and striking and the good, hot-blood kill, he strove to take off, but only the one wing came up, winnowing with a hiss, and drove him over on to his side in the sand. After these futile trials he would rage and clatter. But gradually he learned to believe that he could not fly, that his life must now be that of the discharged nestling again. Denied the joy of space, without which the joy of loneliness was lost, the joy of battle and killing, the blood lust, became his whole concentration. It was his hope, as he charged feeding gulls, that they would turn and offer battle, but they never did. The sandpipers at his approach fled peeping, or, like a quiver of arrows shot together, streamed out over the surf in a long curve. Once, pent beyond bearing, he disgraced himself by shrieking challenge at the businesslike heron which flew south every evening at the same time. The heron did not even turn his head, but flapped and glided on.

Hook's shame and anger became such that he stood awake at night. Hunger kept him awake also, for these little leavings of the gulls could not sustain his great body in its renewed violence. He became aware that the gulls slept at night in flocks on the sand, each with one leg tucked under him. He discovered also that the curlews and the pipers, often mingling, likewise slept, on the higher remnant of the bar. A sensation of evil delight filled him in the consideration of protracted striking among them.

There was only half of a sick moon in a sky of running but far-separated clouds on the night when he managed to stalk into the center of the sleeping gulls. This was light enough, but so great was his vengeful pleasure that there broke from him a shrill scream of challenge as he first struck. Without the power of flight behind it, the blow was not murderous, and this newly discovered impotence made Hook crazy, so that he screamed again and again as he struck and tore at the felled gull. He slew the one, but was twice knocked over by its heavy flounderings, and all the others rose above him, weaving and screaming, protesting in the thin moonlight. Wakened by their clamor, the wading birds also took wing, startled and plaintive. When the beach was quiet again, the flocks had settled elsewhere, beyond his pitiful range, and he was left alone beside the single kill. It was a disappointing victory. He fed with lowering spirit.

Thereafter he stalked silently. At sunset he would watch where the gulls settled along the miles of beach, and after dark he would come like a sharp shadow among them, and drive with his hook on all sides of him, till the beatings of a poorly struck victim sent the flock up. Then he would turn vindictively upon the fallen and finish them. In his best night he killed five from one flock. But he ate only a little from one, for the vigor resulting from occasional repletion strengthened only his ire, which became so great at such a time that food revolted him. It was not the joyous, swift, controlled hunting anger of a sane hawk, but something quite different, which made him dizzy if it continued too long, and left him unsatisfied with any kill.

Then one day, when he had very nearly struck a gull while driving it from a gasping yellowfin, the gull's wing rapped against him as it broke for its running start, and, the trailing wing failing to support him, he was knocked over. He flurried awkwardly in the sand to regain his feet, but his mastery of the beach was ended. Seeing him, in clear sunlight, struggling after the chance blow, the gulls returned about him in a flashing cloud, circling and pecking on the wing. Hook's plumage showed quick little jets of irregularity here and there. He reared back, clattering and erecting the good wing, spreading the great, rusty tail for balance. His eyes shone with a little of the old pleasure. But it died, for he could reach none of them. He was forced to turn and dance awkwardly on the sand, trying to clash bills with each tormentor. They banked up quealing and returned, weaving about him in concentric and overlapping circles. His scream was lost in their clamor, and he appeared merely to be hopping clumsily with his mouth open. Again he fell sidewards. Before he could right himself he was bowled over, and a second time, and lay on his side, twisting his neck to reach them and clappering in blind fury, and was struck three times by three successive gulls, shrieking their flock triumph.

Finally he managed to roll to his breast, and to crouch with his good wing spread wide and the other stretched nearly as far, so that he extended like a gigantic moth, only his snake head, with its now silent scimitar, erect. One great eye blazed under its level brow, but where the other had been was a shallow hole from which thin blood trickled to his russet gap.

In this crouch, by short stages, stopping to turn and drive the gulls up repeatedly, Hook dragged into the river canyon and under the stiff cover of the bitter-leafed laurel. There the gulls left him, soaring up with great clatter of their valor. Till nearly sunset Hook, broken-spirited and enduring his hardening eye socket, heard them celebrating over the waves.

When his will was somewhat replenished, and his empty eye socket had stopped the twitching and vague aching which had forced him often to roll ignominiously to rub it in the dust, Hook ventured from the protective lacings of his thicket. He knew fear again, and the challenge of his remaining eye was once more strident, as in adolescence. He dared not return to the beaches, and with a new, weak hunger, the home hunger, enticing him, made his way by short hunting journeys back to the wild wheat slopes and the crisp oaks. There was in Hook an unwonted sensation now, that of the ever-neighboring possibility of death. This sensation was beginning, after his period as a mad bird on the beach, to solidify him into his last stage of life. When, during his slow homeward passage, the gulls wafted inland over him, watching the earth with curious, miserish eyes, he did not cower, but neither did he challenge, either by opened beak or by raised shoulder. He merely watched carefully, learning his first lesson observing the world with one eye.

At first the familiar surroundings of the bend in the river and the tree with the dead limb to which he could not ascend aggravated his humiliation, but in time, forced to live cunningly and half-starved, he lost much of his savage pride. At the first flight of a strange hawk over his realm he was wild at his helplessness, and kept twisting his head like an owl, or spinning in the grass like a small and feathered dervish, to keep the hateful beauty of the wind rider in sight. But in the succeeding weeks, as one after another coasted his beat, his resentment declined, and when one of the raiders, a haughty yearling, sighted his up-staring eye and plunged and struck him dreadfully, and only failed to kill him because he dragged under a thicket in time, the second of his great hungers was gone. He had no longer the true lust to kill, no joy of battle, but only the poor desire to fill his belly.

Then truly he lived in the wheat and the brush like a ground owl, ridden with ground lice, dusty or muddy, ever half-starved, forced to sit hours by small holes for petty and unsatisfying kills. Only once during the final months before his end did he make a kill where the breath of danger recalled his valor, and then the danger was such as a hawk with wings and eyes would scorn. Waiting beside a gopher hole, surrounded by the high yellow grass, he saw the head emerge and struck, and was amazed that there writhed in his clutch the neck and dusty coffin-skull of a rattlesnake. Holding his grip, Hook saw the great thick body slither up after, the tip an erect, strident blur, and writhe on the dirt of the gopher's mound. The weight of the snake pushed Hook about, and once threw him down, and the rising and falling whine of the rattles made the moment terrible, but the vaulted mouth, gaping from the closeness of Hook's gripe, so that the pale, envenomed sabres stood out free, could not reach him. When Hook replaced the grip of his beak with the grip of his talons, and was free to strike again and again at the base of the head, the struggle was over. Hook tore and fed on the fine, watery flesh and left the tattered armor and the long, jointed bone for the marching ants.

When the heavy rains returned he ate well during the period of the first escapes from flooded burrows, and then well enough, in a vulture's way, on the drowned creatures. But as the rains lingered, and the burrows hung full of water, and there were no insects in the grass and no small birds sleeping in the thickets, he was constantly hungry, and finally unbearably hungry. His sodden and ground-broken plumage stood out raggedly about him, so that he looked fat, even bloated, but underneath it his skin clung to his bones. Save for his great talons and clappers, and the rain in his down, he would have been like a handful of air. He often stood for a long time under some bush or ledge, heedless of the drip, his one eye filmed over, his mind neither asleep nor awake, but between. The gurgle and swirl of the brimming river, and the sound of chunks of the bank cut away to splash and dissolve in the already muddy flood, became familiar to him, and yet a torment, as if that great, ceaselessly working power of water ridiculed his frailty, within which only the faintest spark of valor still glimmered. The last two nights before the rain ended he huddled under the floor of the bridge on the coastal highway and heard the palpitant thunder of motors swell and roar over him. The trucks shook the bridge so that Hook, even in his famished lassitude, would sometimes open his one great eye wide and startled.

V

After the rains, when things became full again, bursting with growth and sound, the trees swelling, the thickets full of song and chatter, the fields, turning green in the sun, alive with rustling passages, and the moonlit nights strained with the song of the peepers all up and down the river and in pools in the fields, Hook had to bear the return of the one hunger left him. At times this made him so wild that he forgot himself and screamed challenge from the open ground. The fretfulness of it spoiled his hunting, which was now entirely a matter of patience. Once he was in despair, and lashed himself through the grass and thickets trying to rise, when that virgin scent drifted for a few moments above the current of his own river. Then, breathless, his beak agape, he saw the strong suitor ride swiftly down on the wind over him, and heard afar the screaming fuss of the harsh wooing in the alders. For that moment even the battle heart beat in him again. The rim of his good eye was scarlet, and a little bead of new blood stood in the socket of the other. With beak and talon he ripped at a fallen log, made loam and leaves fly from about it.

But the season of love passed over to the nesting season, and Hook's love hunger, unused, shriveled in him with the others, and there remained in him only one stern quality befitting a hawk, and that the negative one, the remnant, the will to endure. He resumed his patient, plotted hunting, now along a field on the land of the Japanese farmer, but ever within reach of the river thickets.

Growing tough and dry again as the summer advanced, inured to the family of the farmer, whom he saw daily stooping and scraping with sticks in the ugly, open rows of their fields, where no lovely grass rustled and no life stirred save the shameless gulls which walked at the heels of the workers, gobbling the worms and grubs they turned up, Hook became nearly content with his shard of life. The only longing or resentment to pierce him was that he suffered occasionally when forced to hide at the edge of the mile-long bean field from the wafted cruising and the restive, down-bent gaze of one of his own kind. For the rest he was without flame, a snappish, dust-colored creature, fading into the grasses he trailed through and suited to his petty way.

At the end of that summer, for the second time in his four years, Hook underwent a drouth. The equinoctial period passed without a rain. The laurel and the rabbit brush dropped dry leaves. The foliage of the oaks shriveled and curled. Even the night fogs in the river canyon failed. The farmer's red cattle on the hillside lowed constantly, and could not feed on the dusty stubble. Grass fires broke out along the highway and ate fast in the wind, filling the hollows with the smell of smoke, and died in the dirt of the shorn hills. The river made no sound; scum grew on its vestigial pools, and turtles died and stank among the rocks. The dust rode before the wind, and ascended and flowered to nothing between the hills, and every sunset was red with the dust in the air. The people in the farmer's house quarreled, and even struck one another. Birds were silent, and only the hawks flew much. The animals lay breathing hard for very long spells, and ran and crept jerkily. Their flanks were fallen in, and their eyes were red.

At first Hook gorged at the fringe of the grass fires on the multitudes of tiny things that came running and squeaking. But thereafter there were the blackened strips on the hills, and little more in the thin, crackling grass. He found mice and rats, gophers and ground squirrels and even rabbits, dead in the stubble and under the thickets, but so dry and fleshless that only a faint smell rose from them, even on the sunny days. He starved on them. By early December he had wearily stalked the length of the eastern foothills, hunting at night to escape the voracity of his own kind, resting often upon his wings. The queer trail of his short steps and great horned toes zigzagged in the dust and was erased by the wind at dawn. He was nearly dead, and could make no sound through the horn funnels of his clappers.

Then one night the dry wind brought him, with the familiar, lifeless dust, another familiar scent, troublesome, mingled and unclear. In his vision-dominated brain he remembered the swift circle of his flight a year past, crossing in one segment, his shadow beneath him, a yard cluttered with crates and chickens, a gray barn, and then again the ploughed land and the stubble. Traveling faster than he had for days, impatient of his shrunken sweep, Hook came down to the farm. In the dark, wisps of cloud blown among the stars over him, but no moon, he stood outside the wire of the chicken run. The scent of fat and blooded birds reached him from the shelter, and also, within the enclosure was water. At the breath of the water, Hook's gorge contracted and his tongue quivered and clove in its groove of horn. But there was the wire. He stalked its perimeter and found no opening. He beat it with his good wing, and felt it cut but not give. He wrenched at it with his beak in many places, but could not tear it. Finally, in a fury which drove the thin blood through him, he leaped repeatedly against it, beating and clawing. He was thrown back from the last leap as from the first, but in it he had risen so high as to clutch with his beak at the top wire. While he lay on his breast on the ground, the significance of this came upon him.

Again he leapt, clawed up the wire, and as he would have fallen, made even the dead wing bear a little. He grasped the top and tumbled within. There again he rested flat, searching the dark with quick-turning head. There was no sound or motion but the throb of his own body. First he drank at the chill metal trough hung for the chickens. The water was cold, and loosened his tongue and his tight throat, but it also made him drunk and dizzy, so that he had to rest again, his claws spread wide to brace him. Then he walked stiffly, to stalk down the scent. He trailed it up the runway. Then there was the stuffy, body-warm air, acrid with droppings, full of soft rustlings as his talons clicked on the board floor. The thick, white shapes showed faintly in the darkness. Hook struck quickly, driving a hen to the floor with one blow, its neck broken and stretched out stringily. He leaped the still pulsing body and tore it. The rich, streaming blood was overpowering to his dried senses, his starved, leathery body. After a few swallows the flesh choked him. In his rage he struck down another hen. The urge to kill took him again, insanely, as in those nights on the beach. He could let nothing go; balked of feeding, he was compelled to slaughter. Clattering, he struck again and again. The henhouse was suddenly filled with the squawking and helpless rushing and buffeting of the terrified, brainless fowls.

Hook reveled in mastery. Here was game big enough to offer weight against a strike, and yet unable to soar away from his blows. Turning in the midst of the turmoil, cannily, his fury caught at the perfect pitch, he struck unceasingly. When the hens finally discovered the outlet and streamed into the yard to run around the fence, beating and squawking, Hook followed them, scraping down the incline, clumsy and joyous. In the yard the cock, a bird as large as he and much heavier, found him out and gave valiant battle. In the dark, and both earth-bound, there was little skill, but blow upon blow and only chance parry. The still squawking hens pressed into one corner of the yard. While the duel went on a dog, excited by the sustained scuffling, began to bark. He continued to bark, running back and forth along the fence on one side. A light flashed on in an uncurtained window of the farmhouse, and streamed whitely over the crates littering the ground.

Enthralled by his old battle joy, Hook knew only the burly cock before him. Now in the farthest reach of the window light they could see each other dimly. The Japanese farmer, with his gun and his lantern, was already at the gate when the finish came. The great cock leapt to jab with his spurs, and, toppling forward with extended neck as he fell, was struck and extinguished. Blood had loosened Hook's throat. Shrilly he cried his triumph. It was a thin and exhausted cry, but within him as good as when he shrilled in mid-air over the plummeting descent of a fine foe in his best spring.

The light from the lantern partially blinded Hook. He first turned and ran directly from it, into the corner where the hens were huddled. They fled apart before his charge. He essayed the fence, and on the second try, in his desperation, was out. But in the open dust the dog was on him, circling, dashing in, snapping. The farmer, who at first had not fired because of the chickens, now did not fire because of the dog, and, when he saw that the hawk was unable to fly, relinquished the sport to the dog, holding the lantern up in order to see better. The light showed his own flat, broad, dark face as sunken also, the cheekbones very prominent, and showed the torn-off sleeves of his shirt and the holes in the knees of his overalls. His wife, in a stained wrapper and barefooted, heavy black hair hanging around a young, passionless face, joined him hesitantly, but watched, fascinated and a little horrified. His son joined them too, encouraging the dog, but quickly grew silent. Courageous and cruel death, however it may afterwards sicken the one who has watched it, is impossible to look away from.

In the circle of the light Hook turned to keep the dog in front of him. His one eye gleamed with malevolence. The dog was an Airedale, and large. Each time he pounced Hook stood ground, raising his good wing, the pinions torn by the fence, opening his beak soundlessly, and at the closest approach hissed furiously and at once struck. Hit and ripped twice by the whetted horn, the dog recoiled more quickly on several subsequent jumps, and, infuriated by his own cowardice, began to bark wildly. Hook manœuvred to watch him, keeping his head turned to avoid losing the foe on the blind side. When the dog paused, safely away, Hook watched him quietly, wing partially lowered, beak closed, but at the first move again lifted the wing and gaped. The dog whined, and the man spoke to him encouragingly. The awful sound of his voice made Hook for an instant twist his head to stare up at the immense figures behind the light. The dog again sallied, barking, and Hook's head spun back. His wing was bitten this time, and with a furious side blow he caught the dog's nose. The dog dropped him with a yelp, then, smarting, came on more warily as Hook propped himself up from the ground again between his wings. Hook's artificial strength was waning, but his heart still stood to the battle, sustained by a fear of such dimension as he had never known before, but only anticipated when the arrogant young hawk had driven him to cover. The dog, unable to find any point at which the merciless, unwinking eye was not watching him, the parted beak waiting, paused and whimpered again.

"Oh, kill the poor thing," the woman begged.

The man, though, encouraged the dog again, saying, "Sick him, sick him."

The dog rushed bodily. Unable to avoid him, Hook was bowled down, snapping and raking. He left long slashes, as from the blade of a knife, on the dog's flank, but, before he could right himself and assume guard again, was caught by the good wing and dragged, clattering and seeking to make a good stroke from his back. The man followed them to keep the light on them, and the boy went with him, wetting his lips with his tongue and keeping his fists closed tightly. The woman remained behind, but could not help watching the diminished conclusion.

In the little palely shining arena, the dog repeated his successful manœuvre three times, growling but not barking, and when Hook thrashed up from the third blow both wings were trailing, and dark, shining streams crept on his black-fretted breast from the shoulders. The great eye flashed more furiously than it ever had in victorious battle, and the beak still gaped, but there was no more clatter. He faltered when turning to keep front; the broken wings played him false even as props. He could not rise to use his talons.

The man had tired of holding the lantern up, and put it down to rub his arm. In the low, horizontal light the dog charged again, this time throwing the weight on his forepaws against Hook's shoulder, so that Hook was crushed as he struck. With his talons up, Hook raked at the dog's belly, but the dog conceived the finish, and furiously worried the feathered bulk. Hook's neck went limp, and between his gaping clappers came only a faint chittering, as from some small kill of his own in the grasses.

In this last conflict there had been some minutes of the supreme fire of the hawk whose three hungers are perfectly fused in the one will; enough to burn off a year of shame.

Between the great sails the light body lay caved and perfectly still. The dog, smarting from his cuts, came to the master and was praised. The woman, joining them slowly, looked at the great wingspread, her husband raising the lantern that she might see it better.

"Oh, the brave bird," she said.

Hildegarde Flanner
"Hawk Is a Woman"

I saw a hawk devour a screaming bird,
Devour the little ounce sugared with song.
First bent and ate the pretty eyes both out,
One eye and twice, stooping to taste the pang.
Then her dripping tongue she cleaned, then
Into the winsome breast she plied her beak,
Took at a gulp the rosy heart, a pinch
Of too great innocence, drank the whole lark
Down, the inmost blood down, licked the lark down
With vicious dainty pick, oh the damned thief!
To break! into the beating bird! and tear
The veins out, out the joy, flesh out of life.
May hawk be hawked upon, I say,
May she be spied and nailed upon the ground
And feel herself divided and devoured
To ease the gullet of some casual fiend.
She, she! before her agony lapse quite,
Before her breast is eaten to her back,
May she, the very she, may that hawk hear
The ugly female laughter of a hawk.

HORSE

Equus caballus

Family Equidae

Height: to 6 ⅔'; Weight: to 2,000 lb

Habitat:

Ranches, farms, semirural and rural stables, open rangeland

Range:

Common throughout California; feral populations exist in Modoc, Lassen, Inyo, and Kern Counties

Comments:

Horses were once common in North America before they became extinct in the region at the end of the Ice Age. The species was re-introduced to the continent by Europeans. It is thought that horses—once hunted as a source of meat—were domesticated in about 2,000 B.C., although earlier dates have been proposed.

Horses have been bred by humans for a variety of purposes, among them riding, racing, herding, and hauling. As a result, horses vary widely in size and color, but typically they all sport short-haired coats, a ridge of stiff hair along the back of the neck (the mane), and a long-haired tail. Long and slender legs support their barrel-shaped bodies. Feral horses tend to be smaller than their domesticated relatives.

Horses graze on grasses and will eat the leaves of various plants and shrubs; domestic horse diets are often supplemented with hay and grain. Social groups usually feature a dominant male and a number of females and their offspring. In the wild, small groups may form larger herds, which in some areas may damage wildlife habitat and compete with domestic livestock.

Although primarily valued for their working and racing abilities and—in the show world—for their conformation, the horse has also long been a beloved companion animal.

Lincoln Steffens
from "A Boy on Horseback"

My life on horseback from the age of eight to fifteen was a happy one, free, independent, full of romance, adventure, and learning, of a sort. Whether my father had any theory about it or was moved only by my prayers I do not know. But he did have some ideas. He took away my saddle, for example. My mother protested that I had suffered enough, but he insisted and he gave me reasons, some for himself, some for me. He said I would be a better horseman if I learned to ride without stirrups and a saddle-horn to keep my balance. The Indians all rode bareback, and the Comanches, the best horsemen on the plains, used to attack, clinging out of sight to the far side of their horses and shooting under their necks.

"We had to shoot a Comanche's horse to get the fellow," he said, "and even then the devil would drop behind his dead pony and shoot at us over the carcass."

I consented finally to having my beautiful saddle hung high in the harness room until I could sit my horse securely. The result was that I came to prefer to ride bareback and used the saddle only for show or for games and work that needed stirrups and a horn, as in picking up things off a box on the ground or handling cattle (calves) with a rope.

That, however, was but one detail. I had begun about that time to play boys' games: marbles, tops, baseball, football, and I can see now my father stopping on his way home to watch us. He used to wag his head; he said nothing to me, but I knew he did not like those games. I think now that he thought there was some gambling in them, and he had reason to dread gambling. It was a vice that hung over from the mining days in California, and the new business men were against it. They could not have it stopped because "Frank" Rhodes, the political boss, was the keeper of a famous gambling-house; he protected business men, but also he protected his own business. They could not fight Frank too openly, but they lost money and they lost clerks and cashiers through the gambling hells. My father had had to discharge a favorite bookkeeper on account of his heavy play at the gaming-tables. He may have given me the pony to keep me from gambling games or to get me up off the streets and out into the country. There was another result, however, which he did not foresee.

After that blessed pony loped into my life, I never played those trading games which, as I see them now, are the leads not merely to gambling but to business. For there goes on among boys an active trade in marbles, tops, knives, and all the other tools and properties of boyhood. A born trader finds himself in them, and the others learn to like to trade. My theory is that those games are the first lessons in business: they cultivate the instinct to beat the other fellows on 'Change and so quicken their predatory wits. Desirable or no, I never got that training; I never had any interest in, I have always had a distaste for, business, and this my father did not intend. I remember how disappointed he was later when he offered to stay in his business till I could succeed him and I rejected the "great opportunity" with quick scorn—"Business! Never."

My pony carried me away not only from business but from the herd also and the herding habits of mind. The tendency of the human animal to think what others think, say what the mob says, do what the leaders do or command, and, generally, go with the crowd, is drilled in deep at school, where the playground has its fashions, laws, customs and tyrannies just as Main Street has. I missed that. I never played "follow the leader," never submitted to the ideals and the discipline of the campus or, for that matter, of the faculty; and so, ever since, I have been able to buy stocks during a panic, sell when the public was buying; I could not always face, but I could turn my back on, public opinion. I think I learned this when, as a boy on horseback, my interest was not in the campus; it was beyond it; and I was dependent upon, not the majority of boys, but myself and the small minority group that happened to have horses.

I began riding alone. When I mounted my pony the morning after I got him I knew no other boys that had horses, and I did not think of anybody else. I had a world before me. I felt lifted up to another plane, with a wider range. I could explore regions I had not been able to reach on foot. Sacramento is protected from high water in the rivers by levees which send the overflow off to flood other counties. I had visited these levees on foot and wondered what was beyond them. Now I could ride over them and the bridges to—anywhere, I thought. The whole world was open to me. I need not imagine it any more, I could go and see.

I was up early to water, feed, and clean the pony before breakfast. That meal, essential for the horse, was of no importance to me. I slighted it. My father, cautioning me not to work a horse till he had fed fully, said I had plenty of time to eat myself. But I could not eat. I was too excited, too eager, and when I was free to rise from the table I ran out to see if the pony was through his breakfast. He wasn't. I watched him; he was in no hurry. I urged him a bit, but he only lost time looking around at me curiously, and then slowly resumed his meal. My sisters came out to see me off, and one of them rebuked my impatience with a crude imitation of a grown-up.

"The *pony* eats like a gentleman," she said, as if I cared about gentlemen. Something my father had said hit me harder. He said that teamsters, vaqueros, and Indians fed more and longer when they were in a hurry to get off on a long, hard run than on other days; they foresaw that they must be "fortified with food." It took nerve, he admitted, to eat that way, but those fellows had nerve. They could control their animals so perfectly because they had self-control. They didn't force a horse, even in a pursuit. They changed the gait often and went long stretches at a walk. And they could shoot straight, especially in a fight or a battle, because they never became fidgety.

I didn't know it then, but I can see now, of course, that my father was using my horse to educate me, and he had an advantage over the school teachers; he was bringing me up to my own ideals; he was teaching me the things my heroes knew and I wanted to learn. My mother did not understand that. When she came out to the stable, I was anticipating the end of the pony's meal by putting on his saddle blanket and surcingle, and telling my sisters where I was going.

"Don't ride too far the first day," she said. "You will get hungry and sore."

Awful! But I got away at last, and I rode—in all directions. Intending to do one levee that day, and the others in succession the next two days, I rode over them all that morning. I rode over the first one to the American River, and I was disappointed. The general character of the earth's surface did not change much even in that great distance and the change was for the worse—sand and muddy brush. I turned back and rode over the opposite levee, and I could hardly believe it—the land on the other side was like the land on this side. I rode into town again and went across the bridge over the Sacramento River to Yolo County, and that was not different. By that time I was hungry, very hungry, and I came home. Also I was a little hot and uncomfortable in the seat. I was late for lunch, but my mother had kept things warm for me, good things, and she did not ask me very bad questions. Where had I gone? I told her that. What had I seen? I could not tell her that. I had gone to the horizon and seen nothing new, but I did not know that myself well enough to report it to anybody else. Nor could I answer her inquiry for the cause of my depression. Only I denied that I was sore, as she suggested. No, no, not that. I had fed my horse and rubbed him down; when I had eaten I went out and watered and walked him. Then I cleaned him till my sisters came home, and then we all cleaned him.

The next day I was sore, so sore I could hardly sit or walk, but having lied about it, I had to prove it; so I rode off again, in pain, but bravely as a cowboy or an Indian taking torture; only I did not go far. I stopped, dismounted, and let my pony feed on some grass under the trees of East Park. I lay there, and no, I did not think; I imagined things. I imagined myself as all sorts of persons, a cowboy, a trapper, a soldier, a knight, a crusader—I fancied myself as the hero of every story I had read. Not all on this one day. From the day my pony came to me I seem to have spent many, many hours playing around in my imagination, which became the most active faculty of my mind. For, as I say, I was alone much of the time. I learned to like to be alone, and that pleasure I come back to always, even now. When I am tired of the crowd I go off somewhere by myself and have a good time inside my mind.

❦ STELLER'S JAY ❦

Cyanocitta stelleri

Family Corvidae

Length: 12–13 ½"

Habitat:

Trees in coniferous forests and, less frequently, in deciduous areas

Range:

Northern and central Coast Ranges, northern Sierra Nevada, southern California mountains; may move to lower elevations in winter

Comments:

The Steller's jay is easily recognized by its dark gray crest. Its upper throat, head, and back are also dark; the rest of the body is blue, and the wings and tail have black bars. Sometimes this bird—the only crested jay in the West—is mistakenly called a blue jay, which typically lives east of the Rocky Mountains.

An opportunist, the Steller's jay is omnivorous, foraging on acorns, pine seeds, and nuts. But this bold bird also eat insects, scavenges food scraps at campsites, and begs for handouts from human beings. The Steller's jay is highly social, and in a mob will antagonize predators such as hawks.

The Steller's jay may warble, but it also calls out with a series of penetrating, coarse notes—"shaak, shaak, shaak"—which often warn other birds of approaching danger.

William Dawson
from *The Birds of California*

It is a true word which says, "It takes a thief to catch a thief." For, to do him justice, it is usually the Steller Jay who is first to make discovery and outcry if there is any mischief afoot in the woods. Time and again we have had our attention called to the presence of deer or foxes or Horned Owls, which would entirely have escaped our notice had it not been for the zealous proclamations of these birds.

Be sure, also, that the jay is keeping tab on your own movements. If he is feeling hilarious that morning, and he usually is, he will greet the explorer boisterously; but if he "has his doots," he will trail after silently in the tree-tops, "takin' notes" instead. Upon discovery the Steller Jay sets up a great outcry and makes off through the thickets shrieking lustily. A favorite method of retreat is to flit up into the lower branches of a fir tree, and, keeping close to the trunk, to ascend the succeeding limbs as by a spiral staircase. The bird, indeed, takes a childish delight in this mad exercise, and no sooner does he quit one tree-top than he dashes down to a neighboring tree to run another frenzied gamut.

The diet of these jays is highly varied. They will "try anything once," and so, tiring of bugs and slugs, they are not averse to sampling corn, cabbage leaves, or, best of all, potatoes. While their depredations do not figure much in the larger scheme of things, their attentions to pioneer enterprises and modest "clearings" are a little exasperating. The birds have observed the tedious operations of the gardener in planting, and know precisely where the coveted tubers lie. Bright and early the following morning they slip to the edge of the clearing, post one of their number as lookout, then silently deploy upon their ghoulish task. If they weary of potatoes, sprouting peas or corn will do. Or perhaps there may be something interesting at the base of this young tomato plant. And when the irate farmer appears upon the scene, the marauders retire to the forest shrieking with laughter at the discomfitted swain. Ay! there's the rub! We may endure injury but not insult. Bang! Bang!

As a connoisseur of birds' eggs, too, the Steller Jay enjoys a bad eminence. The sufferers in this case are chiefly the lesser song birds; but no eggs whatever are exempt from his covetous glance, if left unguarded.

It is well known that the gentleman burglar takes a conscientious pride in the safety and welfare of his own home. Nothing shall molest *his* dear ones. The jay becomes secretive and silent as the time for nest-building approaches. The nest is well concealed in a dense thicket of fir saplings, or else set at various heights in the larger fir trees. If one but looks at it before the complement of eggs is laid, the locality is deserted forthwith. If, however, the enterprise is irretrievably launched, the birds take care not to be seen in the vicinity of their nest, unless they are certain of its discovery, in which case they call heaven and earth to witness that the man is a monster of iniquity, and that he is plotting against the innocent. The youngsters, too, quickly learn to assume the attitude of affronted innocence. At an age when most bird-babies would make a silent get-away under cover of the parental defense, young Steller jays will turn to and berate the stranger in common with their parents, with all the virtuous zeal of ordained elders.

Louise Wagenknecht
from *White Poplar, Black Locust*

Bird of the bitter bright grey golden morn… —Algernon Charles Swinburne

Tommy had just passed his first birthday when Daddy called us inside one evening as he came home from work. He set his black lunchpail on the table, flipped open the latches, and slowly turned back the lid. Inside were a pair of black shoe-button eyes, a black beak wide open with hunger and indignation, and a couple of tentative, electric blue feathers, lost in a mound of gray fuzz. The young Steller's jay, fallen from the nest, squawked, and loudly. And so we met Perky.

We ran over to Nana's and borrowed an old bird cage; we found an eye dropper and opened a jar of Tommy's strained liver, and after several hours of chaos, Perky sat snuggled in a nest of torn newspaper, eyes shut. He was the first real pet Elizabeth and I ever had, and from the beginning we knew he wasn't ours to keep. "You'll have to let him go when he gets old enough to fly," Daddy told us. But of course, by that time, he was used to us, and even after he was free of the cage, and roosted high in the locust tree at night, he still came fluttering down to the front porch in the mornings, his "WAAAK!" alerting us all. He begged for food, long after he could pick up ants on his own.

There never was a day that I was not afraid for Perky. The odds in Hilt did not favor young birds. There were boys with BB guns; there were cats; there were cars. But for enough time to let us become too fond of him, Perky led a charmed life.

That summer, Aunt Jo and Uncle Carl were living in an apartment in Ashland. Carl was out of the Air Force and working as the night chef at the Medford Country Club. Jo was pregnant, the baby due in October, and she was lonely in the daytime, so I was sent to stay with her for a couple of weeks. We went shopping at Woolworth's together, and to the movies, and on Sunday to services at a Presbyterian Church, because it was within walking distance. We sat through hellfire-and-brimstone sermons, while Jo inhaled her smelling salts and rolled her eyes.

I read all of Genesis and Exodus from Jo's white leather-bound Bible, enthralled by the narratives. In the evenings Jo and I watched television and ate popcorn and discussed babies. In the afternoons, I worried about Perky, and wrote letters to Elizabeth asking her how he was. I put the letters in the mailbox at the foot of the driveway and watched the mailman open the box and remove my letters and shove them into his capacious bag.

I picked up the little apples that fell off the tree outside the back door and bowled them down the wheel ruts of the driveway, so that they bounced over the curb and out onto the four-lane highway, to be squished by cars. I wrote more letters, asking how Tommy was, amazed to realize that I actually missed him.

While I was gone, our house in Hilt was painted. The Company, in the throes of some visiting executive's notion that the town looked "run-down," had pushed through a plan to paint all the houses in town. The idea that Hilt's wood-frame cottages should—almost forty years after their construction—be painted struck Daddy as a remarkably bad idea. "That dry wood will soak up a lot of paint; it'll take at least three coats before the job looks decent, and they won't want to buy that much paint."

He was right. Only the Front Street houses received three coats, plus a contrasting color for the trim. The rest received a single spray-painted layer, on body and trim alike. Beneath the thin patina of paint, the old wood soon showed through.

When the Company painters approached Daddy with color cards and asked which color he preferred, he told them that he preferred that it not be painted at all. Just paint the window trim white again, and it'll look nice and rustic, he told them. But they only stared at him, and under the silent reproach of their we-just-work-here-Mr.-Brannon gaze, he finally pointed to a color sample.

So I came home to find the house painted a startling light blue, and not until I saw the quirk around Daddy's mouth as we drove down into Hilt from the highway did I realize the joke. Our house was perched on a little rise at the south edge of town. Driving down into town from the highway a mile above, our house was, for every traveler, the first and most visible glimpse of Hilt. And it now looked exactly like a giant robin's egg with a porch.

Perky was hopping around the garden as we drove up, and as I approached he flew up onto my shoulder. His beak was blue. He had had a wonderful time when the painters were there, landing on their white overalls and pecking at their brass buttons and suspender hooks. And he had, of course, landed on the rims of the open paint cans and tried to drink the paint. "Well, he only did it once," Elizabeth consoled me. "He's into everything these days."

Perky had real feathers now, and there was no doubt that he could fly. More and more, he flew around town, extending his territory. He rode on Liz's shoulder up to Marin's one day and flew into the kitchen, lit on Tony's coffee cup, and took a swig. On his own expeditions, he tried to follow someone as they opened a screen door, and the door slammed on his beak, stunning him, and throwing the beak out of alignment. He startled housewives on their way to the store, as he landed in their hair, squawking.

I had been gone for two weeks, and everyone had survived without me, even Perky, a bird so trusting that his life was one long narrow escape. I spent the last nights of summer sleeping out on the lawn in my sleeping bag, and in the early morning, high above me in the locust tree, I heard Perky singing his imitations of robins and orioles, in the high sweet notes seldom heard from jays.

He began picking up pieces of colored glass in the alleys and tucking them into the holes in the pecky cedarwood fence between our yard and Johnson's. He was careless enough to roost on that fence in the afternoons, and twice Ruthie saved him from a cat about to pounce. And one day, of course, he disappeared.

We did not find him until October, when the little that was left of him turned up in the dry bed of Hilt Creek, recognizable at once because there were no other Steller's jays in town—they were a forest bird—and because of the distinctive beak. We should have taken him into the woods ourselves, and picnicked somewhere where the Steller's jays were, and left him there, I thought. A Bible verse, read that summer, ran through my mind: "Let me not see the death of the child."

On my way home from school the next day, I carried a handkerchief, and walking back up the creek bed, I scraped up the remains of beak and claw and feather with a wood chip. Walking back toward the alley, the light dry burden clutched in my hand, I was ambushed by Mike Trinca, who leapt out from the piles of old tires behind his Uncle Bob's service station and unleashed a barrage of crab apples at me. I ran, fleeing the missiles, ashamed of my cowardice, knowing that if Daddy learned of it, he would tell me what he had told me last year, when the boys threw clods of dirt at me.

"They'll keep throwing things at you until you beat one of them up," he had said. "If you don't have enough courage to do that, don't come crying to us." I was afraid of an actual physical conflict, and it made me ashamed. I said no more about the incidents, which continued. But this was too much. Mike, I was convinced, had killed my blue jay, knowing that Perky was mine, and had thrown the apples at me just to taunt me about it.

The next morning at school, I tapped Mike on the shoulder as he was hanging up his jacket, and when he turned around, I punched him as hard as I could in the mouth and kept on punching. Mike staggered backwards into the coats, tripping over someone's rubber boots. But although he was a year my junior, Mike was as tall as I was and heavier. He would never have punched a girl unprovoked, but after a moment's wild puzzlement, he evidently decided he was dealing with an unprecedented situation and began to fight back, fists whirling as he landed a hard punch on my ear that slammed the ear piece of my glasses into my skull. I grabbed his shirt and yanked and swung my fist at his eye socket, jamming my knuckles in the process. He fell on top of me, landing punches on my ribs, and I felt my head slam onto the linoleum tiles just as Mrs. Jeter grabbed Mike by his shirt collar and hauled him upright.

Sitting in the principal's office, watching the stunned look on Mr. Rhodes's face as he slowly pried the story out of me, I felt strangely peaceful. I didn't think I would be punished for hitting Mike, but if I was, I didn't care. Mr. Rhodes kept me sitting across from his desk until noon, then sent me home. I had a torn dress, a bruised face, and a new reputation. No one ever threw anything at me again. When Mother told Daddy, he only nodded. "The boy asked for it," was all he said.

That evening, Daddy dug a grave for Perky in the nasturtium bed and dropped beak, feathers, bones, and handkerchief inside, tamping everything down with a big round piece of river-washed granite and leaving it there as a headstone.

A few days later, I heard another boy bragging that he had shot a bluejay in town that summer and I knew that I had found the real culprit. I had never told David about Perky, precisely because I knew he had a BB gun, and I feared the generalized meanness of boys.

That fall, as baseball season gave way to football, eight or ten of us gathered on Sunday afternoons in David's yard to play tackle football, with the sidewalk as the fifty-yard line. I made sure of tackling David as often as I could, driving his knees into the morass, slamming him to the ground until my coat was covered with dirt and the shredded remnants of dead damp leaves and streaked with the green blood of the mashed and dying lawn.

∽⌇ DESERT HORNED LIZARD ⌇∽

Phrynosoma platyrhinos

Family Phrynosomatidae

Length: 3–5 ⅜"

Habitat:

Arid landscapes with rocks or scrub vegetation; sandy, gravelly soil

Range:

Eastern and southeastern California

Comments:

The desert horned lizard, often called a "horned toad" because of its squat size and head armor, looks almost like a dragon. It is red, tan, or dark gray, and flat-bodied with short spines surrounding its head. A row of scales encircles its trunk, and the scales on its underside are smooth. The sides of its head are colored with wavy crossbands, and its neck has dark spots. It has five clawed toes on each of its four legs, and a short, broad tail.

The desert horned lizard is diurnal. It hibernates in the fall by burying itself in sand and emerges in the spring when it is warm. Mornings it basks in the sun, and when sufficiently warmed up, forages for food. Its diet includes a variety of arthropods, including spiders, ants, sow bugs, and ticks.

The desert horned lizard mostly depends on camouflage for safety and will sit quietly when discovered; if near vegetation, it may instead seek cover. If the ground becomes too hot, it will seek shade and, in the evening, it digs a hole in the sandy soil in which to spend the night.

William Saroyan
from *My Name Is Aram*

My uncle Melik was just about the worst farmer that ever lived. He was too imaginative and poetic for his own good. What he wanted was beauty. He wanted to plant it and see it grow. I myself planted over one hundred pomegranate trees for my uncle one year back there in the good old days of poetry and youth in the world. I drove a John Deere tractor too, and so did my uncle. It was all pure aesthetics, not agriculture. My uncle just liked the idea of planting trees and watching them grow.

Only they wouldn't grow. It was on account of the soil. The soil was desert soil. It was dry. My uncle waved at the six hundred and eighty acres of desert he had bought and he said in the most poetic Armenian anybody ever heard, Here in this awful desolation a garden shall flower, fountains of cold water shall bubble out of the earth, and all things of beauty shall come into being.

Yes, sir, I said.

I was the first and only relative to see the land he had bought. He knew I was a poet at heart, and he believed I would understand the magnificent impulse that was driving him to glorious ruin. I did. I knew as well as he that what he had purchased was worthless desert land. It was away over to hell and gone, at the foot of the Sierra Nevada mountains. It was full of every kind of desert plant that ever sprang out of dry hot earth. It was overrun with prairie dogs, squirrels, horned toads, snakes, and a variety of smaller forms of life. The space over this land knew only the presence of hawks, eagles, and buzzards. It was a region of loneliness, emptiness, truth, and dignity. It was nature at its proudest, driest, loneliest, and loveliest.

My uncle and I got out of the Ford roadster in the middle of his land and began to walk over the dry earth.

This land, he said, is my land.

He walked slowly, kicking into the dry soil. A horned toad scrambled over the earth at my uncle's feet. My uncle clutched my shoulder and came to a pious halt.

What is that animal? he said.

That little tiny lizard? I said.

That mouse with horns, my uncle said. What is it?

I don't know for sure, I said. We call them horny toads.

The horned toad came to a halt about three feet away and turned its head.

My uncle looked down at the small animal.

Is it poison? he said.

To eat? I said. Or if it bites you?

Either way, my uncle said.

I don't think it's good to eat, I said. I think it's harmless. I've caught many of them. They grow sad in captivity, but never bite. Shall I catch this one?

Please do, my uncle said.

I sneaked up on the horned toad, then sprang on it while my uncle looked on.

Careful, he said. Are you sure it isn't poison?

I've caught many of them, I said.

I took the horned toad to my uncle. He tried not to seem afraid.

A lovely little thing, isn't it? he said. His voice was unsteady.

Would you like to hold it? I said.

No, my uncle said. You hold it. I have never before been so close to such a thing as this. I see it has eyes. I suppose it can see us.

I suppose it can, I said. It's looking up at you now.

My uncle looked the horned toad straight in the eye. The horned toad looked my uncle straight in the eye. For fully half a minute they looked one another straight in the eye and then the horned toad turned its head aside and looked down at the ground. My uncle sighed with relief.

A thousand of them, he said, could kill a man, I suppose.

They never travel in great numbers, I said. You hardly ever see more than one at a time.

A big one, my uncle said, could probably bite a man to death.

They don't grow big, I said. This is as big as they grow.

They seem to have an awful eye for such small creatures, my uncle said. Are you sure they don't mind being picked up?

I suppose they forget all about it the minute you put them down, I said.

Do you really think so? my uncle said.

I don't think they have very good memories, I said.

My uncle straightened up, breathing deeply.

Put the little creature down, he said. Let us not be cruel to the innocent creations of Almighty God. If it is not poison and grows no larger than a mouse and does not travel in great numbers and has no memory to speak of, let the timid little thing return to the earth. Let us be gentle toward these small things which live on the earth with us.

Yes, sir, I said.

I placed the horned toad on the ground.

Gently now, my uncle said. Let no harm come to this strange dweller on my land.

The horned toad scrambled away.

These little things, I said, have been living on soil of this kind for centuries.

Centuries? my uncle said. Are you sure?

I'm not sure, I said, but I imagine they have. They're still here, anyway.

My uncle looked around at his land, at the cactus and brush growing out of it, at the sky overhead.

What have they been eating all this time? he shouted.

I don't know, I said.

What would you say they've been eating? he said.

Insects, I guess.

Insects? my uncle shouted. What sort of insects?

Little bugs, most likely, I said. I don't know their names. I can find out tomorrow at school.

WESTERN FENCE LIZARD

Sceloporus occidentalis

Family: Iguanidae

Length: 3 ½"

Habitat:

> Found in a wide variety of habitats, including coastal sage and chaparral and forested foothills

Range:

> Throughout California, except in some deserts; from the coast to elevations of 6,000'

Comments:

> One of the most common lizards in California, the western fence lizard is often seen on top of rocks, fence posts, and walls, where it basks in sunshine. Also called a "blue-belly," this lizard is brown or grayish, with spots, chevrons, or stripes on its back; underneath, blue patches mark the throat and ventral sides.
>
> The western fence lizard preys on insects and spiders and is, in turn, preyed upon by snakes and birds. Near suburban settings, it may also be stalked by cats and dogs. When threatened, the western fence lizard may detach the tip of its tail—which grows back—in order to distract predators. The male of the species is territorial, and it typically does "push ups" in order to display its blue patches and to ward off outsiders.
>
> Researchers have recently discovered that the blood of western fence lizards contains a substance that kills Lyme disease. When infected nymphal ticks feed on the blood of western fence lizards, the disease may be "cleansed" from the nymph before it matures into an adult. This factor may explain why Lyme disease is as yet less common in California than elsewhere.

David Mas Masumoto
"Lizard Dance"

While weeding, I feel something tickle my calf. Without stopping my shovel, I brush the back of my leg. It happens again and I assume the clumps of johnsongrass I dug out are rolling off their pile, the thick stalks and stems attacking their killer in a vain attempt at revenge. Finally, I shake my right leg, and the thing bolts upward.

Immediately I throw down my shovel and stamp my feet. The adrenaline shoots into my system and my heart races. I initiate my lizard dance, shaking my leg, pounding my feet, patting my pants as the poor creature runs wild up my leg. The faster I spin and whirl, the more confused the lizard becomes and the more frantically he scrambles up and down the dark caverns of my pant leg.

In the middle of my dance, I begin laughing, recalling the familiar feel of a lizard running up my pants, through my shirt, and down my sleeves. My body dances uncontrollably to the feel of its tiny feet and little claws grabbing my skin. I try to slow down, knowing the lizard will too if we both relax.

But as the creature scampers up higher and higher my imagination runs wild. Vulnerable body parts flash in my mind.

If other workers were around, they would laugh, watching me tug at my belt, frantically trying to drop my pants. With luck, I won't open a crevice in my shorts, inviting the lizard into another dark hiding place. Instead he'll be attracted to daylight, leap out of my crotch, and tumble to the ground, dazed for a moment before scampering into the safety of weeds and undergrowth.

I enjoy the return of lizards to my farm. They were plentiful in my youth, soaking up the rays of the sun, eating bugs and insects, living happily in the patches of grasses and weeds. Then we disked and plowed their homes and sprayed to kill most of their food. The lizards left.

I didn't plan on raising lizards, but they're part of a natural farm landscape. Besides, their presence reminds me of my childhood. I can't return to those days but I can try and foster new life on the farm, along with laughter and the lizard dance.

LOUSE

Pediculus humanus humanus and Pediculus humanus capitis

Family Pediculidae

Length: $\frac{1}{16}$–$\frac{1}{4}$"

Habitat:

Human bodies, temporarily on clothes and/or bedding

Range:

Common throughout California

Comments:

The human louse is grayish with a pear-shaped, flat body. It has short, strong legs for gripping onto its host. It hides in folds and seams of clothing, from which it crawls onto skin to feed on human blood.

The louse attaches its eggs to clothing, and the eggs hatch in approximately eight days. The louse matures in less than two weeks. The human head louse *(Pediculus humanus capitis)* glues its eggs, or nits, onto human hair. The female can lay ten eggs per day, fastening each one to a different hair, making them difficult to dislodge. The human body louse, *Pediculus humanus humanus*, glues its eggs to clothing.

Infestations of lice cause uncomfortable skin irritations and itching. Outbreaks of head lice are common among schoolchildren. More serious side effects include various diseases, particularly typhus.

G. Ezra Dane
from *Ghost Town*

It was one day in the rainy winter of '54 and '55, and too wet to work in the mines, so the boys begun to wander in early down at the Long Tom. By noon all the tables was full and the gambling got more exciting as the day wore on. Some of the boys set right there at the tables from morning through all the day and on into the evening, without stopping except to take on a drink or to make room for more.

If you once get the gambling fever, you know, in a place like that, the longer you keep at it, the higher the fever gets. That fever's catching and it'll spread through a crowd like any other fever. So monte, faro, seven-up, and the different brands of poker got too slow for some, and they begun laying bets on any chance that offered. At some of the tables they was betting on the turn of a card, and they was one crowd having a spitting tournament at the stove. Then they was some fellows betting which of two flies on the wall would move first, and others at the door laying bets whether or not the next man to come in would be Irish. But the greatest bet in betting history was laid that night by young Ad Pence. An inspiration it was, no less.

"Boys," says Ad, pounding on the bar to get the attention of the crowd, "Boys," says he, "luck's been agin me so far, but I've got five hundred here that says I've a louse that can beat, in a fair race, any louse that ever cut his teeth on any miner's hide."

He'd caught a good lively one and held him up for all the boys to see.

"I say this louse is the champeen," says Ad, "for I've been chasing him around my carcass for a week and I've only just caught up with him. Five hundred backs him against all comers."

Well, at that all the games stopped short, and everybody crowded up to the bar where Ad was showing off this champeen louse. But none of the boys would admit that he kept this kind of stock and it begun to look as though nobody was going to take the bet. Then a stranger, a big Irishman with a red beard, come elbowing his way through the crowd and up to the bar where Ad was standing.

"Will ye let me have a look at that louse?" he says.

So Ad held it out and the stranger squinted at it from one side and then from the other. "A dainty crayther indade he is," says he, "but I think he's no racer. His belly's too low and his legs are too short by a long ways. Now wait just a bit and I'll have something to show ye."

So the stranger put his hand inside his shirt, and scrabbled around in there for a minute, and when he pulled it out again, between his thumb and finger he held a struggling louse.

"Me boy," he says, "your five hundred is as good as gone. But before I take it from ye, I want ye to have a good look at *this* louse. Ye'll never see the likes of him again. Ye say yours is the champeen, but ye've only had him a wake, and he has not so much as a name. I say he's but a mongrel. Now *this* one is the greatest racing louse in all the world, and he has the most distinguished pedigray that ever a louse did boast. And I don't want to be taking your money under any false pretenses, so I'm going to tell ye his history, and when ye've heard it, if ye want to withdraw, I'll freely let ye do so.

"Just before me old grandfather died, back in Ireland, he called me to his bedside and he said to me: 'Grandson,' says he, 'I'm a pore man. I've no money to lave ye, nor any property. But there's wan threasure I have, Grandson,' says the old man, 'Katie, the finest little seam squirrel in all of Ireland, and a direct discindent of one that fed on Saint Patrick.

"'Take her, Grandson,' says he, 'kape good care of her and fade her well, and she'll surely bring ye luck.'

"Now, me boy, this louse ye see here is Larry, Katie's great-great-great-grandson, and the blood of Saint Patrick himself runs in his veins, so he's bound to bring me luck. And to show the faith I have in him and in Holy Saint Patrick, bejayziz, I'll lay a thousand to that five hundred ye bet on yer mongrel louse! Now, do ye still want to make the bet?"

"I do," says Ad. "Your louse may be good, but I know what mine can do from long chasing of him, and my bet on him still stands."

So Ad and the stranger placed their stakes with Doc Johns, and side betting begun in the crowd.

"There can be no race without a racetrack," says the stranger, and he calls to the bar-tender. "Bring us a plate," he says. "Now, boys, the middle's the start, the edge is the goal, and the first little pants rabbit over the rim is the winner."

So the bar-tender brought the plate, and the stranger felt of it. "No louse," says he, "would ever set a good pace on this cold plate. Let's hate it up a bit, and then you'll see them kick up their heels and run."

So they heated the plate piping hot over the stove and set it on a table where all could see. And when Doc Johns counted off: "One, two, three, go!" each man dropped his louse in the middle of the plate and they were off, a-scrambling and a-jumping because it was so hot, you know. The boys was cheering and yelling and standing on chairs to see, and laying bets right and left.

Well, neck and neck it was at the start acrost the bottom of the plate, but Ad's louse pulled ahead a bit and he was the first to reach the rise of the rim. Then come the last hard pull for the edge. He started up the rise, but when he got about half-way up he lost his footing on the slippery rim and slid down again. So he backed up and he took another run for it, and got up a little further, but again he slid back. He was a game one, that louse was. He tried it again and again, but he couldn't quite make it. No sir, it was on that last hard pull up the rim of the plate that the blood of Saint Patrick begun to tell, for Larry, the stranger's lucky louse, he started up slow and careful, and he kept on a-pulling and a-scrambling and up and up he went and *over* the edge to victory and into his master's hand. A hero he was, for sure!

The fellows jumped down from the tables then and Jack White, he says: "Three cheers for Larry and the blood of Saint Patrick!" So the boys roared out the three cheers. And they *was* cheers too, for them young fellows didn't have no colds, nor consumption neither.

Well, then Doc Johns paid over the fifteen hundred dollars to the stranger, and Ad went up to shake his hand. "Stranger," he says, "it was a fair race, and the best louse won. The money's yours and I don't begrudge it to you. But I've one request to make of you, stranger, and if you'll grant it, I'll be forever grateful."

"And what may that be?" says the stranger.

"Just let me borrow Larry till tomorrow," says Ad.

"But what for?" says the stranger. "Why might ye be wanting to borry me pet?"

"Why, man!" says Ad, "I want to improve my breed!"

MOSQUITO

Ochlerotatus melanimon

Family Culicidae

Length: up to ¼"

Habitat:
Still bodies of water, from water-filled leaves to lakes, irrigated pastures, and seasonal waterfowl habitats

Range:
Common throughout inland California, especially the Central Valley and the Sierra Nevada

Comments:
The mosquito is a delicate fly easily identified by its slender legs and proboscis—a long set of mouthparts for piercing a food source. *Ochlerotatus melanimon*, the mosquito common in the Central Valley, is brown to tan. Its wings are scaled and fold over the abdomen. The male has feathery antennae in comparison to the female's.

The female must have a blood meal before it can produce eggs; it preys on humans and other mammals like cattle, horses, and dogs. Male mosquitoes do not feed on blood but on nectar, which female mosquitoes may also feed on.

Up to 150 eggs are laid on damp soil or at the base of grasses that will be flooded at a later time; eggs can sustain drying and will hatch once there is water. It takes four to ten days for a larva (or "wiggler") to emerge as an adult, and multiple generations can be produced by one female from March to November. The first frost generally kills adult *Ochlerotatus melanimon*.

The mosquito is considered a pest and can be harmful to humans; *Ochlerotatus melanimon* has been known to spread various viruses, including the Western Equine Encephalitis virus. Other types of mosquitos in California include *Ochlerotatus nigromaculis, Ochlerotatus dorsalis*, and *Culex pipiens*.

James M. Hutchings
from *Scenes of Wonder and Curiosity in California*

The Sacramento boat, we see, is going straight forward, and will soon enter the Sacramento River, up which her course lies; while ours is to the right—past "New York of the Pacific," a place now containing only two or three small dilapidated houses, but which was once intended by speculators to be the great commercial emporium of this coast—up the San Joaquin.

The evening being calm and sultry, it soon becomes evident that, if it is not the height of the musquito season, a very numerous band are out on a freebooting excursion; and, although their harvest-home song of blood is doubtless very musical, it is matter of regret with us to confess that, in our opinion, but few persons on board appear to have any ear for it. In order, however, that their musical efforts may not be entirely lost sight of, they—the musquitos—take pleasure in writing and impressing their low refrain, in red and embossed notes, upon the foreheads of the passengers, so that he who looks may read, "Musquitos!" when, alas! such is the ingratitude felt for favors so voluntarily performed, that flat-handed blows are dealt out to them in impetuous haste; and blood, blood, blood, and flattened musquitos, are written, in red and dark brown spots, upon the smiter; and the notes of *those* singers are heard no more!

MOUNTAIN LION

Felis concolor

Family Felidae

Length: 6–9'; Weight: 150–230 lb

Habitat:

Forested and brushy areas; occasionally sighted in urban areas

Range:

Throughout California

Comments:

The mountain lion—also known by the names cougar, panther, painter, puma, and catamount—is the largest cat in California. Its head is small for the size of its body, which is pale brown or sandy in color. The mountain lion also possesses a long, usually black-tipped tail.

The mountain lion is an important predator, serving as a check against burgeoning deer populations. The big cat primarily hunts at night, although it will also hunt by day in remote areas. The mountain lion is strongly territorial, with some male cats staking claims of up to one hundred square miles. It feeds primarily on deer—which it can outrun over short distances—but will also take other animals for food, including coyotes, beavers, and even skunks. It may cover the carcass of an animal it doesn't eat completely and revisit the cache several times. A mountain lion that lives near urban areas may feed on domestic cats, and in more rural regions, it may prey on domestic stock. Rarely will a mountain lion attack a human being, but isolated incidents do occur.

Mountain lions are generally stealthy animals, preferring to sneak up on their prey before running it down and leaping onto its back. Usually silent, mountain lions do produce a variety of calls, including growls, hisses, and a particularly shrill mating call, "which has been likened to a woman's scream," according to one authority.

Charles Bukowski
"the lady and the mountain lion"

it was hardly a wilderness area
but it was countryside
and there had been a paucity of
rainfall—also some housing
construction on the
hillsides.

small game was dying
out.
the coyotes were the first of
the famished to
arrive
looking for
chickens
cats
anything.

in fact, a group attacked
a man on horseback
tearing his arm
but he
escaped.

then
in a park
there was the lady who
left her car to
go to the public
restroom.

she had closed the stall
door
when she heard a

soft
sound,
the stealth of
padded
feet.

then
as she sat there
the mountain lion stuck
his head under the
stall door.

a truly beautiful
animal.

then
the head withdrew, the cat
knocked over a trash can, circled,
emitted a slow
growl.

the lady climbed up
on the toilet
then grasped an overhead
pipe
and
swung herself completely up
(fear creates abnormal
acts) and sat where
she could watch
the cat.

at once
the cat put his
paws up
on the wash basin
stuck his head in
there
and lapped at a dripping
spigot.

then
he sank
low upon the floor
crouched
facing the doorway

then
zing
was gone
out of there.

then
at last
the lady began
screaming.

when the people
arrived
the cat was nowhere to be
seen.

the story made the
newspapers and the television
stations.

Charles F. Lummis
"The California Lion"

Of all animate creation, science recognizes the cat family as the most perfect workmanship. No other animal—not even Man—is so unimprovably adjusted to its environments, so absolutely fitted for the life it has to lead. Even evolution, the supreme, slow Afterthought, has found nothing to better in the *felidae*....

No other animal remained so unchanged through the geologic aeons; no other is so unchangeable now. Domesticated for as many millenniums as the dog—and therefore far longer than any other quadruped—he stands in look, in motion, in dignity and independence unchanged from the beginning of the world. He is today the most archaic of all living types; and to the scientist that means that the type was practically perfect. If there had been any room for improvement, Nature would have found it out a few million years ago. He is still a tiger, whatever his size; loving his family and his friends but owning no master, never a sycophant, always independent and a hunter.

In despite of the closet naturalist and the traveled confounder, mankind from its own infance has half unconsciously realized this feline perfection. In all ages and all climes the greatest cat has ranked as "king of beasts." The Hottentot in his Kraal, the Inca in his cyclopean fortress, the literature of every civilized nation—all have agreed in this one point as upon few others.

The greatest cat of the Western Hemisphere is the jaguar, the most beautiful animal, superficially, in the world. But he is the American tiger, not a lion, in appearance and in character. He is burliest of all *felidae*, and terrible as a Royal Bengal.

The American lion is *felis concolor*—the puma, cougar, mountain-lion or California lion. His build is essentially leonine, not tigerish; and so are his color and his character. He is most supple of all the great cats. The lither body and lack of mane make him a very different presence from his old-world namesake; but he is very much like the African lioness....

The California lion is not a coward and not a fool. He has learned what civilized man is; he *sabes* "gun." The reflections upon his honor because he has learned this lesson are not creditable to the intelligence of his critics. All the higher animals have learned it, and have become prudent within half a century; only the bull and the average man continue to charge upon the red rag and cold steel of Fate.

I know the puma not only in the cage but in his habitat; and every student with that acquaintance respects not only his armature but his character. Barring the jaguar (which does not range north of Mexico) he is the most beautiful creature in the New World; the most graceful, the most dignified, the most superbly competent. He is the highest type of sinewy strength, of agility, of dexterity, of balanced power. Stalking his prey, he is more graceful than a perfect woman, and inevitable as the End. In repose,

he is the last word of contained force. Noblest of all is he when he promenades—"walking with himself," as my *paisano* friends have it; *paseandose*, not for prey, but just for joy of his legs. I have studied all the large animals of the New World in their native haunts; and there is none other so lordly. The jaguar, for all his peerless beauty of hide, is a lubber afoot compared to the puma. No cat can be called clumsy—but Don Jaguar is a burly prize-fighter beside the lithe magic of Puma.

Felis concolor is practically a Spanish-American—for while he is of the same species as the Eastern panther, only a closet naturalist educated on stuffed skins could confound the two. He ranges throughout the Rockies from Montana to New Mexico; and thence south all the way to Chile—and even further. And since human life first began on this continent, the puma has been revered by his aboriginal neighbors. He is still the highest fetich of the Pueblos, as he was of the Incas; and his sculptured image is among the prehistoric ruins all the way from Colorado to Peru.

It is curious that the bear should have been chosen as the California emblem. It is not distinctive—for no other quadruped is so universally distributed. There are bears in every country in the world except the few where civilization has exterminated them. And a generation ago there were bears in every State of the Union. The adoption anyhow of so clumsy, uncleanly, monkey-brained, hoglike and hog-rooting a brute, probably the least respectable of all the feral types—a grub-digging, berry-picking, bee-robbing, carrion-contented duffer—is hardly more creditable to the observation of the electors than our national choice of the thievish bird whose last claims to romance or even respect were laughed out of court by Mayne Reid a generation ago, and will never be rehabilitated.

⤳ POCKET MOUSE ⤳

Chaetodipus fallax; *also* ***Perognathus fallax***

Family Heteromyidae

Length: 6 ⅜–7 ⅞"; Weight: ½–⅓ oz

Habitat:

Dry, sandy, and chaparral areas

Range:

Southwestern California, within the vicinity of San Diego County

Comments:

The San Diego pocket mouse is covered with rough hair and spines. It is dark brown above, with black spines on its rump and white spines on its hips. Its underparts are white and its tail is dark above with a lighter stripe below. Its tail is about one inch shorter than its body and is used as a rudder for balance when the animal runs. During slow locomotion it is quadrupedal, but when it accelerates—it can gallop up to 8 miles per hour—it uses both of its hind legs simultaneously.

A solitary creature, the San Diego pocket mouse is intolerant even of its own species, and little is known about many of its habits. It appears to be granivorous and carries seeds in fur-lined pouches inside its cheeks. Seeds are an important source of moisture, and as temperatures rise, the pocket mouse tends to eat seeds that contain high amounts of moisture.

The San Diego pocket mouse stores its seeds in extensive burrow systems with separate passages reserved for food storage. It remains in its burrows for most of the day and emerges to look for food at night. During the winter it goes through a decreased state of activity, but no true hibernation occurs. The San Diego pocket mouse squeaks when in danger.

Chaetodipus fallax was known as *Perognathus fallax* until 1983, when the genus for all spiny pocket mice was changed to *Chaetodipus.*

Steve Kowit
"Perognathus fallax"

When I went to the shed to check for water damage
after the last rains,
I found a tiny gray mouse, dead
among the rubbish of an old carton,
& lifting out the rags & jars, came
on his mate, backed in a corner, tiny
and alive. Beside her—ears
barely visible flecks, tails nothing
but tendrils of gray thread—two nurslings:
one curled asleep by her snout,
& the other awake at her nipple;
the three together no larger, I'd guess,
than the height of my thumb.
I took the box into the yard,
where there was more light,
& where the cats weren't lurking,
& lifted out the rest of the detritus—
a shredded pillow, cans of varnish
& spray paint—beneath which I found, woven
out of what must have been pieces
of cotton, chewed cardboard, & small twigs,
some sort of ramshackle nest.
Now, with nowhere to hide,
she scurried behind it, a pup still at her dugs,
& looked up at me, into my eyes,
the way one of my cats might
who'd been cornered, or as might
one of my own kind, pleading—
her gaze wholly human, wholly intelligible.
It's uncanny, isn't it,
how much alike we all are?
The next morning,
when I went to the pump house
where I'd set the carton for safety,
I was amazed to see the perfect
filigreed globe into which
she had rewoven her nest overnight—
From a port at its top, her tiny snout,

& those two bright eyes
peering anxiously up into my face.
I just stood there: I could hardly believe
how exquisite that nest was,
& how happy I was to see her.
The crumbs of seed I had dropped in
were gone, & I couldn't help but think
how nice it would be
to keep them there, safe from the hawks,
feed them whatever they liked—
but for only a moment.
Then took out my knife
& sliced a small hole in the cardboard,
an inch or so from the bottom,
& the next time I went back they were gone.
I was sorry to see the thing empty.
Is that stupid of me? *Perognathus*
 fallax: the San Diego pocket mouse,
according to my *Audubon*
Guide to North American Mammals—
which was the last week of March,
the whole yard given over to mountain lilac
& sage & alyssum
& out by the wood fence, that stand of iris,
too tattered, I'd thought, to survive
all those hard rains,
but which had.
& under my feet, alive, but so tiny
one hardly noticed,
a hundred species of wild flower:
saffron & white & pink & mauve & blood red.

MULE

Equus caballus x Equus asinus

Family Equidae

Height: to 5 ⅜'; Weight: 400–500 lb

Habitat:

Ranches, farms, semirural and rural stables

Range:

Common throughout California

Comments:

A mule is the sterile, hybrid offspring of a male donkey and a female horse. At first glance, it resembles the donkey more, with a thick head and long ears, though its body and height are more reminiscent of the horse. Its coat is usually brown, although it may be almost any color that horses and donkeys have.

Mules have been bred from ancient times to draw wagons and carry heavy loads. They are surefooted, patient, and possessed of prodigious endurance. Although they can be trained to any of the work done by horses and donkeys, they are particularly good at high-jumping. The "Coon Hunter's Jump" is a sport that derives from hunters jumping strings of pack mules across fences.

John Randolph Spears
from *Illustrated Sketches of Death Valley*

The "largest, most capacious, and most economical wagons ever built were manu-factured on the Mojave Desert, for use in Death Valley."

The tourist among the deserts of Nevada and California will hear a good many curious statements from the scattered population he will find there—the one quoted above among the rest—and if he have any interest in horses or teaming, he will find the subject of desert transportation worth inquiry. There is probably nothing like it in all the world.

I got my first glimpse of desert transportation at the Nevada Salt & Borax Co.'s works, at Rhodes' Marsh, on the Carson & Colorado Railroad, Esmeralda County, Nev. The works for producing borax from the crude material, found in the marsh there, used nut-pine as fuel, and the wood was cut on a mountain-top, twelve miles away, piled up on a bench at the head of a cañon, and drawn thence in wagons to the works. One of these wagons was standing empty in a wood-yard when I visited the marsh, and, although not the largest in use, it was a sight to make an Eastern teamster gasp. The tops of the wheels came just level with the eyes of a tall man.

Over the divide at Teels' Marsh, some nine miles away, I found more wagons of the same kind, and, finally, down at the mining-camp of Candelaria and the little village of Columbus, where there is another borax marsh, I saw what they called wood-trains—all loaded—trains, so to speak, of two great wagons coupled together and piled high with wood.

The woodsman of the East counts his load great when he has piled two cords on the easy-running bob-sleds in winter-time, but here the wood-hauler piles from five to six cords on each wagon, couples two of them together, and draws the train down the rocky defiles and winding cañons of the mountain-side and across the sandy plains, where the wheels of an ordinary Eastern farm wagon, with its load, would cut in six inches deep.

Of course, no one pair of horses, nor any combination of horses, known to Eastern teamsters, could move, let alone haul, such a load. The swell young gentlemen who handle the ribbons over two pairs of horses, in front of a Newport coach, and the dignified driver guiding four pairs of heavy grays before a New York City safe truck, think themselves drivers of rare skill, and so they are. But the fuel hauler of the desert commonly drives twelve horses, with the aid of a single rope in place of reins, and never has less than ten before him.

And yet he is but "a raw-hide" driver, when compared with those who had charge of the Death Valley borax teams.

When, in 1883, the manufacture of borax was first undertaken at the marsh in Death Valley, one of the best-known men in the desert region was Charles Bennett. He had taken up a claim on an oasis in the Pahrump Valley, in Southern Nevada, and had made a ranch of it that he afterward sold for $20,000. Here he lived, hundreds of miles from the nearest town, with the Piutes only for neighbors, unless, indeed, the scattered white Arabs of the desert—renegade whites and squaw wives—and one or two white families, who lived at springs, from twenty to 100 miles away, could be called neighbors.

But in spite of this curious taste in the selection of a home, Bennett thrived on his ranch, and accumulated plenty of horses, mules, and cattle, with money in the bank at Los Angeles, through furnishing supplies to prospectors and trading with the Indians. He learned about the doings in Death Valley, and before the fire was built under the pans, had made a contract to haul the product over the desert to Mojave Station, on the Southern Pacific Railroad, as well as to freight the supplies from the railroad to the workmen in Death Valley.

Before the end of the year, when his contract expired, the company making the borax concluded they could do the freighting more satisfactorily with their own teams than by contract, and, accordingly, J. S. W. Perry, now superintendent of the Pacific Coast Borax Company's borate-mines in the Calico Mountains, and who had before that been employed in Mojave in the borax business, was put at work organizing a system of transportation over the desert, which should be adequate for the safe handling of all the product of the Death Valley region.

Some of the difficulties in the way of carrying out the company's plans may be mentioned, but scarce described so as to be fully comprehended by one who has not seen the desert to be crossed. Between Mojave and the valley proper there were but three springs of water. The road from the railway station led away over the sandy plain, in an easterly direction, toward a peak locally known as Granite Mountain, but called Pilot Butte in the reports of the California State Mineralogist, and by the early prospectors as well. It was just 50 ½ miles across this desert—a desert where the sand-laden wind forever blows, and the sun pours down with intolerable fierceness in summer—to the first spring, which was called Black Water. Beyond Black Water, 6 ½ miles away, was Granite Spring, at the foot of Pilot Butte, and the next spring was Lone Willow, twenty-six miles away, at the foot of one of the peaks of the Panamint Range. These last two spaces between springs were comparatively short distances between waters, but the next dry space was worst of all, for it was fifty-three miles to Mesquite Well, near the lower end of Death Valley.

And yet experience had demonstrated that a loaded team could only travel from fifteen to seventeen miles in a day. There was, of course, but one way in which those fifty-mile stretches could be crossed, and that was by hauling water for men and animals for the three days required in the passage between springs. Nor was that all. The desert does not produce a mouthful of food of any kind. Grain and hay had to be hauled as well as water.

There were other obstacles along the trail. It is a mountainous country. The road leaves Death Valley by what is known as Windy Gap. This gap is really what is known in that country as a wash. It is the bed of torrents that come pouring down after a cloud-burst on the mountain top. Volumes of water, in foaming waves twenty feet high, are said to be common enough, and others much higher are told about by the white Arabs. When a wave has passed, boulders are found scattered in all directions, gullies are cut out, and at the best only a bed of yielding sand is found for the wheels to roll over. Worse yet, this bed of sand rises on an average grade of one hundred feet to the mile for forty miles, while the grade for short distances is four times as much.

The entire length of this desert road between Death Valley and Mojave is 164 ½ miles. There was, of course, in all that distance no sign of human habitation. In case of sickness, accident or disaster, either to themselves or the teams, the men could not hope for help until some other team came along over the trail.

The first thing done by Mr. Perry was to obtain, by inspection or correspondence, the dimensions of all varieties of great wagons used by Pacific coast freighters. With these and the load carried by each wagon spread out before him, he proceeded to design the wagons.

The task he had set for himself was the building of ten wagons so large that any of them would carry at least ten tons. The reader who is familiar with railroads, in fact any reader who has traveled at all by rail, must have seen these legends painted on the sides of freight cars: "Capacity 28,000 lbs." "Capacity 40,000 lbs." (rarely) "Capacity 50,000 lbs." With this in mind, consider that these wagons for hauling borax out of Death Valley were to haul ten tons, or half a car-load each—that a train of two wagons was to carry a load, not for one of the old-style, but for one of the modern, well-built freight cars, and carry the load, too, not over a smooth iron tramway, but up and down the rocky defiles and cañons of one of the most precipitous mountain ranges in the world, the Panamint. Because these were probably the largest wagons ever used, and because they were and still are completely successful, space may well be given to their dimensions in detail. They were as follows:

The hind wheel was seven feet in diameter, and its tire was eight inches wide and an inch thick. The forward wheel was five feet in diameter, with a tire like that on the rear wheel. The hubs were eighteen inches in diameter by twenty-two inches long. The spokes were made of split oak, five and a half inches wide at the butt, and four inches wide at the point. The felloes were made double, each piece being four by four inches large in cross section, and the two being edge-bolted together. The forward axle-trees were made of solid steel bars, three and one quarter inches square in cross-section, while the rear axles were three and a half inches square. The wagon beds were sixteen feet long, four feet wide, and six feet deep. The tread of the wagon the width across the wheels was six feet. Each wagon weighed 7,800 pounds, and the cost of the lot was about $9,000, or $900 each.

It is worth while to once more compare these wagons with the best modern freight car. The best freight car for use on a steel track weighs 27,000 pounds, and carries a load of 50,000 pounds. Note that the car weighs more than half the load. Two of these Death Valley wagons very often carried 45,000 pounds, and sometimes 46,000 pounds of cargo, exclusive of water and feed for men and team, while their combined weight was but 15,600 pounds, or about one third of their load. Moreover, all of the ten were in constant use for five years without a single breakdown. The works in Death Valley were then closed down, but two of the wagons have been in constant use since, and are at this date (1892) running from the Borate Mine in the Calico Mountains to Daggett Station on the Atlantic & Pacific Railroad, where they bid fair to have an experience equal to that of the wonderful one-horse shay.

The building of the wagons was but the beginning of the work, though it should be said here that the building was all done in Mojave Village by men working by the day—it was not a contract job. While the wagons were building, the road had to be divided up into what might be called days' journeys. The heavy loads were to be brought in from Death Valley, and since only supplies for the workmen were to be carried out, the wagons would have but light loads one way. Of course the teams would not travel so far in a day with a full load as with a light one. Moreover they could not travel so far on the long up-grades, like that in Windy Gap, as they could down the long grade from Granite Spring toward Mojave. So the matter was figured over, and ten stations were established at intervals along the whole route, where the teams could stop for the night when coming in loaded to Mojave, while certain other stations were established for resting places on the way out to Death Valley, these last being located with a view of making a team travel further when light than when loaded.

So far as possible these stations were established at the few springs found along the route. Elsewhere dry camps had to be made. Here the natural lack of water was overcome by a system of wheeled water tanks, very much like the tanks of street sprinklers. These were made to hold 500 gallons each, and were towed by the teams from the springs to the dry camps, and from the dry camps back to the springs to be filled again when empty. They were necessarily made of iron, because a wooden tank would dry out and fall to pieces when partly empty.

Then, in the language of the desert Arab, the springs were developed. Some holes were cleaned out and enlarged. At others that were not easily accessible from the best trail to be followed by the wagons, pipes were put in and the water run down to convenient tanks. At all the stations from two to four feed boxes were built of lumber, each large enough to hold four bales of hay and six bags of barley, barley being the grain used on the desert as oats and corn are used in the East. The teams bound out to the valley filled the feed boxes, and then emptied them coming in. The greatest distance made by a team in cool winter weather, on a down grade with no load, was twenty-two miles. The shortest run for hot weather was about fourteen miles.

But it should be said here, that for the three months in the heat of the summer, from the middle of June until the middle of September, no teaming could be done at all. It was not possible for either man or beast to stand the terrific heat of even the Mojave Desert, not to mention Death Valley.

The teams consisted of eighteen mules and two horses. As was said, the man who handles four trained horses before a society coach, or eight huge Percherons before a safe-carrying truck, may think himself a pretty good driver, but in the desert, to use the desert term, he would be a sick raw-hide beside the man who steers eighteen mules with a jerk-line. To compare the one with the other is like comparing a Corinthian yachtsman, or the deck-hand of a harbor scow, to the captain of a Black Ball liner, if we may use a nautical simile in a story of the desert.

In building the desert freight train, the front wagon receives a tongue of ordinary length, while from the rear axle projects a little wrought-iron tongue about three feet long. The second wagon has a tongue, say six feet long, with a stout vertical ring on the end of it, which, when the two wagons are coupled together, slides over the three-foot tail of the front wagon. Then, to hold the two wagons together, a stout chain runs from the front axle of one to the front axle of the other.

The horses and mules are harnessed up in pairs. The horses are attached to the wagon at the tongue, and a great, handsome 2,800-pound team it is—gentle, obedient, and strong as a locomotive. Ahead of them stretch the mules, their double-trees geared to a chain that leads from a forward axle. The most civilized pair are placed in the lead and the next in intelligence just ahead of the tongue, while the sinful, the fun loving, and the raw-hides fill in between. The nigh leader has a bridle with the strap from the left jaw shorter than the other, and from this bridle runs a braided cotton rope a half an inch in diameter, through fair-leaders on each mule to the hand of the driver, who sits on a perch on the front end of the wagon box just eight feet above the ground. That rope is known as the jerk-line, and its length is not far from 120 feet. The team that draws the desert freight train stretches out for more than 100 feet in front of the wagon.

If historians and poets have been justified in writing rapturously about the Arab and his steed, what may we not say of the Death Valley teamster and his mules? To see him soar up over the front wheel to his perch, tilt his hat back on a rear corner of his head, gather in the slack of a jerk-line, loosen the ponderous brake, and awaken the dormant energies of the team with "Git up, ——— ——— you; git up," is the experience of a tourist's life-time. And when at the end of a journey, the teamster pulls up beside the dump with the mules in a line so straight that a stretched string would touch the ear of every mule on either side of the chain, as has often been done, one wants to be introduced and shake hands, as with "one whom lesser minds make boast of having seen." And when one sees the mules settle forward in their collars, feeling gently of their load, until at last the chain stretches as firm as an iron bar, and with one accord start the train of well-nigh 60,000 pounds weight almost as though it was naught, he wants to be introduced and shake hands with the mules, too—that is, figuratively speaking. Their intelligence is such that he would be proud of a speaking acquaintance with them, but if he knew the mules he would be a little shy about getting within hand-shaking range.

It is wonderfully interesting, too, to watch the mules as they turn a sharp corner in a cañon, or on a trail where it rounds a sharp turn on the mountain side. Span after span, near the end of the tongue, often without a word from the driver, will jump over the long chain and pull away on a tangent that the heavy load may be dragged around. Even then the novice wonders how they succeed, for some of the curves are so sharp that the leaders pull in one direction while the wagons are traveling very nearly in an opposite one.

In their short journey after fuel, the drivers of the ten-horse teams often manage their outfits alone. It is but a day's trip from the village to the wood camp and back; but in freighting over the desert with a twenty-animal team, every driver has an assistant called a swamper. The swamper's duties are multifarious. On a down-grade, he climbs to a perch on the rear wagon and puts on the brake; on the up-grade, he reasons with and throws rocks at the indolent and obstreperous mules. As meal-time approaches he kicks dead branches from the grease brush along the route, and pulls up sage-brush roots for fuel. When the outfit stops, he cooks the food while the driver feeds the animals, and when the meal is over, washes the dishes, which, with the food, are carried in a convenient box in the wagon.

The mules get their grain from boxes which are arranged to be secured to the wagon tongue and between the wheels, when feeding. They eat their hay from the ground. Beyond feeding and watering, the animals get no care—they curry themselves by rolling on the sand, and rolling with cyclonic vigor, at that. The cloud of dust raised when an outfit of mules starts in for a lark is suggestive of a Death Valley sand storm, and there is nothing to compare with their cries of glee after the rolling is done. The work is not wearing on the animals. It is common and polite to say to a driver, when a thin or scrawny mule is seen in a big team: "Been getting a raw hide, hey?" which, being interpreted, means: "Ah, I observe you have recently purchased an animal unaccustomed to the work."

Quite as interesting as the teams and the freight trains of the desert are the men who handle them. The drivers receive from $100 to $120 per month, and the swampers about $75. They furnish their own food and bedding. The bill of fare served at a desert freight camp includes bacon, bread, and beans for a foundation, with every variety of canned goods known to the grocery trade for the upper strata. They carry Dutch ovens for their baking, pans for frying, and tin kettles for stewing. On the whole, however, they do not eat much fancy canned stuff, and a cobbler made of canned peaches serves for both pie and cake.

"We don't care much for gimcracks, but we're hell on grub. The gimcracks don't stay by ye," as one said. They rarely carry liquor for use on the road. I observed that empty bottles on some of the desert trails were as thick as good resolutions on the road to sheol, but the teamster did not empty or leave them there. They had served to cheer the road for gentlemen en route to inspect Breyfogle, Gunsight lead, and Peg-Leg mines, discovered by enthusiastic eaters of grub-stakes.

This is not to say, however, that the teamster is a disciple of Neal Dow, or the Woman's Christian Temperance Union. While the five trains were running regularly between Death Valley and Mojave, the chief care of Superintendent Perry was to keep them moving regularly. He had the road so divided that the teams went out to the valley, got loaded, and returned to Mojave on the twentieth day at 3 o'clock with a precision that was remarkable. At Mojave the teamster was allowed to have the rest of the day and night to himself, and it usually happened that when the hour of starting came next day, he rolled in instead of soared to his perch and then, as he blinked his eyes and pawed the jerk line, said:

"Git hep-th-th-th-th yongithop."

It is a matter of record that the mules understood him, nevertheless that, in fact, these long eared, brush tailed tugs of the desert never did but once fail to understand the driver, no matter what his condition. On that occasion the driver, instead of getting drunk, had gone to hear an evangelist preach, and had been converted. Next morning, it is said, when he mounted the wagon and invited the team to go on, the mules, with one accord, turned their heads over their shoulders, cocked forward their ears and stared at him. He had omitted the customary *emphasis* from his command.

It is a curious fact—a fact that a thoroughbred Kansas boomer will scarcely believe in—that the building of a railroad to a desert mining camp invariably decreases the life and activity seen on the streets and among the business houses. The railroad benefits the mine owners, but injures everyone else. The explanation is simple, however. Before the railroad reaches the active camp, all the supplies are brought by teams, and so are the mails and the passengers. When the railroad comes, the teamsters and swampers drive away to return no more, and the railroad brings none to take their place. In fact, it would take a pretty lively citizen to fill the place of a departed teamster, in any event.

"There was a faro bank running most of the time at Mojave. It was a good thing for us, for the teamsters could go broke in one night and be ready to go out over the road in the morning," said Supt. Perry.

That was by no means a heartless remark, as it seems to be at first blush, for if the teamster did not gamble away his money, he was sure to get drunk and spend it in ways more harmful, while if by any chance he got the wages of two months in his pocket at once, he would rush off to Los Angeles for a spree that would take a fortnight or more to recover from. The teamsters are, with rare exceptions, unmarried men.

The life of a teamster on the desert is not only one of hardship, it is in places extremely dangerous. Mention has been made of the grades up which the loads must be dragged. There are other grades down the mountains, like the one, for instance, on the road from Granite Spring toward Mojave, where the plunge is not only steep, but the road-bed is as hard as a turnpike. The load must go down, and so when the brink is reached the driver throws his weight on the brake of the front wagon, the swamper handles the brake on the rear one, and away they go, creaking, and groaning, and sliding, till the bottom is reached. If the brake holds, all is well, but now and then a brake block gives way, and such a race with death as then begins can not be seen elsewhere. With yells and curses, the long team is started in a gallop, an effort is made to swing them around up the mountain-side, a curve is reached, an animal falls, or a wheel strikes a rock or a rut, and, with thunderous crash, over go the great wagons, and the teamster who has stuck to his post goes with them. There are many graves on the desert of men who died with their boots on, but some of them hold men who were killed while striving to guide a runaway freight team in a wild dash down the side of a desert mountain.

As one may suppose, the effect of desert life upon the teamsters is almost every way deteriorating. The men who drove from Mojave were out twenty days for each half day in the settlement, and the settlement itself was but a collection of shanties on as arid a part of the desert as can be found outside of Death Valley. They were not men of education or very wide experience. Their topics of conversation were few. The driver and his swamper had very little to say to each other. To all intents and purposes each lived a solitary life. Being thus alone they grew morose and sullen. Their discomforts by night and their misery by day in the desert heat added to their ill nature. They became in a way insane. It was necessary whenever a team came in to inquire of each man separately whether he was perfectly satisfied with the other, and whether a change was desired or would be objected to. If the least ill will was displayed by one toward the other, a new swamper was provided, lest a fight follow on the desert and one kill the other. Even the greatest precaution could not prevent murder. The soil at Saratoga Springs, in the Amargosa Valley, is stained with blood, a human corpse once swung from a telegraph pole in Daggett, and a rounded pile of stones in Windy Gap is marked "Grave of W. M. Shadley," all because human flesh and human brain could not endure the awful strife of life on the desert. Because these are phases, and illustrative phases, of life on the desert, the stories of these crimes should be told.

Fortunately the stories are but brief. A team was coming in to the railroad from the borax works in the Amargosa Valley. At Saratoga Springs they stopped for the night. There the teamster and swamper quarreled, and the swamper hit the teamster on the back of the head with a shovel, as he sat by the camp fire, killing him at once.

Then the swamper buried the body close by the spring and lay down to sleep by the grave. In the morning he hitched up the team and started to drive in. But he was no teamster, and soon had the mules in a tangle, and the wagons, big as they were, overturned, the fall breaking the swamper's leg. In this condition he crawled about among the animals and turned them all loose save one horse, which he somehow mounted and rode away over the long, hot divide, with the broken limb swinging about and the broken bones grinding together, till he reached the works once more.

His terrible condition and untrue story of the trouble with the teamster awakened the deepest sympathy—a feeling which lasted until he had been sent in a buckboard, a journey of 105 miles over the desert, to a surgeon. When the workmen came to dig up the body of the teamster, that it might be removed to a healthful distance from the spring, they found he had been foully struck from behind, and they wanted to lynch the murderer. But they did not do it, and because of the discomforts and dangers of a trip over the desert, neither the coroner or the district attorney of the county would investigate the matter.

Daggett's only lynching was due to the murder of a teamster. His swamper, for some fancied wrong, was moping about the village, drowning his care in liquor. Another teamster advised him to kill the offender. Early next morning someone passing the blacksmith shop heard groans behind it, and there was found the offending teamster alive, but with his skull crushed. Beside him lay one of the huge spokes used in building wheels for desert wagons. One end was covered with blood and the hair of the dying teamster.

Two nights later, when it appeared that the justice was about to turn the swamper loose for want of direct evidence of guilt, a masked mob took both the swamper and the teamster who had advised the crime, from the lock up. The telegraph poles at Daggett have a single cross-arm. Two ropes were thrown over one of these arms, and nooses in the ends were put about the necks of the two prisoners. Both men had until this time thought the movement a bluff to frighten them into confession. Now they would have begged for mercy, but before the trembling lips could gasp half a sentence the tightening ropes lifted them from the ground.

However, it was really but a bluff on the teamster. He was soon lowered to the ground and advised to leave town. He left. The swamper now "holds down a six-foot claim on the mesa," just beyond the village limits.

~ GIANT PACIFIC OCTOPUS ~

Enteroctopus dofleini

Family Octopodidae

Length: 9 ¾–16'; Weight: 22–110 lb

Habitat:

Found in rocky tide pools; in low, intertidal zone water; and in depths up to 1,650'

Range:

Common in California coastal waters

Comments:

The giant Pacific octopus is one of the largest octopods in the world. It is a reddish to brownish animal with wrinkly, folded skin and, like other octopods, it can change color. It consists of a head—with a brain, sense organs, and a mouth—and a foot specialized into eight arms with two alternating rows of suckers. The arms of the giant Pacific octopus— three to five times its body length—surround a mouth equipped with a beak for the octopus to kill and tear apart its prey. It has eyes high on each side of its head, which is as broad as its body.

It moves quickly through the water by jetting backward with arms trailing or, when on the ocean bottom, crawling with its arms. An ink gland that opens into the mantle cavity allows it to squirt a cloud of ink at a predator in order to confuse it and make a speedy escape.

The giant Pacific octopus's diet includes shrimp, crabs, abalone, and smaller octopods. Its predators include seals, sea otters, and sharks. It is also commercially hunted.

The giant Pacific octopus, like other octopuses, is highly intelligent. It has been observed to solve experiments using short- and long-term memory and can distinguish between shapes and patterns. It is even able to open jars after observing how it is done.

Walter Nordhoff
from *The Journey of the Flame*

Sailors, about our campfire, talked much of the octopus of this Vermilion Sea, which have arms twenty feet long with suckers of the roundness of a silver dollar for holding their prey. These suckers are spaced every six inches the length of the arms. These rulers of the surf hide in seaweed at the entrance of harbors, or rivers, or any place frequented by men. There they wait like monstrous sea spiders, ready to throw out an arm at their prey, as we cast a riata at a cow. Where this arm catches, there it holds, since the suckers, once fastened, never relax their grip except by the animal's will.

The octopus is lead colored, smooth and slippery as an eel, with a hide like a bull's for strength and arms strong enough to throttle a whale, as our pearl fishers have seen it do. Its enormous red, greedy eyes are all which can be easily seen in the sea, and then probably too late to ensure safety from its tentacles.

When the octopus is in the mood, or hungry, it rises from our Vermilion Sea below a small boat and fastens its body to the keel, thus holding the vessel against motion by oarsmen or sails. While some of the crew of such a captured boat trim sails or make frantic efforts with oars, the rest pray or, cursing, draw their knives. One snaky arm seizes an oar, another fastens on the mast, while others, rising stealthily from the sea on all sides, seem to warn the prey against jumping into the water with any hope of thus avoiding death. These arms progress like giant inchworms, never releasing their grasp, but ever extending their reach.

Crew and passengers fight as Spaniards ever battle against death, but knives are of little use against cork-like flesh, and blows rebound from the octopus as from rubber. No sooner is an oar freed for use as a weapon than another arm rises and takes it from the man who struck.

Except for the greater fear of stopping his story, I would have shrieked aloud as some sailor thus told how an unseeing tentacle at last touches a man, and how his comrades shrink from the cowering victim as from the living dead. Other tentacles instantly tie the man's struggling arms and jerking legs. Then, its victim being well trussed for delivery, a great round body rises from the sea. With dull, piggish eyes the monster approves its arms' selection, and, gazing into its vast, champing parrot's beak, the condemned man sees his fate.

Those left in the boat, exhausted by fear, without oars, their sails in shreds, are fearful to risk their arms in water; for at times such octopuses run in pairs. Nevertheless, so eager are those sailors left alive to be elsewhere that they paddle themselves to shore with their bare hands.

～ SEA OTTER ～

Enhydra lutris

Family Mustelidae

Length: 2 ½'–6'; Tail: 10–12"; Weight: 25–80 lb

Habitat:

Coastal waters near shore, especially rocky shallows with kelp beds

Range:

Common mostly off the coast from Monterey Bay to Big Sur

Comments:

The sea otter is dark brown, with a yellow or gray head and nape. Older males sometimes have white heads. The sea otter has a relatively short, tapering tail and an incredibly thick fur coat that provides warmth in its cold environment and traps air for buoyancy.

An aquatic animal, the sea otter eats, sleeps, mates, and gives birth in the water. If in a hurry, the sea otter swims on its stomach, but it is generally seen floating on its back. At night the sea otter wraps itself in kelp to secure its position in the water. Its hind feet serve as flippers, making the animal clumsy on land.

The sea otter diet consists mainly of abalone, sea urchins, crabs, and fish. Sea otters can dive underwater from four to five minutes in search of food. When the sea otter emerges with its meal, it uses a rock to crack open shellfish while floating on its back. It is a playful animal, often interrupting mealtime to frolic underwater.

Hunted for their pelts, sea otters were feared extinct by 1911. In 1938, they were rediscovered off the coast south of Carmel, and today the population in the Monterey Bay is approximately one thousand, and there are herds off the coast of southern Alaska and near the Aleutian Islands as well.

Charles Melville Scammon
from *The Marine Mammals of the North-Western Coast of North America*

The most valuable fur-bearing animals inhabiting the waters of the North-western Coast of North America are the Sea Otters. They are found as far south as twenty-eight degrees north latitude, and their northern limits include the Aleutian Islands. Although never migrating to the southern hemisphere, these peculiar amphibious animals are found around the isolated points of southern Kamschatka, and even to the western Kuriles, a chain of islands that separates the Okhotsk Sea from the north-eastern Pacific. The length of the full-grown animal may average five feet, including the tail, which is about ten inches. The head resembles that of the Fur Seal. The eyes of the Sea Otter are full, black, and piercing, and exhibit much intelligence. The color of the female, when "in season," is quite black; at other periods, it is a dark brown. The males are usually of the same shade, although, in some instances, they are of a jet, shining black, like their mates. The fur is of a much lighter shade inside than upon the surface, and, extending over all, are scattering, long, glistening hairs, which add much to the richness and beauty of the pelage. Some individuals, about the nose and eyes, are of a light brown, or dingy white. The ears are less than an inch in length, quite pointed, standing nearly erect, and are covered with short hair. Occasionally, the young are of a deep brown, with the ends of the longest hairs tipped with white, and, about the nose and eyes, of a cream color.

The mating season of the Sea Otter is not known, as the young are met with in all months of the year; hence, it is reasonable to suppose they differ from most other species of fur-bearing marine mammalia in this respect. The time of gestation is supposed to be eight or nine months.

The hind feet, or flippers, of the animal are webbed, much like the seal's. Its fore legs are short, the fore paws resembling those of a cat, being furnished with five sharp claws, as are the posterior flippers.

The oldest and most observing hunters about Point Grenville (in latitude 47° 20′) aver that the "Sea Otter is never seen on shore unless it is wounded." Nevertheless, we have accounts of their being found on the Aleutian Islands when the Russians were first engaged in the fur trade, and the animals are still occasionally taken, while asleep upon the rocks. We quote the following from Coxe's work on *Russian Discoveries between Asia and America, and the Conquest of Siberia*, published in 1780: "Of all these furs, the skins of the Sea Otters are the richest and most valuable. These animals resort in great numbers to the Aleutian and Fox islands; they are called by the Russians *Boobry Morfki*, or sea beavers, on account of the resemblance of their fur to that of the common beaver. They are taken four ways: struck with darts as they are sleeping upon their backs in the sea; followed by boats and hunted down until they are tired; surprised in caverns; and taken in nets." They are possessed of much sagacity, have great powers of scent, and are exceedingly imbued with curiosity. Their home is nearly as much in the water as that of some species of whales; and as whalers have their favorite "cruising-grounds," so, likewise, do the Otter-hunters have their favorite hunting-grounds, or points where the objects of pursuit are found in greater numbers than along the general stretch of the coast. About the sea-board of Upper and Lower California, Cerros, San Geronimo, Guadalupe, San Nicolas, and San Miguel islands, have been regarded as choice places to pursue them; and farther northward, off Cape Blanco, on the Oregon coast, and Point Grenville and Gray's Harbor, along the coast of Washington Territory. At the present day, considerable numbers are taken by whites and Indians about those northern grounds. Thence, to the northward and westward, come a broken coast and groups of islands, where the animals were, in times past, hunted by the employés of the Hudson's Bay Company and Russian-American Company, and where they are still pursued by the natives inhabiting those rock-bound shores. These interesting mammals are gregarious, and are frequently seen in bands numbering from fifty up to hundreds. When in rapid movement, they make alternate undulating leaps out of the water, plunging again, as do seals and porpoises. They are frequently seen, too, with the hind flippers extended, as if catching the breeze to sail or drift before it.

They live on clams, crabs, and various species of crustacea, and sometimes small fish. When the Otter descends and brings up any article of food, it instantly resumes its habitual attitude—on the back—to devour it. In sunny days, when looking, it sometimes shades its eyes with one fore paw, much in the same manner as a person does with the hand. The females rarely have more than a single one at a birth—never more than two—which are "brought forth upon the kelp," say the white hunters, that abounds at nearly all points known as their favorite resorting-places. The mothers caress and suckle their offspring seemingly with much affection, fondling them with their fore paws—reclining, in their usual manner—and frequently uttering a plaintive sound, which may have given rise to the saying that "Sea Otters sing to quiet their young ones," and gives some credence to the suggestion that the human-like actions of the animal originated the story about mermaids. But when they are startled, they rise perpendicularly half their length out of the water; and if their quick, sharp eyes discern aught to cause alarm, the cubs are seized by the mouth, and both mother and offspring instantly disappear under water. Males and females are sometimes seen curled up in such shapelessness as to present no appearance of animal form. When in this posture they are said to be sleeping.

Sea Otters are rarely seen far from shore, their home being among the thick beds of kelp near the beach, or about outlying rocky reefs and islets. Point Grenville, however, seems to be an exception, as there is no kelp in sight from the shore.

PURSUIT AND CAPTURE.—About the period of the establishment of Fort Astoria, near the mouth of the Columbia River, and for many succeeding years, the Sea Otter hunters along the coasts of California and Oregon were made up from nearly all the maritime nations of Europe and America, as well as from the different tribes of natives that dwelt near the sea-shore. Those of the former were hardy spirits, who preferred a wild life and adventurous pursuits, rather than civilized employment. The distance coasted in their lightly constructed boats, the stealthy search for the game, and when discovered, the sharp shooting chase, gave these hunting expeditions a pleasant tinge of venture. Moreover, the taking of Sea Otters on the coasts of the Californias was prohibited by the Mexican government, and the hunters were aware that, if detected, the penalty would be severe; hence, they ever kept a watchful eye on all vessels seen, which were carefully avoided or cautiously approached.

A peculiar sort of boat is used by the hunters, called an "Otter-canoe." It is fifteen feet long, nearly five wide, and eighteen inches deep. It is sharp at each end, with flaring sides, and but little sheer. Still, these boats are excellent "sea-goers," and are regarded as unsurpassed for landing through the surf, their shape being peculiar. So, likewise, are the paddles for propelling them, which are short, with very broad blades—they being better adapted for use in the thick beds of kelp. The outfit, when going on a cruise, is limited to nearly the barest necessities. Three men usually go in one boat—two to paddle, and one to shoot; the latter having two or three favorite rifles, with a supply of ammunition. A little tea, coffee, sugar, flour, or ship-bread is provided, adding pipes and tobacco, and, as a great luxury, perhaps a keg of spirits completes their equipment.

All being in readiness, they leave the quiet waters of the harbor, and put to sea, following the general trend of the land, but at times making a broad deviation, to hunt about some islands, miles from the main land. When an Otter is seen within rifle-shot, instantly the hunter fires; and if only wounding the animal, it dives under the water, but soon re-appears, to be repeatedly shot at until killed. Sometimes, three boats will hunt together. Then they take positions, one on each side, but in advance of the third, and all three in the rear of where the animal is expected to be seen. It is only the practiced eye of the experienced men that can detect the tip of the animal's nose peering above water, and frequently disguised by a leaf of kelp. Occasionally, a large band is met with. Then every exertion is made to keep them within the triangle formed by the boats; and, at such times, a deal of rapid and sharp shooting ensues, and many a bullet sings through the air, or skips over the water, almost as near the pursuers as the animals pursued. However, six, eight, or a dozen Otters are sometimes secured before the main body disperses; and it is rarely any accident occurs by reckless firing.

From day to day, if the weather is pleasant, they cruise in search of the animals landing to pass the night at different places well known to them, behind some point or rock that breaks the ocean swell. The landings are made by watching the successive rollers as they break upon the beach, and when a favorable time comes, the boat, under dexterous management, glides over the surf with safety to the shore. It is then hauled up clear of the water, and turned partially over for a shelter, or a tent is pitched. A fire is made of drift-wood, or, if this fail, the dry stalks of the cactus, or a bunch of dead chaparral, serves them; and, if their provisions should be getting short, an excursion is made up some one of the many ravines or intervals—perhaps to a stagnant water-pool, where the deer and antelope in that arid region resort to quench their parching thirst. The unerring rifle brings one to the ground, when out comes the hunter's knife, and cutting the choice pieces from the creature, he sallies back again to camp, and soon has the venison broiling over the coals, and, in due time, it is added to their evening meal, which is partaken of with hearty relish; then follow the pipes, which are enjoyed as only those men of free and easy life can enjoy them. Relieved from all care, these adventurers talk of past exploits or frolics, and finally roll themselves in their blankets for a night's invigorating sleep in the open air. At daybreak they are all awakened by the screams of sea birds and the barking of coyotes, attracted by the scent of the encampment. The morning repast over, they again embark in their cockle-shell boats, launch through the surf, gain the open sea, and paddle or sail along the shores in search of "Otter signs." But the scarcity of Otters on the old hunting-grounds has developed the character of these fearless hunters, who, in order to still maintain their game-life, have again reluctantly taken to their pigmy sea-craft—a small vessel of forty tons—in which they have stretched across the Pacific to the western Kuriles (the extreme geographical limit of the breeding-grounds), and now successfully pursue them around those rugged islands during summer, returning again to the California shores with their rich booty as winter approaches.

HUNTING FROM THE SHORE.—From San Francisco northward, as far as Juan de Fuca Strait, the hunting is chiefly prosecuted by shooting the animals from the shore; the most noted grounds being between Gray's Harbor and Point Grenville—a belt of low coast, lying within the parallels of 46° and 48°, north latitude.

The white hunter builds his two log-cabins; one, near the southern limits of his beat, and the other at its northern terminus near Point Grenville. During the prevalence of the southerly winter gales he takes up his quarters at the last named station, as the game is found there more frequently; but when the summer winds sweep down from the north he changes his habitation, and pursues the animals about the breakers of Gray's Harbor. From early dawn until the sun sinks beneath the horizon, the hunter, with rifle in hand and ammunition slung across his shoulder, walks the beach on the lookout for "a shot." The instant one is seen, crack goes the rifle; but it is seldom the animal is secured by one fire. A Sea Otter's head bobbing about in the restless swell is a very uncertain mark; and if instantly killed, the receding tide or adverse wind might drift the animal seaward: so that, even if it eventually drifts to shore, it may be far out of sight from the hunters by day, or be thrown on the rocks by the surge during the night, and picked up by some of the strolling Indians who run the beach in quest of any dead seal or Otter that may come in their way.

The difficulty in shooting from the shore, when the marksman stands nearly on a level with the ever-changing swell, has always been an aggravating annoyance; to avoid which, the hunters now use a sort of ladder, or, as it may be termed, two ladders, joined near the upper ends by a hinge, spreading at the lower ends, forming a triangle—when placed on the beach or in the edge of the water—on which the hunter climbs in order to gain elevation. The ladders are made of light material, so that they can be easily carried at any time, should the sea be ruffled by a local wind or waves from seaward. When an Otter is seen, up go the ladders, and up goes the hunter to the topmost round, and fires. The shot is repeated very quickly, if the first does not take effect; and ball after ball is sent after the animal, until it is far out of reach. It is estimated that the best shooters average at least twenty-five shots to every Otter obtained, and that about one half the number killed are secured by the rightful owners; but, when once in their possession, it is quickly fleeced of its valuable skin, which is stretched on the walls of the cabin to dry. It is no unusual occurrence for the hunter to pass a week traveling up and down the beach, and he may shoot sixty or more rounds, and, perhaps, kill several Otters; but, owing to "bad luck," not one may be secured—the carcass either drifting to sea, or to shore, possibly, with the flowing night-tide, and the object so patiently and eagerly sought for is at last stealthily appropriated by some skulking savage.

Notwithstanding their propensity to purloin, the Indians of the North-western Coast not only occasionally shoot the Sea Otters, as do the whites, but in the months of July and August, when calm weather prevails, they capture them by night. A small canoe is chosen for the purpose, and the implement used to capture the animals is a spear of native make, composed of bone and steel, fitted to a long pole by a socket. Four chosen men make the crew for the canoe. Near the close of day, a sharp lookout is kept for any band of the animals that may have been seen from the shore, and their position accurately defined before beginning the pursuit. All being in readiness, as the shade of evening approaches, they launch their pigmy craft upon the calm sea, and three men paddle in silence toward the place where the Otters were seen, while the fourth takes his station in the bow. He is either a chief, or some one distinguished in the chase. He watches intently for the sleeping Otters. As soon as one is descried, the canoe is headed for it, and, when within reach, the spear is launched into the unwary creature. In its efforts to escape, it draws the spear from the pole. There is a small but strong cord connecting the spear and pole, which admits them to separate a few feet, but does not free the Otter. The animal dives deeply, but with great effort, as the unwieldy pole greatly retards its progress. The keen-eyed savage traces its course, in the blinding darkness, by the phosphorescent light caused by the animal's transit through the water; and when it rises upon the surface to breathe, it is beset with clubs, paddles, and perhaps another spear, and is finally dispatched, after repeated blows or thrusts. The conflict arouses the whole band, which instantly disappear; so that it is seldom more than one is secured. As soon as the hunt is over, the animal is brought on shore, the skin taken off and stretched to dry, and, when ready for market, the lucky owner considers himself enriched to the value of ten or fifteen blankets, and the flesh is devoured as a choice article of food.

The mode of capturing the Sea Otters between Point Grenville and the Aleutian Islands varies with the different native tribes inhabiting that coast. The Aleutians, dressed in their water-proof garments, made from the intestines of seals, wedge themselves into their *baiarkas* (which are constructed with a light, wooden frame, and covered with walrus or seal skin), and, donning their hunting caps, plunge through the surf that dashes high among the crags, and, with almost instinctive skill, reach the less turbulent ground-swell that heaves in every direction. These aquatic men are so closely confined by the narrow build of their boats, and keeping motion with them, too, that their appearance suggests the idea that some undescribed marine monster had just emerged from the depths below. Once clear of the rocks, however, the hunters watch diligently for the Otters. The first man that gets near one darts his spear, then throws up his paddle by way of signal; all the other boats forming a circle around him, at some distance. The wounded animal dives deeply, but soon returns to the surface, near some one of the *baidarkas* forming the circle. Again the hunter that is near enough hurls his spear and elevates his paddle, and again the ring is formed as before. In this way the chase is continued until the capture is made. As soon as the animal is brought on shore, the two oldest hunters examine it, and the one whose spear is found nearest its head is entitled to the prize.

The number of Sea Otter skins taken annually is not definitely known, but from the most authentic information we can obtain, the aggregate for the past three years has been five thousand, one thousand of which came from the Kurile Islands; and, valuing each skin at fifty dollars, amounts to the sum of two hundred and fifty thousand dollars.

Whether these very valuable fur animals have decreased in numbers within the past few years, is questionable. The hunting of them on the coast of California is no longer profitable for more than two or three hunters, and we believe of late some seasons have passed without any one legitimately engaging in the enterprise; notwithstanding, off Point Grenville, which is an old hunting-ground, sixty Otters were taken by only three hunters during the summer of 1868—a great annual increase over many past years. It is said the Russian-American Company restricted the number taken yearly by the Aleutian Islanders, from whom the chief supply was obtained, in order to perpetuate the stock. Furthermore, may it not be that these sagacious animals have fled from those places on the coasts of the Californias where they were so constantly pursued, to some more isolated haunt, and now remain unmolested?

GREAT HORNED OWL

Bubo virginianus

Family Strigidae

Length: 1 ½–2'; Wingspan: 3–5'

Habitat:

Woodlands, cities, parks, deserts; nests in trees, caves, or on the ground

Range:

Common throughout California

Comments:

The great horned owl, sometimes called the "cat owl," is distinguished by its fluffy ear tufts, large head, and bulky shape, which may appear hunched when at rest. Chiefly dark brown and with a bright white throat, this owl also has piercing yellow eyes set within distinctive facial disks. It is the only large North American owl with "horns" of feathers, which actually have nothing to do with hearing.

Generally solitary, the great horned owl is a nocturnal hunter that usually hunts from a perch, although it may also glide slowly above the ground in search of prey. While it enjoys excellent nighttime vision, its hearing is so acute it can locate prey even in total darkness. Great horned owls feed on small mammals—rats, mice, squirrels, even skunks—and occasionally they take birds such as quails and ducks.

Their call is a series of three to eight deep hoots, the second and third shorter and more rapid.

Yokuts
"The Man and the Owl"

A man and his wife were traveling. They camped overnight in a cave. They had a fire burning. Then they heard a horned owl *(hutulu)* hoot. The woman said to her husband: "Call in the same way. He will come and you can shoot him. Then we will eat him for supper." The man got his bow and arrows ready and called. The owl answered, coming nearer. At last it sat on a tree near the fire. The man shot. He killed it. Then his wife told him: "Do it again. Another one will come." Again he called and brought an owl and shot it. He said: "It is enough now." But his wife said: "No. Call again. If you call them in the morning they will not come. We have had no meat for a long time. We shall want something to eat tomorrow as well as now." Then the man called. More owls came. There were more and more of them. He shot, but more came. The air was full of owls. All his arrows were gone. The owls came closer and attacked them. The man took sticks from the fire and fought them off. He covered the woman with a basket and kept on fighting. More and more owls came. At last they killed both the man and the woman.

~ CALIFORNIA QUAIL ~

Callipepla californica

Family Phasianidae

Length: 9 ½–11"

Habitat:

Open woodlands, foothills, chaparral, and stream valleys; prefers permanent water source; nests on the ground

Range:

Common throughout California, including the coastal inlands and mountains to 8,500'

Comments:

The distinctive *Callipepla californica* (formally *Lophortyx californica*) was adopted as the state bird of California in 1931. Recognized easily by the black, tear-shaped plume hanging in front of its forehead, the California quail is typically pale brown. Males have a chestnut crown and white eyebrows and necklace. Females have smaller plumes and lack the white necklace and eyebrows.

California quail form coveys, consisting of up to two hundred birds, which may be seen scurrying along the ground or taking flight when startled. Quail may roost in trees to rest or to avoid danger. They generally feed in the morning and eat seeds, fruits, and insects.

One of the California quail's calls is a loud "chi-ca-go."

John Steinbeck
"The White Quail"

Late in the afternoon, when the sun had gone behind the hill, there was a time Mary called the really-garden-time. Then the high school girl was in from school and had taken charge of the kitchen. It was almost a sacred time. Mary walked out into the garden and across the lawn to a folding chair half behind one of the lawn oaks. She could watch the birds drinking in the pool from there. She could really *feel* the garden. When Harry came home from the office, he stayed in the house and read his paper until she came in from the garden, star-eyed. It made her unhappy to be disturbed.

The summer was just breaking. Mary looked into the kitchen and saw that everything was all right there. She went through the living room and lighted the laid fire, and then she was ready for the garden. The sun had just dropped behind the hill, and the blue gauze of the evening had settled among the oaks.

Mary thought, "It's like millions of not quite invisible fairies coming into my garden. You can't see one of them, but the millions change the color of the air." She smiled to herself at the nice thought. The clipped lawn was damp and fresh with watering. The brilliant cinerarias threw little haloes of color into the air. The fuchsia trees were loaded with blooms. The buds, like little red Christmas tree ornaments, and the open blooms like ballet-skirted ladies. They were so *right*, the fuchsias, so absolutely right. And they discouraged the enemy on the other side, the brush and scrubby, untrimmed trees.

Mary walked across the lawn in the evening to her chair, and sat down. She could hear the birds gathering to come down to the pool. "Making up parties," she thought, "coming to my garden in the evening. How they must love it! How I would like to come to my garden for the first time. If I could be two people—'Good evening, come into the garden, Mary.' 'Oh, isn't it lovely.' 'Yes, I like it, especially at this time. Quiet, now, Mary. Don't frighten the birds.'" She sat as still as a mouse. Her lips were parted with expectancy. In the brush the quail twittered sharply. A yellowhammer dropped to the edge of the pool. Two little flycatchers flickered out over the water and stood still in the air, beating their wings. And then the quail ran out, with funny little steps. They stopped and cocked their heads, to see whether it was safe. Their leader, a big fellow with a crest like a black question mark, sounded the bugle-like "All clear" call, and the band came down to drink.

And then it happened, the wonderful thing. Out of the brush ran a white quail. Mary froze. Yes, it was a quail, no doubt of it, and white as snow. Oh, this was wonderful! A shiver of pleasure, a bursting of pleasure swelled in Mary's breast. She held her breath. The dainty little white hen quail went to the other side of the pool, away from the ordinary quail. She paused and looked around, and then dipped her beak in the water.

"Why," Mary cried to herself, "she's like me!" A powerful ecstasy quivered in her body. "She's like the essence of me, an essence boiled down to utter purity. She must be the queen of the quail. She makes every lovely thing that ever happened to me one thing."

The white quail dipped her beak again and threw back her head to swallow.

The memories welled in Mary and filled her chest. Something sad, always something sad. The packages that came; untying the string was the ecstasy. The thing in the package was never quite—

The marvelous candy from Italy. "Don't eat it, dear. It's prettier than it's good." Mary never ate it, but looking at it was an ecstasy like this.

"What a pretty girl Mary is. She's like a gentian, so quiet." The hearing was an ecstasy like this.

"Mary dear, be very brave now. Your father has—passed away." The first moment of loss was an ecstasy like this.

The white quail stretched a wing backward and smoothed down the feathers with her beak. "This is the me that was everything beautiful. This is the center of me, my heart."

❧ RABBIT ❧

Lepus californicus

Family Leporidae

Length: 18 ¼–25"; Tail: 2–4 ¼"; Weight: 3 ¼–8 lb

Habitat:

Open areas such as prairies, meadows, and fields

Range:

Common throughout California

Comments:

The black-tailed jackrabbit has gray or sandy fur peppered with black above and white on its underside. Its tail has a black stripe above with a white border. Its long ears—up to six inches—are brown with black tips. The black-tailed jackrabbit has a lean build and long legs.

The black-tailed jackrabbit is actually not a rabbit but a hare. Like other hares (and unlike rabbits), it makes no maternity nest and its young are born furred and with their eyes open.

During the day, the black-tailed jackrabbit generally spends its time resting in dense vegetation, becoming active in the late afternoon. It feeds in loose groups and eats different kinds of plants—such as alfalfa—in the summer and woody, dried vegetation in the winter or during a drought. Its ears can detect the faint sounds of predators, and when alarmed the jackrabbit remains very still. It usually does not walk, but hops five to ten feet at a time and up to twenty feet when panicked, sometimes reaching speeds of thirty to thirty-five miles per hour. When hopping at a moderate speed, the jackrabbit's fourth or fifth jump will be higher to allow for a view of its surroundings. This hare flashes its white underside at an enemy—usually a coyote, bobcat, fox, or owl—to perhaps warn other jackrabbits of danger and confuse its predators. It also may stop to give a danger warning to other jackrabbits by thumping its hind feet. A jackrabbit can also swim using a kind of "doggy-paddle" with all four feet.

Although usually quiet animals, this hare can squeal and make distinct noises when fighting, distressed, or assembling its young.

Frank LaPena
"Rabbit Crazy"

Rabbit laughed and slapped his knees
Oh lord you're really something
and mouse laughed back

They were talking how rabbit
got so many girls and what it takes
to keep them happy

It must be something real good, "Yeah
for a ninety year old…" he's saying
but he's really 62
which ain't bad for a rabbit

"They are from 18 to old…"
He's talking of his women
I wonder who "they" are
and what he means by "old"

One time, rabbit to show
his friendship offered to
let mouse use his name
for one of rabbit's children

Mouse's wife said
she would beat him
if that happened
and mouse and rabbit laughed

They laughed as they talked
of women and babies
and what it takes to be
a crazy rabbit or a lover man

∼⨼ COMMON RACCOON ⨽∼

Procyon lotor

Family Procyonidae

Length: 24–37"; Tail: 7 ½–16"; Weight: 12–48 lb

Habitat:

    Found in forests, near streams, and in cities and rural areas

Range:

    Common throughout California

Comments:

    The common raccoon is gray-brown or orange-brown with a grayish underbody. Its distinctive markings include a black "mask" outlined in white around its eyes and four to six alternating black stripes along its bushy tail.

    The common raccoon is omnivorous and will eat almost anything. Nuts, berries, fruits, crayfish, rodents, fish, frogs, and bird eggs can all be a part of the common raccoon's diet. They have also been known to adapt to the presence of humans by eating trash or roadkill. Raccoons are often seen using their paws to wash their food in water or rub it with their dry paws before eating it, probably to feel for inedible matter to discard.

    The common raccoon is an accomplished climber, having the unique ability to descend trees either backward or forward by inverting its hind feet 180 degrees. On the ground it usually walks, but it can also run up to fifteen miles per hour and swim well. Its nimble fingers can manipulate a variety of tasks, including turning doorknobs and opening refrigerators.

    The common raccoon is mainly nocturnal and solitary and, while active in warmer seasons, it spends most of the winter in a den. Its vocalizations include purrs, whimpers, snarls, and screams.

Kenneth Rexroth
"Raccoon"

The raccoon wears a black mask,
And he washes everything
Before he eats it. If you
Give him a cube of sugar,
He'll wash it away and weep.
Some of life's sweetest pleasures
Can be enjoyed only if
You don't mind a little dirt.
Here a false face won't help you.

ᴖᴔ RAT ᴔᴖ

Rattus rattus

Family Muridae

Length: 12 ¾"–18"; Tail: 6 ⅜–10 ⅛"; Weight: 4–12 ⅜ oz

Habitat:

  Mostly seaports and buildings

Range:

  Common inland near the California coast

Comments:

The black rat has many subspecies, not all of which are black. All have long tails and large ears. The black rat was accidentally introduced into North America by the Jamestown colonists in 1609 and spread from there throughout the continent. It is common on ships and is continually reintroduced into seaports. The black rat probably originated in Southeast Asia, and does best in warm climates.

Primarily nocturnal, the black rat is active throughout the year. It is omnivorous but prefers eating grain. It is considered a pest and damages millions of dollars of goods each year, especially in docks and warehouses, where it contaminates with droppings consumables it does not eat. Although occurrences are rare today, diseases such as the plague can be spread from black rats to humans through fleas.

The black rat is a skillful climber and often nests in the upper stories of buildings, as well as in vines and trees. The black rat is very opportunistic and is a quick learner. Cats, dogs, and snakes are predators of the black rat.

William K. McGrew
"The Rats of Sacramento"

Not that the rats of Sacramento in 1850 were individually, as moral beings, more deserving of obloquy than those of any other place on the Pacific Coast,—and that is not saying much in their favor,—it was their appalling numbers that gave them an overshadowing prominence in the list of local calamities. San Francisco had its legions, but for everyone in the bay city Sacramento could master ten, if appearances were not very deceiving. They pervaded everything—everywhere. They were a paramount influence and consideration in all local economies—public and private. If there was no special legislation concerning them, it was because of the bewildering magnitude of the subject, and the incapacity of the average legislative mind to grasp it. Whether from a sense of fairness in the matter of a division of time and opportunities with man and other animals, or in the expedient conformity to the law which impels the most lawless criminal to regard the right of others in the presence of an alternate peril, they were less assertive during the day than they were at night; but, day or night, whether in active service or dreaming away their hours of idleness in temporary seclusion, their influence was always felt, always visible, always wearing on the moral endurance of us who claim to be their superiors. While they were on duty, there was no place too exclusive for their vandalism. They were ravenous to a miracle, and what they could not eat they destroyed, simply because they could. It was not a question of right with them, but an arbitrary exercise of qualities which a high-minded being would scorn to possess.

Such were the rats of Sacramento in the year of grace, one thousand eight hundred and fifty, and there were millions and millions and millions of them.

I asked Captain (afterwards General) John A. Sutter one day if the country had always been so rat-ridden. He replied: "No, the rats are aliens—not all, for there were some here before these came, but they were unambitious, unprogressive,—like the Indians of the missions, content to merely exist, on almost any terms. This diffusive, invading, prolific kind, this besom of destruction, came with the gold-seekers, passengers on the same vessels. Their dominion here coordinates with that of your people. They hold by right of conquest, as you do."

"And purchase, too, Captain," I interrupted. "The United States Government, you remember, paid Mexico fifteen million dollars for the territory."

"True," the Captain continued, "as an emollient to the American conscience. But, if there had been no money consideration, the sequel would have been the same."

"Manifest Destiny?" I interposed, with an interrogative accent.

"Well, manifest something. I will not be categorical," Sutter responded. "Before the gold excitement the social air of California was serene, like our climate, genial in its warmth during the day and made delicious by the cool zephyrs of evening. The Spanish-speaking natives, content with their *frijoles* and *tortillas*, enjoyed a perpetual sweet do-nothing, reserving all of their energies for the fandango and the periodical rodeos. Rats were merely sporadic. Coyotes were the only plague, and even they were not entirely beyond control. When the world opened upon us its Pandora's box, there was the genesis of evil."

"Good as well, Captain," I remarked.

"Yes," he said: "much good came too. But we are speaking now of rats. There are rats with four legs and biped rats. There are rats with tails and rats without tails. The tail-bearing quadruped is the lesser evil—of rats. It yields to necessities, and is restricted to the limit of its physical powers. Your biped overcomes necessities,— extends indefinitely the limit of its cupidity, and to accomplish his end, employs explosive forces that might shatter a planet. The rat you complain of brought his wife along with him, and a single pair increase to a million in two years. That is the truth with regard to their propagation. They multiply more rapidly than any other animal except the rabbit."

"How are you to get rid of them?"

"The Sacramento River will, in all probability solve that problem. You've not seen an inundation yet. The little freshet of last winter was a mere suggestion. Wait!"

The fires and floods of 1851 fulfilled Captain Sutter's prophecy.

A few years ago I was traveling by rail from Brighton to London on one of those compartment contrivances that embalm in the conservative English mind the cherished memories of their ancient stagecoach. An elderly Englishman shared with me the monopoly of a smoking compartment. He was a hale, brisk, brightened septuagenarian, and still loyal to his pipe—in England, the open sesame to the social department of a man's nature, if he has a social department. He filled his pipe and searched through his pocket and satchel for a match; but finding none, he turned to me with a half-apologetic air and said: "Beg pardon, sir. Can you favor me with a match?"

I gave him my match-case and at the same time handed him a cigar.

"Ah! an American I perceive! I thank you very much indeed."

"Why an American?" I asked.

His reply was a genuine surprise to me, coming from a Briton.

"For two reasons," he said. "In the first place, an Englishman on the move almost always smokes a pipe,—seldom a cigar. Good cigars here are very dear as well as rare. In the second place, if an Englishman does smoke cigars, he rarely ever offers one to a stranger. Almost every American I meet offers me a cigar, if he smokes himself."

"You are correct in your conjecture. I am an American," I said.

"I thought so. And pray, what part of the States are you from, may I ask?"

"California," I replied.

"Oh, California, indeed! And how long have you lived there?"

"Off and on since 1849."

"You don't tell me!" he exclaimed, grasping my hand. "Why, I'm a forty-niner myself!"

"Yes? How long were you there, and what kind of a time did you have?"

"Oh, I'll tell you. I'm so glad to meet an old forty-niner! Isn't this lucky? I was down in Australia when the gold-fever broke out and was among the first to sail from there. I wasn't a convict nor a Sydney duck. We entered San Francisco bay in September, 1849. I and my party went directly up to the mines about Hangtown, and some of us had pretty fair luck. I skirmished around on the Stanislaus, at Murphy's Camp, Mokelumne Hill, Shaw's Flat, and got up as far as Gold Run and Rough and Ready. At last I happened on a rich claim and took out about two thousand pounds—ten thousand dollars in your money—in six weeks. I thought that was doing pretty well. And having had some experience in the volatile quality of gold—for, before that, one day I would have lots and the next day I would be that broke—I made a bee-line for the Bay, intending to take passage in the first vessel that sailed from 'Frisco to an Australian port or to England—I did not care which. I was obliged to stay over night in Sacramento, and that did the business for me. I had never heard anything about the trouble between the squatters, or, as they styled themselves, the pre-emptors—and those who claimed title under the Mexican grant to Sutter. Some fellow at the hotel where I was stopping offered to sell me Sacramento lots for from ten to twenty dollars apiece. There was a fortune in it, he said, and the opportunity would never occur again. In three months, they would readily bring from three hundred to one thousand dollars each.

"I asked him why he was selling them at such low figures, if they would mount up into the hundreds and thousands so rapidly. His reply appeared to me to be perfectly satisfactory. He said that he owned a large number of lots, and that by putting improvements on some the value of the others would be greatly enhanced. So he had determined to dispose of a few at merely nominal prices, to persons who would build, and it would also furnish him with ready money for the same purpose. I bought twenty lots at an average cost of fifteen dollars. In other words, I bit and got bitten.

"I was now a fixture in Sacramento for at least six months, if not for a longer time. But, then, just see the money I was going to make. I counted on selling my lots for at least eight hundred or one thousand dollars apiece. I built a house that cost me two thousand dollars and it wasn't much of a house either.

"While waiting for my lots to soar, it was desirable that I should be employed at something that would pay current expenses and leave my little capital intact. Somebody said that the meat business was better than a mine. It suited me, although I didn't know a hind-quarter from the neck, nor tail from tongue. An outlay of fifty pounds put me in as neat a meat-shop as there was in Sacramento. An impecunious fellow–countryman, who said he had been a butcher in Adelaide, came along and I hired him to take charge of my business at two dollars a day, with board and lodging. He was glad to get it—and well he might be, for although apparently sober, he was lazy and trifling. He did know, however, how to saw off a steak and to prospect around among the ravines and gulches and ledges of a beef carcass. I commenced business with a small stock, and had out a big cloth sign:—

N. S. WALES
METROPOLITAN MARKET
Fresh Meat Every Day
Kept On Ice

"You see, I hadn't lived among you Yankees for nothing. My name wasn't Wales, and I hadn't an ounce of ice about the establishment."

"'N. S. Wales,' then, was a purely fictitious name?" I suggested.

"So far as I was concerned, yes. It really stood for New South Wales, the Australian province I sailed from for California. I took the one from a shop firm in Sacramento, styled 'Galena & Dubuque,' which I was told were simply the names of two towns somewhere on the Upper Mississippi River."

My companion paused in his narrative long enough to produce a small pocket-wallet and hand me from it a neat card bearing his name and address—"Peter Augustus Morneywaite, No. —, St. George's Terrace, East Croydon, Surrey." I gave him one of my cards in exchange.

Continuing, Mr. Morneywaite said: "I felt now that I was fairly launched into business. But there was one factor in the economic constituent of Sacramento that I had not taken into account."

"What was that?" I asked.

"Rats," he replied. "Did you ever hear of Sacramento rats?"

"I have, and seen them, too."

"Well," he continued. "I lived in a small room back of my shop. It was my kitchen, dining-room, bedroom and parlor—everything. I was merchant, cook, and chambermaid, all under one skin. I thought I was wise—but I wasn't. I thought I was going to be a millionaire,—but it didn't come to pass. Why? Why, mainly because of rats—and other things. The rats were cunning. They didn't throw me into a feverish state of alarm right away, and cause me to create safeguards against them. They knew that I would open with a small stock and increase it with the growth of my business. So they held off for a while.

"Customers came, and from a single side of beef, my stock grew in two weeks, until you might have thought that I slaughtered a whole herd every day. My provisions were not molested. I grew careless. A few rats came nosing around occasionally, but they satisfied themselves from the waste-box. They were well-behaved rats,—kind-hearted, honest rats. They were not going to make a nuisance of themselves. They won my confidence and I trusted them. I had never taken their census, and did not know that there were millions of them. I thought there were only a few hundred thousands. A double-barreled shot-gun stood in one corner of my room. I awoke early one morning, and saw from my bunk a dozen rats sitting in a circle around it. They appeared to take a deep interest in the thing, but left suddenly when I showed signs of life.

"A little incident occurred about this time that made me think that there might be something more in a Sacramento rat than mere depravity. One day, I left the shop in the care of my young man, and strolled a short distance below town. A bayou barred my further progress, and I seated myself on the bank, without any definite aim, and fell into a reverie. I sat there as quiet as a kingfisher. Did you ever see a kingfisher waiting for a chance to dive after something? They are as motionless as if they were dead and stuffed. Well, presently a rat came down from the brush upon the opposite bank. It was followed by another and another until there were five at the water's edge. They appeared to hold a consultation, and then separated, trotting independently up and down the stream, as if they were looking for something. Then they held another consultation. There appeared at first to be a difference in a patch of tules. I could see that there was something going on in there. After a little while they came out, each dragging a bulrush, which they deposited together at the place where they held their first council, and close to the water's edge. Then, they went to work as if they were trying to do something they had never done before and didn't know exactly how to manage it. They launched their tules into the water one by one, and almost drowned themselves in a vain effort to construct a raft out of them. One big fellow acted as a superintendent; but he didn't appear to know anything more about ship-building than the others did, and their tales floated away with the stream. There seemed to be a good deal of dissatisfaction among them, and finally the workers struck. Mr. Superintendent delivered an excited harangue and worked himself into a frenzy. At last, he rushed up into the jungle and returned presently with another detachment of a half-dozen. I resolved to remain quiet and see what all this meant.

"A little while was spent in reconnoitering, and then the whole posse started off together up the stream. In less than ten minutes they came swimming down with a big chunk of wood which they steered to the place they seemed to have fixed upon for an embarcadero. They held it securely as close to shore as they could get, owing to the shoaling of the water, while the superintendent galloped up the bank and into the jungle again. When he appeared it was at the head of a procession of a dozen or more, dragging the apparently dead body of one of their comrades. The movements of the pall-bearers were not sufficiently solemn for a funeral occasion, and I observed during their frequent pauses in the descent that the corpse was still languidly alive, but either helplessly sick or disabled.

"It was now becoming evident that the floating chunk was to be used for transportation purposes, and in this connection a serious problem had to be solved—one that required brain as well as muscular force. How was the sick rat to be transferred from shore to the float, across water two feet wide and deepening from one inch at the edge to six outside? The thing was becoming intensely interesting, and if I had had a dozen double-barreled shot-guns I would not have interrupted the proceedings. I was anxious to see how much wisdom a rat could muster, and besides they were engaged in a noble work.

"You may not believe me when I tell you how they managed it; but I assure you it is a fact, every word of it. You know that a rat can stand on its hind feet and lift its head high up, though it can't do much walking in that posture. Well, these fellows formed two lines about six inches apart, all standing erect, and a dozen rats in each line, the largest taking the deepest water, and two got up on the float. Then those on shore lifted the patient gently with their teeth and passed it on to the next two, and they to the next, and so on until it reached the float, where it was taken by those on board and dragged up to the high and dry upper deck, the two attendants remaining with the patient to prevent it from sliding off into the water during the voyage across the stream. It required the united efforts of the escort, swimming and pushing behind and alongside, to hold the float against the current and direct its course almost straight across. They landed a short distance below where I sat, and in a better harbor than that from which they started. The same tenderness and skill they had before displayed was exercised in landing the patient and getting it up to the top of the steep bank, when they disappeared among the weeds and brush, leaving me wrapt in wonder and admiration at the human qualities that so disreputable a thing as a rat can display when it is in the right mood.

"I returned to my shop with a better opinion of rats than I ever had before or since. A little later on they entirely forfeited my good opinion and I only wanted the opportunity to revel in a carnival of their extermination.

"Soon after this side-show at the bayou the rats began to grow troublesome at the shop. The reason why they had not paid their respects to my stock of meat was simply because my house was new and built almost air-tight, a few only having found a way in, and they kept it a secret. Now they came through a dozen private entrances of their own creation, and soon made it apparent that their ideas of honesty were unorthodox. My young man had warned me against them, but between a misplaced confidence in the animals themselves and a mistaken belief that everything that a rat would pine for was out of their reach, I adopted no extraordinary measures for protection.

"One night I went to a fandango at Sutter's fort, leaving the shop in charge of my clerk. The festivities, which had a sort of religious significance, being the festival of some saint, were kept up all night. The decorations and performances were extremely unique and elaborate and attracted a large crowd of spectators, most of whom remained to see the affair through. I left at three o'clock in the morning, and on arriving home was surprised at finding the shop front-door standing open. Upon entering I was instantly assailed by something that threw me backward to the floor and almost smothered and crushed me with its weight as it passed like a great wave over my prostate form. For a few moments the house seemed to be coming to pieces, and it was at least a minute, though it seemed an hour, before I was allowed to regain my feet. Terrified, I retreated from the house and hunted up one of the night patrol, to whom I related the circumstances as they occurred and impressed me. He went back with me to the shop and with his little bull's-eye lantern lighted, got behind me as we approached the door. I reversed the order of the procession and invited him as a matter of courtesy to go in first. I assured him of the glory there was in it, and he accepted the honor. The little bull's-eye lantern was brought

into service and flashed its ray upon festoons of bare bones hanging from the hooks
and stripped to whiteness. What a spectacle! Whole carcasses had disappeared!

The officer said: "Rats! The rats have ruined you, man!"

"'Rats?' I said. 'I thought it was an elephant—two of them. They've eaten up my
whole stock!'

"He asked me how much meat I had.

"I said, 'A whole herd. Why, look at the bones!'

"'Where's your young man?' he asked.

"'Blamed if I know,' I replied. 'I expect they have eaten him up, too.'

"We went into the living-room to see if he was there. I expected to find the
fellow's bones fleshless in the bunk, but there was no trace of him there.

"A glance around disclosed the fact that my provisions had gone the way of the
beef. On the floor an empty flour-sack lay in shreds. Flour was scattered all over the
room. The bacon was eaten up, except the rind. Every crumb of bread was devoured.
Coffee and tea were strewed broadcast, and mixed up with sugar. Candle, tallow, soap,
bacon-grease, baking-powders, shoe-blacking, flour, dried apples, shot and salt were
mixed up and spread about in daubs. The rats had held a high jinks, and I had paid the
expense. The money-till in the shop was empty.

"As the morning wore on, the patrolman and I continued our investigations and
learned that my young man had patronized a saloon pretty liberally the night before
and had left it about eleven o'clock as drunk as a lord. He probably then returned
to the shop, cleaned out the till, and decamped, leaving the front-door open. At all
events, I never saw or heard of him from that day to this. He didn't get much out
of the till, for I seldom left enough in it over night to pay a thief for his trouble of
sneaking in.

"I resolved to renew my stock and continue the business, and went the next
morning to a corral just outside of town to look at some beef cattle. On returning I
found my door broken open and the house in charge of men who barred my entrance
and asked what I wanted.

"I thought that was cool, and said I wanted to go into my house. I demanded to
know who they were and why they were here. I was given to understand that I was a
squatter and would have to emigrate from these particular premises.

"This was the first intimation I ever had of any dispute about land-titles. I ran off
to a lawyer with my deeds. He looked at them and told me that I had only a squatter's
title, which wasn't worth the paper it was written on. My whole batch of lots was in the
same category. The lawyer charged me fifty dollars for this piece of information. I went
back to the house and demanded pay for my improvements. The men laughed at me and
asked me if I would take a check on Priest, Lee & Co. Perhaps you remember them?"

I did,—the scamps!

"Well, that was adding insult to injury. However, I was generously permitted to
remove all my personal effects. I had an auction sale and left Sacramento. Shortly after
that the squatter riots occurred and in the litigation that followed, Sutter's grant was
sustained and I was out and injured.

"I did clerical work for a shipping firm in San Francisco for about a year and then returned to my old home in England, a wiser if not richer man. Still I often feel as if I would love to see California again."

The train had now arrived at East Croydon where Mr. Morneywaite took leave of me with a hearty shake of the hand, expressing his great pleasure at having met with an old forty-niner.

I complimented him on his intimate acquaintance with Sacramento rats, but especially upon his *strict fidelity to facts.*

~⚬~ WESTERN RATTLESNAKE ~⚬~

Crotalus viridis

Family Viperidae

Length: 16"–4' 2"

Habitat:

Forests, grasslands, and brush-covered and rocky areas to 11,000'

Range:

Throughout northern and central California and along the coast

Comments:

The Western rattlesnake has dark brown blotches down the center of its back, which is marked with whitish or yellowish lines forming ovals or diamond shapes that eventually narrow near the tail into crossbands. Size varies greatly, but most individuals grow to around three feet long. The tail has a rattle, or a series of flattened, interlocking segments of horn, which create a rattling noise when shaken. Each time the snake sheds its skin it gains a new segment of rattle.

A venomous species, the Western rattlesnake has retractable hollow fangs in its upper jaw. Its poison is a mix of proteins that immediately acts on its prey's blood tissue. It detects its prey by using the heat-sensitive pits on each side of its head. The Western rattlesnake primarily eats small mammals, ground-nesting birds, and other small animals.

When this snake is bothered, it lifts its head above its coils and rattles its tail. It is most active in the late day and night during the summer. Individuals have been known to live as long as nineteen years.

Charley Brown
"The Girl Who Married Rattlesnake"

At a place called Cobowin there is a large rock with a hole in it and there were many rattlesnakes in this hole. At Kalesima nearby there was a village with four large houses. In one of these large houses which had a center pole there lived a girl. This was in the spring of the year when the clover was just right to eat. This girl went out to gather clover and one of the rattlesnakes watched her. When she had a sufficient amount of this food she took it home and gave it to her mother.

Rattlesnake went to the village and when he had approached very near to the house he transformed himself into a young man with a head-net on his head and fine beads around his neck. He made himself look as handsome as possible. Then he climbed up onto the top of the house and came down the center pole. He went to this girl and told her that he wanted to marry her and he remained there with the family. The following morning he went home again. This he did for four days. On the fifth evening he came back but this time he did not change his form. He simply went into the house and talked just as he had before. The girl's mother said that there was someone over there talking all the time. She made a light and looked over in the place where she heard the sound, and there was Rattlesnake. He shook his head and frightened her terribly. She dropped the light and ran.

On the following morning Rattlesnake took the girl home with him and she remained there. Finally this girl had four children and as they grew up, whenever they saw any of the people from the village, they would say to their mother, "We are going to bite those people." But she would say, "No, you must not do that. Those are your relatives." And the children would do as she told them.

Now these four rattlesnake boys were out playing around one day as they grew a little older. Finally they became curious. They came in and asked their mother, "Why do you not talk the way we do? Why are you so different?"

"I am not a rattlesnake," she replied. "I am a human being. I am different from you and your father."

"Are you not afraid of our father?" asked the boys. "No," she answered.

Then the oldest of the rattlesnake boys said that he had heard the other rattlesnakes talking and that they too thought it strange that she was so different from them and that they were going to investigate and see just why it was that she was so different. They were going to crawl over her body and find out why she was so different from themselves. She was not at all afraid; when the rattlesnakes all came they crawled over her and she was not alarmed in any way.

Then she said to her oldest boy, "It is impossible for you to become a human being and I am not really a human being any longer, so I am going back to my parents and tell them what has happened." She did go home and she said to her parents, "This is the last time that I shall be able to talk to you and the last time that you will be able to talk with me." Her father and mother felt very sad about this, but they said nothing. Then the daughter started to leave, but her mother ran after her and caught her right by the door, brought her back into the house and wept over her because she was so changed. Then the girl shook her body and suddenly she was gone. No one knew how or where she went, but she really went back to Rattlesnake's house where she has lived ever since.

Bill Hotchkiss
"Rattlesnakes"

For years I looked for them, killed them, smashed them with stones.
I cured one hide, made a belt of it, would have eliminated
The species if I'd had my way. Poisonous bastards, killers,
I thought. A snake had bitten my dog King: I carried him three miles
Home, crying, waited for news from the vet.
                                        It came.

Dead.

   I hunted them then, blew them apart with my grandfather's
Old four-ten shotgun. Hated them.
                              One evening, just at sundown,
I cut over Screwball Hill on my way home, came up a brushy draw
In late red light of sunset, to the canal, and I thought
About rattlesnakes and water, how they always seem to be
      somewhere near it,
Thought about what a good place this was for *Crotalus atrox*.

Was considering this when I leaped the canal, took a step further
In dim light, felt something soft, tensile beneath my foot.
My brain screamed *Snake!* and I lunged backward, arms out,
Into the ditch. Cold water cleared my mind, the old hatred returned.
I climbed from the canal, found a club, and went snake hunting.

In the dimness I saw him, back under manzanita, coiled now—
Buzzing, warning me. I'd have to crawl in after him—I gauged
The space, what my chances were, what his were. I didn't move.

Stared at him.
        He was coiled, ready.
                    Enemy.
                        And I
Was a man with a club, intent upon acting out an ancient
Antagonism.

      But my anger vanished in the pale red light
That seemed to set chaparral aflame, seemed to envelope
The rattler in a crimson halo.

        Beautiful.

                I remembered
My dog, but that was years since.
                Life and death, the process
Of generation, unutterable mystery, a serpent that gleamed
In redness of failing light.

      Standoff.

          His chance,
There, under closeness of manzanita thicket, as good as mine:
No possible victory. I could kill him, but he might kill me,
And I knew it.
      "All right, then," I said, "I'll make a bargain
With you. You hear me, snake? I'll leave you alone if you'll
Leave me alone. I don't have anything you want, and you
Don't have anything I want. We'll both keep watch on the other.
There's bad blood between us. But the world's simpler
If we just stay out of each other's way. What do you think,
Buzztail, is it a deal?"
      The light was gone: only
Shadows now, tall white firs in the gully above, and a mile
Of woods between me and home.

         I started to throw away my club,
Then thought better of it. I could no longer see the rattler
At all—but I guessed he was gone, slipping silently
Over dry leaves, perhaps not even hurrying, intent, serpentine,
Twisting and slithering into timeless night.

KING SALMON

Oncorhynchus tshawytscha

Family Salmonidae

Length: to 4'10"; Weight: 30 lb

Habitat:

    Oceans in mid-depths or near surface; coastal streams

Range:

    In California, from the Sacramento River northward

Comments:

The largest of the Pacific salmon, the Chinook salmon is greenish blue to black above and silvery white below. It has irregular black spots on its back and smooth striations on its rays.

Also called the king salmon, the Chinook salmon feeds near the bottom of the ocean on crustaceans and fish, such as anchovies, herrings, and sand lances. It spends five to seven years at sea and then spawns in large rivers. The major spawning occurs in spring or fall, and the mature salmon die soon afterward.

The Chinook salmon stays in freshwater for only short periods of time. It can recognize its home stream by the odor, and migrates up and down the coast using visual cues. Unfortunately, dams can block salmon runs completely.

The Chinook salmon is the most prized ocean sport fish throughout the Pacific, from Alaska down to northern California. It is also the most common salmon in California and helps support commercial troll fishery.

Alexandre Dumas
from *A Gil Blas in California*

In certain places the Sacramento is half a mile wide; the average depth is three or four metres, the result being that ships to 200 tons can navigate it. In the Sacramento are found great quantities of salmon which are also numerous throughout its affluents. The salmon leave the sea in spring and ascend the river in swarms for about 500 miles. By following the main stream no obstacles are encountered, but on beyond, whether following the Sacramento or venturing up its affluents, their ascent is impeded by cascades, by dams made by the Indians or erected by farmers for some definite purpose, or even by gold-seekers, exploiting the rivers.

Here the fish struggle in vain to cross these bars or barricades. When approaching the limb of a tree or a rock which might retard their progress, they approach, swim along it, dart underneath, trace an arc, then mustering every ounce of strength, jump frequently twelve or fifteen feet up in the air. Their leap is always so gauged that they will fall into the upper waters toward which they are moving.

Freeman House
from *Totem Salmon*

Sometimes your storyline is
the only line you have to Earth.
    —Sharon Doubiago

I am alone in a sixteen-foot trailer by the side of a river. It is New Year's Eve, 1982. The door to the banged-up rig stands open, and when the radio is off I can hear water in the river splashing endlessly over cobbles. The oven is on full blast. Its door hangs open too. The heat rises to the ceiling in layers, ending at the level of my chest. My face is hot, but my ankles and knees are cold and damp. On the radio the Grateful Dead and fifteen thousand celebrants woozily greet the new year at the Oakland Coliseum. Ken Nordine's deep beatnik baritone drones on. Ken Kesey babbles. Any moment now, Bill Graham, undressed as Baby Time, will be lowered from the rafters. The band lurches through the music, loses the thread entirely, and after a long time finds it again, the beat loose and insouciant throughout. The band seems to say, "See? Told you we could find it again." It all makes sense with enough LSD, I suppose, and I have sometimes lived my life as the Grateful Dead plays its music, drifting in and out of the right way to be, risking everything on an exploratory riff. But tonight I am focused and full of purpose. My only drug is a poorboy of red port, which I sip cautiously.

I turn the radio off and listen. Then, to hear better, I turn the lights off too. I am listening to the water. If you listen carelessly, the water in a rushing river sounds like a single thing with a great fullness about it. But when you begin to try to sort out the sound of one thing *within* the sound of the water, the moving water breaks into a thousand different sounds, some of which are in the water and some of which are in your mind. Individual boulders rolling along the bottom. The Beatles singing *ya-na-na-na*. The one sound breaks itself into separate strands that intertwine with each other like threads in a twisted rope. Some strands are abandoned as new ones are introduced, making a strange and hypnotic music. Listening to running water is a quick route to voluntary hallucination.

Among the many voices of the water, I am trying to distinguish the sound of a king salmon struggling upstream. It is a foolish undertaking and it never works. I hear a hundred fish for every one that is actually there, and then miss the one that is. The only sure way to locate a fish in this realm of sensation is to walk to the river's edge and play your light along the surface of the water where it passes through the weir. The king salmon may be large or small, it may weigh three pounds or thirty. If it has swum into the pen above the weir, I will pull the long latchstring that releases the gate that closes the mouth of the weir, so the fish can go neither upstream nor down. This doesn't happen very often in 1982.

A little more than three years ago, a state fisheries biologist told us that this race of native king salmon is done for. I am still not totally sure he wasn't right. The state Department of Fish and Game is spread thin. They can't afford to expend their scarce resources on a river that has next to no hope of continuing to produce marketable salmon for a diminishing fishing fleet. But a small number of residents of the remote little valley have not been able to bring themselves to stand by and watch while one more race of salmon disappears, especially the one in the river that runs through their lives. They have begun with little idea of what can be done. They've talked to other people like themselves, and also to ranchers, loggers, academic biologists, and commercial fishers. They have read books and sent away for obscure technical papers. They've developed a scheme that they hope will enhance the success of the spawning of the wild fish. Through stubborn persistence they've convinced the state to let them have a go at it.

By the last night of 1982, this little group has grown into a cohort of several dozen residents who are spending a great deal of time trying to forge a new sort of relationship to the living processes of their home place. We also have learned to deal with bureaucracies outside that place, and we have incorporated as the Mattole Watershed Salmon Support Group. We have raised money. We have entered into contracts. We are inventing our strategies as we go along.

I am part of that cohort. I am tending a weir with an enclosed pen behind it that is meant to capture wild salmon in order to fertilize and incubate their eggs. I am working by myself, which is unusual. Normally a crew of two or three would share these long nights. Most often, David and/or Gary, two of the people who initiated the effort, would be here. But it's a holiday. Everyone else has pressing engagements. The fish, however, know nothing of holidays. The spawning season is almost over, and we few who care for the salmon haven't come anywhere close to reaching the goals we have set for ourselves this year.

———

(Now, nearly twenty years later, we find ourselves with lots of company—hundreds in our own watershed and thousands in other places all over North America—and I write out of curiosity as to what motivated people, myself included, to act in such a way. It is my hope that by the time you close this book we will both have some of the answers.)

———

The weir looks like fish weirs have always looked on this coast, a fence angled upstream across the river from either bank at enough of a bias against the current so that it will not offer more resistance than it can endure. It closes off passage upstream except through a one-foot opening at its apex. In earlier times, a fisher with a net or spear might have stood behind or above the opening. For our purposes, the opening serves as the doorway to a trap, or to a pen. Although built from materials manufactured elsewhere, it has a funky look; it blends in. Panels of redwood one-by-one, grape stakes in another life, are spaced at one-inch intervals horizontally and lashed to metal fence posts pounded into the river bottom. Each panel has a chickenwire apron attached at its bottom. The aprons are held to the bottom by sandbags, gravelbags really, each one weighing about forty pounds. Filling and hauling the bags two at a time takes up most of the two-hour drill required for three or four people to install the temporary structure.

The salmon's progress upstream is one of many marvels of the salmonid life cycle. The grace and strength required to overcome waterfalls and other blockages, the stamina to endure floodwaters, the systematic persistence necessary to thread the maze that a big logjam presents—these are attributes so wondrous that we must consider them in the same realm as the mysterious intelligence that allows the creature to distinguish between the smell of her particular natal stream and the smell of the rest of the world of water. But when the fish swims into an enclosure that requires her to seek an exit *downstream*, she becomes slow and seemingly confused. It will usually take her some hours to discover the downstream exit that she found so quickly before, when it was the passage upstream. Her slow meanders seem now to lack purpose; escape from the trap, when it comes, seems almost accidental. It is as if nothing matters now that the path to the spawning gravels is blocked.

I had argued with my coworkers that we should take advantage of this weakness. We humans have little enough advantage dealing with such a marvelously functional aquatic creature, and I am a person who loves his sleep. Salmon have yet to recognize that we are trying to help them; they continue to evade us. We are social workers whose clients decline to be served. Use our terrestrial, linear intelligence, I said, to fashion traps that would hold the fish until morning. Wait to handle them until after a second cup of coffee. And we had, for two years, fashioned beautiful traps to stand at the mouth of the weir. The traps had been built from the same grape stakes as the weir panels, and they had cleverly hinged plywood covers opening out from either side of the top. A three-quarter-inch cable slung all the way across the river from the top of the gorge at either side allowed a running block to be installed. Another line running through the block attached the traps to a hand-operated winch for installing the heavy hulks of the things in their exact locations, or for pulling them out quickly when the level and velocity of the rising water threatened to tear them apart or sweep them away.

But there was something about the traps—the sound that the waters made passing through so much enclosure, or perhaps the shadow that the things cast in the liquid boil below—that seemed to prevent the fish from entering. We had observed fish moving at dusk work their way right up to the mouth of a trap and then, in an instant, turn and disappear downstream. When they did enter and stayed for the night, they leaped against the plywood covers looking for a way out, wounding themselves and threatening their precious manifest of unfertilized eggs. Such a trap was too obviously a construct in service of human comfort, and we were, after all, seeking to serve the ends of the other species. Thus we have switched to a system featuring the larger and less secure pen, and the alarm clock set at two-hour intervals, and the muddled brains of the attendants.

———◦———

If the salmon are running in the deep night in December or January, it is likely that the moon is new, that the river is rising, and that the water is clouded with silt. It is probably raining. The salmon will use these elements of obscurity to hide them from predators while they make a dash toward the spawning grounds.

Tonight it is drizzling lightly, the air full of water only just heavy enough to fall to the ground. The drops cut across the beam of my headlamp and seem to be held there motionless, a black-and-white cartoon of rain. In the circle at the end of the beam, the black shag of redwood, and the huckleberry understory is everywhere weighted down with water and dripping.

I am in clumsy chestwaders that weigh seven or eight pounds. The rubber boot-legs join at the crotch and the garment continues up to just above the sternum, where it's held in place by a pair of short suspenders. The suspenders are never adjusted correctly; they are inevitably too tight or too loose. I lurch about like a puppet with too few moveable joints. Long-johns top and bottom against the cold. A Helly-Hansen raincoat and a black knit watch cap put on over the strap that holds my headlamp. To pee, I have to take off the coat, find a place to put it so that it won't get wet on the inside, undo the suspenders and slide the waders down to my knees, unbutton my Levi's, and fish around for the fly of the long-johns. The cap can stay on. I turn my back to the river out of courtesy.

The Mattole River runs through the westernmost watershed in California, cutting down through sea bottoms that have only recently, in geological terms, risen up out of the Pacific. It runs everywhere through deep valleys or gorges carved from the soft young sandstone.

Here, only a few miles from its headwaters, the river looks more like a large creek and is closely contained by steep banks. The fish are spooky during this culminating stage of their lives, which is why they run at night, and in murky water. Any light on the water, any boulder clumsily splashed into the stream, will turn a salmon skittering back toward the nearest hole or brushy overhang downstream. She may not try again until another night, or, in the worst case, will establish a spawning nest—a redd—downstream from the weir, in a place with too much current to allow her eggs to be effectively fertilized.

I inch down the bank crabwise in wet darkness, the gumboot heels of the waders digging furrows in the mud, the fingers and heels of my hands plowing the soaked wet duff.

On the bank of the river at the bottom of the ravine I hold my breath and let my ears readjust to the sounds of the water. I think I can hear through the cascades of sound a systematic plop, plop, plop, as if pieces of fruit are being dropped into the water. Sometimes this is the sound of a fish searching for the opening upstream; sometimes it is not. I breathe quietly and wait. I continue to hear the sound for a period of time for which I have no measure…and then it stops. I wait and wait. I hold my breath but do not hear the sound again. There is a long piece of parachute cord tied to a slipknot that holds open the gate at the mouth of the weir. I yank on the cord and the gate falls closed, its crash muted as the rush of water pushes it the last few inches tight against the body of the weir.

And now that I am no longer trying to sort one sound from another in the sound of the water, it is as if the water has become silent. It is dark. If the world were a movie, this would be cut to black. When I hear the sound I am waiting for, it is unmistakable: the sound of a full-grown salmon leaping wholly out of the water and twisting back into it. My straining senses slow down the sound so that each of its parts can be heard separately. A hiss, barely perceptible, as the fish muscles itself right out of its living medium; a silence like a dozen monks pausing too long between the strophes of a chant as the creature arcs through the dangerous air; a crash as of a basketball going through a plate glass window as he or she returns to the velvet embrace of the water; and then a thousand tiny bells struck once only as the shards of water fall and the surface of the stream regains its viscous integrity.

I flick on my headlamp and the whole backwater pool seems to leap toward me. The silver streak that crosses the enclosure in an instant is a flash of lightning within my skull, one which heals the wound that has separated me from this moment—from any moment. The encounter is so perfectly complex, timeless, and reciprocal that it takes on an objective reality of its own. I am able to walk around it as if it were a block of carved stone. If my feelings could be reduced to a chemical formula, the experience would be a clear solution made up of equal parts of dumb wonder and clean exhilaration, colored through with a sense of abiding dread. I could write a book about it.

———

The coevolution of humans and salmon on the North Pacific Rim fades into antiquity so completely that it is difficult to imagine a first encounter between the two species. Salmon probably arrived first. Their presence can be understood as one of the necessary preconditions for human settlement. Pacific salmon species became differentiated from their Atlantic ancestors no more than half a million years ago. Such adaptations were a response to their separation from their Atlantic salmon parent stock by land bridges such as the one that has periodically spanned the Bering Strait. By the time the Bering Sea land bridge last emerged, twelve thousand to twenty-five thousand years ago, in the Pleistocene epoch, the six species of Pacific salmon had arrived at their present characteristics and had attained their distribution over the vast areas of the North Pacific. As the ice pack retreated, the species continued to adapt ever more exactly as stocks or races—each finely attuned to one of the new rivers and to recently arrived human predators. If indeed humans first arrived in North America after crossing that land bridge from Asia, the sight of salmon pushing up the rivers of this eastern shore would have served as proof that this place too was livable.

On this mindblown midnight in the Mattole I could be any human at any time during the last few millennia, stunned by the lavish design of nature. The knowledge of the continuous presence of salmon in this river allows me to know myself for a moment as an expression of the continuity of human residence in this valley. Gone for a moment is my uncomfortable identity as part of a recently arrived race of invaders with doubtful title to the land; this encounter is one between species, human and salmonid. Such encounters have been happening as long as anyone can remember: the fish arrive to feed us and they do so at the same time every year and they do so with an obvious sense of intention. They come at intervals to feed us. They are very beautiful. What if they stopped coming?—which they must if we fail to relearn how to celebrate the true nature of the relationship.

For most of us, the understanding of how it might have been to live in a lavish system of natural provision is dim and may be obscured further by the scholarship that informs us. Our understanding of biology has been formulated during a time of less diversity and abundance in nature; our sense of relationship is replaced by fear of scarcity. By the time the anthropologists Alfred Kroeber and Erna Gunther were collecting their impressions of the life of the Native Americans of the Pacific Northwest, early in the twentieth century, the great salmon runs that had been an integral part of that life had already been systematically reduced. It may be this factor that makes the rituals described in their published papers seem transcendent and remote: ceremonial behavior that had evolved during a long period of dynamic balance has become difficult to understand in the period of swift decline that has followed.

It seems that in this part of the world, salmon have always been experienced by humans very directly as food, and food as relationship: the Yurok word for salmon, *nepu*, means "that which is eaten"; for the Ainu, the indigenous people of Hokkaido Island, the word is *shipe*, meaning "the real thing we eat." Given the abundance and regularity of the provision, one can imagine a relationship perceived as being between the feeder and those fed rather than between hunted and hunter. Villages in earlier times were located on the banks of streams, at the confluence of tributaries, because that is where the food delivers itself. The food swims up the stream each year at much the same time and gives itself, alive and generous.

It is not difficult to capture a salmon for food. My own first memory of salmon is of my father dressed for work as a radio dispatcher, standing on the low check dam across the Sacramento River at Redding and catching a king salmon in his arms, almost accidentally. The great Shasta Dam, which when completed would deny salmon access to the headwaters of the river, was still under construction. Twenty years later, as an urbanized young man, I found myself standing with a pitchfork, barefooted, in an inland tributary of the Klamath River, California's second largest river system. The salmon were beating their way upstream in the shallow water between my legs. Almost blindly, my comrades and I speared four or five of them. When the salmon come up the river, they come as food and they come as gift.

Salmon were also experienced as *connection*. At the time of year when the salmon come back, drawn up the rivers by spring freshets or fall rains, everyone in the old villages must have gained a renewal of their immediate personal knowledge of why the village was located where it was, of how tightly the lives of the people were tied to the lives of the salmon. The nets and drying racks were mended and ready. Everyone had a role to play in the great flood of natural provision that followed. The salmon runs were the largest annual events for the village community. The overarching abundance of salmon—their sheer numbers—is difficult to imagine from our vantage point in the late twentieth century. Nineteenth-century firsthand accounts consistently describe rivers filled from bank to bank with ascending salmon: "You could walk across the rivers on their backs!" In the memory of my neighbor Russell Chambers, an octogenarian, there are stories of horses refusing to cross the Mattole in the fall because the river had for a time become a torrent of squirming, flashing, silvery salmon light.

It is equally difficult to imagine a collective life informed and infused by the exuberant seasonal pulses of surrounding nature over a lifetime, over the lifetime of generations. But for most of the years in tribal memory of this region's original inhabitants, the arrival of salmon punctuated, at least once annually, a flow of provision that included acorn and abalone in the south, clams and berries and smelt in the north, venison and mussels and tender greens everywhere. Humans lived on the northwest coasts of North America for thousands of years in a state of lavish natural provision inseparable from any concept of individual or community life and survival.

Human consciousness organized the collective experience as an unbroken field of being: there is no separation between people and the multitudinous expressions of place manifested as food.

But each annual cycle is punctuated also by winter and the hungry time of early spring, and in the memory of each generation there are larger discontinuities of famine and upheaval. Within the memory of anyone's grandmother's grandfather, there is a catastrophe that has broken the cycle of abundance and brought hard times. California has periodic droughts that have lasted as long as a human generation. And there are cycles that have longer swings than can be encompassed by individual human lifetimes. Within any hundred-year period, floods alter the very structure of rivers. Along the Cascadian subduction zone, which stretches from Vancouver Island to Cape Mendocino in California, earthquakes and tidal waves three to five hundred years apart change the very nature of the landscape along its entire length. Whole new terraces rise up out of the sea in one place; the land drops away thirty feet in another. Rivers find new channels, and the salmon become lost for a time.

Even larger cycles include those long fluctuations of temperature in the air and water which every ten or twenty thousand years capture the water of the world in glaciers and the ice caps. Continents are scoured, mountain valleys deepened, coastlines reconfigured, human histories interrupted. These events become myths of a landscape in a state of perpetual creation; they are a part of every winter's storytelling. The stories cast a shadow on the psyche and they carry advice, which cannot be ignored. Be attentive. Watch your step. Everything's alive and moving.

On a scale equivalent to that of the changes caused by ice ages and continental drift are the forces set loose by recent European invasions and conquests of North America, the exponential explosion of human population that drives this history, and the aberrant denial of the processes of interdependence, which has come to define human behavior during this period.

Somewhere between these conflicting states of wonder—between natural provision erotic in its profligacy and cruel in its sometimes sudden and total withdrawal—lies the origins of the old ways. Somewhere beyond our modern notions of religion and regulation but partaking of both, human engagement with salmon—and the rest of the natural world—has been marked by behavior that is respectful, participatory, and ceremonial. And it is in this way that most of the human species has behaved most of the time it has been on the planet.

King salmon and I are together in the water. The basic bone-felt nature of this encounter never changes, even though I have spent parts of a lifetime seeking the meeting and puzzling over its meaning, trying to find for myself the right place in it. It is a *large* experience, and it has never failed to contain these elements, at once separate and combined: empty-minded awe; an uneasiness about my own active role both as a person and as a creature of my species; and a looming existential dread that sometimes attains the physicality of a lump in the throat, a knot in the abdomen, a constriction around the temples. They seem important, these various elements of response, like basic conditions of existence. I am smack in the middle of the beautiful off-handed description of our field of being that once flew up from my friend David Abram's mouth: that we are many sets of eyes staring out at each other from the same living body. For the instant, there is a part of that living body which is a cold wet darkness containing a pure burst of salmon muscle and intelligence, and containing also a clumsy human pursuing the ghost of a relationship.

I have left the big dip net leaning against the trailer up above the river. I forget that the captured fish is probably confused and will not quickly find its way out of the river pen. I race up the steep bank of the gorge as if everything depends upon my speed. My wader boots, half a size too large, catch on a tree root and I am thrown on my face in the mud. The bank is steep and I hit the ground before my body expects to, and with less force. I am so happy to be unhurt that I giggle absurdly. Why, tonight, am I acting like a hunter? All my training, social and intellectual, as well as my genetic predisposition, moves me to act like a predator rather than a grateful, careful guest at Gaia's table. Why am I acting as if this is an encounter that has a winner and a loser, even though I am perfectly aware that the goal of the encounter is to keep the fish alive?

I retrieve the dip net and return more slowly down the dark bank to the river. Flashing the beam of my headlamp on the water in the enclosure, I can see a shape darker than the dark water. The shape rolls as it turns to flash the pale belly. The fish is large—three or maybe four years old. It seems as long as my leg.

Several lengths of large PVC pipe are strewn along the edge of the river, half in the water and half out. These sections of heavy white or aquamarine tubing, eight, ten, and twelve inches in diameter, have been cut to length to provide temporary holding for a salmon of any of the various sizes that might arrive: the more closely contained the captured creature, the less it will thrash about and do injury to itself. I remove from the largest tube the perforated Plexiglas endplate held in place by large cotter pins.

I wade into the watery pen. Nowhere is the water deeper than my knees; the trap site has been selected for the rare regularity of its bottom and for its gentle gradient. The pen is small enough so that anywhere I stand I dominate half its area. Here, within miles of its headwaters, the river is no more than thirty feet across. The pen encloses half its width. I wade slowly back and forth to get a sense of the fish's speed and strength. This one seems to be a female, recently arrived. When she swims between my feet I can see the gentle swollen curve from gill to tail where her three to five thousand eggs are carried. She explores this new barrier to her upstream migration powerfully and methodically, surging from one side of the enclosure to another. Using the handle of the net to balance myself against the current, I find the edge of the pen farthest from the shore, turn off the headlamp, and stand quietly, listening again.

The rain has stopped. Occasionally I can hear her dorsal fin tear the surface of the water. After a few minutes I point my headlamp downward and flick the switch. Again the surface of the water seems to leap toward me. The fish is irritated or frightened by the light, and each of her exploratory surges moves her farther away from me, closer to the shore.

The great strength of her thrusts pushes her into water that is shallower than the depth of her body and she flounders. Her tail seeks purchase where there is none and beats the shallow water like a fibrillating heart. The whole weight of the river seems to tear against my legs as I take the few steps toward her. I reach over her with the net so that she lies between me and the mesh hoop. I hold the net stationary and kick at the water near her tail; she twists away from me and into the net. Now I can twist the mouth of the net up toward the air and she is completely encircled by the two-inch mesh. I move her toward deeper water and rest.

There are sparks of light rotating behind my eyes. The struggle in the net translates up my arms like low-voltage electricity. The weight of the fish amplified by the length of the net's handle is too much. I use two hands to grasp the aluminum rim at either side of the mouth of the net, and I rest and breathe. After a bit, I can release one side of the frame and hold the whole net jammed against my leg with one hand. I reach for the PVC tube and position its open mouth where I want it, half submerged and with the opening pointing toward us. I move the net and the fish around to my left side and grasp through the net the narrow part of her body just forward of her tail—the peduncle—where she is still twice the thickness of my wrist.

I only have enough strength to turn the fish in one direction or another; were I to try and lift her out of the water against her powerful lateral thrashing, I would surely drop her. The fish is all one long muscle from head to tail, and that muscle is longer, and stronger, than any muscle I can bring to bear. I direct her head toward the tube, and enclose tube and fish within the net. I drop the handle of the net, and move the fish forward, toward the tube.

There is a moment while I am holding the salmon and mesh entwined in elbow-deep water when everything goes still. Her eyes are utterly devoid of expression. Her gills pump and relax, pump and relax, measured and calmly regular. There is in that reflex an essence of aquatic creaturehood, a reality to itself entire. And there is a sense of great peacefulness, as when watching the rise and fall of a sleeping lover's chest. When I loosen my grasp, she swims out of the net and into the small enclosure.

Quickly, trembling, I lift the tail end of the tube so that her head is facing down into the river. I slide the Plexiglas endplate into place and fasten it, and she lies quietly, the tube just submerged and tethered to a stout willow. I sit down beside the dark and noisy river, beside the captured female salmon. I am sweating inside my rubber gear. The rain has begun again. I think about the new year and the promise of the eggs inside her. I am surrounded by ghosts that rise off the river like scant fog.

✤ SHEEP ✤

Ovis aries

Family Bovidae

Height: 25–50"; Weight: 44–440 lb

Habitat:

    Pastures and open rangeland

Range:

    Common throughout rural and semirural regions of California

Comments:

Sheep were among the first animals to be domesticated, with some evidence suggesting that the process began nine thousand to eleven thousand years ago. Breeding for wool quality and other characteristics has yielded more than two hundred breeds of domestic sheep, as well as a number of varieties resulting from crossbreeding. Sheep are now raised all over the world, valued primarily for their milk, meat, and wool.

Because of the variety of breeds, their physical characteristics vary. Their color varies from white to dark brown, and they often have dark faces with pointed, narrow muzzles. Domestic breeds may or may not have horns.

Sheep are grazing animals, though their diet may be supplemented with hay and grain. In California—as elsewhere—sheep have often been blamed for the destruction of rangeland, since these animals graze very close to the ground. However, in various regions, programs are now in place that use sheep to help control non-native vegetation and other unwanted growth.

Mary Austin
"The Flock"

The earliest important achievement of ovine intelligence is to know whether its own notion or another's is most worth while, and if the other's, which one. Individual sheep have certain qualities, instincts, competencies, but in the man-herded flocks these are superseded by something which I shall call the flock-mind, though I cannot say very well what it is, except that it is less than the sum of all their intelligences. This is why there have never been any notable changes in the management of flocks since the first herder girt himself with a wallet of sheepskin and went out of his cave dwelling to the pastures.

Understand that a flock is not the same thing as a number of sheep. On the stark wild headlands of the White Mountains, as many as thirty Bighorn are known to run in loose, fluctuating hordes; in fenced pastures, two to three hundred; close-herded on the range, two to three thousand; but however artificially augmented, the flock is always a conscious adjustment. As it is made up in the beginning of the season, the band is chiefly of one sort, wethers or ewes or weanling lambs (for the rams do not run with the flock except for a brief season in August); with a few flock-wise ones, trained goats, the *cabestres* of the Mexican herders, trusted bell-wethers or experienced old ewes mixed and intermeddled by the herder and the dogs, becoming invariably and finally coördinate. There are always Leaders, Middlers, and Tailers, each insisting on its own place in the order of going. Should the flock be rounded up suddenly in alarm it mills within itself until these have come to their own places.

If you would know something of the temper and politics of the shepherd you meet, inquire of him for the names of his leaders. They should be named for his sweethearts, for the little towns of France, for the generals of the great Napoleon, for the presidents of Republics,—though for that matter they are all ardent republicans,— for the popular heroes of the hour. Good shepherds take the greatest pains with their leaders, not passing them with the first flock to slaughter, but saving them to make wise the next.

There is much debate between herders as to the advantage of goats over sheep as leaders. In any case there are always a few goats in a flock, and most American owners prefer them; but the Frenchmen choose bell-wethers. Goats lead naturally by reason of a quicker instinct, forage more freely, and can find water on their own account. But wethers, if trained with care, learn what goats abhor, to take broken ground sedately, to walk through the water rather than set the whole flock leaping and scrambling; but never to give voice to alarm as goats will, and call the herder. Wethers are more bidable once they are broken to it, but a goat is the better for a good beating. Echenique has told me that the more a goat complains under his cudgelings the surer he is of the brute's need of discipline. Goats afford another service in furnishing milk for the shepherd, and, their udders being most public, will suckle a sick lamb, a pup, or a young burro at need.

It appears that leaders understand their office, and goats particularly exhibit a jealousy of their rights to be first over the stepping-stones or to walk the teetering log-bridges at the roaring creeks. By this facile reference of the initiative to the wisest one, the shepherd is served most. The dogs learn to which of the flock to communicate orders, at which heels a bark or a bite soonest sets the flock in motion. But the flock-mind obsesses equally the best trained, flashes as instantly from the Meanest of the Flock.

Suppose the sheep to scatter widely on a heather-planted headland, the leader feeding far to windward. Comes a cougar sneaking up the trail between the rooted boulders toward the Meanest of the Flock. The smell of him, the play of light on his sleek flanks startles the unslumbering fear in the Meanest; it runs widening in the flock-mind, exploding instantly in the impulse of flight.

Danger! flashes the flock-mind, and in danger the indispensable thing is to run, not to wait until the leader sniffs the tainted wind and signals it; not for each and singly to put the occasion to the proof; but to run—of this the flock-mind apprises—and to keep on running until the impulse dies faintly as water-rings on the surface of a mantling pond. In the wild pastures flight is the only succor, and since to cry out is to interfere with that business and draw on the calamity, a flock in extremity never cries out.

Consider, then, the inadequacy of the flock-mind. A hand-fed leader may learn to call the herder vociferously, a cosset lamb in trouble come blatting to his heels, but the flock has no voice other than the deep-mouthed pealings hung about the leader's neck. In all that darkling lapse of time since herders began to sleep by the sheep with their weapons, affording a protection that the flock-mind never learns to invite, they have found no better trick than to be still and run foolishly. For the flock-mind moves only in the direction of the Original Intention. When at shearings or markings they run the yearlings through a gate for counting, the rate of going accelerates until the sheep pass too rapidly for numbering. Then the shepherd thrusts his staff across the opening, forcing the next sheep to jump, and the next, and the next, until, Jump! says the flock-mind. Then he withdraws the staff, and the sheep go on jumping until the impulse dies as the dying peal of the bells.

By very little the herder may turn the flock-mind to his advantage, but chiefly it works against him. Suppose on the open range the impulse to forward movement overtakes them, set in motion by some eager leaders that remember enough of what lies ahead to make them oblivious to what they pass. They press ahead. The flock draws on. The momentum of travel grows. The bells clang soft and hurriedly; the sheep forget to feed; they neglect the tender pastures; they will not stay to drink. Under an unwise or indolent herder the sheep going on an accustomed trail will over-travel and under-feed, until in the midst of good pasture they starve upon their feet. So it is on the Long Trail you so often see the herder walking with his dogs ahead of his sheep to hold them back to feed. But if it should be new ground he must go after and press them skillfully, for the flock-mind balks chiefly at the unknown.

If a flock could be stopped as suddenly as it is set in motion, Sanger would never have lost to a single bear the five hundred sheep he told me of. They were bedded on a mesa breaking off in a precipice two hundred feet above the valley, and the bear came up behind them in the moonless watch of night. With no sound but the scurry of feet and the startled clamor of the bells, the flock broke straight ahead. The brute instinct had warned them asleep but it could not save them awake. All that the flock-mind could do was stir them instantly to running, and they fled straight away over the headland, piling up, five hundred of them, in the gulch below.

In sudden attacks from several quarters, or inexplicable man-thwarting of their instincts, the flock-mind teaches them to turn a solid front, revolving about in the smallest compass with the lambs in the midst, narrowing and in-drawing until they perish by suffocation. So they did in the intricate defiles of Red Rock, where Carrier lost two hundred and fifty in '74, and at Poison Springs, as Narcisse Duplin told me, where he had to choose between leaving them to the deadly waters, or, prevented from the spring, made witless by thirst, to mill about until they piled up and killed threescore in their midst. By no urgency of the dogs could they be moved forward or scattered until night fell with coolness and returning sanity. Nor does the imperfect gregariousness of man always save us from ill-considered rushes or strangulous in-turnings of the social mass. Notwithstanding there are those who would have us to be flock-minded.

It is probably that the obsession of this over-sense originates in the extraordinary quickness with which the sheep makes the superior intelligence of the leader serve his own end. A very little running in the open range proves that one in every group of sheep has sharper vision, quicker hearing, keener scent; henceforth it is the business of the dull sheep to watch that favored one. No slightest sniff or stamp escapes him; the order for flight finds him with muscles tense for running.

The worth of a leader in close-herded flocks is his ability to catch readily the will of the herder. Times I have seen the sheep feeding far from the man, not knowing their appointed bedding-place. The dogs lag at the herder's heels. Now as the sun is going down the man thrusts out his arm with a gesture that conveys to the dogs his wish that they turn the flock toward a certain open scarp. The dogs trot out leisurely, circling widely to bring up the farthest stragglers, but before they round upon it the flock turns. It moves toward the appointed quarter and pours smoothly up the bill. It is possible that the leaders may have learned the language of that right arm, and in times of quietude obey it without intervention of the dogs. It is also conceivable that in the clear silences of the untroubled wild the flock-mind takes its impulse directly from the will of the herder.

Almost the only sense left untouched by man-herding is the weather sense. Scenting a change, the sheep exhibit a tendency to move to higher ground; no herder succeeds in making his flock feed in the eye of the sun. While rain falls they will not feed nor travel except in extreme desperation, but if after long falling it leaves off suddenly, night or day, the flock begins to crop. Then if the herder bears not the bells nor wakes himself by that subtle sense which in the outdoor life has time to grow, he has his day's work cut out for him in the rounding-up. A season of long rains makes short fleeces.

Summers in the mountains, sheep love to lie on the cooling banks and lick the snow, preferring it to any drink; but if falling snow overtakes them they are bewildered by it, find no food for themselves, and refuse to travel while it lies on the ground. This is the more singular, for the American wild sheep, the Bighorn, makes nothing of a twenty-foot fall; in the blinding swirl of flakes shifts only to let the drifts pile under him; ruminates most contentedly when the world is full of a roaring white wind. Most beasts in bad weather drift before a storm. The faster it moves the farther go the sheep; so if there arises one of those blowy days that announce he turn of the two seasons, blinding thick with small dust, at the end of a few hours of it the shepherd sees the tails of his sheep disappearing down the wind. The tendency of sheep is to seek lower ground when disturbed by beasts, and under weather stress to work up. When any of his flock are strayed or stampeded, the herder knows by the occasion whether to seek them up hill or down. Seek them he must if he would have them again, for strays have no faculty by sense or scent to work their way back to the herd. Let them be separated from it but by the roll of the land, and by accident headed in another direction, it is for them as if the flock had never been. It is to provide against this incompetency that the shepherd makes himself markers, a black sheep, or one with a crumpled horn or an unshorn patch on the rump, easily noticeable in the shuffle of dust-colored backs. It is the custom to have one marker to one hundred sheep, each known by his chosen place in the flock which he insists upon, so that if as many as half a dozen stray out of the band the relative position of the markers is changed; or if one of these conspicuous ones be missing it will not be singly, because of the tendency of large flocks to form smaller groups about the best worth following.

I do not know very well what to make of that trait of lost sheep to seek rock shelter at the base of cliffs, for it suits with no characteristic of his wild brethren. But if an estray in his persistent journey up toward the high places arrives at the foot of a tall precipice, there he stays, seeking not to go around it, feeding out perhaps and returning to it, but if frightened by prowlers, huddling there to starve. Could it be the survival, not of a wild instinct,—it is too foolish to have been that,—but of the cave-dwelling time when man protected him in his stone shelters or in pens built against the base of a cliff, as we see the herder yet for greater convenience build rude corrals of piled boulders at the foot of an overhanging or insurmountable rocky wall? It is yet to be shown how long man halted in the period of stone dwelling and the sheep with him; but if it be assented that we have brought some traces of that life forward with us, might not also the sheep?

Where the wild strain most persists is in the bedding habits of the flock. Still they take for choice, the brow of a rising hill, turning outward toward the largest view; and never have I seen the flock all lie down at one time. Always as if by prearrangement some will stand, and upon their surrendering the watch others will rise in their places headed to sniff the tainted wind and scan the rim of the world. Like a thing palpable one sees the racial obligation pass through the bedded flock; as the tired watcher folds his knees under him and lies down, it passes like a sigh. By some mysterious selection it leaves a hundred ruminating in quietude and troubles the appointed one. One sees in the shaking of his sides a hint of struggle against the hereditary and so unnecessary instinct, but sighing he gets upon his feet. By noon or night the flock instinct never sleeps. Waking and falling asleep, waking and spying on the flock, no chance discovers the watchers failing, even though they doze upon their feet; and by nothing so much is the want of interrelation of the herder and the flock betrayed, for watching is the trained accomplishment of dogs.

The habit of nocturnal feeding is easily resumed, the sheep growing restless when the moon is full, and moving out to feed at the least encouragement. In hot seasons on the treeless range the herder takes advantage of it, making the longer siesta of the burning noon. But if the habit is to be resumed or broken off, it is best done by moving to new grounds, the association of locality being most stubborn to overcome.

Of the native instincts for finding water and knowing when food is good for them, herded goats have retained much, but sheep not a whit. In the open San Joaquin, said a good shepherd of that country, when the wind blew off the broad lake, his sheep, being thirsty, would break and run as much as a mile or two in that direction; but it seems that the alkaline dust of the desert range must have diminished the keenness of smell, for Sanger told me how, on his long drive, when his sheep had come forty miles without drink and were then so near a water-hole that the horses scented it and pricked up their ears, the flock became unmanageable from thirst and broke back to the place where they had last drunk. Great difficulty is experienced in the desert ranges in getting the flock to water situated obscurely in steep ravines; they panting with water need, but not even aware of its nearness until they have been fairly thrust into it. Then if one lifts up a joyous blat the dogs and the herder must stand well forward to prevent suffocation by piling up of the flock. You should have heard José Jesús Lopez tell how, when the ten thousand came to water in the desert after a day or two of dry travel, when the first of the nearing band had drunk he lifted up the water call; how it was taken up and carried back across the shouldering brutes to the nearest band behind, and by them flatly trumpeted to the next, and so across the mesa, miles and miles in the still, slant light.

When Watterson ran his sheep on the plains he watered them at a pump, and in the course of the season all the bands that bore the Three Legs of Man got to know the smell pertaining to that brand, drinking at the troughs as they drew in at sundown from the feeding-ground. But when for a price strange bands in passing drank there, he could in no wise prevail upon his own sheep to drink of the water they had left. The flocks shuffled in and sniffed at the tainted drink and went and lay down waterless. The second band drew alongside and made as if to refresh themselves at the troughs, but before they had so much as smelled of it:—

Ba-a-a, Ba-a-a-a! blatted the first flock, and the newcomers turned toward them and lay down. Comes another band and the second takes up the report, not having proved the event but accepting it at hearsay from the first.

Ba-a-a-d, Ba-a-a-d! blat the watchers, and when that has happened two or three times the shepherd gives over trying to make his sheep accept the leavings of the troughs, whatever the price of water, but turns it out upon the sand. Sheep will die rather than drink water which does not please them, and die drinking water with which they should not be pleased. Nor can they discriminate in the matter of poisonous herbs. In the northerly Sierras they perish yearly, cropping the azaleas; Julien lost three or four hundred when wild tobacco *(nicotiana attenuata)* sprang up after a season of flood water below Coyote Holes; and in places about the high mountains there are certain isolated meadows wherein some herb unidentified by sheepmen works disaster to the ignorant or too confiding herder. Such places come to be known as Poison Meadows, and grasses ripen in them uncropped year after year. Yet it would seem there is a rag-tag of instinct left, for in the desert regions where sheep have had a taste of Loco-weed *(astragalus)* which affects them as cocaine, like the devotees of that drug, they return to seek for it and become dopy and worthless through its excess; and a flock that has suffered from milkweed poisoning learns at last to be a little aware of it. Old tales of folklore would have us to understand that this atrophy of a vital sense is within the reach of history. Is it not told indeed, in Araby, that the exhilaration of coffee was discovered by a goatherd from the behavior of his goats when they had cropped the berries?

By much the same cry that apprises the flock of tainted drink they are made aware of strangers in the band. This is chiefly the business of yearlings, wise old ewes and seasoned wethers not much regarding it. One of the band discerns a smell not the smell of his flock, and bells the others to come on and inquire. They run blatting to his call and form a ring about the stranger, vociferating disapproval until the flock-mind wakes and pricks them to butt the intruder from the herd; but he persisting and hanging on the outskirts of the flock, acquaints them with his smell and becomes finally incorporate in the band. Nothing else but the rattlesnake extracts this note of protest from the flock. Him also they inclose in the noisy ring until the rattler wriggles to his hole, or the herder comes with his *makila* and puts an end to the commotion.

It is well to keep in mind that ordinarily when the flock cries there is nothing in particular the matter with it. The continuous blether of the evening round-up is merely the note of domesticity, ewes calling to their lambs, wethers to their companions as they revolve to their accustomed places, all a little resentful of the importunity of the dogs. In sickness and alarm the sheep are distressfully still, only milkweed poisoning, of all evils, forcing from them a kind of breathy moan; but this is merely a symptom of the disorder and not directed toward the procurement of relief.

It is doubtful if the herder is anything more to the flock than an incident of the range, except as a giver of salt, for the only cry they make to him is the salt cry. When the natural craving is at the point of urgency they circle about his camp or his cabin, leaving off feeding for that business; and nothing else offering, they will continue this headlong circling about a boulder or any object bulking large in their immediate neighborhood remotely resembling the appurtenances of man, as if they had learned nothing since they were free to find licks for themselves, except that salt comes by bestowal and in conjunction with the vaguely indeterminate lumps of matter that associate with man. As if in fifty centuries of man-herding they had made but one step out of the terrible isolation of brute species, an isolation impenetrable except by fear to every other brute, but now admitting the fact without knowledge, of the God of the Salt. Accustomed to receiving this miracle on open boulders, when the craving is strong upon them they seek such as these to run about, vociferating, as if they said, In such a place our God has been wont to bless us, come now let us greatly entreat Him. This one quavering bleat, unmistakable to the sheepman even at a distance, is the only new note in the sheep's vocabulary, and the only one which passes with intention from himself to man. As for the call of distress which a leader raised by hand may make to his master, it is not new, is not common to flock usage, and is swamped utterly in the obsession of the flock-mind.

But when you hear shepherds from the Pyrenees speak of the salt call it is no blether of the sheep they mean, but that long, rolling, high and raucous *Ru-u-u-u-u-u* by which they summon the flock to the lick. And this is most curious that no other word than this is recognized as exclusive to the sheep, as we understand "scat" to be the peculiar shibboleth of cats, and "bossy" the only proper appellate of cows. Ordinarily, the herder does not wish to call the sheep, he prefers to send the dogs, but if he needs must name them he cries Sheep, sheep! or *mouton*, or *boregíto*, as his tongue is, or apprises them of the distribution of salt by beating on a pan. Only the Basco, and such French as have learned it from him, troubles his throat with this searching, mutilated cry. If it should be in crossing the Reserve when the rangers hurry him, or on the range when in the midst of security, suddenly he discovers the deadly milkweed growing all abroad, or if above the timber-line one of the quick, downpouring storms begins to shape in the pure aerial glooms, at once you see the herder striding at the head of his flock drawing them on with the uplifted *Ru-u-u-uuuu!* and all the sheep running to it as it were the Pied Piper come again.

Suppose it were true what we have read, that there was once an Atlantis stationed toward the west, continuing the empurpled Pyrenees. Suppose the first of these Pyrenean folk were, as it is written, just Atlantean shepherds straying farthest from that happy island, when the seas engulfed it; suppose they should have carried forward with the inbred shepherd habit some roots of speech, likeliest to have been such as belonged to shepherding—well then, when above the range of trees, when the wild scarps lift rosily through the ineffably pure blue of the twilight earth, suffused with splendor of the alpen glow, when the flock crops the tufted grass scattering widely on the steep, should you see these little men of long arms leaping among the rocks and all the flock lift up their heads to hear the ululating *Ru-u-ubru-u-uuu!* would not all these things leap together in your mind and seem to mean something? Just suppose!

Helen Hunt Jackson
from *Ramona*

At the sheep-shearing sheds and pens all was stir and bustle. The shearing shed was a huge caricature of a summer-house,—a long, narrow structure, sixty feet long by twenty or thirty wide, all roof and pillars; no walls; the supports, slender rough posts, as far apart as was safe, for the upholding the roof, which was of rough planks loosely laid from beam to beam. On three sides of this were the sheep-pens filled with sheep and lambs.

A few rods away stood the booths in which the shearers' food was to be cooked and the shearers fed. These were mere temporary affairs, roofed only by willow boughs with the leaves left on. Near these, the Indians had already arranged their camp; a hut or two of green boughs had been built, but for the most part they would sleep rolled up in their blankets, on the ground. There was a brisk wind, and the gay-colored wings of the windmill blew furiously round and round, pumping out into the tank below a stream of water so swift and strong, that as the men crowded around, wetting and sharpening their knives, they got well spattered, and had much merriment, pushing and elbowing each other in the spray.

A high four-posted frame stood close to the shed; in this, swung from the four corners, hung one of the great sacking bags in which the fleeces were to be packed. A big pile of these bags lay on the ground at foot of the posts. Juan Can eyed them with a chuckle. "We'll fill more than those before night, Señor Felipe," he said. He was in his element, Juan Can, at shearing times. Then came his reward for the somewhat monotonous and stupid year's work. The world held no better feast for his eyes than the sight of a long row of big bales of fleece, tied, stamped with the Moreno brand, ready to be drawn away to the mills. "Now, there is something substantial," he thought; "no chance of wool going amiss in market!"

If a year's crop were good, Juan's happiness was assured for the next six months. If it proved poor, he turned devout immediately, and spent the next six months calling on the saints for better luck, and redoubling his exertions with the sheep.

On one of the posts of the shed short projecting slats were nailed, like half-rounds of a ladder. Lightly as a rope-walker Felipe ran up there, to the roof, and took his stand there, ready to take the fleeces and pack them in the bag as fast as they should be tossed up from below. Luigo, with a big leathern wallet fastened in front of him, filled with five-cent pieces, took his stand in the center of the shed. The thirty shearers, running into the nearest pen, dragged each his sheep into the shed, in a twinkling of an eye had the creature between his knees, helpless, immovable, and the sharp sound of shears set in. The sheep-shearing had begun. No rest now. Not a second's silence from the bleating, baa-ing, opening and shutting, clicking, sharpening of shears, flying of fleeces through the air to the roof, pressing and stamping them down in the bales; not a second's intermission, except the hour of rest at noon, from sunrise till sunset, till the whole eight thousand of Señora Moreno's sheep were shorn. It was a dramatic spectacle. As soon as a sheep was shorn, the shearer ran with the fleece in his hand to Luigo, threw it down on a table, received his five-cent piece, dropped it in his pocket, ran to the pen, dragged out another sheep, and in less than five minutes was back again with a second fleece. The shorn sheep, released, bounded off in another pen, where, light in the head no doubt from being three to five pounds lighter on their legs, they trotted around bewilderedly for a moment, then flung up their heels and capered for joy.

~∾ DESERT TARANTULA ∾~

Aphonopelma chalcodes

Family Theraphosidae

Length: Male 2–2 ½"; Female 2–2 ¾"

Habitat:

　Desert soil

Range:

　Common throughout southern California

Comments:

　The desert tarantula is a large, hairy spider. It is gray to dark brown, with a brownish black, bristly abdomen. It has a large middle pair of eyes surrounded by three smaller eyes. Its legs have two claws and a patch of hair underneath. The bristles on the abdomen break off easily and irritate the skin of the spider's prey.

　The desert tarantula is a primarily nocturnal animal, usually spending its time in dark cavities or burrows during the day. Its burrow is usually lined with silk, but unlike many other spiders, the desert tarantula does not spin a web to catch prey. At night, it emerges from its burrow to hunt by touch. It feeds on lizards, insects, and small animals such as mice.

　Males are short-lived and are more active than females. They do not molt after they reach maturity, but females do. Females can live up to twenty years in captivity. The desert tarantula is generally reluctant to attack people, but its venom is no more dangerous than a bee sting.

George Wharton James
from *The Wonders of the Colorado Desert*

The tarantula *(Mygale avicularia)* is occasionally seen on the desert. It is nothing but a large, hairy, overgrown spider. There are two or three different species, but except to the entomologist the differences seem slight. They belong to the trapdoor spider family.

The great foe to the tarantula is a hornet or wasp-like insect called the tarantula hawk *(Pompilius formosus)*. The female, when ready to lay her eggs, flies eagerly about looking for a tarantula. As soon as she sees the great, hairy-bodied spider, she alights upon it and with the speed of a flash of lightning darts her sting into it. There must be some preservative quality in the poison she injects, for, while the insect dies, its body does not decompose nor dry out. It has not yet served its purpose. Digging a hole some five inches deep the hawk now rolls the body of the tarantula into it, and deposits her eggs either in or on the body. She now closes up the nest. When the larvae leave the egg they find themselves supplied with food enough to last until they are fully grown. All the transformations occur in the underground nest, and finally the adult insect emerges after reaching its perfect stage.

∽ CALIFORNIA ∽ WESTERN TOAD

Bufo boreas halophilus

Family Bufonidae

Length: 2 ½–5"

Habitat:

Grasslands and woodlands, meadows, gardens, parks, and near streams

Range:

Common throughout California, except desert areas

Comments:

The California western toad is dusky gray or green, with dark blotches and a white or cream stripe down the middle of its back. It is a subspecies of the western toad and has a wider head and lighter markings than its relative. Red-tinged warts surrounded by black blotches on its skin secrete a milky, poisonous substance that protects it from predators.

The diet of the western toad consists of insects such as bees, flies, beetles, grasshoppers, and moths. It will also eat spiders and earthworms.

Usually nocturnal, the California western toad is only rarely seen during the day. It is not found in cold weather and is solitary. Unlike other toads, the California western toad has no vocal sac and a weak voice.

David Rains Wallace
from "Gardening with Pests"

The other major burrow dwellers in my garden are completely beneficial, since they don't dig burrows, just live in them. In late spring my wife and I began to think we had Peeping Toms. Startling loud rustling sounds were coming from below our windows at night. We went out with a flashlight and found several of the biggest, fattest toads I'd ever seen, crawling out from under the house. They looked as large as dinner plates—like lumpy, flattened clods of earth that somehow had sprouted eyes and legs and started hopping around. The toads promptly moved into the gopher's burrow system in the garden, where, judging from their girth, they must have eaten thousands of earwigs, moths, beetles, and other nocturnal insects. I'd go out at night with a flashlight and see what appeared to be a pair of black eyes sparkling solemnly from the earth itself—as though my garden had grown sense organs—until I discerned the outline of the toad's body around the eyes, its warty hide having taken on the same flat, pebbly contours of the ground where it crouched at the entrance to a gopher tunnel.

Toads didn't turn up only at night. There was one gopher hole in a bean patch from which—when I watered the patch after sunset—would regularly emerge a dignified toad that I half expected to be carrying a towel and bar of soap, ready for its daily shower, although I suppose the real reason for its emergence was that it didn't like being flooded in its resting place. Another time, I dug up a stony patch in the garden to fill a hole in the driveway. When I poured a bucketful of this soil on the driveway, one of the "stones" bounced and squeaked indignantly, then waddled off and somehow inserted itself into an inch-wide crevice in a pile of boards—quite an astonishing feat, since the toad itself was at least six inches wide. It just flattened out and *flowed* between the boards.

❧ RAINBOW TROUT ❧

Oncorhynchus mykiss

Family Salmonidae

Length: to 4'; Weight: to 53 lb

Habitat:

Ocean or lakes and freshwater streams and rivers, at mid-depths and near the surface

Range:

Common throughout California; steelhead are found in the Pacific as far south as San Luis Obispo County, and rainbow trout prefer coastal streams but can be found in inland lakes, where they are often stocked

Comments:

The rainbow trout is metallic blue above and silvery white below. It has small black spots on its back, sides, and most fins. A spawning male also has a distinctive red to pink band running down its sides. Its head is short and the inside of its mouth is white.

Sea-run rainbow trout are called steelhead. They migrate extensively, spending two to four years in the home stream before going out to sea for three years. Typically, they spawn in home streams during fall or winter, and most adults survive spawning. The rainbow trout is a popular sport fish and is often caught by humans for food.

Richard Brautigan
from *Trout Fishing in America*

The creek was made narrow by little green trees that grew too close together. The creek was like 12,845 telephone booths in a row with high Victorian ceilings and all the doors taken off and all the backs of the booths knocked out.

Sometimes when I went fishing in there, I felt just like a telephone repairman, even though I did not look like one. I was only a kid covered with fishing tackle, but in some strange way by going in there and catching a few trout, I kept the telephones in service. I was an asset to society.

It was pleasant work, but at times it made me uneasy. It could grow dark in there instantly when there were some clouds in the sky and they worked their way onto the sun. Then you almost needed candles to fish by, and foxfire in your reflexes.

Once I was in there when it started raining. It was dark and hot and steamy. I was of course on overtime. I had that going in my favor. I caught seven trout in fifteen minutes.

The trout in those telephone booths were good fellows. There were a lot of young cutthroat trout six to nine inches long, perfect pan size for local calls. Sometimes there were a few fellows, eleven inches or so—for the long distance calls.

I've always liked cutthroat trout. They put up a good fight, running against the bottom and then broad jumping. Under their throats they fly the orange banner of Jack the Ripper.

Also in the creek were a few stubborn rainbow trout, seldom heard from, but there all the same, like certified public accountants. I'd catch one every once in a while. They were fat and chunky, almost as wide as they were long. I've heard those trout called "squire" trout.

It used to take me about an hour to hitchhike to that creek. There was a river nearby. The river wasn't much. The creek was where I punched in. Leaving my card above the clock, I'd punch out again when it was time to go home.

I remember the afternoon I caught the hunchback trout.

A farmer gave me a ride in a truck. He picked me up at a traffic signal beside a bean field and he never said a word to me.

His stopping and picking me up and driving me down the road was as automatic a thing to him as closing the barn door, nothing need be said about it, but still I was in motion traveling thirty-five miles an hour down the road, watching houses and groves of trees go by, watching chickens and mailboxes enter and pass through my vision.

Then I did not see any houses for a while. "This is where I get out," I said.

The farmer nodded his head. The truck stopped.

"Thanks a lot," I said.

The farmer did not ruin his audition for the Metropolitan Opera by making a sound. He just nodded his head again. The truck started up. He was the original silent old farmer.

A little while later I was punching in at the creek. I put my card above the clock and went into that long tunnel of telephone booths.

I waded about seventy-three telephone booths in. I caught two trout in a little hole that was like a wagon wheel. It was one of my favorite holes, and always good for a trout or two.

I always like to think of that hole as a kind of pencil sharpener. I put my reflexes in and they came back out with a good point on them. Over a period of a couple of years, must have caught fifty trout in that hole, though it was only as big as a wagon wheel.

I was fishing with salmon eggs and using a size 14 single egg hook on a pound and a quarter test tippet. The two trout lay in my creel covered entirely by green ferns, ferns made gentle and fragile by the damp walls of telephone booths.

The next good place was forty-five telephone booths in. The place was at the end of a run of gravel, brown and slippery with algae. The run of gravel dropped off and disappeared at a little shelf where there were some white rocks.

One of the rocks was kind of strange. It was a flat white rock. Off by itself from the other rocks, it reminded me of a white cat I had seen in my childhood.

The cat had fallen or been thrown off a high wooden sidewalk that went along the side of a hill in Tacoma, Washington. The cat was lying in a parking lot below.

The fall had not appreciably helped the thickness of the cat, and then a few people had parked their cars on the cat. Of course, that was a long time ago and the cars looked different from the way they look now.

You hardly see those cars any more. They are the old cars. They have to get off the highway because they can't keep up.

That flat white rock off by itself from the other rocks reminded me of that dead cat come to lie there in the creek, among 12,845 telephone booths.

I threw out a salmon egg and let it drift down over that rock and WHAM! a good hit! and I had the fish on and it ran hard downstream, cutting at an angle and staying deep and really coming on hard, solid and uncompromising, and then the fish jumped and for a second I thought it was a frog. I'd never seen a fish like that before.

God-damn! What the hell!

The fish ran deep again and I could feel its life energy screaming back up the line to my hand. The line felt like sound. It was like an ambulance siren coming straight at me, red light flashing, and then going away again and then taking to the air and becoming an air-raid siren.

The fish jumped a few more times and it still looked like a frog, but it didn't have any legs. Then the fish grew tired and sloppy, and I swung and splashed it up the surface of the creek and into my net.

The fish was a twelve-inch rainbow trout with a huge hump on its back. A hunchback trout. The first I'd ever seen. The hump was probably due to an injury that occurred when the trout was young. Maybe a horse stepped on it or a tree fell over in a storm or its mother spawned where they were building a bridge.

There was a fine thing about that trout. I only wish I could have made a death mask of him. Not of his body though, but of his energy. I don't know if anyone would have understood his body. I put it in my creel.

Later in the afternoon when the telephone booths began to grow dark at the edges, I punched out of the creek and went home. I had that hunchback trout for dinner. Wrapped in cornmeal and fried in butter, its hump tasted sweet as the kisses of Esmeralda.

Austen D. Warburton
"Steelhead, the Trickster"

Coyote was the trickiest person on land, and Steelhead was his counterpart in the water. Each could move faster in his own element than anyone else. Neither was dependable. Both would cheat and steal and play mean tricks on other people.

One day in Haw-Kay-Maw (the tenth month–acorn time) two Indians were going up the Klamath River in a canoe. They came to a swift riffle and had to pole the boat. This made for very slow progress. While they were moving slowly up the river, Steelhead rushed up beside the boat. He was on his way with many others to the spawning waters, the small streams flowing into the Klamath. Steelhead was born in one of these small streams and was now going back.

Steelhead said to the two men in the canoe, trying to tantalize them: "You slow jess like ole woman. Why ain't you go more fast? Pole he's too slow. Why ain't you use paddle? I guess we gon to run race, ain't et." The Indians wisely refused. Steelhead then said, "You watch me, I kin walk fast on top of water." After skimming on top of the water as far as one can throw a flat rock, Steelhead came back to the canoe and began to banter the two men again and to show off by jumping over the boat, darting around it, etc. The men by this time were quite provoked with the performance.

One of the Indians had a white eye, caused by a briar getting into it when he was a boy, and he could not see with it. This man said to Steelhead: "You are so smart and can do so many things and boast so much, can you see that mosquito on that redwood tree on the other side of the river?" Steelhead said: "No, I no see em. What he do?"

"Wal, he cleanet off hees legs now, cos sun he go to sleep pitty soon. Den hee's go eat blood some place. You no kin see it?"

"No, I no see et."

"Wal, I gimmet to you my white eye en you gimmet to me you black eye. We make trade."

Steelhead traded and put the white eye in his head, then looked for the mosquito and said, "I no kin see dat mosquito."

The Indian replied, "No use to look cos white eye hees no good."

Steelhead tried to trade back but the Indian wouldn't do it. The Indian he told to

Steelhead, "All time all buddy he make laff fer me cos I got white eye that time. Now hees goan make laff fer you cos you got white eye. Any time somebody he got too smart, den hees goan git too sorry too, jess like coyote when he put his tail in fire and hees too sorry for hees tail and you just like coyote. Now you goan be too sorry for you white eye. Better you go up river now."

~ TURKEY VULTURE ~

Cathartes aura

Family Cathartidae

Length: 26–32"; Wingspan: 5–6'

Habitat:

> Common over desert and scrub regions and mountains; does not build nests, but commonly hides eggs in sheltered spots on the ground and sometimes on a cliff ledges or in caves

Range:

> In spring and summer, found throughout California; in fall and winter, more common in coastal and southern California

Comments:

> Occasionally miscalled a "buzzard," the turkey vulture has a featherless, red head—small for the size of its body—and a yellow, hooked beak suitable for tearing flesh. Its body is mostly black and its wings are two-toned when seen from below: black with grayish flight feathers.
>
> While soaring, the turkey vulture forms a shallow V with its wings and will rock back and forth in the air searching out food, which it does not kill but scavenges for. It has a highly developed sense of smell—an unusual trait for a bird—and locates carrion using both sight and smell. At night, turkey vultures may assemble at communal roosts in trees or other tall perches.
>
> The turkey vulture is usually quiet but may grunt or hiss if threatened.

Robinson Jeffers
"Vulture"

I had walked since dawn and lay down to rest on a bare hillside
Above the ocean. I saw through half-shut eyelids a vulture wheeling high
    up in heaven,
And presently it passed again, but lower and nearer, its orbit narrowing, I
    understood then
That I was under inspection. I lay death-still and heard the flight-feathers
Whistle above me and make their circle and come nearer.
I could see the naked red head between the great wings
Bear downward staring. I said, "My dear bird, we are wasting time here.
These old bones will still work; they are not for you." But how beautiful he looked,
    gliding down
On those great sails; how beautiful he looked, veering away in the sea-light over
    the precipice. I tell you solemnly
That I was sorry to have disappointed him. To be eaten by that beak and become
    part of him, to share those wings and those eyes—
What a sublime end of one's body, what an enskyment; what a life after death.

George Sterling
"The Black Vulture"

Aloof within the day's enormous dome,
He holds unshared the silence of the sky.
Far down his bleak, relentless eyes descry
The eagle's empire and the falcon's home—
Far down, the galleons of sunset roam;
His hazards on the sea of morning lie;
Serene, he hears the broken tempest sigh
Where cold sierras gleam like scattered foam.

And least of all he holds the human swarm—
Unwitting now that envious men prepare
To make their dream and its fulfillment one,
When, poised above the caldrons of the storm,
Their hearts, contemptuous of death, shall dare
His roads between the thunder and the sun.

247

∽ LONG-TAILED WEASEL ∽

Mustela frenata

Family Mustelidae

Length: 11–22"; Weight: 3–9 oz

Habitat:

Fairly open, brushy areas, including forests, mountains, and farmland

Range:

Common throughout California

Comments:

One of the most widespread carnivores, the long-tailed weasel has a long body, short legs, and fine, chocolate brown fur, with a pale yellow or white underside. The weasel often has a white or light-colored face, or sometimes just a white patch between the eyes. One of its signature characteristics is its long, black-tipped tail.

A skilled predator with highly developed scent glands, the long-tailed weasel prefers eating warm-blooded vertebrates, including a variety of small mice, voles, shrews, rats, pocket gophers, ground squirrels, chipmunks, and small birds. Although it prefers small prey, it can also kill animals several times its weight, such as rabbits. It also occasionally eats bees.

The long-tailed weasel captures its prey by clutching the back or neck and biting at the skull and ears with the sharp edges of its canines. It moves from burrow to burrow in search of food, sometimes plunging under snow, and will store food when it is abundant. The weasel makes dens from the abandoned burrows of other mammals and constructs nests of hair from prey.

A playful animal, the long-tailed weasel runs by a series of bounds. It also produces many different vocalizations, including screeches and purrs.

Sally Carrighar
from *One Day on Beetle Rock*

A cry from the Steller's Jay reached the Weasel. It was like a touch on a spring. Out of the den instantly, she stretched herself up, her eyes glittering, darting everywhere, trying to see what enemy of the bird was making him so angry. There was a rush of wings as four more jays flew in to aid the screamer. The Weasel often stirred commotion similar to this. She was not the one who had done it now, but if there was going to be a fight she wanted to see it and if possible to join it.

The jays grew even more excited, for they had lost the object of their hunt. They tossed themselves through the branches of a pine, peering everywhere over the Rock. The Weasel found what they sought—a wildcat crouching under an edge of the granite. A figure of wonderful tense stillness was the cat. Watching her, the Weasel swayed with emotion, her ears, her eyes, her pointed tail, her very fur electric. She saw the wildcat wait, quiet but alert, w hile the voices of the jays grew less and less belligerent. Finally they ceased. When there had been no outcry for some time, the smooth round body slipped from its crevice, into a gully and out of sight. A moment later it appeared at the gully's end, a shadow sliding across the gravel to the brush.

The Weasel flung impatient eyes around her. She was charged with energy and once more had no chance to spend it. The human creatures had partly risen during the jays' noise. Now they were lying down again, composing themselves, but the Weasel could not escape so easily from her emotion. She prowled over the ground, sniffed for a promising scent, but found none. Still restless, she withdrew into the burrow, to lie with her body in the tunnel, her little triangular head at the entrance where she could watch for something to battle or to chase.

The lustre of the moon was dulled by the gray of the dawn, and no pocket of full darkness now remained, not even in the underbrush or the depths of the trees. A few chirps rose from high nests, but as yet no pewee droned, no chickaree's query rang from the pines. After the jays ceased screaming, most of the sounds were lifeless—a small wind knifing through the oak leaves, and the pricking of stiff needles against bark.

All around the Weasel, animals were sleeping. The hunters of the night were drawing long breaths from tired flanks, their eyelids nerveless and their faces empty of expression. Other animals were breathing lightly now. Soon they will waken, stretch, rise, suddenly leap for a fly or perhaps pounce on a leaf mistaken for a mouse. They will feel it good to have their muscles speeded by an inward fire, just as the Weasel does. For them, the fire will burn out later; then they will be glad to lay their tired legs on their beds. Each satisfaction in its time, and no resistance to the loss of any. For the Weasel, though, the fire will not die. Her nerves cry always for more and more intensity—for wilder winds, for colder air, for faster streams, for sharper scents! In the wilderness most animals' needs are answered, and strain is balanced by repose. But the Weasel never quite relaxes, since her longing for sensation seldom can be filled completely.

Her taut nerves had been stretched still tighter by the restricted life she had led while her kits were small. Through the rest of the year she gained some peace by being always on her way to a new place. There were boundaries to the territory where she wandered, but she never returned to a meadow or grove or granite field until the season had moved along and given it a different look and to some extent a different population.

Quick roamer that she was, she found her food by covering much ground lightly. She cleared out the slow, the weak, and the injured prey, and then went on. By June eighteenth, however, she had stayed at Beetle Rock for thirty-seven days. Long since, she had found the easier victims, and now was forced to hunt with a sickening persistence. The very sight of the Rock—hard, gray, unmoving—was like pressure on a bruise.

The Weasel's den, too, was now almost uninhabitable. It had been a good one this year. The Weasel had got it by eating the gopher that had dug it. The central chamber already had been prepared for a brood of young, with a lining of grass and roots, to which was added gradually the fur of mice. Six side burrows branched from the nest compartment. The tidy Weasel used them for discarding refuse. The entrance had been well built, hidden at first beneath a crust of rain-stiffened leaves. But the crust was broken down. The whole burrow was going to pieces, and the nest was becoming intolerably crowded as the five kits neared full growth.

The dawn on June eighteenth was colorless and cold. Above the canyon staggered a bat, its flight abrupt and senseless to an eye that could not see the insects it pursued. A late owl flapped to rest. The breeze drew across the Weasel's nose a tassel of scents, but none of them interesting: the bitter odor from an anthill, the dried blood of a deer mouse slain by the owl, and smell signs left on a bear-tree. The Weasel noted these and remained where she was. Then she caught another scent, from the black oak overhead. It was faint but exciting—the clean, sweet spiciness of purple finches!

A flock of the birds had flown to the tree on the previous evening, while the Weasel was away. Now they were stirring for a farther flight, beginning to layer their feathers and to stretch their wings. Cautiously the Weasel crept up the trunk of the oak and stepped onto one of the branches. The canny finches were perched at the outermost ends. Twig by twig the Weasel approached them. The branch is bending a little, now, under her weight. Two of the sleepy birds are almost in her grasp. But she cannot spring; the bough here is so light that she must coil her body around it to keep her balance. It dips. The birds are warned and the whole flock bursts from the tree.

The sharp fights of the earlier night, and the prey that had filled the stomachs of the Weasel and all her brood, were too far past to be remembered. She only sensed that she was tortured with disappointments. She stood at the entrance of her burrow and looked again around the Rock, empty of life except for the sleeping human figures. Finally, more in disgust than fatigue, she turned into the tunnel and the nest.

While the weasels slept, the sun rose and became warm, and the daytime animals began their frank and visible play. Only three or four bounds from the den, chipmunks raced on the Rock, the Lizard searched for insects, a junco sang, and a butterfly dangled above a clump of golden-throated gilia. A chickaree danced through the branches of the nearest pine, continually calling in his high, sweet bark.

There was a little time of wary silence when the human creatures threw off their blankets, stood up and stretched, and walked to the rim of the Rock. But they paid more attention to the canyon view than to the scores of eyes that watched them from the pines, the manzanita, and the nooks in the granite. As soon as they took up their blankets and strolled towards the bordering forest, they were followed by a wave of small bright sounds.

The weasels, down in the cool dark earth, lay with their bodies coiled together, breathing softly into one another's fur. But their graceful sleep was jolted. The nest was shaken by a series of great thumps, slight at first but quickly becoming violent.

Two of the smaller weasels were so exhausted that they did not waken, but the mother and three larger kits streamed out. They saw the white rump of a deer who was bounding down the slope, alighting each time with a force that would have collapsed the den if he had struck it. His passage was a crashing—the earth resounding, fallen branches snapping under his feet, and gravel rolling.

The animals' calls and movements all had ceased. But after the deer had disappeared and the forest had been empty of sounds for a moment, a chirp was heard from an oak tree and a chickaree dropped a cone from the top of a pine. Among the leaves a wing flashed and a fluffy tail unfurled. Soon the creatures were frisking more recklessly than ever, relieved to feel again that they were safe.

A golden-mantled squirrel made the mistake of jumping over a log without stopping on top to see what was on the other side. He came down at the mouth of the weasels' den, in the very midst of the four who had awakened. The squirrel had seen them before he touched the ground, and had twisted his body so that he was able instantly to dodge back towards the Rock. But the mother Weasel cleared the log on his heels and caught him.

The two fought back and forth across the granite. The squirrel was larger, the Weasel faster; in fury they were matched. Every breath of the squirrel was a shriek of rage and protest.

In this battle the Weasel must really spend herself. Now the two are together, now apart, streaking away side by side. Together again, they claw and hiss feverishly; their teeth flash and grope for each other. The Weasel has caught the squirrel around the haunches. All her attention is given to coiling herself around his body. She shifts her hold until it is more and more secure and her teeth can approach the base of the squirrel's skull. Finally she sinks them in a precise and fatal puncture.

The feast is shared by all the family except the two still sleeping in the den.

Now the Rock is indeed quiet. Gone are the junco's song, the chickarees' barks, and the quick brown scallops of the chipmunks bouncing among the boulders. No jay screams. This is one of the times when the undependable jays have failed to call a warning. If they saw the flight of the golden-mantled squirrel, and its end in the whirl of cinnamon and yellow fur, they watched without a flutter or a sound.

HUMPBACK WHALE

Megaptera novaengliae

Family Balaenopteridae

Length: 43–46'; Weight: 27 ½–33 tons

Habitat:
   Polar to tropical waters; coastal and deep waters during migration

Range:
   Common off the coast of California, especially around Monterey Bay

Comments:
   The humpback whale has dark bluish-black coloring on the upper part of its body, with paler patches below. Its pectoral fins, or flippers, are one-third of its total body length, making them the longest flippers of any animal. The flippers also have knobs on them. These knobs and the color variations on the rest of the animal—especially on the tail—make it possible to identify individual humpbacks.

   Humpback whales migrate from cold waters rich with food during the summer, spring, and fall and travel to warmer, coastal waters in the winter for calving. Whales generally travel off the California coast in summer and fall for feeding. They prefer to migrate along coastlines and in groups.

   Humpback whales feed on plankton, plant and animal life near the ocean's surface, and large schools of fish. One of their food-gathering methods is to form a small group and then blow underwater bubbles to herd fish.

   The humpback whale is a vocal creature, making sounds ranging from squeals to rumbles. The male humpback has a "song" that can last up to thirty minutes and is used to attract females, warn off other males, or be a kind of sonar to detect other whales. Like other whales, the humpback "breaches" the water—perhaps to create sound waves—and can generate almost enough force to accelerate its massive body out of the water. Once mostly out, it twists and falls back on the water with a huge splash.

Richard Henry Dana, Jr.
from *Two Years Before the Mast*

After lying about a week in San Pedro, we got under way for San Diego, intending to stop at San Juan, as the southeaster season was nearly over, and there was little or no danger.

This being the spring season, San Pedro, as well as all the other open ports upon the coast, was filled with whales, that had come in to make their annual visit upon soundings. For the first few days that we were here and at Santa Barbara, we watched them with great interest, calling out, "There she blows!" every time we saw the spout of one breaking the surface of the water; but they soon became so common that we took little notice of them. They often "broke" very near us, and one thick, foggy night, during a dead calm, while I was standing anchor watch, one of them rose so near that he struck our cable, and made all surge again. He did not seem to like the encounter much himself, for he sheered off, and spouted at a good distance. We once came very near running one down in the gig, and should probably have been knocked to pieces or thrown sky-high. We had been on board the little Spanish brig, and were returning, stretching out well at our oars, the little boat going like a swallow; our faces were turned aft (as is always the case in pulling), and the captain, who was steering, was not looking out, when, all at once, we heard the spout of a whale directly ahead. "Back water! Back water, for your lives!" shouted the captain; and we backed our blades in the water, and brought the boat to in a smother of foam. Turning our heads, we saw a great, rough, humpbacked whale slowly crossing our fore foot, within three or four yards of the boat's stem. Had we not backed water just as we did, we should inevitably have gone smash upon him, striking him with our stem just about amidships. He took no notice of us, but passed slowly on, and dived a few yards beyond us, throwing his tail high in the air. He was so near that we had a perfect view of him, and, as may be supposed, had no desire to see him nearer. He was a disgusting creature, with a skin rough, hairy, and of an iron-gray color. This kind differs much from the sperm, in color and skin, and is said to be fiercer. We saw a few sperm whales; but most of the whales that come upon the coast are finbacks and humpbacks, which are more difficult to take, and are said not to give oil enough to pay for the trouble. For this reason, whaleships do not come upon the coast after them. Our captain, together with Captain Nye of the *Loriotte*, who had been in a whaleship, thought of making an attempt upon one of them with two boats' crews; but as we had only two harpoons, and no proper lines, they gave it up.

During the months of March, April, and May, these whales appear in great numbers in the open ports of Santa Barbara, San Pedro, &c., and hover off the coast, while a few find their way into the close harbors of San Diego and Monterey. They are all off again before midsummer, and make their appearance on the "offshore ground." We saw some fine "schools" of sperm whales, which are easily distinguished by their spout, blowing away, a few miles to windward, on our passage to San Juan.

David Rains Wallace
"Humphrey: Goodwill Ambassador"

The odyssey of Humphrey the humpback whale is a measure of the depth of public concern for whales. Humphrey was a young whale who, for an unknown reason, left his southward-migrating pod in October 1985 and swam into San Francisco Bay. In the next few weeks, he wandered inland through San Pablo Bay, the Carquinez Straits, and into the mouth of the Sacramento River. From there, he pushed on upstream into Cache Slough, a marshy tributary of the Sacramento, where he stopped.

A few decades ago, a wayward whale like Humphrey probably would not have gotten much public attention, and might have been killed for target practice. Humphrey's reception was worthy of royalty: crowds turned out to see and cheer him wherever he appeared. Fearful that long immersion in fresh water would harm him, scientists, government officials, and private citizens worked hard to help him return to the ocean. They tried first to draw him back downstream by banging on metal pipes lowered into the water. When that only succeeded in moving him a few miles downriver, they tried luring him downstream by playing humpback-whale feedings sounds from a boat.

On first hearing the sounds, Humphrey slapped the water surface with his tail, possibly a sign of irritation, but then he began to follow the boat downstream, covering fifty miles in one day, as far as Angel Island. He breached (jumped clear out of the water), a possible sign of high spirits, and everyone expected him to swim out through the Golden Gate. Instead, he turned around and started back inland again. An armada of small boats rushed to bar his way, and the recorded feeding sounds eventually turned him back toward the Pacific. As he swam out under the Golden Gate, a crowd on the bridge exuberantly urged Humphrey on and finally waved good-bye to him, some of them in tears.

Skeptics wondered whether a whale who behaved as oddly as Humphrey would have much chance of surviving. Possibly, he was ill or deranged. Humphrey does seem to be surviving, however. A whale with the same fluke configuration (the pattern of black and white markings on the tail fins or flukes) as Humphrey was photographed off Point Reyes a few dozen miles north of the Golden Gate in August of 1986.

Humpback whales are rorquals, relatives of the larger blue whales. (The word *rorqual* refers to the pleated grooves these whales have on their throats, which allow them to open their mouths to engulf plankton.) Humpbacks reach a length of fifty feet. They are a cosmopolitan species, various populations spending warm seasons feeding in far northern or far southern waters, then moving into tropical waters for breeding.

Because they migrate close to coasts and are relatively slow swimmers compared to other rorquals, humpbacks have been heavily hunted, and are now classified as endangered. An estimated ten thousand remain alive.

Concern about whales has become a worldwide phenomenon. The Visited Nations Environmental Program has a Global Plan of Action for Marine Mammal Conservation, which includes management of benign research on whales in the Indian Ocean Whale Sanctuary and a far-reaching plan for maintaining safe habitat for marine mammals worldwide. Whale watching has emerged as a multimillion-dollar industry in the United States and is growing in nations such as Mexico and Sri Lanka.

KILLER WHALE

Orcinus orca

Family Delphinidae

Length: Males to 23'; Females to 21'; Weight: 6–10 tons

Habitat:

Deep oceanic waters and coastal shallows

Range:

Common off the coast of California

Comments:

The largest member of the dolphin family, the killer whale is easily recognized by its distinctive black-and-white coloring, and particularly the conspicuous white patches over its eyes. Behind the dorsal fin is a light-colored section called the "saddle."

The killer whale is a highly social animal that travels in groups called "pods," which may contain as many as one hundred individuals. These pods are matriarchal, and calves tend to stay with their mothers for life. Whales in pods often hunt together, forcing large numbers of fish into a concentrated location for feeding. The killer whale will also hunt seals and other marine mammals, as well as birds, other whale species, and squids.

Like other toothed whales, killer whales use echolocation—bouncing sound off of objects—to determine their location. Although their worldwide population is unknown, they are thought to be vulnerable to chemical pollution and other contaminants, which may lead to illness and reproductive difficulties.

Robinson Jeffers
"Orca"

Sea-lions loafed in the swinging tide in the inlet, long fluent creatures
Bigger than horses, and at home in their element
As if the Pacific Ocean had been made for them. Farther off shore the island-rocks
Bristled with quiet birds, gulls, cormorants, pelicans, hundreds and thousands
Standing thick as grass on a cut of turf. Beyond these, blue, gray, green, wind-straked,
    the ocean
Looked vacant; but then I saw a little black sail
That left a foam-line; while I watched there were two of them, two black triangles,
    tacking and veering, converging
Toward the rocks and the shore. I knew well enough
What they were: the dorsal fins of two killer-whales: but how the sea-lions
Low-floating within the rock-throat knew it, I know not. Whether they heard or
    they smelled them, suddenly
They were in panic; and some swam for the islands, others
Blindly along the granite banks of the inlet; one of them, more pitiful, scrabbled
    the cliff
In hope to climb it: at that moment black death drove in,
Silently like a shadow into the sea-gorge. It had the shape, the size, and it seemed
    the speed
Of one of those flying vipers with which the Germans lashed London. The water
    boiled for a moment
And nothing seen; and at the same moment
The birds went up from the islands, the soaring gulls, laborious pelicans, arrowy
    cormorants, a screaming
And wheeling sky. Meanwhile, below me, brown blood and foam
Striped the water of the inlet.
                    Here was death, and with terror, yet it looked
    clean and bright, it was beautiful.
Why? Because there was nothing human involved, suffering nor causing; no lies, no
    smirk and no malice;
All strict and decent; the will of man had nothing to do here. The earth is a star, its
    human element
Is what darkens it. War is evil, the peace will be evil, cruelty is evil; death is not evil.
    But the breed of man
Has been queer from the start. It looks like a botched experiment that has run wild
    and ought to be stopped.

∾ GRAY WOLF ∾

Canis lupus

Family Canidae

Height: 26–38"; Length: 4'3"–6'9"; Weight: 57–167 lb

Habitat:

Forests and plains; avoids deserts

Range:

Extirpated species

Comments:

The gray wolf has a very large build, long legs, and a deep chest. Its fur is usually gray with black patches, but sometimes its coat is all white or all black. Its face is bicolored, with a white lower half and dark patches around the eyes. The gray wolf also has well-developed canines and a long, bushy, black-tipped tail.

A carnivore, the gray wolf mostly hunts hoofed mammals, like sheep, deer, and caribou, but it also eats beavers and rabbits, and sometimes it eats berries, birds, fish, and insects. The gray wolf tends to gorge when food is abundant, and can go two weeks without food when prey is scarce. It hunts at night, mostly in family groups, which allows it to prey on animals many times its size.

Gray wolves are social animals that usually form pairs and packs of up to fifteen. The packs are hierarchical, tend to avoid each other, and often travel great distances. In addition to howling, which is used to keep packs together, the gray wolf also whines, yelps, growls, and barks. It does not use traditional shelters but does form maternity dens.

Intolerant of coyotes, gray wolves will suppress coyote populations whose range overlaps their own. Human beings, who have sensationalized encounters with the gray wolf, are its only predators, although in actuality, the animal generally fears humans. In California, gray wolves used to prey on livestock, which led to their being trapped and poisoned into extinction within the state. They were last seen wild in California in 1924.

Jack London
from *White Fang*

Not only was White Fang adaptable by nature, but he had travelled much, and knew the meaning and necessity of adjustment. Here, in Sierra Vista, which was the name of Judge Scott's place, White Fang quickly began to make himself at home. He had no further serious trouble with the dogs. They knew more about the ways of the Southland gods than did he, and in their eyes he had qualified when he accompanied the gods inside the house. Wolf that he was, and unprecedented as it was, the gods had sanctioned his presence, and they, the dogs of the gods, could only recognize this sanction.

Dick, perforce, had to go through a few stiff formalities at first, after which he calmly accepted White Fang as an addition to the premises. Had Dick had his way, they would have been good friends; but White Fang was adverse to friendship. All he asked of other dogs was to be let alone. His whole life he had kept aloof from his kind, and he still desired to keep aloof. Dick's overtures bothered him, so he snarled Dick away. In the north he had learned the lesson that he must let the master's dogs alone, and he did not forget that lesson now. But he insisted on his own privacy and self-seclusion, and so thoroughly ignored Dick that that good-natured creature finally gave him up and scarcely took as much interest in him as in the hitching-post near the stable.

Not so with Collie. While she accepted him because it was the mandate of the gods, that was no reason that she should leave him in peace. Woven into her being was the memory of countless crimes he and his had perpetrated against her ancestry. Not in a day nor a generation were the ravaged sheep-folds to be forgotten. All this was a spur to her, pricking her to retaliation. She could not fly in the face of the gods who permitted him, but that did not prevent her from making life miserable for him in petty ways. A feud, ages old, was between them, and she, for one, would see to it that he was reminded.

So Collie took advantage of her sex to pick upon White Fang and maltreat him. His instinct would not permit him to attack her, while her persistence would not permit him to ignore her. When she rushed at him he turned his fur-protected shoulder to her sharp teeth and walked away stiff-legged and stately. When she forced him too hard, he was compelled to go about in a circle, his shoulder presented to her, his head turned from her, and on his face and in his eyes a patient and bored expression. Sometimes, however, a nip on his hind-quarters hastened his retreat and made it anything but stately. But as a rule he managed to maintain a dignity that was almost solemnity. He ignored her existence whenever it was possible, and made it a point to keep out of her way. When he saw or heard her coming, he got up and walked off.

There was much in other matters for White Fang to learn. Life in the Northland was simplicity itself when compared with the complicated affairs of Sierra Vista. First of all, he had to learn the family of the master. In a way he was prepared to do this. As Mit-sah and Kloo-kooch had belonged to Gray Beaver, sharing his food, his fire, and his blankets, so now, at Sierra Vista, belonged to the love-master all the denizens of the house.

But in this matter there was a difference, and many differences. Sierra Vista was a far vaster affair than the tepee of Gray Beaver. There were many persons to be considered. There was Judge Scott, and there was his wife. There were the master's two sisters, Beth and Mary. There was his wife, Alice, and then there were his children, Weedon and Maud, toddlers of four and six. There was no way for anybody to tell him about all these people, and of blood-ties and relationship he knew nothing whatever and never would be capable of knowing. Yet he quickly worked it out that all of them belonged to the master. Then, by observation, whenever opportunity offered, by study of action, speech, and the very intonations of the voice, he slowly learned the intimacy and the degree of favor they enjoyed with the master. And by this ascertained standard, White Fang treated them accordingly. What was of value to the master he valued; what was dear to the master was to be cherished by White Fang and guarded carefully.

Thus it was with the two children. All his life he had disliked children. He hated and feared their hands. The lessons were not tender that he had learned of their tyranny and cruelty in the days of the Indian villages. When Weedon and Maud had first approached him, he growled warningly and looked malignant. A cuff from the master and a sharp word had then compelled him to permit their caresses, though he growled and growled under their tiny hands, and in the growl there was no crooning note. Later, he observed that the boy and girl were of great value in the master's eyes. Then it was that no cuff nor sharp word was necessary before they could pat him.

Yet White Fang was never effusively affectionate. He yielded to the master's children with an ill but honest grace, and endured their fooling as one would endure a painful operation. When he could no longer endure, he would get up and stalk determinedly away from them. But after a time, he grew even to like the children. Still he was not demonstrative. He would not go up to them. On the other hand, instead of walking away at sight of them, he waited for them to come to him. And still later, it was noticed that a pleased light came into his eyes when he saw them approaching, and that he looked after them with an appearance of curious regret when they left him for other amusements.

All this was a matter of development, and took time. Next in his regard, after the children, was Judge Scott. There were two reasons, possibly, for this. First, he was evidently a valuable possession of the master's, and next, he was undemonstrative. White Fang liked to lie at his feet on the wide porch when he read the newspaper, from time to time favoring White Fang with a look or a word—untroublesome tokens that he recognized White Fang's presence and existence. But this was only when the master was not around. When the master appeared, all other beings ceased to exist so far as White Fang was concerned.

White Fang allowed all the members of the family to pet him and make much of him; but he never gave to them what he gave to the master. No caress of theirs could put the love-croon into his throat, and, try as they would, they could never persuade him into snuggling against them. This expression of abandon and surrender, of absolute trust, he reserved for the master alone. In fact, he never regarded the members of the family in any other light than possessions of the love-master.

Also White Fang had early come to differentiate between the family and the servants of the household. The latter were afraid of him, while he merely refrained from attacking them. This because he considered that they were likewise possessions of the master. Between White Fang and them existed a neutrality and no more. They cooked for the master and washed the dishes and did other things, just as Matt had done up in the Klondike. They were, in short, appurtenances of the household.

Outside the household there was even more for White Fang to learn. The master's domain was wide and complex, yet it had its metes and bounds. The land itself ceased at the county road. Outside was the common domain of all gods—the roads and streets. Then inside other fences were the particular domains of other gods. A myriad laws governed all these things and determined conduct; yet he did not know the speech of the gods, nor was there any way for him to learn save by experience. He obeyed his natural impulses until they ran him counter to some law. When this had been done a few times, he learned the law and after that observed it.

But most potent in his education were the cuff of the master's hand, the censure of the master's voice. Because of White Fang's very great love, a cuff from the master hurt him far more than any beating Gray Beaver or Beauty Smith had ever given him. They had hurt only the flesh of him; beneath the flesh the spirit had still raged, splendid and invincible. But with the master the cuff was always too light to hurt the flesh. Yet it went deeper. It was an expression of the master's disapproval, and White Fang's spirit wilted under it.

In point of fact, the cuff was rarely administered. The master's voice was sufficient. By it White Fang knew whether he did right or not. By it he trimmed his conduct and adjusted his actions. It was the compass by which he steered and learned to chart the manners of a new land and life.

In the Northland, the only domesticated animal was the dog. All other animals lived in the Wild, and were, when not too formidable, lawful spoil for any dog. All his days White Fang had foraged among the live things for food. It did not enter his head that in the Southland it was otherwise. But this he was to learn early in his residence in Santa Clara Valley. Sauntering around the corner of the house in the early morning, he came upon a chicken that had escaped from the chicken-yard. White Fang's natural impulse was to eat it. A couple of bounds, a flash of teeth and a frightened squawk, and he had scooped in the adventurous fowl. It was farm bred and fat and tender; and White Fang licked his chops and decided that such fare was good.

Later in the day, he chanced upon another stray chicken near the stables. One of the grooms ran to the rescue. He did not know White Fang's breed, so for weapon he took a light buggy-whip. At the first cut of the whip, White Fang left the chicken for the man. A club might have stopped White Fang, but not a whip. Silently, without flinching, he took a second cut in his forward rush, and as he leaped for the throat the groom cried out, "My God!" and staggered backward. He dropped the whip and shielded his throat with his arms. In consequence, his forearm was ripped open to the bone.

The man was badly frightened. It was not so much White Fang's ferocity as it was his silence that unnerved the groom. Still protecting his throat and face with his torn and bleeding arm, he tried to retreat to the barn. And it would have gone hard with him had not Collie appeared on the scene. As she had saved Dick's life, she now saved the groom's. She rushed upon White Fang in frenzied wrath. She had been right. She had known better than the blundering gods. All her suspicions were justified. Here was the ancient marauder up to his old tricks again.

The groom escaped into the stables, and White Fang backed away before Collie's wicked teeth, or presented his shoulder to them and circled round and round. But Collie did not give over, as was her wont, after a decent interval of chastisement. On the contrary, she grew more excited and angry every moment, until, in the end, White Fang flung dignity to the winds and frankly fled away from her across the fields.

"He'll learn to leave chickens alone," the master said. "But I can't give him the lesson until I catch him in the act."

Two nights later came the act, but on a more generous scale than the master had anticipated. White Fang had observed closely the chicken-yards and the habits of the chickens. In the night-time, after they had gone to roost, he climbed to the top of a pile of newly hauled lumber. From there he gained the roof of a chicken-house, passed over the ridgepole and dropped to the ground inside. A moment later he was inside the house, and the slaughter began.

In the morning, when the master came out on to the porch, fifty white Leghorn hens, laid out in a row by the groom, greeted his eyes. He whistled to himself, softly, first with surprise, and then, at the end, with admiration. His eyes were likewise greeted by White Fang, but about the latter there were no signs of shame nor guilt. He carried himself with pride, as though, forsooth, he had achieved a deed praiseworthy and meritorious. There was about him no consciousness of sin. The master's lips tightened as he faced the disagreeable task. Then he talked harshly to the unwitting culprit, and in his voice there was nothing but godlike wrath. Also, he held White Fang's nose down to the slain hens, and at the same time cuffed him soundly.

White Fang never raided a chicken-roost again. It was against the law, and he had learned it. Then the master took him into the chicken-yards. White Fang's natural impulse, when he saw the live food fluttering about him and under his very nose, was to spring upon it. He obeyed the impulse, but was checked by the master's voice. They continued in the yards for half an hour. Time and again the impulse surged over White Fang, and each time, as he yielded to it, he was checked by the master's voice. Thus it was he learned the law and ere he left the domain of the chickens, he had learned to ignore their existence.

"You can never cure a chicken-killer." Judge Scott shook his head sadly at the luncheon table, when his son narrated the lesson he had given White Fang. "Once they've got the habit and the taste of blood…" Again he shook his head sadly.

But Weedon Scott did not agree with his father.

"I'll tell you what I'll do," he challenged finally. "I'll lock White Fang in with the chickens all afternoon."

"But think of the chickens," objected the judge.

"And furthermore," the son went on, "for every chicken he kills, I'll pay you one dollar gold coin of the realm."

"But you should penalize father, too," interposed Beth.

Her sister seconded her, and a chorus of approval arose from around the table. Judge Scott nodded his head in agreement.

"All right." Weedon Scott pondered for a moment. "And if, at the end of the afternoon, White Fang hasn't harmed a chicken, for every ten minutes of the time he has spent in the yard, you will have to say to him, gravely and with deliberation, just as if you were sitting on the bench and solemnly passing judgment, 'White Fang, you are smarter than I thought.'"

From hidden points of vantage the family watched the performance. But it was a fizzle. Locked in the yard and there deserted by the master, White Fang lay down and went to sleep. Once he got up and walked over to the trough for a drink of water. The chickens he calmly ignored. So far as he was concerned they did not exist. At four o'clock he executed a running jump, gained the roof of the chicken house and leaped to the ground outside, whence he sauntered gravely to the house. He had learned the law. And on the porch, before the delighted family, Judge Scott, face to face with White Fang, said slowly and solemnly, sixteen times, "White Fang, you are smarter than I thought."

But it was the multiplicity of laws that befuddled White Fang and often brought him into disgrace. He had to learn that he must not touch the chickens that belonged to other gods. Then there were cats, and rabbits, and turkeys; all these he must let alone. In fact, when he had but partly learned the law, his impression was that he must leave all live things alone. Out in the back-pasture, a quail could flutter up under his nose unharmed. All tense and trembling with eagerness and desire, he mastered his instinct and stood still. He was obeying the will of the gods.

And then, one day, again out in the back-pasture, he saw Dick start a jackrabbit and run it. The master himself was looking on and did not interfere. Nay, he encouraged White Fang to join in the chase. And thus he learned that there was no taboo on jackrabbits. In the end he worked out the complete law. Between him and all domestic animals there must be no hostilities. If not amity, at least neutrality must obtain. But the other animals—the squirrels, and quail, and cottontails, were creatures of the Wild who had never yielded allegiance to man. They were the lawful prey of any dog. It was only the tame that the gods protected, and between the tame deadly strife was not permitted. The gods held the power of life and death over their subjects, and the gods were jealous of their power.

Life was complex in the Santa Clara Valley after the simplicities of the Northland. And the chief thing demanded by these intricacies of civilization was control, restraint—a poise of self that was as delicate as the fluttering of gossamer wings and at the same time as rigid as steel. Life had a thousand faces, and White Fang found he must meet them all—thus, when he went to town, in to San Jose, running behind the carriage or loafing about the streets when the carriage stopped. Life flowed past him, deep and wide and varied, continually impinging upon his senses, demanding of him instant and endless adjustments and correspondences, and compelling him, almost always, to suppress his natural impulses.

There were butcher-shops where meat hung within reach. This meat he must not touch. There were cats at the houses the master visited that must be let alone. And there were dogs everywhere that snarled at him and that he must not attack. And then, on the crowded sidewalks, there were persons innumerable whose attention he attracted. They would stop and look at him, point him out to one another, examine him, talk to him, and, worst of all, pat him. And these perilous contacts from all these strange hands he must endure. Yet this endurance he achieved. Furthermore he got over being awkward and self-conscious. In a lofty way he received the attentions of the multitudes of strange gods. With condescension he accepted their condescension. On the other hand, there was something about him that prevented great familiarity. They patted him on the head and passed on, contented and pleased with their own daring.

But it was not all easy for White Fang. Running behind the carriage in the outskirts of San Jose, he encountered certain small boys who made a practice of flinging stones at him. Yet he knew that it was not permitted him to pursue and drag them down. Here he was compelled to violate his instinct of self-preservation, and violate it he did, for he was becoming tame and qualifying himself for civilization.

Nevertheless, White Fang was not quite satisfied with the arrangement. He had no abstract ideas about justice and fair play. But there is a certain sense of equity that resides in life, and it was this sense in him that resented the unfairness of his being permitted no defence against the stone-throwers. He forgot that in the covenant entered into between him and the gods they were pledged to care for him and defend him. But one day the master sprang from the carriage, whip in hand, and gave the stone-throwers a thrashing. After that they threw stones no more, and White Fang understood and was satisfied.

One other experience of similar nature was his. On the way to town, hanging around the saloon at the cross-roads, were three dogs that made a practice of rushing out upon him when he went by. Knowing his deadly method of fighting, the master had never ceased impressing upon White Fang the law that he must not fight. As a result, having learned the lesson well, White Fang was hard put whenever he passed the cross-roads saloon. After the first rush, each time, his snarl kept the three dogs at a distance, but they trailed along behind, yelping and bickering and insulting him. This endured for some time. The men at the saloon even urged the dogs on to attack White Fang. One day they openly sicked the dogs on him. The master stopped the carriage.

"Go to it," he said to White Fang.

But White Fang could not believe. He looked at the master, and he looked at the dogs. Then he looked back eagerly and questioningly at the master.

The master nodded his head. "Go to them, old fellow. Eat them up."

White Fang no longer hesitated. He turned and leaped silently among his enemies. All three faced him. There was a great snarling and growling, a clashing of teeth and a flurry of bodies. The dust of the road arose in a cloud and screened the battle. But at the end of several minutes two dogs were struggling in the dirt and the third was in full flight. He leaped a ditch, went through a rail fence, and fled across a field. White Fang followed, sliding over the ground in wolf fashion and with wolf speed, swiftly and without noise, and in the center of the field he dragged down and slew the dog.

With this triple killing his main troubles with dogs ceased. The word went up and down the valley, and men saw to it that their dogs did not molest the Fighting Wolf.

Julian H. Steward
"The Theft of Pine Nuts"

Coyote was a contrary, funny fellow who always changed his mind. He lived with Wolf, his older brother, in the desert east of the Sierra Nevada.

One day, Coyote and Wolf lay around at their camp. Coyote said to his brother, "What is it that smells good? It smells good like something good to eat." The people had no pine nuts at that time. Coyote said to his brother, "Brother, I think I had better go and see about this." Coyote was good-looking. He would try to do anything, but he spoiled everything he did.

Coyote went to the place toward the east from which the smell had come. He was a stranger in that country. The people who dwelled there were A'na.[1] They lived on pine nuts. When Coyote arrived, they said to one another, "Here is a stranger. You people had better hide your food." They took the nuts and put them in the roofs of their houses, hiding them in the cracks of the supports near the smokeholes. They said, "You people had better feed this stranger pine-nut mush, but make it as thin as you can with water."

They gave Coyote some pine-nut mush, made very thin. Every swallow of it tasted good to him. He did not know whether to drink it all down or to take it back to his home. He sat down and drank a little, then looked around for the nuts. There were many shells on the floor, but he could not find any whole nuts. He ran home to his brother. He ran all day.

When he reached home, he said to his brother, "I went over to that place to eat some pine nuts and they tasted good." They decided that all the people—Rat, Eagle,

[1] Birds which eat pine nuts. Their cry is "a'na a'na." These are some species of mountain bluebird.

[2] A small, gray, sage bird.

Deer, Mountain Sheep, Chipmunk, Sau'awini'[2]—should go over to the country of the pine nuts. They started out and arrived that night. Then they began to play the hand game with the A'na people. They played all night. Coyote sang, "Upija, upija, upija [Go to sleep, go to sleep, go to sleep]" in a monotonous chant. Toward morning, all the A'na people went to sleep.

Then Mouse, Woodpecker, and the others began to look for the pine nuts. Mouse searched everywhere and finally found them. But they were so deep in the cracks of the roof supports that he could not get them out. Yellowhammer succeeded in getting the nuts out, and then flew back to his own country with them. Coyote and Wolf followed him.

When the A'na woke up, their pine nuts were gone. When the A'na woke up and found that their pine nuts had been stolen, they said, "Our pine nuts are gone. Those people stole our pine nuts. We had better chase them." One of them said, "We had better make ice walls which they cannot climb over." The A'na made an ice wall grow up in front of Coyote, Wolf, and their people as they were on their way home. They could not get over it. Coyote said, "Let's try. I think I can knock this wall down by running against it." Coyote ran against it but fell back flat on the ground. He tried again with no better success. Then Mountain Sheep said, "I think I can knock it down. I can butt pretty hard." He tried but failed.

Every member of the tribe except the Crows tried to knock the wall down but none could do it. The Crows sat on one side looking on. Wolf said, "Well, there are those little black people there. It is their turn to try it now. They will have to try." Coyote said, "Little people like that? What can they do?" One of the Crows got up and flew around and around and around. He flew up into the air, so high that the people could hardly see him. Then he came down at full speed and hit the ice wall so hard that it broke all to pieces. Coyote tried to be the first man to go through the wall, but his brother kicked him back. All the people went through and Coyote was last man. He said, "Why did you do that to me? I was the first to find the pine nuts. I ought to go ahead."

They went through the ice wall safely, and then took turns at packing the pine nuts. After a while, the A'na caught up with them. They caught up with Wolf and killed him first because he was the leader. Then they killed Coyote. Pack Rat was getting tired. His brother[3] tried to carry him, but he got tired, too, and they both were killed. After a while, all the people were killed except Hawk. Hawk had a sore leg and he hid the pine nuts in the sore. When the A'na caught up with him, they seized him, broke his legs, and threw them away. They killed him, but did not know that he had the pine nuts.

After awhile, Wolf came back to life again. He woke up his brother, Coyote, and they went on and woke up all those who had keen killed. They all went on home and arrived there safely.

When they got home, Wolf said to his brother, "You shall plant these pine nuts." He showed Coyote how to plant the seeds. He filled his mouth with pine nuts and

[3] *Also Rat, another species.*

chewed them up. Then he blew them out and scattered the seeds over the country. Pine-nut trees sprang up everywhere. But when Coyote filled his mouth with pine nuts, he chewed them up and swallowed them. He only spat out his saliva, and where this fell juniper trees grew. Coyote eats juniper berries now.

This is how the pine nuts come to be here.

After this, the people were going to turn into animals. Wolf said to his brother, "You are going to be a coyote. You will be a stealer." He became a coyote and now he steals and eats everything. Wolf said, "I am going to be a wolf and chase deer." He changed into a wolf and chases deer today. Birds, rats, chipmunks, squirrels, and all the other people turned into the animals and birds that they are today.

Wolf was going to make moccasins with the soles only stuck on, but Coyote said, "You had better sew on the soles, and sing a little while you are doing it."

Wolf said, "I am going to kill deer, and I am going to smoke before I ever kill one. I am going to be that way. In that way, even if I kill deer they will continue to increase.

ACORN WOODPECKER

Melanerpes formicivorus

Family Picidae

Length: 8–9 ½"

Habitat:

Oak and oak-pine forests; nests in cavities dug out of dead or living tree trunks and limbs

Range:

Resident in northern California, the Coast Ranges south from San Francisco, and the western Sierra foothills

Comments:

The acorn woodpecker has a bright red cap, white forehead and throat, black back, and mostly black wings. Flight reveals its white rump and white wing patches.

These birds subsist chiefly on acorns and other nuts during winter and on insects during summer. They cache acorns in trees and poles by drilling neat holes into tree bark and firmly jamming an acorn into each hole, creating granaries of up to fifty thousand acorns. These granaries hold enough food to last the winter and may be shared and defended by social groups of up to fifteen members.

Acorn woodpeckers are cooperative breeders and could be described as "polygynandrous"— pairs might breed alone, but males and females from previous broods often help.

Their call is a sharp, repetitive "ja-cob."

Ursula K. Le Guin
"What Is Going On in the Oaks around the Barn"

The Acorn Woodpeckers
are constructing an Implacable
Pecking Machine to attack oaks
and whack holes to stack acorns in.

They have not perfected
it yet. They keep cranking
it up ratchet by ratchet
by ratchet each morning
till a Bluejay yells, "SCRAP!"
and it all collapses
into black-and-white flaps and flutters
and redheads muttering curses
in the big, protecting branches.

❧ AUTHOR SKETCHES ❧

Mary Austin (1868–1934) published her first book in 1903—the successful *The Land of Little Rain*, a collection of short sketches about the southern California deserts. *The Flock* (1906) and *Lost Borders* (1909) complete a trilogy.

Ambrose Bierce (1842–1914?) began his literary career in San Francisco and quickly became known for his black humor, irony, morbidity, and satire. "To the Happy Hunting Grounds" is from Bierce's 1892 poetry collection, *Black Beetles in Amber*. The circumstances surrounding his death are unclear; in 1914 he informed friends he intended to join Pancho Villa's forces in Mexico, and he was never heard from again.

T. C. Boyle (b. 1948) is the award-winning author of seventeen books of fiction, including 1995's *The Tortilla Curtain,* which examines race relations between white, upper-middle-class Americans and poor Mexican illegal immigrants in southern California. It won France's "Prix Médicis étranger" for the best foreign novel in 1997.

Richard Brautigan (1935–1984), commonly associated with the San Francisco Beat movement, wrote primarily humorous sketches, many of which have been collected in short books such as *Trout Fishing in America* (1967).

William Bright (b. 1928), anthropologist and linguist, has contributed to over twenty-five books and was from 1965 to 1987 the editor of *Language*, the journal of the Linguistic Society of America. *A Coyote Reader* (1993) reflects his interest in translating Native American myths.

Charley Brown (n.d.) told the story of "The Girl who Married Rattlesnake" in the northern Pomo language sometime after the turn of the century.

Edwin Bryant (1805–1869) moved to Kentucky from Massachusetts, where he became a journalist and later led a wagon train to the West Coast. In 1848, he published his account of the trip, *What I Saw in California: By Wagon from Missouri to California.*

Charles Bukowski (1920–1994) illustrated in his poetry and prose the oppressive metropolitan environments of America. "The lady and the mountain lion" (1988) is from his 1992 work, *The Last Night of the Earth Poems.*

Gelett Burgess (1866–1951) was the editor of and a major contributor to the bohemian San Francisco–based *Lark* magazine. Burgess published "The Purple Cow" in *Lark*, along with other silly rhymes and cartoons.

Sally Carrighar (1898–1985) was born in Ohio and spent much of her childhood outdoors, eventually making her way to California, where she became a nature writer. *One Day on Beetle Rock* (1944) is based on her observations at the real Beetle Rock in Sequoia National Park.

Walter Van Tilburg Clark (1909–1971) is known for his vivid descriptions of Western settings. His first novel, *The Ox-Bow Incident* (1940), evokes timeless themes of law and society and was met with critical praise. Clark followed his success with other books and short stories, including "Hook" (1940).

Richard Henry Dana, Jr. (1815–1882) became a sailor at age nineteen, setting off from Boston to California. He spent about sixteen months in California, an experience he detailed in *Two Years Before the Mast: A Personal Narrative of Life at Sea* (1841).

G. Ezra Dane (1904–1941) presents a series of authentic gold rush–era stories in *Ghost Town* (1941) through the voice of a single narrator, an Old Timer who sits on a stump and recalls the good old days, when trust and hospitality were cardinal virtues.

William Heath Davis (1822–1909) came from a Boston ship-owning family and was one of the founders of "New Town" San Diego. His book *Sixty Years in California* (1889) provides a vivid portrait of early California.

William Dawson (1873–1928) was an ornithologist, oologist, and minister. His monumental four-volume *The Birds of California: A Complete, Scientific and Popular Account of the 580 Species and Subspecies of Birds Found in the State* was published in 1923. He also wrote about the birds of Florida and Ohio.

Jim Dodge (b. 1945) published his first novel in 1983; *Fup* tells the story of an alcoholic grandfather, orphaned grandson, and a mallard duck who is too big to fly. Dodge's other novels include *Not Fade Away* (1987) and *Stone Junction: An Alchemical Potboiler* (1990), and he is also the author of four poetry chapbooks.

Alexandre Dumas (1802–1870), a French novelist who never came to California, wrote *Un Gil Blas en Californie* (1852) in the style of a young Frenchman's firsthand experiences during the California gold rush. *A Gil Blas in California* was translated into English in 1933.

Hildegarde Flanner (1899–1987), the pseudonym of June Hildegarde Flanner Monhoff, settled in California in the 1920s. Flanner wrote poems, essays, and one-act plays. An early environmental advocate, Flanner's love of nature is apparent and runs throughout her work.

Jessie Benton Fremont (1834–1902) worked as a travel writer, memoirist, and co-author of her husband John Fremont's expedition reports through the American West. In her 1887 memoir, *Souvenirs of My Time*, she tells of her childhood in Washington, D.C., as the daughter of Senator Thomas Hart Benton, and also of her elopement with Fremont and the couple's vast travels.

Gerald Haslam (b. 1937) was born in Bakersfield, California, and the majority of his writings are set within the state. His literary influences include his grandmother's stories, the people he grew up with, his schooling, and his various jobs, which ranged from ranching in Utah to working in the oil fields of California's Central Valley. Haslam's major works include *Okies: Selected Stories* (1975) and *Condor Dreams and Other Stories* (1994).

Robert Hass (b. 1941) won the 1973 Yale Series of Younger Poets Award for his first book of verse, *Field Guide*. Hass has since published criticism and translations, and from 1995 to 1997 he served as U.S. Poet Laureate and poetry consultant to the Library of Congress.

Bill Hotchkiss (b. 1936) is a critic, novelist, editor, publisher, poet, and amateur carpenter. His works include the collection of verse *I Hear the Coyote* (1997).

Freeman House (n.d.) was inspired to write *Totem Salmon* (1999) by his own experiences as a commercial fisherman and tugboat owner/operator, as well as twenty years of living in the Mattole River valley. He is the co-founder of the Mattole Watershed Salmon Support Group and the Mattole Restoration Council.

James M. Hutchings (1820–1902) immigrated to America from England in 1848 and became a wealthy miner during the California gold rush. After losing his money in a bank failure, he made a second fortune in publishing, beginning with his periodical, *The California Monthly*, and, later, his book *Scenes of Wonder and Curiosity in California*.

Helen Hunt Jackson (1830–1885) gained fame through her poetry, but it was her 1884 novel, *Ramona*, that brought her to prominence. She was also a historian, children's author, travel writer, and vocal advocate for the better treatment of Native Americans.

George Wharton James (1858–1923) came west from his native England in the 1870s, eventually becoming a public lecturer. He was especially interested in southern California and the Southwest, writing *The Wonders of the Colorado Desert* (1906) and *Through Ramona's Country* (1909).

Robinson Jeffers (1887–1962) settled with his wife, Una Jeffers, in Carmel in 1914. There Jeffers developed his poetic style and became renowned for his narrative verse. The California landscape was essential to his work, as reflected in "Vulture" and "Orca."

Steve Kowit (b. 1938) is the author of several collections of poetry, including *The Dumbbell Nebula* (1999). In addition to his work as a poet, he has authored a guide to writing poetry and is an animal rights advocate.

Frank LaPena (b. 1937) was born in San Francisco. As a young man he became interested in his Nomtipom Wintu heritage, and his poetry and art focus on the traditions of his ancestors. LaPeña is active in preserving Native arts.

Ursula K. Le Guin (b. 1929), a California native, publishes everything from children's literature to young adult novels to adult science fiction. "What Is Going on in the Oaks around the Barn" is included in *Buffalo Gals and Other Animal Presences* (1987), a collection of writings about animals.

Jack London (1876–1916), a California native, sought to portray Western consciousness in his writings. *White Fang* (1906) was London's companion piece to his *Call of the Wild* (1903).

Charles F. Lummis (1859–1928)—author, anthropologist, editor, and historian—was especially interested in the Native American culture of the American Southwest. By 1891, he was publishing almost one book per year of either history, verse, or fiction.

Barry Lopez (b. 1945) often describes the landscapes of the American West and the relationship between humans and nature. Native American myths also significantly influence his work, as evidenced in his *Giving Birth to Thunder, Sleeping with His Daughter: Coyote Builds North America* (1977).

David Mas Masumoto (b. 1954), a writer and farmer in Del Rey, California, explores in his first major work, *Epitaph for a Peach* (1995) his family's commitment to their farm and desire to produce fine quality fruits. Masumoto's most recent publication is *Letters to the Valley* (2004).

William K. McGrew (n.d.) published "The Rats of Sacramento" in *Overland Monthly and Out West Magazine* in 1900.

Alejandrina Murillo Melendres (n.d.) told "Coyote Baptizes the Chickens" in the Diegueno language. It was translated by Maria Aldama and Leanne Hinton and adapted by William Bright.

Joaquin Miller (1839–1913), born Cincinnatus Hiner Miller, was known as "The Poet of the Sierra." His writings include *Songs of the Sierras* (1871) and *Life Amongst the Modocs* (1873).

Harriet Monroe (1860–1936) was a freelance writer for the *Chicago Tribune* as well as the founder and editor of *Poetry: A Magazine of Verse*, which provided a forum for poets during the poetry renaissance of the early twentieth century.

John Muir (1838–1941), a prominent figure in the American conservation movement, was born in Scotland and immigrated to America in 1849. He arrived in California in 1868 and explored Yosemite Valley, the Central Valley, and the Sierra Nevada, using his experiences to write the book *My First Summer in the Sierra* (1911).

Gladys Nomland's (n.d.) "Origin of Abalone" appeared in *Bear River Ethnography*, published in 1938.

Walter Nordhoff (1855–1937) published *The Journey of the Flame* in 1933 under the pseudonym Antonio de Fierro Blanco. The story of Baja California as told through the fictional Don Juan Obrigón is a framed narrative: it is told by an old man, written down by another, and then translated.

Ishmael Reed (b. 1938) is the award-winning author of many works of fiction, nonfiction, and poetry. His satirical, original style has established him as one of California's most original writers.

Kenneth Rexroth (1905–1982), a leader in the San Francisco Poetry Renaissance of the 1960s, included several of his humorous poems about animals in his 1963 collection, *Natural Numbers: New and Selected Poems*. Rexroth was also known as a translator, essayist, and painter.

Arnold R. Rojas (1896–1988) chronicled the lives and legends of California's vaqueros in a series of books for which material was collected "around the campfire and in the bunkhouse on winter nights." *These Were the Vaqueros: The Collected Works of Arnold R. Rojas* was published in 1974.

Floyd Salas (b. 1931) attended the University of California on a boxing scholarship and soon found that boxing and writing complemented each other, both requiring what he describes as "dedication, durability, and courage." His works include his 1996 memoir *Buffalo Nickel*, the 1978 novel *Lay My Body on the Line*, and 1996's book of verse *Color of My Living Heart*.

William Saroyan (1908–1981) was the son of Armenian immigrants and often wrote about the immigrant experience in America. *My Name Is Aram*, a collection of short stories, was published in 1940.

Charles Melville Scammon (1825–1911), a sea captain, whaler, and naturalist, wrote his major literary and scientific work, *The Marine Mammals of the North-Western Coast of North America*, in 1874. It remains a major primary source about whaling in the nineteenth century and was the first major contribution to the knowledge of cetaceans.

John Randolph Spears (1850–1936) was the first professional journalist to visit, photograph, and report on Death Valley. Spears's *Illustrated Sketches of Death Valley and Other Borax Deserts of the Pacific Coast* appeared in 1862 and is considered an important literary and historical account of the region.

Lincoln Steffens (1886–1936) was one of America's most famous and influential "muckrakers," or journalists who investigated and exposed pervasive political, social, and corporate corruption. Steffens's *Autobiography* (1931) is a passionate recounting of his early childhood through his years as a reporter examining the conditions that breed corruption, power, and misery.

John Steinbeck (1902–1968) was born in the Salinas Valley of California, an agricultural region that provided the backdrop for many of his works, including "The Gift" (1937), "The White Quail" (1938), and *Cannery Row* (1945). His most famous novel, *The Grapes of Wrath* (1939), won the Pulitzer Prize, and Steinbeck himself received the Nobel Prize for Literature in 1962.

George Sterling (1869–1926), although originally from New York, is most often identified with San Francisco. He devoted himself to poetry and published *The Testimony of the Suns and Other Poems* in 1903. Despite this success, he felt he was not appreciated outside California, and, faced with financial difficulties and depression, he committed suicide in 1926.

Julian H. Steward (1902–1972), a social anthropologist credited with new theories on cultural ecology and multilinear evolution, published a variety of works, including *Theory of Culture Change* (1955).

Mark Twain (1835–1910), the pseudonym of Samuel Langhorne Clemens, spent most of the 1860s in Nevada and California. He wrote "The Celebrated Jumping Frog of Calaveras County" (1865) while working as a reporter in San Francisco.

Georgiana Valoyce-Sanchez (n.d.) is a member of the Coastal Band of the Chumash Nation. She currently teaches American Indian literature and Native American women's literature at California State University at Long Beach.

Louise Wagenknecht (b. 1949) grew up at the end of the 1950s lumber boom that devastated her community, Hilt, near the California-Oregon border. Her memoir, *White Poplar, Black Locust*, describes the transformation of the town as the lumber mills go out of business.

David Rains Wallace (b. 1945) has written on everything from the varied ecosystems of Central America (his 1997 *The Monkey's Bridge: Mysteries of Evolution in Central America*) to backyard ecosystems (1986's *The Untamed Garden and Other Personal Essays*).

Austen D. Warburton (1917–1995) was a lawyer, civic leader, and art patron. He collected Native American art and artifacts, participated in the excavation of several pre-Columbian sites in California and the Southwest, and wrote extensively about Native American culture.

Darryl Babe Wilson (b. 1939), the son of A'juma'wi and Atsuge'wi Indians in northern California, had a childhood steeped in Native American tradition. His acclaimed autobiography, *The Morning the Sun Went Down*, was published in 1998.

The Yokuts are a Native American people with up to fifty separate tribes and many dialects. Their homeland is southern California and they are noted for their basketry and pictographs.

∼ TIMELINE ∼

By Christie Genochio

"A Long Time Ago"	Coyote created the world, then called a council of all the animals (including Lion, Grizzly Bear, Cinnamon Bear, Buck, Mountain Sheep, Mouse, Eagle, Mole, and so on) to get started on the creation of Man.
Proterozoic Era (2.5 billion to 543 million years ago)	Shelled invertebrates and fauna appear in California.
Permian Period (290 to 248 million years ago)	The earliest dinosaurs appear in North America.
10,000 years ago	Evidence indicates the first people arrive in California, where they encounter the last of the Pleistocene animals, such as giant condors, native horses, and saber-toothed cats.
8,000 years ago	According to Peter J. Bryant of the University of California, Irvine, final extinction of native North American horses occurs, most likely due to early game hunting and late Pleistocene (Ice Age) glaciations.
700 AD	Lake Cahuilla forms in the Salton Sink due to silting of the Colorado River. The lake creates a habitat for freshwater fish and mollusks, which were harvested by native people.
1493	Columbus's second voyage to the Americas brings Spanish horses, reintroducing the caballoid horse to the New World. The first European equines arrive at the Virgin Islands that year, and in 1519 another group reaches the continent, starting in Mexico.
1540	The Colorado River delta is first explored by Melchior Diaz and his Spanish comrades.

1741	Russians come to Alaska, where they find sea otters and harvest their pelts; English and American hunters and trappers soon join in the Pacific fur trade.
1700s	Europeans introduce livestock, including sheep, goats, horses, and poultry, to the missions, ranchos, presidios, and other immigrant outposts. Some of these animals escape and begin feral populations, and many non-native species damage the local environments through activities including overgrazing.
1769	A bedraggled group of Spanish Franciscan missionaries and soldiers arrives on the shores of San Diego Bay on July 1; Padre Junipero Serra and Governor Gaspar de Portola arrive on mules. By July 16, Father Serra and his company establish Mission San Diego de Alcalá, the first of the Alta California missions, signaling the advent of European cattle husbandry, agriculture, and animal domestication north of Mexico.
1786	French explorer Jean François de la Pérouse enters Monterey Bay and finds himself surrounded by whales: "They spouted every half minute within half a pistol shot of our frigates and caused a most annoying stench."
1790s	The California condor becomes a target for hunters; settlers shoot, poison, capture, and collect condor eggs and reduce their food supply by hunting antelope, elk, and other condor prey. Ultimately the population begins a steep decline, hovering near extinction in the 1980s.
1817	Russian explorer Otto von Kotzebue enters a San Francisco Bay Area marsh and finds that the "geese, ducks, and snipes were so tame that we might have killed great numbers with our sticks."
1826	Jedediah Smith leads trappers to California to hunt beavers, which were then abundant in the Sacramento and San Joaquin Rivers.
1833	Passing through Benecia, fur trapper and future founder of Yountville George Yount reports, "The deer, antelope, and noble elk held quiet and undisturbed possession of all that wide domain, from San Pablo Bay to Sutter's Fort....The above named animals were numerous beyond all parallel. In herds of many hundreds they might be met, so tame that they would hardly move to open the way for the traveler to pass."

1848	On January 24, James Marshall discovers gold on the American River, where Sutter had sent him and twenty other men to build a sawmill.
1849	During the height of the gold rush, forty-niners create a huge demand for meat and a growing market for elk, bighorn sheep, deer, bears, and quail, all of which are slaughtered in enormous numbers for the mining camps. Overgrazing and drought changes parts of California's landscape by destroying native grassland; indigenous grasses also continue to dwindle.
1850	California's human population is recorded at 92,597.
1851–1854	During a three-year visit to San Francisco, writer J. D. Borthwick reports that "the market was well-supplied with every description of game—venison, elk, antelope, grizzly bear, and an infinite variety of wild fowl."
1850s	Immigrants settle in the Tulare Basin; Tulare Lake was the largest body of fresh water west of the Great Lakes, providing a fertile environment for local wildlife. European settlers displace the Yokuts Indians and transform the landscape by felling trees, killing native game, establishing a cattle industry, and spreading foreign grasses.
1850–1878	California oyster fishery is established when gold prospectors from the East Coast arrive in the state. Market pressure impacts the state's shellfish resources, straining the only native oyster populations of *Ostrea conchaphila (Ostrea lurida)* and requiring the transplantation of oyster beds from Shoalwater Bay in Washington state, as well as from Mexico and states on the Eastern Seaboard.
1857	Lieutenant Edward F. Beale journeys from Texas to California using camels as pack animals bearing loads from seven hundred to one thousand pounds each. "Certainly there never was anything so patient and enduring and so little troublesome as this noble animal…, so perfectly docile and quiet that they are the admiration of the whole camp." After arriving at Tejon Ranch, Beale tested their snow and cold endurance; according to his report, several camels rescued a stalled wagon loaded with provisions, traversing snow and ice, despite the failure of six strong mules to complete the same task.
1860	Settlers begin modifying Central Valley waterscapes; between 1860 and 1930, according to modern environmental scientist Andrew N. Cohen, "97 percent of the Sacramento–San Joaquin River Delta's

350,000 acres of tidal marsh were diked, drained, and plowed." In northern California, Tule and Klamath Lakes undergo a similar process. Large wetland habitats are thus greatly diminished as dams, reservoirs, and other instream structures block the movement of aquatic creatures, such as salmon and steelhead fish, which are unable to reach their natal streams to spawn.

1865   Mark Twain pens "The Celebrated Jumping Frog of Calaveras County" about Dan'l Webster, a California red-legged frog who loses a leaping contest when a stranger loads his mouth with buckshot. The red-legged frog was the largest frog in the state until the introduction of the bullfrog in 1896, and is today listed as a threatened species.

1868   John Muir arrives in San Francisco in March. In May of 1869, after working as a ferry operator, sheepherder, and bronco buster in the Sierra foothills, rancher Pat Delaney offers Muir a summer job caring for sheep in the mountains.

1870   Lake Merritt, the United States's first wildlife refuge, is established in Oakland.

1870s   Streams diverted for irrigation in the 1850s grow into a more elaborate artificial water system as stock raising gives way to grain farming. The King River and its tributaries are diverted for crop support, disturbing the habitat of innumerable animals, and most of Tulare Lake has vanished by 1922.

1874   When a marsh is drained on the Miller–Lux ranch in present-day Kern County, workers discover a small herd of tule elk. Henry Miller, the ranch owner, orders protection for these animals on his land. After sixteen years, extensive crop and pastoral damage cause Miller to request that the elk be relocated, which results in the tragic killing and injury of several of the creatures during the capture and release. Twenty-one tule elk made it to Sequoia National Park, but by 1926 the entire population had died out.

1877   Professor William Denton identifies a tooth from the La Brea tar pits that suggests the palaeontological significance of the location (in present-day Los Angeles). Excavations that take place between 1906 and 1915 unearth around 2 million specimens and fossils of plants and animals from the Pleistocene era (40,000 to 8,000 years ago).

1878	The first Fish and Game Commission begins overseeing wildlife protection, but due to limited funds and personnel, regulations are not actively enforced.
1900	The Lacey Act is passed, allowing the federal government to adopt measures for the restoration of scarce and nearly extinct birds and game, as well as to introduce non-native birds in certain localities.
1905	A temporary diversion of the Colorado River, intended to replace the water from a silt-blocked canal, is breached by floodwaters such that the river alters its course and flows into the Salton Sink.
1906	George Wharton James explores the flooded Salton Sea and reports large concentrations of waterfowl, pelicans, and other avian inhabitants of the area. The elevation of the Salton Sea is recorded at 195 feet below sea level.
1906	A herd of horses panics and flees in the moments preceding the April 18 San Francisco earthquake, contributing to superstitions that animals can predict seismic activity. According to Helmut Tributsch's *When the Snakes Awake: Animals and Earthquake Prediction,* bizarre behavior in dogs, cats, livestock, possums, rats, birds, fish, reptiles, and insects has been linked to changes in electrical charges and in the earth's magnetic field, and to other such elemental indicators.
1913	President Woodrow Wilson approves the Raker Bill, authorizing the transformation of Hetch Hetchy Valley into a reservoir and thereby drowning the valley's flora and fauna and removing the habitat and resources of neighboring wildlife. John Muir battles the project until his death on December 24, 1914.
1914	The California Academy of Sciences takes over tule elk relocation efforts and moves 235 elk to twenty-two locations within the state; unfortunately, by 1940 only three herds continue to thrive.
1918	The United States's Migratory Bird Treaty Act prohibits commercial shooting of waterfowl.
1920	Californians number 3,426,861.
1922	The last known California grizzly bear is killed, ending hopes of the species' natural repopulation.

| 1923 | The Michael M. O'Shaughnessy Dam is finished and the Hetch Hetchy Reservoir is established. |

1923   California law re-enforces the Migratory Bird Treaty Act, but overharvesting of birds continues well into the 1950s. On average, 200,000 birds are annually harvested and sold until the law is properly enforced.

Early 1920s   Petaluma, a town of fewer than five thousand residents, becomes home to a socialist community of American Jewish chicken farmers. By the 1930s the town is considered the "Egg Basket of the World," largely thanks to the several hundred Jews striving to unite left-wing ideals with chicken-wing cultivation. These were, according to journalist Sue Fishkoff, "idealists, socialists, Jews from the shtetls of Eastern Europe and the sweatshops of New York's Lower East Side, young men and women who dreamed of escaping urban poverty and mixing their labor with the soil of the earth."

1928   May 15, Ub Iwerks creates Mickey Mouse, to whom Walt Disney lends his voice, in the debut short film *Plane Crazy*.

1928   On May 19 and 20, the city of Angel's Camp in Calaveras County holds the first Jumping Frog Jubilee to celebrate the famous Mark Twain story. Approximately fifteen thousand people attend. In response, the California Fish and Game Commission begins protective regulation of native frogs in 1933, and in 1995 the 39 District Agricultural Association adopts the "Frog Welfare Policy." Today, the Calaveras County Fair and Jumping Frog Jubilee welcomes thirty-five thousand visitors and over two thousand frogs.

1929   The California Department of Fish and Game begins experimental plantings of Pacific oysters *(Crassostrea gigas)* in a number of locations, primarily in Tomales Bay, Elkhorn Slough, and the San Francisco–area bays. The success of several of these plantings demonstrates that the imported Pacific oyster seed is commercially viable in California.

1939   The "Picture Animal Top Star of the Year (PATSY) Award" is created by the Hollywood office of the American Humane Association to honor animal actors following the tragic death of a horse during the filming of Tyrone Power's *Jesse James*. The first award is given in 1951 to Francis the mule of *Francis the Talking Mule* and its six spin-offs. Other recipients include Arnold Ziffel, the pig from *Green*

Acres; Higgins the dog (as Benji); and Lassie.

1939   The Federal Reorganization Act creates the U.S. Fish and Wildlife Service.

1940   California's population grows to 6,907,387.

1946   The International Convention for the Regulation of Whaling is held and yields the International Whaling Commission.

1947   California's Wildlife Conservation Law passes.

1950   California's population is recorded at 10,586,223.

1950   Timber workers spot large footprints near their logging camps. In 1958, bulldozer operator Jerry Crew finds more footprints in Humboldt County and makes a cast of one of the prints, then has his photo taken with the "Bigfoot" evidence for the local newspaper. Willow Creek, at the center of Humboldt, has since declared itself the "capital of Bigfoot country" and is home to a wooden carving of the mythical beast.

1951   When Clint Eastwood bids to become mayor of Carmel in 1986, Reagan comments, "What makes him think a middle-aged actor, who's played with a chimp, could have a future in politics?" Reagan himself co-starred with Bonzo the Chimp in *Bedtime for Bonzo* in 1951.

1958   According to the inland southern California newspaper *The Press-Enterprise,* legend has it that one November night, while driving through a forest near his Riverside home, Charles Wetzel saw a six-foot-tall creature with no nose, no ears, a beak-like mouth, and fluorescent eyes glaring at him in the dark. Today the figure is referred to as the Riverside Bridge Monster.

1960   The Committee for the Preservation of Tule Elk is formed. In 1971 it enacts a law to control population growth and relocation.

1961   The California Department of Fish and Game predicts the Salton Sea will die in the next twenty or thirty years due to increasing salinity levels.

1962   First appearing as a serial in *The New Yorker,* Rachel Carson's

Silent Spring exposes the hazards of DDT as a modern addition to the food chain. Subsequent banning of the chemical allows the recovery of eagles and other avian wildlife.

1966   The Federal Endangered Species Protection Act passes.

1967   President Ronald Reagan accepts the gift of a baby elephant named Gertie (bought through the Harrods department store) from Crown Prince Leka of Albania and donates it to the Sacramento Zoo. However, when offered a mule by another dignitary, he declined, saying, "I'm afraid I can't use a mule. I have several hundred up on Capitol Hill."

1969   The city of Bishop, California, celebrates its first Mule Days, an annual Memorial Day event. The small town in the eastern Sierra Nevada gathers for a combination of mule presentations, tests of skills, and a Wild West show to kick off packing season and to prove, according to organizers, that "anything a good horse can do, a good mule can do better."

1969   The Endangered Species Conservation Act broadens the previous Protection Act.

1970   California passes a state Endangered Species Act, establishing a process of identifying and restoring rare and endangered species. The California Species Preservation Act also passes, requiring "inventories of threatened fish and other wildlife."

1972   The U.S. government passes the Marine Mammal Protection Act.

1980   The human population of California reaches 23,667,764.

1980   The Federal Fish and Wildlife Conservation Act defends non-game wildlife.

1984   Approximately five thousand birds die in and around the San Francisco Bay when the tanker *Puerto Rican* spills 1.5 million gallons of oil into the bay.

1987   State and federal officials and the Condor Recovery Team trap the last California condors and place them in the Los Angeles Zoo, where they enter a captive-breeding program.

1989   The Loma Prieta earthquake hits northern California on October 17. Prior to the quake, James Berkland, a retired U.S. Geological

Survey geologist from San Jose, claims he can predict earthquakes based upon the number of "lost pet" ads, which he argues correlate to the lunar-tide cycles that influence earthquakes.

1990   California's population reaches 29,760,021.

1990   The California Wildlife Protection Act states: "There is an urgent need to protect the rapidly disappearing wildlife habitat that supports California's unique and varied wildlife resources."

1992   Increasing levels of salt and other substances lead to the death of 150,000 eared grebes at the Salton Sea. Two years later, another 20,000 grebes die.

1992   The first captive-reared California condors are released.

1994   The Point Reyes Bird Observatory (PRBO), founded in 1965, contracts with the California Department of Fish and Game Office of Spill Prevention and Response to develop protocols for oiled wildlife processing.

1995   The California sea otter population peaks at 2,400 but begins to decline shortly thereafter; the trend continues to this day.

1999   The California condor population reaches 158, and the bird's status as an Endangered Species—and not an Extinct one—is considered stable.

2000   California's population reaches 33,871,648.

2000   Pilot projects for saving the Salton Sea are approved, and the Salton Sea Restoration Project gets underway.

2004   Census figures reveal that 3,700 tule elk now live in twenty-two separate herds thanks to a dramatic population increase enacted by the Tule Elk Interagency Task Force (established in 1977) and its Management Plan for the Conservation of Tule Elk.

2006   Baby brown pelicans, most two to four months old, emaciated, and too weak to fly, wash up on California beaches; biologists speculate that the young pelicans may be victims of intense competition for food after a particularly successful breeding season. The Federal Fish and Wildlife Service is considering removing brown pelicans from the endangered species list, since their numbers have rebounded significantly in recent years.

∼ᴏᆖ SELECTED REFERENCES ᆖᴏ∼

Among the many online and print sources consulted for this anthology, the following were especially useful:

Alden, Peter, et al. *National Audubon Society Field Guide to California*. New York: Knopf, 1998.

Bean, Walton. *California: An Interpretive History*. 2nd Ed. New York: McGraw-Hill, 1968.

Behler, John R., and F. Wayne King. *National Audubon Society Field Guide to Reptiles and Amphibians*. 1970. New York: Knopf, 2005.

Burnie, David, and Don E. Wilson, eds. *Animal: The Definitive Guide to the World's Wildlife*. 2001. New York: DK Publishing, 2005.

Cogswell, Howard L. *Water Birds of California*. Berkeley: University of California Press, 1977.

Eschmeyer, William N., Earl S. Herald, and Howard Hammann. *A Field Guide to Pacific Coast Fishes of North America*. Boston: Houghton Mifflin, 1983.

Gilbert, Carter R., and James D. Williams. *National Audubon Society Field Guide to Fishes*. 1983. New York: Knopf, 2005.

Jameson, E. W., Jr., and Hans J. Peeters. *Mammals of California*. Rev. Ed. Berkeley: University of California Press, 2004.

MacMahon, James A. *Deserts*. New York: Knopf, 1985.

Meinkoth, Norman A. *National Audubon Society Field Guide to Seashore Creatures*. 1981. New York: Knopf, 2004.

Milne, Lorus, and Margery Milne. *National Audubon Society Field Guide to Insects and Spiders*. 1980. New York: Knopf, 2004.

National Geographic Society. *Field Guide to the Birds of North America*. Washington, D.C.: National Geographic Society, 1983.

Peterson, Roger Tory. *A Field Guide to Western Birds*. 2nd Ed. New York: Houghton Mifflin, 1961.

Schoenherr, Allan A. *A Natural History of California*. 1992. Berkeley: University of California Press, 1995.

Starr, Kevin. *California: A History*. New York: Modern Library Chronicles, 2005.

Thelander, Carl G., ed. *Living on the Edge*. Santa Cruz: BioSystems Books, 1994.

Whitaker, John O., Jr. *National Audubon Society Field Guide to North American Mammals*. Rev. Ed. New York: Knopf, 1996.

~ PERMISSIONS ~

Mary Austin. "The Flock" and "The Go-Betweens," from *The Flock* by Mary Austin. Boston: Houghton Mifflin Company, 1906.

Ambrose Bierce. "To the Happy Hunting Grounds," from *Black Beetles in Amber* by Ambrose Bierce. San Francisco: Western Authors Publishers, 1892.

T. Coraghessan Boyle. "Pilgrim at Topanga Creek," from *The Tortilla Curtain* by T. Coraghessan Boyle. New York: Penguin Books. Copyright © 1995 by T. Coraghessan Boyle. Used by permission of Viking Penguin, a division of Penguin Group (USA) Inc.

Richard Brautigan. "The Hunchback Trout," from *Trout Fishing in America* by Richard Brautigan. Boston: Houghton Mifflin. Copyright © 1968 by Richard Brautigan. Reprinted by permission of Houghton Mifflin Company/Seymour Lawrence. All rights reserved.

William Bright. "Coyote's Journey," translated by William Bright, from *American Indian Culture and Research Journal*, January 4, 1980. Reprinted in *The Way We Lived: California Indian Stories, Songs, and Reminiscences*, edited by Malcolm Margolin. Berkeley: Heyday Books, 1981. Copyright © 1981 by William Bright. Reprinted by permission of the translator.

Charley Brown. "The Girl Who Married Rattlesnake" by Charley Brown, from *The Way We Lived: California Indian Stories, Songs, and Reminiscences*, edited by Malcolm Margolin. Berkeley: Heyday Books, 1981.

Edwin Bryant. Excerpt from *What I Saw in California: Being the Journal of a Tour* by Edwin Bryant. New York: New Appleton, 1848.

Charles Bukowski. "The Lady and the Mountain Lion," from *The Last Night of the Earth Poems* by Charles Bukowski. Copyright © 1992 by Charles Bukowski. Reprinted by permission of HarperCollins Publishers.

Gelett Burgess. "The Purple Cow" and "The Purple Cow: Suite," from *The Burgess Nonsense Book* by Gelett Burgess. New York: Frederick A. Stokes Co., 1901.

Sally Carrighar. Excerpt from *One Day on Beetle Rock* by Sally Carrighar. New York: Knopf. Copyright © 1944 and renewed 1972 by Sally Carrighar. Copyright © 1943, 1944 by the Curtis Publishing Company. Used by permission of Alfred A. Knopf, a division of Random House, Inc.

Walter Van Tilburg Clark. "Hook" by Walter Van Tilburg Clark, from *The Atlantic Monthly* 166:2, August 1940. Copyright © 1940 by Walter Van Tilburg Clark. Reprinted by permission of International Creative Management, Inc.

Richard Henry Dana. Excerpt from *Two Years Before the Mast* by Richard Henry Dana. New York: Harper, 1840.

G. Ezra Dane. Excerpt from *Ghost Town* by G. Ezra Dane. New York: Knopf. Copyright © 1941 by G. Ezra Dane, renewed in 1969 by Deborah Dane Baker and Diana Dane Dajani. Reprinted by permission of Diana Dane Dajani.

William Heath Davis. Excerpt from *Sixty Years in California* by William Heath Davis. San Francisco: A. J. Leary, 1889.

William Leon Dawson. Excerpt from *The Birds of California* by William Leon Dawson. San Diego: South Moulton, Co., 1923.

Jim Dodge. Excerpt from *Fup* by Jim Dodge. New York: Simon and Schuster. Copyright © 1983 by Jim Dodge. Reprinted by permission of the author.

Alexandre Dumas. Excerpt from *A Gil Blas in California* by Alexandre Dumas, translated by Marguerite Eyer Wilbur. Santa Ana: Fine Arts Press, 1948.

Hildegarde Flanner. "Hawk Is a Woman," from *Poems Collected and Selected* by Hildegarde Flanner. Santa Barbara: John Daniel. Copyright © 1988 by Hildegarde Flanner. Reprinted by permission of Daniel and Daniel Publishers, Inc.

Jessie Benton Fremont. "My Grizzly Bear," from *Far West Sketches* by Jessie Benton Fremont. Boston: Lothrop, 1890.

Gerald Haslam. "Condor Dreams," from *Condor Dreams and Other Stories* by Gerald Haslam. Reno: University of Nevada Press. Copyright © 1994 by Gerald Haslam. Reprinted by permission of University of Nevada Press.

Robert Hass. "On the Coast Near Sausalito," from *Field Guide* by Robert Hass. New Haven: Yale University Press. Copyright © 1973 by Robert Hass. Reprinted by permission of Yale University Press.

Bill Hotchkiss. "Rattlesnakes," from *I Hear the Coyote* by Bill Hotchkiss. Murphy, OR: Castle Peak Editions. Copyright © 2002 by Bill Hotchkiss. Reprinted by permission of the author.

Freeman House. Excerpt from *Totem Salmon* by Freeman House. Boston: Beacon Press. Copyright © 1999 by Freeman House. Reprinted by permission of Beacon Press, Boston.

James Hutchings. Excerpt from *Scenes of Wonder and Curiosity in California* by James Hutchings. London: Chapman and Hall, 1895.

Helen Hunt Jackson. Excerpt from *Ramona* by Helen Hunt Jackson. Boston: Roberts Brothers, 1884.

George Wharton James. Excerpts from *Wonders of the Colorado Desert* by George Wharton James. Boston: Little Brown, 1906.

Robinson Jeffers. "Vulture," from *Selected Poetry of Robinson Jeffers* by Robinson Jeffers. New York: Random House. Copyright © 1963 by Garth Jeffers and Donnan Jeffers. Used by permission of Random House, Inc. "Orca," from *The Double Axe* by Robinson Jeffers. New York: Random House. Copyright © 1948 by Robinson Jeffers. Reprinted by permission of Jeffers Literary Properties.

Steve Kowit. *"Perognathus fallax,"* from *The Dumbbell Nebula* by Steve Kowit. Berkeley: Heyday Books/Roundhouse Press. Copyright © 2000 by Steve Kowit. Reprinted by permission of the author.

Frank LaPena. "Rabbit Crazy" by Frank LaPena, from *The Dirt Is Red Here: Art and Poetry from Native California,* edited by Margaret Dubin. Berkeley: Heyday Books. Copyright © 2002 by Frank LaPena. Reprinted by permission of the author.

Ursula K. Le Guin. "What Is Going On in the Oaks around the Barn," from *Buffalo Gals and Other Animal Presences* by Ursula K. LeGuin. Santa Barbara: Capra Press. Copyright © 1990 by Ursula K. LeGuin. Reprinted by permission of the author and the author's agents, the Virginia Kidd Agency, Inc.

Jack London. Excerpt from *White Fang* by Jack London. New York: Macmillan, 1906.

Barry Lopez. "A Reflection on White Geese," from *Crossing Open Ground* by Barry Lopez. New York: Vintage. Copyright © 1982 by Barry Lopez. Reprinted by permission of SSL, Sterling Lord Literistic, Inc. Charles Lummis. "The California Lion" by Charles Lummis, from *Land of Sunshine*, Volume 2, 1895.

David Mas Masumoto. Excerpt from *Epitaph for a Peach* by David Mas Masumoto. New York: HarperCollins. Copyright © 1995 by David Mas Masumoto. Reprinted by permission of HarperCollins Publishers.

William K. McGrew. "The Rats of Sacramento" by William K. McGrew, from *Overland Monthly* 36:23, September 1900.

Alejandrina Murillo Melendres. "Coyote Baptizes the Chickens" by Alejandrina Murillo Melendres and Leanne Hinton, translated by Maria Aldama and Leanne Hinton, from *Coyote Stories*, edited by William Bright. Chicago: University of Chicago Press, 1978. Copyright © 1978 by The University of Chicago Press.

Joaquin Miller. "The Grizzly as Fremont Found Him," from *True Bear Stories* by Joaquin Miller. Chicago and New York: Rand McNally, 1900. Excerpt from *Life Amongst the Modocs* by Joaquin Miller. Hartford: American Publishing Company, 1874.

Harriet Monroe. "The Water Ouzel" by Harriet Monroe, from *The Second Book of Modern Verse,* edited by Jesse B. Rittenhouse. Boston: Houghton Mifflin Company, 1919.

John Muir. "Biters," from *My First Summer in the Sierra* by John Muir. New York: Houghton Mifflin, 1911. "The Bee-Pastures" and "The Water-Ouzel," from *The Mountains of California* by John Muir. New York: The Century Company, 1894.

Gladys Nomland. "Origin of the Abalone" by Gladys Nomland, from *Bear River Ethnography*. Berkeley: University of California Anthropological Records Vol. 2, No. 2, 1938.

Walter Nordhoff. Excerpt from *The Journey of the Flame* by Walter Nordhoff. Boston: Houghton Mifflin. Copyright © 1933 by Walter Nordhoff. Reprinted by permission of Brandt and Hochman Literary Agents, Inc.

Ishmael Reed. "My Thing Abt Cats," from *New and Collected Poems, 1964–2006* by Ishmael Reed. New York: Carroll and Graf Publishers. Copyright © 1966 by Ishmael Reed. Permission granted by Lowenstein-Yost Associates, Inc.

Kenneth Rexroth. "Raccoon," from *Selected Poems* by Kenneth Rexroth. Norfolk: New Directions. Copyright © 1940, 1956 by Kenneth Rexroth. Reprinted by permission of New Directions Publishing Corp.

Arnold R. Rojas. Excerpt from *California Vaqueros* by Arnold R. Rojas. Fresno: Academy Library Guild, 1953.

Floyd Salas. "To Sergie My Sweet Old Dog Who Died in Old Age," from *The Holy Earth Megascene* by Floyd Salas. San Francisco: Peeramid Press. Copyright ©1982 by Floyd Salas. Reprinted by permission of the author.

William Saroyan. "The Pomegranate Trees," from *My Name Is Aram* by William Saroyan. New York: Harcourt, Brace. Copyright © 1940 by William Saroyan. Used by permission of the Trustees of Leland Stanford Junior University.

Charles Melville Scammon. Excerpt from *The Marine Mammals of the North-Western Coast of North America* by Charles Melville Scammon. New York: G. P. Putnam's Sons, 1874.

John Spears. Excerpt from *Illustrated Sketches of Death Valley* by John Spears. Chicago: Rand McNally, 1892.

Lincoln Steffens. Excerpt from "A Boy on Horseback," from *The Autobiography of Lincoln Steffens* by Lincoln Steffens. New York: Harcourt, Brace and Co. Copyright © 1931 by Harcourt, Inc., and renewed in 1959 by Peter Steffens. Reprinted by permission of Harcourt.

John Steinbeck. Excerpts from *Cannery Row* by John Steinbeck. New York: Viking. Copyright © 1945 by John Steinbeck, renewed © 1973 by Elaine Steinbeck, John Steinbeck IV, and Thom Steinbeck. "The White Quail," from *The Long Valley* by John Steinbeck. New York: Viking. Copyright © 1935, renewed © 1963 by John Steinbeck. Both used by permission of Viking Penguin, a division of Penguin Group (USA) Inc.

George Sterling. "The Abalone Song" by George Sterling. San Francisco: Albert Bender, 1937. "The Black Vulture," from *Selected Poems* by George Sterling. New York: H. Holt, 1923.

Julian H. Steward. "The Theft of Pine Nuts," from *Myths of the Owens Valley Paiute* by Julian H. Steward. Berkeley: University of California Press, 1936.

Mark Twain. Excerpt from *Roughing It* by Mark Twain. Hartford, CT: American Publishing Company, 1872. "The Celebrated Jumping Frog of Calavares County," from *The Celebrated Jumping Frog of Calavares County, and Other Sketches* by Mark Twain. New York: CH Webb, 1865.

Georgiana Valoyce-Sanchez. "The Dolphin Walking Stick" by Georgiana Valoyce-Sanchez, from *The Sound of Rattles and Clappers,* edited by Greg Sarris. Tucson: University of Arizona Press. Copyright © 1994 by Georgiana Valoyce-Sanchez. Reprinted by permission of the author.

Louise Wagenknecht. Excerpt from *White Poplar, Black Locust* by Louise Wagenknecht. Lincoln: University of Nebraska Press. Copyright © 2003 by the University of Nebraska Press. Reprinted by permission of University of Nebraska Press.

David Rains Wallace. Excerpt from "Gardening with Pests," from *The Untamed Garden and Other Personal Essays* by David Rains Wallace. Columbus: Ohio State University Press. Copyright © 1986 by David Rains Wallace.

Reprinted by permission of the author. "Humphrey: Goodwill Ambassador," from *Life in the Balance: Companion to the Audubon Television Specials* by David Rains Wallace. New York: Harcourt Brace. Copyright © 1987 by David Rains Wallace. Reprinted by permission of the author.

Austin D. Warburton. "Steelhead, the Trickster," from *Indian Lore of the North California Coast* by Austin D. Warburton. Santa Clara, CA: Pacific Pueblo Press, 1966.

Darryl Babe Wilson. "Dose" from *The Morning the Sun Went Down* by Darryl Babe Wilson. Berkeley: Heyday Books. Copyright © 1998 by Darryl Babe Wilson.

Yokuts. "The Man and the Owls," from *The Way We Lived: California Indian Stories, Songs, and Reminiscences,* edited by Malcolm Margolin. Berkeley: Heyday Books, 1981.

INDEX

Austin, Mary 85, 228

Bierce, Ambrose 97

Boyle, T. C. 59

Brautigan, Richard 242

Bright, William 61

Brown, Charley 213

Bryant, Edwin 107

Bukowski, Charles 168

Burgess, Gelett 52

Carrighar, Sally 249

Clark, Walter Van Tilburg 132

Dana, Richard Henry, Jr. 253

Dane, G. Ezra 162

Davis, William Heath 52

Dawson, William 151

Dodge, Jim 99

Dumas, Alexandre 217

Flanner, Hildegarde 145

Fremont, Jessie Benton 9

Haslam, Gerald 45

Hass, Robert 39

Hotchkiss, Bill 214

House, Freeman 217

Hutchings, James M. 166

Jackson, Helen Hunt 235

James, George Wharton 35, 115, 238

Jeffers, Robinson 247, 257

Kowit, Steve 173

LaPena, Frank 200

Le Guin, Ursula K. 269

London, Jack 259

Lummis, Charles F. 170

Lopez, Barry 119

Masumoto, David Mas 160

McGrew, William K. 204

Melendres, Alejandrina Murillo 66

Miller, Joaquin 12, 105

Monroe, Harriet 74

Muir, John 6, 15, 74

Nomland, Gladys 3

Nordhoff, Walter 186

Reed, Ishmael 41

Rexroth, Kenneth 202

Rojas, Arnold R. 56

Salas, Floyd 90

Saroyan, William 157

Scammon, Charles Melville 188

Spears, John Randolph 176

Steffens, Lincoln 147

Steinbeck, John 33, 129, 197

Sterling, George 4, 247

Steward, Julian H. 265

Twain, Mark 41, 109

Valoyce-Sanchez, Georgiana 94

Wagenknecht, Louise 152

Wallace, David Rains 240, 254

Warburton, Austen D. 244

Wilson, Darryl Babe 68

Yokuts 195

ABOUT THE EDITORS

Terry Beers teaches writing and literature at Santa Clara University, where he is currently a professor in the English department and director of the California Legacy Project. He also serves as the general editor of the California Legacy series of books, co-published by Santa Clara University and Heyday Books, and is the host of the *Your California Legacy* radio anthology on KAZU public radio. He lives in northern Monterey County, where he trains sled dogs.

Emily Elrod graduated from Santa Clara University in 2005 with a B.A. in history and ancient studies and minors in English and medieval and Renaissance studies. A California native, she is looking forward to a publishing career and graduate school in her home state. Emily has two cats, Lizzy and Mr. Darcy.

A California Legacy Book

Santa Clara University and Heyday Books are pleased to publish the California Legacy series, vibrant and relevant writings drawn from California's past and present.

Santa Clara University—founded in 1851 on the site of the eighth of California's original twenty-one missions—is the oldest institution of higher learning in the state. A Jesuit institution, it is particularly aware of its contribution to California's cultural heritage and its responsibility to preserve and celebrate that heritage.

Heyday Books, founded in 1974, specializes in critically acclaimed books on California literature, history, natural history, and ethnic studies.

Books in the California Legacy series appear as anthologies, single author collections, reprints of important books, and original works. Taken together, these volumes bring readers a new perspective on California's cultural life, a perspective that honors diversity and finds great pleasure in the eloquence of human expression.

Series editor: Terry Beers

Publisher: Malcolm Margolin

Advisory committee: Stephen Becker, William Deverell, Charles Faulhaber, David Fine, Steven Gilbar, Ron Hansen, Gerald Haslam, Robert Hass, Jack Hicks, Timothy Hodson, James Houston, Jeanne Wakatsuki Houston, Maxine Hong Kingston, Frank LaPena, Ursula K. Le Guin, Jeff Lustig, Tillie Olsen, Ishmael Reed, Alan Rosenus, Robert Senkewicz, Gary Snyder, Kevin Starr, Richard Walker, Alice Waters, Jennifer Watts, Al Young.

Thanks to the English Department at Santa Clara University and to Regis McKenna for their support of the California Legacy series.

If you would like to be added to the California Legacy mailing list, please send your name, address, phone number, and email address to:

California Legacy Project
English Department
Santa Clara University
Santa Clara, CA 95053

For more on California Legacy titles, events, or other information, please visit www.californialegacy.org.

CALIFORNIA
LEGACY

SCU

Other California Legacy Books

California Poetry: From the Gold Rush to the Present
Edited by Dana Gioia, Chryss Yost, and Jack Hicks

Unfolding Beauty: Celebrating California's Landscapes
Edited with an Introduction by Terry Beers

Gunfight at Mussel Slough: Evolution of a Western Myth
Edited by Terry Beers

Essential Mary Austin
Edited by Kevin Hearle

Essential Muir
Edited by Fred White

Essential Saroyan
Edited by William E. Justice

Lands of Promise and Despair: Chronicles of Early California, 1535–1846
Edited by Rose Marie Beebe and Robert M. Senkewicz

The Anza Trail and the Settling of California
Vladimir Guerrero

Death Valley in '49
William Lewis Manly

The Land of Orange Groves and Jails: Upton Sinclair's California
Edited by Lauren Coodley

And many more!

If you would like to be added to the California Legacy mailing list, please send your name, address, phone number, and email address to:

California Legacy Project
English Department
Santa Clara University
Santa Clara, CA 95053

For more on California Legacy titles, events, or other information, please visit www.californialegacy.org.

HEYDAY INSTITUTE

Since its founding in 1974, Heyday Books has occupied a unique niche in the publishing world, specializing in books that foster an understanding of the history, literature, art, environment, social issues, and culture of California and the West. We are a 501(c)(3) nonprofit organization based in Berkeley, California, serving a wide range of people and audiences.

We are grateful for the generous funding we've received for our publications and programs during the past year from foundations and more than 300 individual donors. Major supporters include: Anonymous; Anthony Andreas, Jr., Audubon, Barnes & Noble bookstores; Bay Tree Fund; S.D. Bechtel, Jr. Foundation; Butler Koshland Fund, California Council for the Humanities; Candelaria Fund; Columbia Foundation; Colusa Indian Community Council; Federated Indians of Graton Rancheria; Wallace Alexander Gerbode Foundation; Richard & Rhoda Goldman Fund; Evelyn & Walter Haas, Jr. Fund; Walter & Elise Haas Fund; Hopland Band of Pomo Indians; James Irvine Foundation; George Frederick Jewett Foundation; LEF Foundation; Michael McCone; Middletown Rancheria Tribal Council; Gordon & Betty Moore Foundation; Morongo Band of Mission Indians; National Endowment for the Arts; National Park Service; Poets & Writers; Rim of the World Interpretive Association; River Rock Casino; Alan Rosenus; San Francisco Foundation; John-Austin Saviano/Moore Foundation; Sandy Cold Shapero; L.J. Skaggs and Mary C. Skaggs Foundation; Victorian Alliance; and the Harold & Alma White Memorial Fund.

Heyday Institute Board of Directors
Michael McCone (chair), Peter Dunckel, Karyn Flynn, Theresa Harlan, Leanne Hinton, Nancy Hom, Susan Ives, Marty Krasney, Guy Lampard, Lee Swenson, Jim Swinerton, Lynne Withey, Stan Yogi

For more information about Heyday Institute, our publications and programs, please visit our website at www.heydaybooks.com.